Lecture Notes in Computer Science

Lecture Notes in Artificial Intelligence   15356

Founding Editor

Jörg Siekmann

Series Editors

Randy Goebel, *University of Alberta, Edmonton, Canada*
Wolfgang Wahlster, *DFKI, Berlin, Germany*
Zhi-Hua Zhou, *Nanjing University, Nanjing, China*

The series Lecture Notes in Artificial Intelligence (LNAI) was established in 1988 as a topical subseries of LNCS devoted to artificial intelligence.

The series publishes state-of-the-art research results at a high level. As with the LNCS mother series, the mission of the series is to serve the international R & D community by providing an invaluable service, mainly focused on the publication of conference and workshop proceedings and postproceedings.

Nardine Osman · Luc Steels
Editors

Value Engineering in Artificial Intelligence

Second International Workshop, VALE 2024
Santiago de Compostela, Spain, October 19–24, 2024
Revised Selected Papers

 Springer

Editors
Nardine Osman
Artificial Intelligence Research Institute
(IIIA-CSIC)
Bellaterra, Spain

Luc Steels
Studio Stelluti
Brussels, Belgium

ISSN 0302-9743   ISSN 1611-3349 (electronic)
Lecture Notes in Artificial Intelligence
ISBN 978-3-031-85462-0   ISBN 978-3-031-85463-7 (eBook)
https://doi.org/10.1007/978-3-031-85463-7

LNCS Sublibrary: SL7 – Artificial Intelligence

This Springer imprint is published by the registered company Springer Nature Switzerland AG
The registered company address is: Gewerbestrasse 11, 6330 Cham, Switzerland

If disposing of this product, please recycle the paper.

Preface

The VALE track (Value Engineering in AI) of the VECOMP 2024 workshop held its second edition at the European Conference on AI (ECAI 2024) in Santiago de Compostela on October 19, 2024. VALE continued its mission to study the development of value-aware AI that can identify and understand a (human's) value system, abide by that value system, and explain its own behavior and that of others in terms of that value system.

A total of 16 full papers were submitted, and a single-blind review was followed. Papers received an average of three reviews each. All papers were positively argued for by most of their reviewers, so all papers were accepted. Instead of being competitive, the objective was to foster in-depth discussions and build a community that supports this young research line.

This year's workshop track brought together a diverse set of researchers to explore issues such as the identification and modeling of values, the practical challenges of embedding values into AI-driven decision-making systems, and the incorporation of human values into a range of application areas.

This year's edition showed a growing focus on the topic of value identification, with research areas ranging from enriching population synthesis with motivational factors like values, conducting user studies to better understand the semantics of bioethical values, using reinforcement learning to learn values relevant to route choice modeling, and exploring how adversarial behavior on social media is grounded in moral value expression.

In this area of value identification, we also noted the use of techniques such as vision and language models to detect values, large language models to uncover the values behind arguments, natural language processing to design value-based agent architectures, and neuro-symbolic approaches for classifying fundamental human values.

Value-driven decision making is naturally a cornerstone in the area of value-aware AI. Papers on this topic focused on presenting a systematic review of value-based decision-making in software agents, modeling moral decision-making based on ethical frameworks, along with growing research in developing strategies for negotiations and deliberations with social values in mind.

Broader ethical challenges in AI were also investigated, with contributions on the pertinent issue of forgetting in explainability, responsible data sharing, and how value-engineering can help address AI risks in general.

The workshop was funded primarily by the EU Pathfinder project VALAWAI, which is part of the 'Awareness Inside' portfolio, with additional support from the MUHAI EU pathfinder project on 'Meaning and Understanding in AI', and the Spanish national VAE project.

December 2024

Nardine Osman
Luc Steels

Organization

Program Committee Chairs

Nardine Osman

Artificial Intelligence Research Institute, CSIC, Spain

Luc Steels

Studio Stelluti, Belgium

Program Committee

Nirav Ajmeri	University of Bristol, UK
Kevin Baum	DFKI Saarbrücken, Germany
Tony Belpaeme	Ghent University, Belgium
Holger Billhardt	Universidad Rey Juan Carlos, Spain
Filippo Bistaffa	Artificial Intelligence Research Institute, CSIC, Spain
Jan Broersen	Utrecht University, The Netherlands
Carlos Carrascosa	Universitat Poltècnica de València, Spain
Dave de Jonge	Artificial Intelligence Research Institute, CSIC, Spain
Sara Degli-Esposti	Institute of Philosophy, CSIC, Spain
Jayati Deshmukh	University of Southampton, UK
Frank Dignum	Umeå University, Sweden
Alberto Fernandez	Universidad Rey Juan Carlos, Spain
Guido Governatori	Central Queensland University, Australia
Stella Heras	Universitat Politècnica de València, Spain
Vicente Julian	Universitat Politècnica de València, Spain
Timotheus Kampik	Umeå University, Sweden
Marin Lujak	Universidad Rey Juan Carlos, Spain
Serena Marchesi	Italian Institute of Technology, Italy
Luis Marcos-Vidal	Hospital del Mar Research Institute, Spain
Sanjay Modgil	King's College London, UK
Juan Carlos Nieves	Umeå University, Sweden
Pablo Noriega	Artificial Intelligence Research Institute, CSIC, Spain
Sascha Ossowski	Universidad Rey Juan Carlos, Spain
Julian Padget	University of Bath, UK
Giulio Prevedello	CSL Sony, France

Contents

Ethical Issues, Including Explainability

Value Identification

Value-Enriched Population Synthesis: Integrating a Motivational Layer

Alba Aguilera[1]([✉])[iD], Miquel Albertí[2][iD], Nardine Osman[1][iD],
and Georgina Curto[3][iD]

[1] Artificial Intelligence Research Institute (IIIA-CSIC), Barcelona, Spain
aaguilera@iiia.csic.es
[2] Universitat de Barcelona, Barcelona, Spain
[3] University of Notre Dame, Notre Dame, USA
https://iiia.csic.es/en-us/

Abstract. In recent years, computational improvements have allowed for more nuanced, data-driven and geographically explicit agent-based simulations. Yet, simulations have struggled to adequately represent the attributes that motivate the actions of the agents. In fact, existing population synthesis frameworks generate agent profiles limited to socio-demographic attributes. In this paper, we introduce a novel value-enriched population synthesis framework that integrates a motivational layer with the traditional individual and household socio-demographic layers. Our research highlights the significance of extending the profile of agents in synthetic populations by incorporating data on values, ideologies, opinions and vital priorities, which motivate the agents' behaviour. This motivational layer can help us develop a more nuanced decision-making mechanism for the agents in social simulation settings. Our methodology integrates microdata and macrodata within different Bayesian network structures. This contribution allows to generate synthetic populations with integrated value systems that preserve the inherent socio-demographic distributions of the real population in any specific region.

Keywords: agent-based modelling · population synthesis · values · social digital twin · bayesian network · motivational attributes · cultural variation

1 Introduction

Agent-based simulations are now widely used in interdisciplinary research, especially to support policy-making in social contexts. When applied to real-life domains, these simulations are evolving towards more nuanced, data-driven models that accurately reflect the complexities of socio-environmental systems. During the outbreak of the COVID-19 pandemic, the importance of accurate simulations in policy-making scenarios became starkly evident. An important body

© The Author(s), under exclusive license to Springer Nature Switzerland AG 2025
N. Osman and L. Steels (Eds.): VALE 2024, LNAI 15356, pp. 3–21, 2025.
https://doi.org/10.1007/978-3-031-85463-7_1

of studies emerged focusing on simulating disease outbreaks and public health interventions, such as lockdowns or mask mandates. These types of models (along with many others focusing on issues like gentrification, spatial inequality or urban ageing) require a reliable representation of agents, the interactions between them and their environment [23].

In such models, the interactions and behaviour of agents are strongly determined by their profile, which usually comprises specific demographic attributes. These attributes must closely resemble the characteristics of the human population they simulate. Ideally, this information would be sourced from census data; however, due to data privacy constraints, only certain open-source data can be employed. To achieve a simplified yet representative depiction of the population in a specific region, population synthesis methods are used. In this context, the most important challenge is to close the gap between the generated population and the actual one [19]. Traditional synthetic populations generate profiles limited to demographic and socioeconomic information [21]. We argue that there is an additional type of data, referred to as motivational attributes in this article, that can enrich population synthesis frameworks, contributing to reflect the complexities of social interactions and decisions. This data includes cognitive and cultural attributes such as values, ideologies, opinions and vital priorities that have a direct impact on the agents' behaviours [53]. We argue that the behaviour of agents, which can either be learnt via machine learning techniques or modelled through mathematical decision-making architectures, can be enhanced by relying on these motivational attributes. Our approach opens the door to the incorporation of numerous frameworks that define and quantify both individual and collective values, such as the cross-cultural Schwartz Theory of Basic Values [53], the evolution of values in line with economic security (or post-materialistic), described by Inglehart [15], the capability approach to human development [55], multiculturalism and the struggle for recognition [57,58], as well as the impact of prejudices [56,60]. In this article, we have focused on incorporating the data obtained by surveys following the frameworks defined by Schwartz's and Inglehart's [1,2,4,5]. By incorporating this data in a population synthesis framework, we are contributing to a line of research that increases the realism of social simulations and motivating researchers in the social domains to use empirical data in their population generation processes [20,30].

People think and behave differently around the world. This is partly due to cultural variation, or the differences among individuals that exist due to some form of social learning [18]. We propose to address this complexity by extending the current demographic-based profile of agents in synthetic populations with the addition of a motivational layer that automatically adapts to the specific region of the case study. The approach therefore facilitates the replication of the model in different regions of the world, working towards policy-oriented research that includes both the Global North and the Global South [22]. This motivation layer contains information about social aspects of the agents' profiles, reflected in the surveys in scope, that potentially motivate behaviour. Decision-making techniques can then rely on these parameters to fine-tune data-driven outcomes, contributing to the "approach to reality" decision-making research direction [14]. However, sources of motivational data are often limited in size and do not cover the whole population's socio-demographic attributes. They require meticulous integration with other data sources to ensure that the synthetic population, which includes both socio-demographic and motivational characteristics, is sufficiently representative within the desired geographical scope.

To bridge this gap, we propose a novel value-enriched population synthesis framework that integrates diverse data sources to generate a population that goes beyond the traditional individual and household layers. Through value learning from existing data, we explore the dependencies between attributes that accurately represent the underlying motivational ones in the population. In particular, by following our methodology, we can generate a synthetic population with a (1) socio-demographic layer and a (2) motivational layer at both the individual and collective levels (see Fig. 1). Our approach aims to be replicable and scalable to a series of case studies. Therefore, we use Bayesian networks that can either be expanded or reduced depending on the data requirements of the study. To overcome data scarcity issues, which is one of the main challenges of population synthesis today, our approach is able to process both macrodata and microdata. We provide a proof of concept for the framework with a use case in the city of Barcelona. We present how we can potentially generate a synthetic population that uniquely characterizes individuals (i.e. their demographic profile along with their value system, ideologies, opinions, worries, priorities, etc.) in a representative manner.

The paper is organized as follows: Sect. 2 underlines the novelty of our work by exploring the state of the art in value-enriched population synthesis. In Sect. 3, we describe the proposed data model and the integration of values into the framework, while in Sect. 4, we explain the formulation of our population synthesis proposal. Section 5 presents a comprehensive application of the framework through a use case for the city of Barcelona. Finally, we conclude with insights into the main implications, limitations, and avenues for future research in Sect. 6.

2   Related Work

Synthetic populations are essential to develop useful applications in an ethical way that does not compromise individual privacy. Numerous works have generated open-source synthetic populations; for the UK [35], the US [36], Canada [32], Ile-de-France (France) [37], Tallinn (Estonia) [38] or some Australian cities [39] (e.g. Sydney, Melbourne and Brisbane), to name a few. These studies rely on two essential components: (i) data sources, such as publicly available microsamples, surveys or government databases, and (ii) population synthesis techniques, which are being constantly refined to match the complex interrelationships between the agent attributes. However, none of these studies have yet incorporated an agents' motivational layer into their frameworks. Adding such a layer could be highly beneficial for models aiming to more accurately represent the complexities of the physical and social environments as a single fabric, a concept recently referred to as Social Urban Digital Twins (SUDTs) [23]. Let us review the main established data sources and synthesis techniques.

Handling data is perhaps the hardest challenge for population synthesis nowadays, especially due to the variability in format, size, level of detail and disaggregation of data sources across different regions. There are a lot of initiatives that work towards data availability and harmonization by offering detailed socio-demographic information, such as IPUMS (International Public Use Micro Samples) [10]. In our case, we are particularly interested in existing surveys on values. These are international research programs devoted to the scientific study of social, political, economic, religious and cultural values of people in the world. Similar surveys exist at the national level, offering practically the same sort of information along different territorial units. For instance, The World Value Survey (WVS) [1], the Europe Value Study (EVS) [2], the European Social Survey (ESS) [3], the Catalonian value survey [4] and the Barcelona value survey [5] contain almost completely harmonized data along continent, country, region, municipality and district. These data sources provide a link between socio-demographic and motivational attributes at different geographic scopes.

The literature categorizes the techniques used to generate synthetic populations into three main groups: synthetic reconstruction, combinatorial optimization, and statistical learning. The choice among the different techniques largely depends on the characteristics of the available data [21]. The first category uses deterministic algorithms that fit and allocate fractions of individuals and/or households to a region, while the second one attempts to reach an optimized solution by randomly drawing from the microsample while minimizing differences in marginals. More recently, researchers have adopted a probabilistic framework instead of a deterministic one, which corresponds to the third category and is the primary focus of this study. This approach searches for the joint distribution of all attributes using partial views available in the data. Within this category, we settle for Bayesian networks because of the main advantages this approach offers: it facilitates replicability (clear and graphical interface) and scalability (easy parallelization for large-size samples). Although many other methods have technically surpassed the capability of sampling a synthetic population, we prioritize successfully merging different data sources rather than the technical accuracy of the method. The foundational application of Bayesian network synthesis can be traced back to [27], followed by other contributions [28,29,34], which constitute our technical starting point.

This study aims to contribute to population synthesis for agent-based models under a social lens. The main novelty of our work is the aggregation of a motivational layer, sourced from social surveys, into the synthetic population. The use case developed for the city of Barcelona is intended to advance the enhancement of the Aporophobia Agent-Based Model (AABM) project [61,62]. The successful addition of motivational attributes into the population signifies the possibility of adjusting the needs-based model [24] decision-making architecture with real-world data.

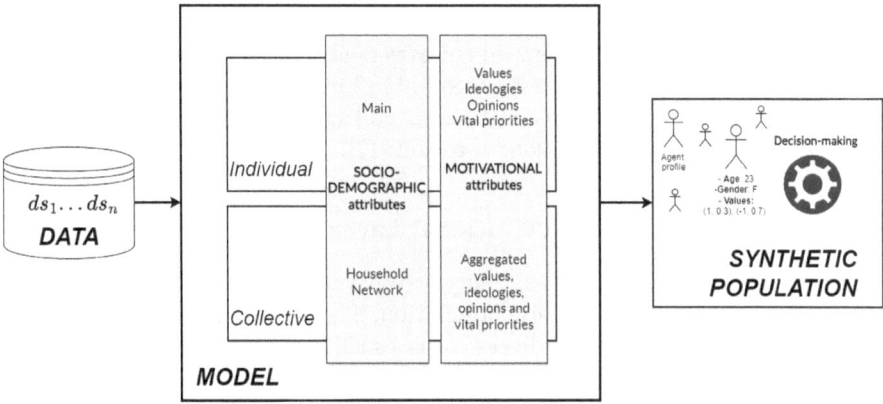

Fig. 1. Workflow scheme. From diverse data sources we extract personal profile attributes and classify them into socio-demographic and motivational layers, represented in blue and pink, at both the individual and collective levels. This information is used to generate comprehensive agent profiles in synthetic populations that help decision-making architectures tune behaviour. (Color figure online)

3   Proposed Data Model

The motivation behind our model is to use diverse data sources to generate comprehensive agent profiles that help decision-making architectures simulate agents' behaviour. In particular, we aim to extend the individual and collective socio-demographic attributes of agents with motivational ones, providing a deeper understanding of the individual's value system that contributes to the agents' actions [53]. The workflow is illustrated in Fig. 1. From the available data sources, denoted as $ds_1, ..., ds_n$, we extract personal attributes and categorize them into two main layers: (i) socio-demographic and (ii) motivational, at both the individual and collective levels. Due to the high dimensionality, particularly of motivational attributes, we further divide the attributes within each layer into types. This allows having an organized overview of the information integrated into the synthetic population.

Socio-demographic attributes, represented in blue, cover the available social, demographic and economic characteristics that define an individual inside a population, a household and a social network. This layer includes "main" attributes at the individual level such as age, gender and nationality, as well as "household" and "network" attributes at the collective level, such as the number of people one lives with, the number of children, detailed information about the household assets and the number of friends. On the other hand, the motivational layer, represented in pink, encompasses attributes that directly impact or motivate behaviour. For this article, they are regrouped into four types: values, ideologies, opinions and vital priorities. This layer includes individual and collective information about prevalent values measured following Inglehart's or Schwartz's theory. Additionally, it includes other motivational attributes such as the alignment with various ideologies, the perceptions on political or economic situations or institutions, the points of view on controversial topics and the vital priorities given to certain aspects of one's life (see Table 2 for further details). These individual motivational attributes can become collective (or consensus) attributes when aggregated or averaged along a region [17].

3.1   Values Within the Motivational Layer

Information extracted from social surveys on values is used to construct the motivational layer of the synthetic population. The surveys are structured along thematic sub-sections covering diverse topics such as vital life priorities, societal well-being, social values and attitudes, religious values, political behaviour and ideology, cultural and national identity, and opinions towards minorities, climate change, migration, etc. [13].

The sections directly related to values in the surveys are linked to the two major human values theories: Inglehart's and Schwartz's. However, keep in mind that surveys can be linked with other theoretical frameworks (such as the ones mentioned in the introduction). Some motivational data sources, such as the ESS [3], use Schwartz's portrait values questionnaire (PVQ-21) [6] to measure the ten fundamental values. In contrast, sources such as WVS [1] or EVS [2], use other methods like Inglehart's materialism/post-materialism (MPM) index [16, 44]. Other regional sources (such as Catalonia's and Barcelona's value surveys) use a combination of both approaches. In all the approaches, respondents' choices are used to quantify their value preferences.

The resulting value preference can be depicted with cultural maps across two predominant dimensions that encompass different values. The Schwartz map [45] includes the dimensions "conservation versus openness to change" and "self-enhancement versus self-transcendence", while the Inglehart-Wezel map [7] features the dimensions "traditional versus secular-rational values" and "survival versus self-expression values." Both maps are represented schematically in Fig. 2, where each specific point indicates a personal value preference.

4   Formulation

In the context of population synthesis under a probabilistic lens, the aim is to infer the underlying joint probability distributions of data, denoted as $P(X_i, .., X_n)$. The random variables $X_i, .., X_n$ are the agent's profile attributes, where each variable X_i is capable of assuming various states x_k. Bayesian networks can embed this joint distribution through two fundamental components: structure and parameters. The structure S captures the dependencies among these variables by connecting them. The parameters δ determine the conditional probability agents have of being assigned a certain attribute given that they have been assigned another one.

Given a set of observational data $\mathcal{D}$, one can either learn the parameters δ when the structure S is known or learn both the structure S and parameters δ.

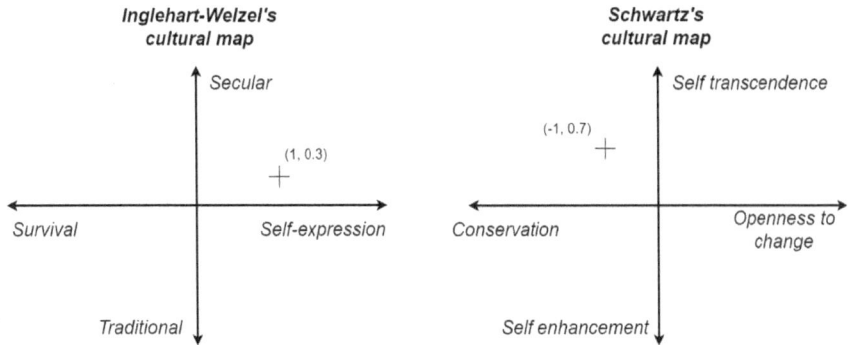

Fig. 2. Simplified depiction of the Inglehart-Welzel's and Schwartz's cultural maps. The points represent a symbolic value preference measured with each value theory along different dimensions.

These processes are known as parameter learning and structural learning, respectively. Our approach employs both methods by (1) crafting an intuitive network based on prior knowledge (knowledge-based model) and (2) using heuristic search techniques to learn an optimal structure (learnt model). These models are then used to sample from the joint probability distribution, obtaining a synthetic dataset where each column is a socio-demographic or motivational attribute and each row uniquely characterizes one individual. The general workflow of a population synthesis process comprises three main steps: (i) data preparation, (ii) model selection and (iii) model validation.

4.1 Data Preparation

Our model is adapted to handle diverse data. We typically encounter two primary data forms: (1) macrodata, which provides information on separate attribute sets but lacks detail on their interdependencies, and (2) microdata, from which we can identify comprehensive interdependencies among attributes. Macrodata can provide information about the conditional probabilities of one, two, or three attributes at most. Relying solely on these conditionals or marginals to produce a representative sample of agents is not feasible, so it is often used as marginal constraints to control the population synthesis process. On the other hand, microdata offers richer insights into the interdependencies between the available attributes (contains their joint distribution) and can be efficiently used to generate a sample. Nevertheless, this microdata can be outdated, lack the needed granularity or contain numerous missing values.

Before data can be integrated into the model, it is essential to select, clean and harmonize the information in it. On one side, the selection of attributes largely depends on the quality of the data. If data on an attribute is substantially incomplete, which is a common situation regarding motivational data, the attribute may be discarded. However, for partially complete data, missing values can be handled either by direct elimination or through imputation techniques [46]. Data harmonization is then required to make diverse datasets compatible and consistent by standardizing and normalizing their values and integrating them into a single, cohesive dataset.

4.2   Model Selection

Following data preparation, the next crucial step is constructing the model that integrates all the selected attributes. These attributes can be organized according to our proposed data model, illustrated in Fig. 1, where attributes are classified within socio-demographic and motivational layers at both the individual and collective levels. Typically, we can associate each layer with one or several data sources that contain the corresponding household, network or motivational attributes. We denote the set of attributes within each data source $ds \in \mathcal{D}$ as X_i^{ds}, where $i = 1, ..., m_{ds}$ and m_{ds} is the total number of attributes selected from a specific data source.

We aim to connect the profile attributes in $\mathcal{D}$ with a structure S and associated parameters δ, representing conditional probabilities between them. In the context of Bayesian networks, various strategies exist for structuring and parameterization, which can differ when dealing with microdata or microdata. Structural learning and parameter learning are straightforward processes for microdata using the common Bayesian network libraries. However, the joint distribution is not attainable for macrodata; only the conditional probabilities of the attributes present separately in each data chunk can be obtained by applying Bayesian estimators of one's choice [9].

To address this limitation, we create two models: one that works solely with microdata (learnt model) and another that can integrate macrodata (knowledge-based model). The main difference between them is how the structure is obtained. While the learnt model incorporates dependencies between attributes directly from data, the knowledge-based model has a predefined structure based on prior knowledge. This combination of models allows for the enrichment of less comprehensive datasets with the robustness of more complete or up-to-date ones. The precise application of the models is detailed in the application through a use case (Sect. 5).

In either of the cases (learnt or crafted), for the attributes in each data source $ds \in \mathcal{D}$, we define a structure S_{ds} and parameters δ_{ds} that connect the attributes within that data source. In other words, S_{ds} is a graph with vertices $\{X_i^{ds}\}_{i=1,...,m_{ds}}$ and directed edges $\{(X_i^{ds}, X_j^{ds})\}_{i,j \in \{1,...m_{ds}\}}$, while δ_{ds} is a set of conditional probability tables $\{P(X_i^{ds} \mid X_j^{ds})\}$ that characterize the dependencies between the attributes described by the S_{ds} structure.

The functioning of our model relies on the combination of various datasets that share a common intersection. We will refer to this set of intersecting variables as the *core* attributes. As all data sources (including surveys, governmental sources and public use microsamples) typically have the same common information integrated, the *core* attributes always correspond to either just individual or individual and collective socio-demographic attributes (e.g. gender, age,

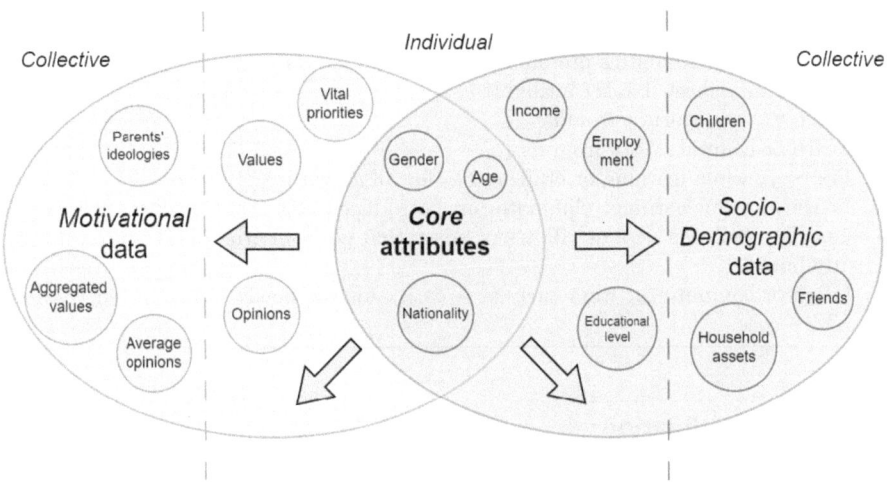

Fig. 3. Representation of the intersection between a set of observational data that contains socio-demographic and motivational information at both the individual and collective levels. As signalled by the edges, from the set of *core* attributes, our procedure allows us to derive the structures or dependencies of all the remaining personal attributes.

nationality, etc.) as shown in Fig. 3. As signalled, by the edges, the rest of the attributes in the socio-demographic and motivational layers are obtained from the *core* attributes.

Let S_{core} refer to the structure connecting the core attributes, learnt or craft from the richest dataset available ds_{rich}. The richest dataset is selected based on various criteria, such as being the largest, the most disaggregated, or the most up-to-date, depending on the specific preferences and requirements of one's study for accurately representing the socio-demographic characteristics of the population. We can use the *core* attributes as a binding factor for the remaining structure, which includes all $X_i^{ds} \notin core$. We do so by fixing S_{core} when learning the other structures, avoiding the overwriting of previously learnt δ_{core} parameters. This approach ensures that the motivational and remaining socio-demographic attributes are linked with the *core* attributes while respecting the probability distributions in each data source. The general procedure to learn the structure and parameters connecting all the attributes is the following.

The final structure is a composition of the structures defined for each data source. The set of nodes is connected through a set of edges, which connect attributes within the same data sources, except from the ones going from the core to other data sources.

Algorithm 1. Procedure to merge attributes contained in different data sources.

1: Find the *core* attributes present in all data sources *ds*.
2: Detect the richest dataset available ds_{rich}.
3: Craft S_{core} or learn it from ds_{rich}.
4: Learn or compute δ_{core} from ds_{rich}.
5: Fix S_{core} while learning or crafting S_{ds} for all *ds* with $X_i^{ds} \notin core$.
6: In the case of learning, eliminate any introduced edge that conflicts with δ_{core}, i.e. edges between *core* attributes or edges that go from other data sources to *core* attributes.
7: Learn or compute δ_{ds} from each $ds \neq ds_{rich}$ for the newly incorporated variables $X_i^{ds} \notin core$.

4.3   Model Validation

Model validation is the process of ensuring the accuracy of the model by comparing the generated synthetic population with the original data. Researchers choose the validation metrics based on the constraints they want to fulfil. In general, these constraints try to ensure that the probability distributions that will eventually be used in population synthesis (whether marginal, conditional, joint, or partially joint) are close enough to the distributions of the real data.

As we are considering an ensemble of different types of data, i.e. macro-data, microdata or a combination of both, we propose to adapt the validation to these different types. Various metrics can be used, such as: (i) Wasserstein distances [49] for evaluating marginal distributions (to be used with macrodata), and (ii) regression lines or SRMSE, described in [27], for evaluating joint distributions (to be used with microdata). The first metric intuitively shows how different two probability distributions are. Concretely, it measures the minimum amount of "work" or effort required to transform one distribution into another. The lower the distance, the closer the distributions. The second comparative approach is regression lines, which help visualize the fit of the synthetic population to the weighted microsample through a frequency plot, where the frequencies of every unique variable combination in the two datasets are plotted against each other. A perfect match is represented by a line of best fit with zero intercept, unit slope, and a correlation coefficient value of one.

5   Application Through Use Case

Following the steps defined in Sect. 4, one can apply our value-enriched population synthesis framework for a specific set of data sources in a region. Once the data is prepared, the models can be created and validated against the original data. The metropolitan area of Barcelona is selected as a proof of concept for our framework. We generate a synthetic population with agents aged from 15 to 74 years old, as motivational data (from existing surveys) is only available for people in that age range.

We use Python's Bayesian network library *pgmpy* [8], which allows for the direct implementation of parameter learning and structural learning techniques. All the project materials can be accessed from the corresponding GitHub public repository. [1]

5.1   Data Preparation

After a thorough analysis of the available data for our selected region, working in close collaboration with local governmental organizations (such as the Open Data department and the Opinion Studies Center of the Government of Catalonia) and non-profit organizations (such as fundació Bofill, which focuses on promoting critical knowledge through education-related studies), we decided upon a set of data sources. The primary data sources considered (and their most updated year of coverage) are: OpenData (2022) [11], IPUMS (2011) [10], Panel fundació Bofill (2012) [12], Barcelona values survey (2021) [5] and Catalonia values survey (2023) [4], which are presented in further detail in Table 1.

Table 1. Selected data sources after attribute selection and harmonization. The size of the data sources, represented by the number of individuals, is listed, along with the maximum geographic scope, the type of data and the models to which the data is fed.

No.	Source	Size	Scope	Type	Model
ds_1	OpenData	1,600,000	Neighborhood	Macrodata	Knowledge-based
ds_2	IPUMS	120,000	Municipality	Microdata	Knowledge-based and learnt
ds_3	Panel	1,500	Census section		
ds_4	Bcn values survey	1,300	District		
ds_5	Cat values survey	3,100	Region		

OpenData [11] is a governmental database, updated annually, that provides socio-demographic macrodata for the entire population of Barcelona up to the neighbourhood level. As a macrodata source, only the knowledge-based model supports it. IPUMS, Panel and value surveys' data are microdata sources, used to feed the learnt and knowledge-based models. IPUMS [10] contains detailed socio-demographic information from the Spanish census at both the individual and collective levels. Panel fundació Bofill's data [12] originates from a longitudinal survey aimed at exploring social inequalities in Catalonia, conducted across households up to the census section level. The Barcelona values survey [5] and the Catalonia values survey [4], conducted every two years up to the district and municipality level, investigate ideological, ethical, or attitudinal questions

---

[1] https://github.com/albaaguilera/Population-Synthesis.

to understand the prevailing value system of the population. We acknowledge that combining data from different years involves a significant assumption, as the populations described may have changed over time. However, the validation process is designed to address this assumption by evaluating the accuracy of the models against all the available data sources. This approach helps us ensure that, despite the temporal differences in the data, the synthetic population does not deviate from the actual characteristics of the population in the region.

Given the set of data sources, a thorough cleaning, harmonization and selection of attributes need to be performed. In our case, we resort to the direct elimination of missing values and the establishment of simplified and standardized states x_k for each variable to ensure consistency. Additionally, the territorial unit node is designed to be flexible, allowing our application to adapt to various spatial scales.

5.2   Model Selection

A summarized classification, definition and description of the selected attributes' is provided in Table 2. The models encompass over seventy variables, a number that can either be reduced or extended to narrow or widen the synthetic agent's profile. We could include as much information as the data sources allow (e.g. workplace sector, extracurricular activities, information about the use of time, the perception of one's health state or social class, detailed information on the household assets, etc.). As explained in Sect. 4, we differentiate between two models: (1) the learnt model (Sect. 5.2) and (2) the knowledge-based model (Sect. 5.2).

Learnt Model. The learnt model draws data from the four microdata sources specified in Table 1. It learns the structures and parameters using the hill climb search method and the expectation maximization estimator [9]. Following the procedure explained in Sect. 4.2, we identify the *core* attributes present in the four datasets. Among the selected datasets, IPUMS stands out as the richest due to its significantly larger interviewed population. Consequently, we learnt both S_{core} and δ_{core} from it. Once this core is established, we add the remaining attributes from the other datasets and learn their structure and parameters, along with their connection with the core attributes. The final learnt model structure is represented in Fig. 4. The structures and parameters S_{ds_3}, δ_{ds_3} and S_{ds_4} δ_{ds_4} encapsulate the dependencies and distributions of the network and motivational attributes, respectively. Furthermore, the remaining structures and parameters S_{ds_5}, δ_{ds_5} can be added as aggregated motivational attributes at the collective level, with a regional scope.

The dependencies identified by the learnt model align with our expectations regarding the connections between profile attributes, indicating that the model is functioning correctly. For instance, within the socio-demographic layer, age emerges as the predominant influencer, as most of the other attributes depend on it. The social network attributes also exhibit a clear structure where friends

Table 2. Summarized classification, definition and description of the selected profile attributes for population synthesis. The attributes are organized into types within the socio-demographic and motivational layers. Note that this simplified table does not specify the 70 attributes comprised in the agent's profile.

Layer	Type	Attribute	Definition	Description
Socio-demographic	Main	D[a]	District	Territorial unit
		G	Gender	Female or male
		A	Age	0–100 years old by groups of 10
		N	Nationality	Spain/rest of EU/rest of the world
		E	Educational level	Last educational level attainment
		U	Unemployment	Registered employed or unemployed
		I	Income	Monthly amount of income
	Household	Hr	Number of people you live with	Number from 0 to 4 or more
		Ch	Children in the household	No children/one or more children
	Network	Fr	Number of friends.	Number from 0 to 3 or more
		X_{Fr}[b]	Friends' main demographic attributes	Friends' age, gender, educational level and nationality
Motivational	Values		Inglehart's materialist/post-materialist index	Degree of materialism, mixed values or post-materialism (1–7)
			Alignment with Schwartz's fundamental values	Degree of agreement or disagreement with the 10 fundamental values (1–5)
	Ideologies		Individual's and parents' ideology	Political spectrum (1–8)
			Alignment with capitalism, socialism, communism and political independence movements	Degree of agreement: agreement, disagreement and indifference (1–3)
			Alignment with feminism, ecologism, multiculturalism and religion	Degree of agreement: agreement, disagreement and indifference (1–3)
	Opinions		Interest on politics, sports, culture, etc.	Degree of interest (1–4)
			View on controversial topics such as immigration, squatting, sustainability, etc.	Multiple options varying with topic
			Confidence in the police, the state, the government, the church, the people, etc.	Degree of confidence (1–4)
	Vital priorities		Importance given to or satisfaction provided by certain aspects of one's life: family, friends, work, personal time and studies	Degree of importance or satisfaction (1–10)

[a] Territorial unit interchangeable for other geographic scopes present in the data sources (e.g. municipality "M", census section "CS" or neighbourhood "N").
[b] X_{Fr} refers to the set of variables describing the demographic profile of the individual's friends (e.g. G_1 being the number one friend's gender).

share similar traits: the characteristics of individuals are found to influence the characteristics of their friends, as observed with attributes such as gender, education, and age. The individual and collective motivational structures, S_{ds_4} and S_{ds_5}, showcase several connections between attributes within the motivational layer and from the socio-demographic one. In the first case, the interdependencies are classified within ideologies, opinions, values and all of them together such as

Learnt model

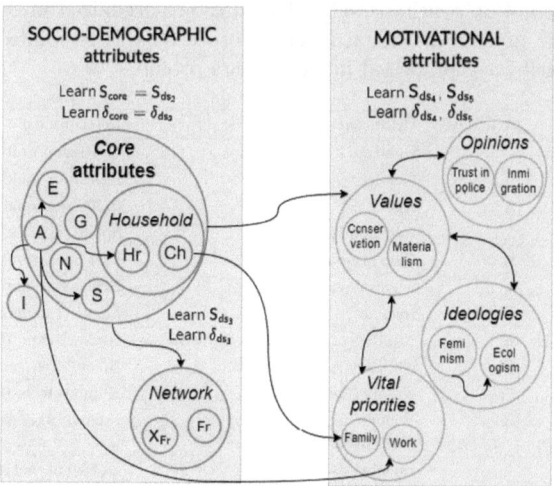

Knowledge-based model

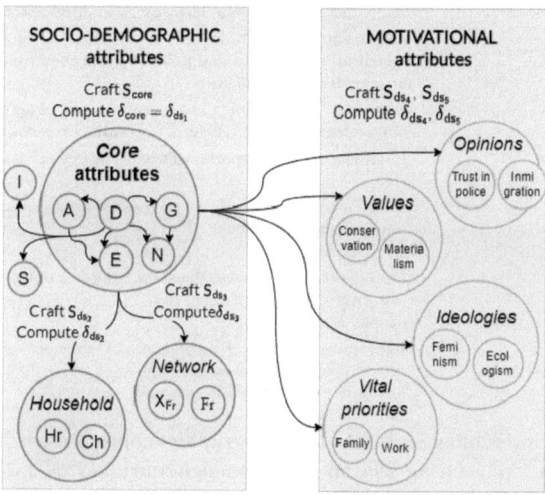

Fig. 4. Schematic representation of the learnt and the knowledge-based model structures, learnt or crafted for each specific data source. The diagrams illustrate several interdependencies within the socio-demographic and motivational layers, as well as outer dependencies between them. Double-headed arrows indicate bidirectional dependencies, meaning that the influence can be mutual between connected attribute types. Note that these diagrams do not depict all the identified connections; only a selection of them is shown for simplicity and clarity.

the parents' ideologies influencing the individual one It is important to highlight that these may vary significantly depending on the city of study, especially those related to politics and trust with institutions.

For a more concrete description of the whole structure learnt by the model, beyond the schematic one provided in Fig. 4, we outline some of the interdependencies (connections between attributes within the same layer) and outer dependencies (connections between attributes from the socio-demographic to the motivational layer). Note that, in the context of dependencies, $a \prec b$ represents the causal relation "b depends on a".

Interdependencies

1. **Socio-demographic layer**
   - Age $\prec$ other main demographic attributes
   - Within network: individual's demographic attributes $\prec$ friend's demographic attributes
2. **Motivational layer**
   - Within ideologies: parents' ideologies $\prec$ individual ideology
   - Within opinions: trust in the monarchy $\prec$ trust in other institutions, opinions about feminism $\prec$ opinion towards ecologism and multiculturalism
   - Within Schwartz's values: benevolence $\prec$ universalism, self-direction $\prec$ stimulation $\prec$ conformity $\prec$ hedonism $\prec$ power $\prec$ achievement
   - Within ideologies, values and opinions: Inglehart's index $\prec$ political ideology, religion $\prec$ tradition, opinion towards immigration $\prec$ security and social trust in people

Outer dependencies

- Between socio-demographic layer and values: nationality $\prec$ religion and opinion about political independence movements, children in the household $\prec$ hedonism
- Between socio-demographic layer and vital priorities: employment status $\prec$ satisfaction with professional and economic aspects, age $\prec$ importance given to work, children in the household $\prec$ importance given to family and social trust in people

Knowledge-Based Model. The knowledge-based model draws data from all the sources listed in Table 1. We establish a basic structure based on prior knowledge, which involves imposing dependencies, available in data, that seem naturally evident between the attributes. We acknowledge the biases that the knowledge-based structure can introduce, but bear in mind that both models defined are intended to complement each other in the validation step. By detecting which model most accurately represents a specific data source, we plan to select that particular structure and parameters for each data source.

The crafted structure is simpler than the learnt one in terms of connections. The *core* attributes (mostly corresponding to main socio-demographic ones) are chosen to influence all the other socio-demographic and motivational attributes. In fact, the structure is geographically rooted: all attributes are influenced by the territorial unit if there is data that allows us to impose so. The final knowledge-based model structure is represented in Fig. 4, where the *core* attributes are the parents of all other attributes. The parameters δ_{ds_1} are computed using the maximum likelihood method, while the other parameters are estimated using expectation maximization. By manually crafting this structure, rather than learning it (feasible only with microdata sources), we can integrate macrodata from ds_1 into the socio-demographic layer. This approach allows us to leverage macrodata that can be more representative than microdata.

6 Conclusions and Future Work

In this paper, we have presented a novel population synthesis framework that incorporates motivational attributes into agent profiles. By feeding from social survey data, our framework connects information about individuals' values, ideologies, opinions and vital priorities to the rest of their socio-demographic attributes, preserving the representativeness of the population. We propose two different models for evaluation: learnt-based and knowledge-based. These structures lead to the generation of synthetic populations with highly detailed motivational attributes at different geographic scopes. Researchers can use these datasets to initialize their simulations with comprehensive agents' profiles and enhance decision-making architectures.

Future work includes developing a hybrid model that leverages the strengths of both the learnt and knowledge-based models: capturing complex variable dependencies effectively while integrating representative and up-to-date macrodata datasets. To achieve this, we will validate the generated synthetic populations against all data sources and compare the performance of the different structures to determine which model's structure most accurately represents each data source selected for the use case. Additionally, the validation should be compared with other emerging machine-learning methods [31,47,48]. Once validated, the synthesized population will be integrated into an agent-based model application. By either creating or extending an already existing decision-making architecture with detailed motivational attributes, we are aiming to model the behaviour of agents closer to real-life complex scenarios.

While agent-based social simulations are always a conceptual simplification of a given social context, their use to inform policy making in sensitive and urgent topics such as poverty mitigation [61] or public health crisis [24] call for a more nuanced analysis and reflection regarding the values that guide the agents' behaviour. Additional future steps will include testing the replicability of the model in other regions with alternative datasets. The article opens the door to operationalize value alignment of agent-based simulations in different contexts and geographical locations as well as to explore how a diversity of values, ideologies, opinions and vital priorities can affect the effectiveness of policy making by conditioning agents' behaviours.

Acknowledgments. This research has been supported by the EU-funded VALAWAI (# 101070930), the Spanish-funded VAE (# TED2021-131295B-C31) and the Rhymas

(# PID2020-113594RB-100) projects. Special thanks to Raül Tormos, Head of Methodology and Research at CEO (*Centre d'Estudis d'Opinió*) Generalitat de Catalunya.

Disclosure of Interests. The authors have no competing interests to declare that are relevant to the content of this article.

References

1. World Values Survey Database. https://www.worldvaluessurvey.org/wvs.jsp
2. European Values Study 2017: Integrated Dataset (EVS 2017), GESIS Data Archive, Cologne. ZA7500 Data file Version 5.0.0. https://doi.org/10.4232/1.13897
3. European Social Survey. https://www.europeansocialsurvey.org/
4. Enquesta de Valors a Catalunya. https://ceo.gencat.cat/ca/estudis/registre-estudisdopinio/estudis-dopinio-ceo/societat/detall/index.html?id=9088
5. Enquesta de Valors Socials Ajuntament de Barcelona - Oficina Municipal de Dades. https://portaldades.ajuntament.barcelona.cat/es/encuestas/21046
6. Portrait Values Questionnaire, 21 items. https://zis.gesis.org/skala/Schwartz-Breyer-Danner-Human-Values-Scale-(ESS)#
7. WVS Cultural Map: 2023 Version Released. https://www.worldvaluessurvey.org/WVSNewsShow.jsp?ID=467
8. Supported Data Types - pgmpy 0.1.23 documentation. https://pgmpy.org/#
9. Structure Learning - pgmpy 0.1.23 documentation. https://pgmpy.org/structure_estimator/base.html
10. Minnesota Population Center. Integrated Public Use Microdata Series, International: Version 7.3. IPUMS, Minneapolis (2020). https://doi.org/10.18128/D020.V7.3
11. Societat i benestar - Open Data Barcelona. https://opendata-ajuntament.barcelona.cat/data/es/organization/societat-i-benestar
12. Panel de Desigualtats Socials a Catalunya-PaD. https://fundaciobofill.cat/panel-de-desigualtats-socials-catalunya-pad
13. European Social Survey European Research Infrastructure (ESS ERIC), ESS round 10 - 2020. Democracy, Digital social contacts, Sikt - Norwegian Agency for Shared Services in Education and Research. https://doi.org/10.21338/NSD-ESS10-2020
14. Liang, X., Luo, L., Hu, S., Li, Y.: Mapping the knowledge frontiers and evolution of decision making based on agent-based modeling. Knowl.-Based Syst. **250**, 108982 (2022)
15. Ronald, I., Christian, W.: Modernization, Cultural Change, and Democracy: The Human Development Sequence. Cambridge University Press, Cambridge (2005)
16. Jacob, J., Bogdan, D.: Post materialism and comparative economic development: do institutions act as transmission channel? Soc. Ind. Res. **148** (2020)
17. Roger, X.L., et al.: Aggregating value systems for decision support. Knowl.-Based Syst. **287**, 111453 (2024)
18. Dov, C.: Cultural variation: considerations and implications. Psychol. Bull. **127**(4), 451 (2001)
19. Chapuis, K., Taillandier, P.: A brief review of synthetic population generation practices in agent-based social simulation. In: Submitted to SSC2019, Social Simulation Conference (2019)
20. Kevin, C., Patrick, T., Alexis, D.: Generation of synthetic populations in social simulations: a review of methods and practices. J. Artif. Soc. Soc. Simul. **25(2)** (2022)

21. Boyam, F., Pascal, G., Pierre, H., Pierre-Olivier, V.: Comparing methods for generating a two-layered synthetic population. Transp. Res. Rec. **2675**(1), 136–147 (2021)
22. Philippe, D., et al.: Recommendations on the Use of Synthetic Data to Train AI Models (2024)
23. Batel, Y., Meirav, A.: The social digital twin: the social turn in the field of smart cities. Environ. Plann. B Urban Anal. City Sci. **50**(6), 1455–1470 (2023)
24. Frank, D., et al.: Analysing the combined health, social and economic impacts of the corovanvirus pandemic using agent-based social simulation. Minds Mach. **30**(2), 177–194 (2020)
25. Peter, C., Rainer, S.: Thirty-three myths and misconceptions about population data: from data capture and processing to linkage. Int. J. Popul. Data Sci. **8**(1) (2023)
26. Stanislav, S.B., Jeppe, R., Francisco, C.P.: How to generate micro-agents? A deep generative modeling approach to population synthesis. Transp. Res. Part C Emerg. Technol. **106** (2019)
27. Lijun, S., Alexander, E.: A Bayesian network approach for population synthesis. Transp. Res. Part C Emerg. Technol. **61**, 49–62 (2015)
28. Aurore, S., Milovs, B.: Travel demand generation using Bayesian networks: an application to Switzerland. Procedia Comput. Sci. **220**, 267–274 (2023)
29. Anugrah, I., Kay, W.A.: Integrating Bayesian network and generalized raking for population synthesis in Greater Jakarta. Reg. Stud. Reg. Sci. **6**(1), 623–636 (2019)
30. Colin, W., Zheng, L., Alicia, G., Yue, Z.: SynC: a unified framework for generating synthetic population with gaussian copula. arXiv preprint arXiv:1904.07998 (2019)
31. Stanislav, S.B., Jeppe, R., Francisco, C.P.: Scalable population synthesis with deep generative modeling. arXiv preprint arXiv:1808.06910 (2018)
32. Manon, P., Manley, E.: A synthetic population for agent-based modelling in Canada. Sci. Data **10**(1), 148 (2023)
33. Na, J., Andrew, T.C., Hamdi, K., Annetta, B., William, G.K.: A method to create a synthetic population with social networks for geographically-explicit agent-based models. Comput. Urban Sci. **2**(1), 7 (2022)
34. Zhou, M., Li, J., Basu, R., Ferreira, J.: Creating spatially-detailed heterogeneous synthetic populations for agent-based microsimulation. Comput. Environ. Urban Syst. **91**, 101717 (2022)
35. Nik, L., Andrew, P.S., Luke, A., Alistair, F., James, V.: An open-source model for projecting small area demographic and land-use change. Geogr. Anal. **54**(3), 599–622 (2022)
36. William, D.W., et al.: Synthesized population databases: a US geospatial database for agent-based models. Methods Report (RTI Press) **2009**(10), 905 (2009)
37. Sebastian, H., Milos, B.: Synthetic population and travel demand for Paris and Île- France based on open and publicly available data. Transp. Res. Part C Emerg. Technol. **130**, 103291 (2021)
38. Serio, A., Claudio, R., Bat-hen, N.: Assignment of a synthetic population for activity-based modeling employing publicly available data. ISPRS Int. J. Geo-Inf. **11**, 148 (2022)
39. Poh Ping, L.: Population synthesis for travel demand modelling in Australian capital cities (2020)
40. Nicholas, G., James, M.M., Alan, D., Kevin, B.K., Jodie, M.: Synthetic population dynamics: a model of household demography. J. Artif. Soc. Soc. Simul. **16**(1), 8 (2013)

41. Oksana, G., et al.: Artificial Populations in Agent-Based Modeling (2023)
42. Friedrich, K.: Heterogeneity in individual adaptation action: modelling the provision of a climate adaptation public good in an empirically grounded synthetic population. J. Environ. Psychol. **52**, 119–135 (2017)
43. Michael, A.H.: Social identity theory. Springer (2016)
44. Ronald, I.: The Silent Revolution: Changing Values and Political Styles Among Western Publics. Princeton University Press, Princeton (1977)
45. Thomas, H., Wolfgang, A.: Value changes in transforming China. Kome Int. J. Pure Commun. Inquiry **2**(1), 1–22 (2013)
46. Muhammad, S.O., Adnan, M.A., Philip, R.P.: A survey on data imputation techniques: water distribution system as a use case. IEEE Access **6**, 63279–63291 (2018)
47. Aemmer, Z., MacKenzie, D.: Generative population synthesis for joint household and individual characteristics. Comput. Environ. Urban Syst. **96**, 101852 (2022)
48. Albiston, G., Osman, T., Brown, D.: A neural network approach for population synthesis. Simulation (2024). https://doi.org/10.1177/00375497241233597
49. Victor, M.P., Yoav, Z.: Statistical aspects of Wasserstein distances. Annu. Rev. Stat. Appl. **6**, 405–431 (2019)
50. Stanislav, S.B., Jeppe, R., Francisco, C.P.: How to generate micro-agents? A deep generative modeling approach to population synthesis. Transp. Res. Part C Emerg. Technol. **106**, 73–97 (2019)
51. Eui-Jin, K., Prateek, B.: A deep generative model for feasible and diverse population synthesis. Transp. Res. Part C Emerg. Technol. **148**, 104053 (2023)
52. Sergio, G., Stanislav, S.B., Francisco, C.P., Jeppe, R.: Prediction of rare feature combinations in population synthesis: application of deep generative modelling. Transp. Res. Part C Emerg. Technol. **120**, 102787 (2020)
53. Shalom, H.S.: An overview of the schwartz theory of basic values. Online Read. Psychol. Cult. **2**(1) (2012)
54. Paul, R.A.: Value change in global perspective. The University of Michigan Press, Ann Arbor (1995)
55. Sen, A.: Development as Freedom. Oxford University Press (2001)
56. Gordon, W.A.: The nature of prejudice. Basic Books (1954)
57. Axel, H.: The Struggle for Recognition. Polity Press (1996)
58. Charles, T.: Multiculturalism and the politics of recognition. Princeton University Press (1931)
59. José, O.: Ideas y Creencias. Ediciones de la Revista de Occidente, Madrid (1942)
60. Kaiyuan, X., Brian, N., Anthony, G.G.: Data from the race implicit association test on the project implicit demo website. J. Open Psychol. Data **2**(1), e3 (2014)
61. Alba, A., Nieves, M., Georgina, C., Nardine, O., Carles, S.: Can poverty be reduced by acting on discrimination? An agent-based model for policy-making. In: AAMAS 2024: Proceedings of the 2024 International Conference on Autonomous Agents and Multiagent Systems (2024)
62. Montes, N., Curto, G., Osman, N., Sierra, C.: An agent-based model for poverty and discrimination policy-making. arXiv preprint arXiv:2303.13994 (2023)

User Study Design for Identifying the Semantics of Bioethical Principles

Manel Rodriguez-Soto[1], Nardine Osman[1(✉)], Carles Sierra[1],
Nieves Montes[2], Jordi Martinez Roldan[3], Rocio Cintas Garcia[4],
Cristina Farriols Danes[4], Montserrat Garcia Retortillo[4],
and Silvia Minguez Maso[4]

[1] Artificial Intelligence Research Institute (IIIA -CSIC), Barcelona, Spain
{manel.rodriguez,nardine,sierra}@iiia.csic.es
[2] Mentice, Barcelona, Spain
[3] Hospital Sant Joan de Déu, Barcelona, Spain
[4] Hospital del Mar Research Institute (IMIM), Barcelona, Spain

Abstract. The topic of value alignment in AI has been gaining significant attention. The ultimate objective is how AI systems can align with human values. One of the main challenges, however, is identifying the relevant values. Some emerging works are focusing on learning relevant values through analysing our statements on social media. In most of these cases, learned values are simply specified through a label such as equality, fairness, or justice. However, the semantics of these values is not studied further. Addressing this gap, we propose a user study that provides us with a systematic approach for learning value semantics. The study is in the context of healthcare and the values of interest are the four fundamental bioethical principles: beneficence, non-maleficence, autonomy, and justice. We conduct a user study to collect the views of medical professionals on the value alignment of synthetic patient cases. We then search the space of candidate functions to find the one that best fits the participants answers, and hence, best describes their view of the value in question.

1 Introduction

The topic of value alignment is gaining a lot of traction lately [6,8,11]. New research lines are emerging that address issues such as how individual values can be aggregated to the level of groups [12]; how arguments that explicitly reference values can be made [3]; how decision making can be value-driven [7,9,21]; and how norms are selected to maximise value alignment [14,19,20]. One of the important challenges, however, is identifying the relevant values that AI needs to align with. There is a growing field on how AI learns human values, with many focusing on analysing our statements on social media [4,13]. In almost all these cases, learned values are simply specified through a label such as *equality*, *fairness*, or *justice*. However, the semantics of these values is not studied further. Recently, we have proposed a formal model for value representation that aims at tackling the issue of value semantics [15]. Values, in this proposal, are no longer treated as labels representing abstract concepts, but as complex taxonomies that take into consideration the relations between value concepts, the importance of value concepts, and the semantics of value concepts. Semantics are provided by linking abstract concepts with formal properties whose satisfaction can be measured. Value semantics essentially define what it means for a given behaviour, whether a single action or an entire interaction, to be aligned with a given value.

However, the issue of learning value semantics arises. Relying on humans to provide these semantics is not always reliable. This paper explains our experience in trying to define the four basic bioethical principle —beneficiency, non-malificiency, autonomy, and justice— and our current user study that is being unrolled to achieve a more systematic approach for extracting these semantics.

Our initial approach was fruitful, but time consuming and not very efficient in eliciting the views of a large number of medical professionals. In our initial approach, our attempt to formalise the semantics of these four bioethical principles was realised through engaging in intensive and lengthy discussions with three medical doctors from Hospital del Mar, Barcelona (the last three authors of this paper). Our interactions, which spanned a period of several months in 2023–2024, allowed us to come up with clear equations for two of the four bioethical principles: beneficency and non-maleficency. However, this labour intensive work allowed us to provide a formal specification that reflects the views of three medical doctors only.

Our current, more systematic, approach is to use replicable questionnaires that can be easily conducted in hospitals at a large scale, allowing us to extract the semantics of these four bioethical principles by taking the point of view of a larger number of medical professionals, both doctors and nurses. By achieving an easily replicable study, this opens the door to comparing the semantics of these bioethical principle for different hospitals, different countries, or even different cultures.

The rest of this paper is divided as follows. Section 2 introduces the four bioethical principles according to the literature of biomedical ethics. Section 3 presents our initial work in defining the semantics of these principles. Section 4 presents our ongoing user study for extracting the semantics of these principles at a large scale, followed by some concluding remarks in Sect. 5.

2   The Four Bioethical Principles

This paper considers that there are four main bioethical principles, following Beauchamp and Childress' principialism [1]. As agreed upon by the biomedical community, at least these four principles provide the best framework for ethical analysis in biomedical scenarios [22]. These four principles are:

1. **Autonomy:** to give value to the considerations and options of autonomous patients, and refrain from putting obstacles to their actions, unless they are clearly harmful to others.
2. **Beneficence:** to ensure that the benefit of the patient is always maximised.

3. **Non-maleficence:** to ensure that no harm is being inflicted on the patient or at least that it is being minimized.
4. **Justice:** to proceed with equity in the distribution of burdens and benefits and treat everyone fairly, equally, and without discrimination.

These principles are sometimes referred to as medical ethical values in the literature [16,17], and as such, we use the words principles and values interchangeably in this paper.

Following Ross's ethical theory, all four values are *prima facie* [18]. That is, there is no explicit ordering between them, and ideally a clinicial should always try to behave as value-aligned as possible with respect to all four values. However, Ross (and later Beauchamp and Childress) acknowledged that always completely aligning with multiple conflicting values would be impossible. Thus, as *prima facie* values, one should always weigh the possible benefits and costs of each medical value according to each value and then decide which is the most appropriate one.

As an example, consider a patient that is suffering from a serious illness and requires an immediate surgery. Following the value of beneficence, the clinician should seek to maximise the benefit of the patient, which means to perform surgery on the patient. However, following the value of non-maleficence the clinician should never produce harm on the patient, or at least minimise the risk of harm. But any surgery has an inevitable degree of risk, and always causes a short-term harm to the patient. Under this dilemma, principialism recommends evaluating the advantages and disadvantages of either performing the surgery or not, in terms of the values in conflict. If the degree of risk of the surgery is low enough while the benefits are almost guaranteed, a clinician then should select to prioritise beneficence over non-maleficence in this specific case.

Next Sect. 3 present our first attempt at formalising these four biomedical values so that they are computationally treatable.

3   Initial Approach

Our first step towards formalising the four biomedical values was to categorise them following the proposed outline by Veatch in [22]. Veatch states that biomedical ethics' four main values can be divided into two categories: *consequence-based* values and *duty-based* values. Recall that value semantics essentially specify what it means for a given behaviour to be aligned with a given value. However, to behave in alignment with a given value has a separate definition for each category, as we show next.

- **Consequence-based values**: An action is aligned with a consequence-based value if its consequences are aligned with that value. In a biomedical context, the degree of alignment with such values is measured by the amount of utility a given action provides to the patient. This category includes the values of *beneficence* (measuring positive utility, good) and *non-maleficence* (measuring negative utility, harm).

– **Duty-based values**: An action is aligned with a duty-based value if and only if it is morally acceptable according to that value, regardless of its consequences. In a biomedical context, actions such as "misinforming the patient" or "disrespecting patient's directives" would not be morally acceptable under any circumstance with respect to the duty-based value of *autonomy*. This category also includes the value of *justice*.

As such, the approach for formalising each of the above value categories is different, as we present next.

3.1 Formalising Consequence-Based Values

We can formalise alignment with a consequence-based value by considering a patient's medical state, described by a set of criteria C, before performing a medical action and comparing it with their medical state after the action is performed, described by the change in criteria C'. Formally, let V be a consequence-based value, then:

$$align(a, \langle C, C' \rangle, V) = f_V(C, C') \tag{1}$$

where a is the medical action taken, and f_V is a function comparing the patient's medical state before and after the action a.

There are two implications from this equation. The first one is that the action taken is irrelevant to the formula since we only care about the consequences. Moreover, this function is taking into account that the outcome of an action is non-deterministic in a medical context, and for that reason we must focus on its consequences.

The second implication is that we can obtain a formal definition of f_V (and thus, of the value it evaluates) by explicitly listing which patient criteria are considered relevant for that specific value and how its change in criteria is evaluated. Assume that we have already agreed on the subset of criteria C_V relevant for a given value V. Then, a possible formula for f_V could be:

$$f_V(C_V, C'_V) = G_V \left(\sum_{i=1}^{|C_V|} g_V^i(c_i, c'_i) \right) \tag{2}$$

where $c_i \in C_V$ and $c'_i \in C'_V$ are different criteria describing the state of the patient before and after the action. Different definitions of the functions g_v^i and G_V could be explored. For example, we can have $g_v^i(x, y) = x - y$ and $G_V(x) = x$, which essentially states that we simply account for the accumulated change for each relevant criterion. If the change in a criterion's evolution was positive (numbers went down after the action was performed), then that would result in a positive alignment, and hence, the change in that criterion's evolution would be contributing to promoting the value V, and vice versa. As such, we see that the range of each criterion needs to be designed and normalised accordingly.

Equation 2 provides us with the formal representation of the consequence-based values, beneficence and non-maleficence. What is then necessary to identify is the set of relevant criteria C_V for each of those values, and the exact definitions of g_v^i and G_V.

Our interactions with the three medical doctors from Hospital del Mar allowed us to identify the potentially relevant patient criteria for the values beneficence and non-maleficence. These are presented in Table 1.

Defining functions g_V and G_V for each value was a more complicated task, and required continued intensive discussions, which was very time consuming and inefficient, especially that the resulting functions would reflect the point of view of the few medical doctors one is working with. For this reason, a more systematic approach has been designed through user studies, which we present in the next section. The user study allows us to define the functions g_V and G_V in an efficient approach that takes into consideration the point of view of a large set of medical professionals, both doctors and nurses.

3.2   Formalising Duty-Based Values

Formalising the alignment of behaviour with a duty-based value is a much more complex task, it requires an understanding of the moral norms that define what is morally acceptable behaviour for that value. The alignment is then dependant on the action and the moral norms that define a duty-based value. Formally, let $\mathbf{V}$ be a duty-based value and $N_{\mathbf{V}}$ be the set of moral norms defining that value $\mathbf{V}$, then:

$$align(a, N_{\mathbf{V}}, \mathbf{V}) = f_{\mathbf{V}}(a, N_{\mathbf{V}}) \tag{3}$$

To compute this alignment, we say it must be based on the degree of satisfying those identified moral norms. So we have:

$$f_{\mathbf{V}}(a, N_{\mathbf{V}}) = \bigoplus_{n \in N_{\mathbf{V}}} (sat(a, n)) \tag{4}$$

where $sat(n)$ describes the degree of satisfaction of action a with moral norm n, and $\bigoplus$ describes some aggregation function that aggregates the different degrees of satisfaction for all moral norms of $\mathbf{V}$.

As such, it becomes critical to understand and formalise these moral norms that define a given value, along with defining the $\bigoplus$ and sat functions.

Our interactions with the medical doctors from Hospital del Mar allowed us to identify the moral norms associated with the value autonomy, which we present below:

norm 1 The patient must be informed of the implications of both receiving and not receiving a given treatment, unless they choose to remain uninformed.
norm 2 The patient's wishes concerning treatments must be respected.
norm 3 The patient must not be coerced or persuaded to accept or reject a treatment.

Our findings are relatively consistent with the literature on that topic [5]. In [5], two norms are represented by our first norm (norm 1): one declares the patient's right to be informed of the consequences of treatments, and the second declares the patient's right to choose not to be informed of treatments' consequences (or the right to remain uninformed). Three norms are represented by our second norm (norm 2): the first declares the right not to be subjected to any treatment without the consent of the patient, the second declares the patient's right to withdraw their consent at any time, and the third states that when the patient is not in a position to express their wishes then their latest wishes (advanced directives) must be respected. We believe our second norm summarises all three situations. Our third norm (norm 3) adds the requirement that a patient must not be coerced or persuaded to accept or reject a treatment, which also appears in the discourse of existing literature.

With the given moral norms identified, the next step is to define the $\oplus$ and sat functions. Concerning the sat function, we assume the results of the sat function to be known and provided by the patient's medical team. This is because the sat function, or the degree of satisfaction of a given action with given moral norm, depends on complex issues, such as understanding the informed consent forms (norm 1), understanding the wishes of the patient with respect to different treatments (norm 2), and identifying whether the patient has been coerced or not in accepting/rejecting a treatment (norm 3). All of this is not straightforward and requires the analysis of natural text in documents (such as the informed consent forms) and live interactions (such as the discussions that a doctor has with a patient and/or his family members). For this reason, in this paper we assume the degree of satisfaction (sat) of these norms to be provided. We rely on the medical professionals' capability of identifying and declaring the satisfaction of these norms. Table 2 presents the variables n_1–n_3, corresponding to the satisfaction of norms 1–3. For the time being, the range of satisfaction of a moral norm is either 1, to represent that the norm was respected, or 0, to represent that the norm was not respected. Future work can introduce degrees of satisfaction, as needed.

As for $\oplus$, one suggested implementation is $\oplus = \sum_{n \in N_{\mathbf{v}}} w_n \cdot sat(a, n)$, where the aggregation is a linear equation that assumes a linear relationship between the degree of satisfaction of the various moral norms, each with a predefined weight w_n.

Once again, trying to elicit the exact definition of $\oplus$ that captures the semantics of autonomy through focus groups is a complicated and time consuming task. We have provided here one possible proposal for $\oplus$. We hope that the user study we are designing will allow us to capture a more comprehensive definition of $\oplus$ that captures the point of view of a large set of medical professionals from Hospital del Mar.

The value justice is much more complex and requires further work. The literature provides open ended discussions and definitions on the topic [5]. For example, it may be understood as ensuring fair treatment and access to resources for all, regardless of their social or economic status. In general, it is about avoiding unjust discrimination based on factors such as race, ethnicity, gender, religion, socioeconomic status, disability, or age. But it may also touch upon topics like holding individuals and institutions responsible for their actions and decisions. What is clear is that justice is the only value that is not solely concerned with the patient in question, but third parties as well. At this stage, no clear moral norms have been identified for the value justice. Through the setup of our user study (the corpus building stage of Sect. 4.2), we will aim at identifying and eliciting moral norms that are relevant for justice. If we do succeed, then a follow up user study can be designed to investigate the functions $\oplus$ and *sat* defining justice for the identified set of moral norms.

4   Proposed User Study

This section proposes a user study for identifying the semantics of the four biomedical values, helping us provide a concrete computational definition of these values that captures the point of view of a large group of medical professionals. In other words, we essentially aim to identify Eqs. 1 and 3 that provide a best representation of the point of view of the medical professionals involved in our study. First, Sect. 4.1 discusses the issue of identifying relevant variables. This step is crucial as these are the variables upon which the equations giving values their semantics will be built upon. Then, Sect. 4.2 illustrates the various stages of our proposed user study and how its results will be used to craft the equations defining the four bioethical values, building on the identified variables.

4.1   Variable Identification

One main requirement for formally defining the formal expression that gives any value its semantics is recognising the potential variables that this expression is built upon. As an example, for formally defining income inequality, the Gini index [10] depends on two variables: the income or wealth values of individuals/households, and the population size (total number of individuals/households). As such, to formally define our four biomedical values, the first step is to identify the relevant variables that define each value. Our initial approach (Sect. 3) has paved the ground for identifying these variables. Interactions with the stakeholders are necessary at this stage.

Given the definitions of beneficence and non-maleficence —ensuring patient benefit is maximised and ensuring no harm is inflicted on the patient [1]—, it becomes clear that the relevant variables for those two bioethical values should be those describing the patient's state, as benefit and harm can be assessed by evaluating the change in the patient's state. However, we cannot depend on variables that are too specific for a given context, such as a given diagnosis or a given field in medicine. For this reason, we set out, in collaboration with the three medical doctors from Hospital del Mar, to identify generic patient variables that can be applied to patients regardless of context, and yet are informative enough to allow medical professionals perform a practical and effective analysis

Table 1. The identified generic (patient) variables related to beneficence and non-maleficence

Variable Name	Variable Description	Variable Range
c_1	**Age:** Specifies the patient's age, specified in intervals representing decades	$\{$0–19, 20–29, ... ,90–99, +99$\}$
c_2	**Complex Chronic Disease (CCD):** Measures if the patient has one or more chronic diseases, with at least one being permanent, leaving lingering disability, being non-reversible, or co-existing with a psychological illness	$\{$Yes, No$\}$
c_3	**Short-term survival (MACA):** Measures if the patient has an advanced chronic disease with an expected survival rate of less than 12–18 months that requires palliative care	$\{$Yes, No$\}$
c_4	**Expected survival:** Provides an estimation, in months, of the expected survival of the patient	$\{<$ 12 months, $>$ 12 months$\}$
c_5	**Frailty Index (Frail-VIG):** Assesses the degree of frailty of the patient	$\{$Low, Moderate, High$\}$
c_6	**Clinical Risk Group (CRG):** Provides a categorical classification that uses administrative data to identify patients with chronic health conditions	$\{$0, 1, 2, 3, 4$\}$
c_7	**Social Support:** Specifies if the patient has social support (from family or friends) to offer support functions (emotional, instrumental, ...)	$\{$Yes, No$\}$
c_8	**Functional independence (Barthel Index):** Measures the capacity of the patient with respect to executing activities of daily living (ADL), such as feeding, bathing, ambulation, bladder and bowel control, ...	$\{$0–20%, 21–60%, 61–90%, 91–99%, 100%$\}$
c_8	**Instrumental activities independence (Lawton Index):** Measures an individual's ability to perform various complex activities that are necessary for independent living, such as using the telephone, shopping, food preparation, housekeeping, laundry, mode of transportation, responsibility for own medications, managing finances,	$\{$0, ..., 8$\}$

(*continued*)

Table 1. (*continued*)

Variable Name	Variable Description	Variable Range
c_9	**Patient's advanced directives:** Specifies, for patients with a decision-making capacity, if there is a signed document or oral communication describing the patient's desires regarding treatment decisions. This includes when the patients identify whom they want to make decisions on their behalf when they cannot do so themselves	{Yes, No}
c_{10}	**Cognitive deterioration:** Specifies if the patient suffers cognitive impairment, such as confusion, memory loss, difficulty understanding or speaking, problems with concentration,	{No deterioration, Low-Moderate, Severe }
c_{11}	**Emotional state:** Specifies whether the patient suffers emotional distress	{Yes, No}
c_{12}	**Discomfort level:** Measures level of pain and physical distress	{Low, Medium, High}

of the patient's state and its evolution. These generic patient variables are listed in Table 1. These variables play a vital role in the definition of consequence-based values, as Eq. 1 shows. The new equations that we intend to identify that capture the point of view of a large group of medical professionals will also build upon these criteria, hence the need for interacting with stakeholders ahead of the user study to identify such criteria. We also hope that qualitative feedback from the user study can confirm whether our identified criteria are comprehensive or lacking in some respects.

Regarding the other two duty-based values (autonomy and justice), and as we noted in Sect. 3, these depend on moral norms. As such, it is necessary to identify and formalise the moral norms that define them.

Given the definition of autonomy, based on some literature on the topic [1, 2, 5] and our discussions with the medical doctors from Hospital del Mar, we were able to recognise the moral norms that define autonomy and the three variables that describe the degree of satisfaction of those norms are presented in Table 2. The equation defining the value of autonomy should be built on these three variables. But we also look forward to qualitative feedback to confirm whether our selected moral norms are comprehensive or lacking in some respects.

Given the definition of justice, we note that justice is even more complicated than autonomy, as alignment with justice cannot be computed at the level of the individual. For example, to assess whether a given action towards a patient is aligned with the value of justice, one of the requirements is to compare it with the actions that similar patients have received. Hence, due to the broadness of the definition of justice, we were not able to identify variables of justice to be

Table 2. The identified generic variables related to autonomy

Variable Name	Variable Description	Variable Range
n_1	The patient's (or their authorised representative's) level of understanding of the instructions provided by the medical professionals	$\{0,1\}$
n_2	The patient (or their authorised representative) being informed about each possible treatment and the consequences of receiving or not that treatment	$\{0,1\}$
n_3	The patient's (or their authorised representative's) independent decision (that s/he has not been coerced/pressured by a third party to accept or reject a given treatment)	$\{0,1\}$

included in our user study, but we hope the user study would shed light on the moral norms that define justice.

4.2 Function Identification

The next step, after identifying the potential relevant variables through interacting with the stakeholders, is to identify the functions that define the bioethical values through these variables: function f_v of Eqs. 1 and 3.

Instead of directly asking stakeholders for their views on these bioethical values and how can we define such functions, as in Sect. 3, we design a user study that would elicit these views through simple questionnaires. This allows us to easily replicate this user study in different departments, hospitals, and so on, to get the different perspectives on the semantics of these bioethical values. In essence, the questionnaires present medical professionals with different patient cases and asks whether the medical professional believes each of the bioethical values was promoted, demoted or not affected for each of those patient cases. The idea is that it is easier for medical professionals to give their opinion on the promotion/demotion of a value when presented with a concrete case. And with these responses, we can then search for the function that best represents the medical professionals' answers; that is, find the function that best describes their perspectives.

The steps for conducting this user study are as follows:

1. **Build a diverse corpus of patient cases**, to be used in the user study.
2. **Select the participants (medical professionals)** for conducting the user study.

3. **Conduct the user study** by asking the selected medical professionals to assess whether each of the bioethical principles was promoted, demoted, or not affected for each of the patients cases they are presented with.
4. **Identify the functions** that describe the semantics of the various bioethical values. This is achieved by finding the functions that best fits the responses of medical professionals.

The remainder of this section is structured with each subsequent subsection covering the different steps of our user study.

Building the Corpus. Obtaining real data is usually a challenge in the medical field, especially when the identified relevant variables refer to information that is usually not digitised in many hospitals. As such, for our user study, we chose to build a corpus of synthetic data.

The objective is to compile a diverse and large number of patient cases, where the patient is defined by his/her relevant variables (in our case, generic patient variables and autonomy-related variables), along with the patient's diagnosis. The patient's diagnosis is concise and described in a few words only, and it is added simply to provide the context for medical professionals to help them with the assessment of patients in the first phase of the user study, when predicting the evolution of a patient's state (see Sect. 4.2). The diagnosis is not relevant (and not presented) in the second phase of the user study, when the promotion/demotion of values is assessed.

To minimise the number of patient cases that each medical professional has to assess in the user study (Step 4), we focus on cases that have the potential of raising a value conflict. In other words, cases that promote one bioethical value while demoting another. We believe such cases might be the most informative ones when it comes to learning the semantics of bioethical values from them.

To create realistic synthetic data, we choose to start with 75 actual patient cases. We are asking five of the medical professionals that we have been collaborating with to assess 15 cases each. They are asked to: 1) identify the cases that might potentially raise value conflicts, 2) identify which actions are the ones that might result in value conflicts, and 3) for each of those cases and their corresponding actions, identify the relevant patient criteria that they believe impact having a value promoted/demoted. In summary, this analysis helps us identify the cases with potential value conflicts, and the relevant actions and patient criteria associated with that potential value conflict. Furthermore, allowing for open-ended responses at this stage allows us to better understand if our list of criteria is comprehensive or not.

With these cases at hand, we plan to generate a larger number of realistic synthetic cases (we are aiming at 150 cases) that will eventually be used in the user study (Step 3). To generate these cases, we essentially take each of the potentially conflicting cases identified above and vary some of their identified relevant variables to create new cases. These new cases will allows us, through the user study, to pinpoint how the relevant variables may impact value promo-

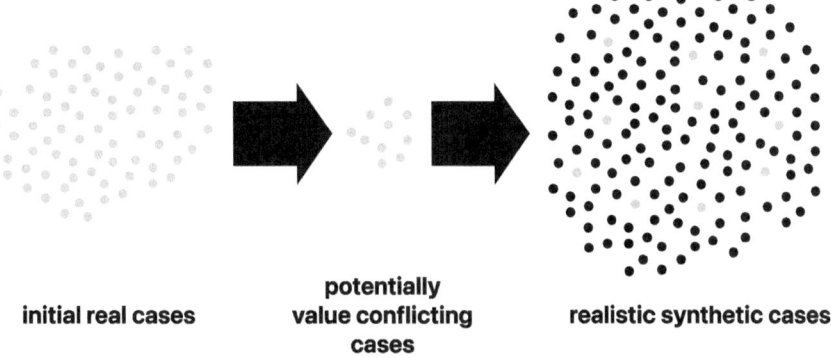

initial real cases   **potentially value conflicting cases**   **realistic synthetic cases**

Fig. 1. Synthesising patient data

tion/demotion, from which we can then try to identify the functions defining the semantics of the four bioethical values (Step 4).

Figure 1 provides us with an illustration on how the 150 patient cases used in the user study are created.

An important issue to note is the need to create cases that span diverse diagnoses. This could help verify whether value promotion/demotion is only affected by the identified relevant variables, or whether the diagnosis plays a crucial role. Our hypothesis, along with that of the medical doctors we are collaborating with, is that the diagnoses is not relevant when considering bioethical values: only the identified relevant variables impact value promotion/demotion. This hypothesis arises despite the fact that doctors are trained to always look at the diagnosis whenever assessing a given patient.

Selecting the Participants. The choice of medical professionals to participate in the user study depends on whose perspective are we interested in obtaining. The semantics of bioethical values can be obtained, for example, for:

- Individual medical professionals, by asking each medical professional to assess a large number of diverse patient examples, which will allow us to extract the function that best defines their view concerning the four bioethical values.
- A hospital department, by asking a number of medical professionals of that department to assess a large number of diverse patient examples.
- A hospital, by having medical professionals from across the various departments of this hospital assess a large number of diverse patient examples.

Of course, we can proceed with this approach to assess the semantics for a given country or geographical region. We can also include and compare the perspective of nurses versus medical doctors.

Our current plans are to include nurses and medical doctors from a range of departments at Hospital del Mar, Barcelona. We plan to recruit 10 medical professionals in totals, with each being asked to assess 15 patient cases from the 150 cases generated in Step 2.

Conducting the User Study. The user study is conducted in two phases. In the first one, participants (selected medical professionals) are presented with a number of patient cases: 15 per professional. Each case consists of patient criteria (variables of Table 1) and a selected action (identified in the earlier stage as potentially raising value conflicts). In this phase, each patient case is being assessed by one professional. The participants are asked to predict the change in patient criteria (specifically those of Table 1) when considering the selected action. At this stage, the diagnosis is presented, as the diagnosis is critical for predicting the evolution of a patient's state. Figure 2 provides an illustration of the questionnaire used in this phase. The parts in red highlight what needs to be filled in by the participants. In this case, how patient criteria evolve. As such, the results of these questionnaires provide us with an expectation of how some of the patients' criteria would evolve for each patient case and selected action.

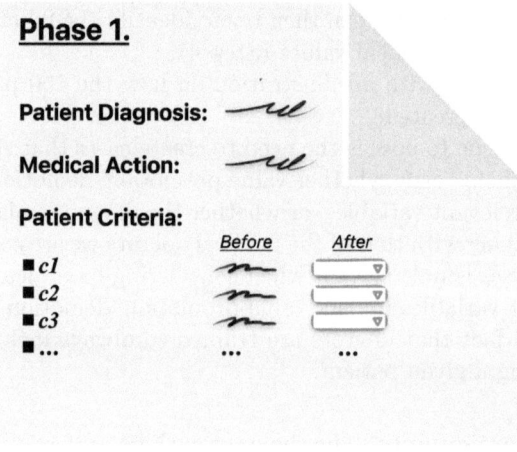

Fig. 2. The user study's questionnaire, phase 1

After the first phase is completed, the second phase starts. In this phase, each participant is presented with 45 patient cases, where each case includes the patient criteria (variables of Tables 1 and 2), a selected action (with potential of introducing value conflicts), and some of the patient criteria (variables of Table 1) resulting from performing the presented action. The diagnosis is not presented in this phase. Here, each patient case is being assessed by three medical professionals. We make sure here that the patient cases presented at this stage to a given participant are different from those assessed by that participant in the first phase. This ensures that knowing the diagnosis and thinking about the evolution of criteria does not influence one's views with respect to value alignment. In this phase, participants are asked to assess whether each of the bioethical values was promoted, demoted, or not affected for each of the patient cases they are presented with. Figure 3 provides an illustration of the questionnaire used

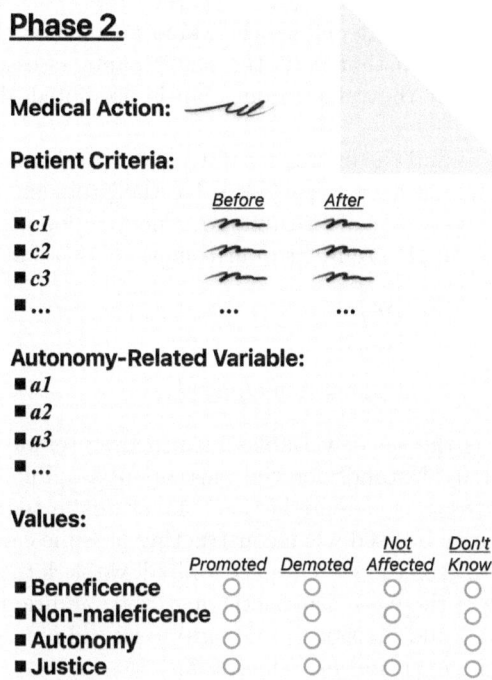

Fig. 3. The user study's questionnaire, phase 2

at this stage. Again, the parts in red highlight what needs to be filled in by the participants. In this case, which values are being promoted/demoted. The results of these questionnaires essentially contain information on how the generic variables (both patient and autonomy related variables identified in Tables 1 and 2) impact value promotion/demotion. The next step will be to find the formal function for each value that fits the data, that is, the function that results in value promotion/demotion that fits the data.

Identifying the Semantics of Bioethical Principles. This subsection describes how we plan to identify and formally define the semantics of a given bioethical principle, or value. The objective is to find the function f_v for a given value v, whether consequence-based or duty-based, that reflects the answers of the participants for that value v.

The search for function f_v can be framed as an optimisation problem over the space of functions $\mathcal{F} : \mathbb{Z}^2 \to \mathbb{R}$ that map a tuple of variables $X = (x_1, ..., x_n, r_v)$ to a real number.

The variables (excluding the last variable r_v) represent the identified relevant criteria for a given value (Tables 1 and 2). In other words, if we are looking for the functions f_b and f_{nm} that define beneficence and non-maleficence, respectively, then we will have $X = (c_1, \ldots, c_n, c'_1, \ldots, c'_n, r_v)$; whereas, if we are looking for a function f_a that defines the value autonomy, then we will have $X = (n_1, n_2, n_3, r_v)$. Recall that r_v is the participants assessment, for a given patient case, on whether the value in question is promoted, demoted, or unaffected.

The objective is to find the expression $f_v(X)$ that best predicts the observed answers that participants have taken. To solve the problem, we implement an Evolutionary Strategy search algorithm. To generate potential candidates for $f(\cdot)$, we start with a simple grammar of arithmetic expressions:

$$Arg := x_1 \mid \ldots \mid x_n \mid r_v \mid z$$
$$Op := + \mid - \mid \cdot \mid /$$
$$Exp := Arg[OpExp]$$

where $\{x_1, \ldots, x_n\}$ is the set of variables identified as relevant to the value in question, $r_v = \{-1, 0, 1\}$ stands for the participant's opinion on whether the value v is promoted ($r_v = 1$), demoted ($r_v = -1$), or unaffected ($r_v = 0$), and $z \in \mathbb{Z}$ is an integer that may be used when constructing possible candidate functions. For the time being, to keep the search space limited, we stick to a simple language that only makes use of the basic arithmetic operators: addition ($+$), subtraction ($-$), multiplication ($\cdot$) and division ($/$). Future work can incorporate additional operators, such as the *max* and *min* operators.

To evaluate how well does a candidate function $f(\cdot)$ fit the user study data, we consider two opposite factors. First, we assess what is the affinity of that function for the experimental data, which we define as $Aff(f)$. One approach for implementing $Aff(f)$ is through the mean absolute error, which computes the distance between the predicted value alignment f and the actual alignment presented in the responses of the user study data. Second, we assess how complex is that function. We favour simpler, less complex expressions. We define the complexity of an expression $Comp(f)$ as the number of operations (Op) required to generate it.

Our proposal then evaluates the suitability of a function by considering its affinity for the user study data and add a penalising factor for the complexity of the expression. The best function that describes the value in question is then obtained through optimisation:

$$f^* = \arg\max_{f \in F}(Aff(f) - (\lambda \cdot Comp(f))) \tag{5}$$

where λ controls the weight of penalisation and F is the set of functions that can be generated with the grammar.

The obtained function f^* that considers the participants' responses r_v for value v essentially describes the semantics of the value v. This could be computed taking into consideration the responses of one participant only, in which case the identified function f_v^* would represent the point of view of that participant. It could also consider the responses r_v of all participants, in which case the identified function f_v^* would represent the point of view of the collective of participants. This collective could be a department, a hospital, or even a geographical region. In our case, we find the function that best describes the point of view of the 10 medical professionals (doctors and nurses) recruited from various departments at Hospital del Mar.

5   Conclusion

With the rising interest in the role of human values in AI and the recent trend of learning these values from our online interactions [4, 13], we notice a striking lack of research on learning the semantics of these values. This paper aims to address this gap by proposing an approach that learns value semantics through user studies eliciting human feedback on value alignment. Our focus is on the medical field, and our participants are medical professionals who are presented with various patient cases. For each case, they assess whether a given action promotes, demotes, or does not affect the value in question. We conducted a user study to evaluate the four bioethical values: beneficence, non-maleficence, autonomy, and justice. Based on the participants' responses, we then explore the space of candidate functions to find the one that best fits the user study answers regarding value alignment. In other words, we identify the function that best describes, computationally, what it means for an action (behaviour) to be aligned with each value.

One primary direction for future work is optimising the creation of synthetic data to improve our user study. Our current approach for building the corpus has been based on medical professional's collaboration for curating a number of cases (75 cases), and then eliciting the professionals' feedback for detecting potentially value conflicting cases. To help improve replicability, we are exploring the creation of synthetic data using ChatGPT. Ongoing work is promising, but naturally, expertise's opinion is still needed to help guide the generation of these cases. Though the involvement of the experts will be less time consuming.

If replicability is achieved, then we plan to apply this user study to a larger number of medical professionals, across different hospitals and geographical areas. This would allow us to analyse how value semantics change across departments, hospitals, or even countries.

Acknowledgments. This work has been supported by the EU-funded VALAWAI (# 101070930) project and the Spanish-funded VAE (# TED2021-131295B-C31) and Rhymas (# PID2020-113594RB-100) projects.

References

1. Beauchamp, T., Childress, J.: Principles of Biomedical Ethics. Oxford University Press (1979)
2. Beauchamp, T.: The 'Four Principles' Approach to Health Care Ethics, pp. 3 – 10. Wiley (2007). https://doi.org/10.1002/9780470510544.ch1

3. Bench-Capon, T., Atkinson, K.: Abstract argumentation and values. In: Simari, G., Rahwan, I. (eds.) Argumentation in Artificial Intelligence, pp. 45–64. Springer US, Boston, MA (2009). https://doi.org/10.1007/978-0-387-98197-0_3

4. Brugnoli, E., Gravino, P., Prevedello, G.: Moral values in social media for disinformation and hate speech analysis. In: Preproceedings of the Value Engineering in AI Workshop, at 26th European Conference on Artificial Intelligence (ECAI 2023) (2023)

5. Casado, M., Baroni, M.: Manual de bioética laica: Cuestiones de salud y biotecnología -. Colección de bioética, Universitat de Barcelona Edicions (2018). https://books.google.es/books?id=LfnBzgEACAAJ

6. Chatila, R., Dignum, V., Fisher, M., Giannotti, F., Morik, K., Russell, S., Yeung, K.: Trustworthy AI. In: Braunschweig, B., Ghallab, M. (eds.) Reflections on Artificial Intelligence for Humanity. LNCS (LNAI), vol. 12600, pp. 13–39. Springer, Cham (2021). https://doi.org/10.1007/978-3-030-69128-8_2

7. Chhogyal, K., Nayak, A.C., Ghose, A., Dam, H.K.: A value-based trust assessment model for multi-agent systems. In: IJCAI, pp. 194–200. ijcai.org (2019)

8. European Commission: ethics guidelines for trustworthy AI (2019). https://digitalstrategy.ec.europa.eu/en/library/ethics-guidelines-trustworthy-ai. Accessed 29 June 2021

9. Cranefield, S., Winikoff, M., Dignum, V., Dignum, F.: No pizza for you: value-based plan selection in BDI agents. In: Proceedings of the Twenty-Sixth International Joint Conference on Artificial Intelligence, IJCAI-17, pp. 178–184. ijcai.org (2017). https://doi.org/10.24963/ijcai.2017/26

10. Damgaard, C.: Gini coefficient (2019). https://mathworld.wolfram.com/GiniCoefficient.html. Accessed 11 June 2024

11. IEEE: IEEE global initiative on ethics of autonomous and intelligent systems (2019). https://standards.ieee.org/industry-connections/ec/autonomous-systems.html. Accessed 29 June 2021

12. Lera-Leri, R., Bistaffa, F., Serramia, M., López-Sánchez, M., Rodríguez-Aguilar, J.A.: Towards pluralistic value alignment: aggregating value systems through l_p-regression. In: Faliszewski, P., Mascardi, V., Pelachaud, C., Taylor, M.E. (eds.) 21st International Conference on Autonomous Agents and Multiagent Systems, AAMAS 2022, Auckland, New Zealand, May 9-13, 2022. pp. 780–788. International Foundation for Autonomous Agents and Multiagent Systems (IFAAMAS) (2022). https://doi.org/10.5555/3535850.3535938, https://www.ifaamas.org/Proceedings/aamas2022/pdfs/p780.pdf

13. Liscio, E., van der Meer, M., Siebert, L.C., Jonker, C.M., Mouter, N., Murukannaiah, P.K.: Axies: identifying and evaluating context-specific values. In: Proceedings of the 20th International Conference on Autonomous Agents and MultiAgent Systems, pp. 799–808. AAMAS 2021, International Foundation for Autonomous Agents and Multiagent Systems, Richland, SC (2021)

14. Montes, N., Sierra, C.: Value-guided synthesis of parametric normative systems. In: Dignum, F., Lomuscio, A., Endriss, U., Nowé, A. (eds.) AAMAS 2021: 20th International Conference on Autonomous Agents and Multiagent Systems, Virtual Event, United Kingdom, 3-7 May 2021, pp. 907–915. ACM (2021)

15. Osman, N., d'Inverno, M.: A computational framework of human values. In: Dastani, M., Sichman, J.S., Alechina, N., Dignum, V. (eds.) Proceedings of the 23rd International Conference on Autonomous Agents and Multiagent Systems, AAMAS 2024, Auckland, New Zealand, 6-10 May 2024, pp. 1531–1539. ACM (2024). https://doi.org/10.5555/3635637.3663013, https://dl.acm.org/doi/10.5555/3635637.3663013

16. Page, K.: The four principles: can they be measured and do they predict ethical decision making? BMC Med. Ethics **13**(1), 10 (2012). https://doi.org/10.1186/1472-6939-13-10
17. Rezler, A.G., Lambert, P., Obenshain, S.S., Schwartz, R.L., Gibson, J.M., Bennahum, D.A.: Professional decisions and ethical values in medical and law students. Acad. Med. **65**(9) (1990)
18. Ross, W.D.: The right and the good. Philosophy **6**(22), 236–240 (1930)
19. Serramia, M., López-Sánchez, M., Rodríguez-Aguilar, J.A.: A qualitative approach to composing value-aligned norm systems. In: Seghrouchni, A.E.F., Sukthankar, G., An, B., Yorke-Smith, N. (eds.) Proceedings of the 19th International Conference on Autonomous Agents and Multiagent Systems, AAMAS 2020, Auckland, New Zealand, 9-13 May 2020, pp. 1233–1241. International Foundation for Autonomous Agents and Multiagent Systems (2020)
20. Sierra, C., Osman, N., Noriega, P., Sabater-Mir, J., Perelló, A.: Value alignment: a formal approach. CoRR abs/2110.09240 (2021). https://arxiv.org/abs/2110.09240
21. di Tosto, G., Dignum, F.: Simulating social behaviour implementing agents endowed with values and drives. In: Giardini, F., Amblard, F. (eds.) Multi-Agent- Based Simulation XIII - International Workshop, MABS 2012, Valencia, Spain, June 4-8, 2012, Revised Selected Papers. LNCS, vol. 7838, pp. 1–12. Springer (2012). https://doi.org/10.1007/978-3-642-38859-0_1, https://doi.org/10.1007/978-3-642-38859-0_1
22. Veatch, R.M.: Reconciling lists of principles in bioethics. J. Med. Philos. Forum Bioeth. Philos. Med. **45**(4–5), 540–559 (2020). https://doi.org/10.1093/jmp/jhaa017, https://doi.org/10.1093/jmp/jhaa017

Value Learning for Value-Aligned Route Choice Modeling via Inverse Reinforcement Learning

Andrés Holgado-Sánchez[1]([✉]) [iD], Javier Bajo[2] [iD], Holger Billhardt[1] [iD],
Sascha Ossowski[1] [iD], and Joaquín Arias[1] [iD]

[1] CETINIA, Universidad Rey Juan Carlos, Madrid, Spain
{andres.holgado,holger.billhardt,sascha.ossowski,joaquin.arias}@urjc.es
[2] Departamento de Inteligencia Artificial, ETSI Informáticos, Universidad
Politécnica de Madrid, Campus de Montegancedo, Madrid 28660, Spain
jbajo@fi.upm.es

Abstract. Acquiring computational specifications of human values is key for building value-aligned and value-aware AI systems. We surveyed methods for learning ethical principles and value-aligned behaviour from human demonstrations or specifications of values. However, to our knowledge, no attempt has been proposed for learning these value specifications from demonstrations, while satisfying the possibly diverse value preferences of different agents. In this work we propose a novel value learning framework (agnostic of specific learning techniques) for (i) learning value groundings (specifications of given values) and (ii) identifying value systems (the particular value preferences of agents) from observed behavior in an application domain. We illustrate our framework in a route choice modeling scenario, using tailored inverse reinforcement learning algorithms. The results show that we can successfully learn value systems that are coherent with observed route choices. Our findings open up intriguing concerns and challenges for future research in the area.

Keywords: Value Alignment · Value Learning · Value Awareness Engineering · Inverse Reinforcement Learning · Route Choice Modeling

1 Introduction

Current directions in AI support the inclusion of values in the decision-making process of agents, mostly focusing on the notion of *value alignment* [9,29]. The goal of value alignment is to ensure that the behavior of AI is aligned (imbued) with human values [38]. Several approaches exist for an AI system to optimize or leverage an acceptable alignment of its actions with a given explicit specifications of values. For instance, there are examples of value-aligned decision making in the context of normative systems [30,45], preference aggregation [18] and reinforcement learning [6,14,37].

© The Author(s), under exclusive license to Springer Nature Switzerland AG 2025
N. Osman and L. Steels (Eds.): VALE 2024, LNAI 15356, pp. 40–60, 2025.
https://doi.org/10.1007/978-3-031-85463-7_3

Russell [38] goes beyond this and synthesises three ambitious principles for designing truly generally value-aligned machines. Machines should not only (1) maximize the realization of human preferences. They also (2) need not know how the preferences are defined; and (3) the preferences should be learned from human behavior. The problem of learning explicit specifications of values under human demonstrations, has been called *value learning* [46].

Different forms of value learning already exist in the literature such as *value inference* [22,24] or *prima facie* duty learning [2,4]. However, to our knowledge, there is no attempt in the literature learning value specifications directly from demonstrations without assumptions on either the value alignment of actions or their preferences. E.g. [47] assumes given rewards measuring value alignment; and [3] uses action preferences as training data with ethical features.

Setting out from a set of previously identified labels of values (without an explicit meaning), in this paper we are interested in learning, from observed behavior, both, the alignment or grounding of specific values in given contexts (the actual meaning of a value in that context) and the particular and possible heterogeneous value preferences (i.e. *value systems* [24,32,43]) of agents that act in such contexts. To address this *value system learning problem*, we set out from a simple value system representation and formally define the notion of value-alignment on top of it.

We test our model and problem formulation in a use case on route choice modeling [33]. Here we assume that different routes in a traffic network (we take a previously studied network from Shanghai (China) [52]) are aligned to different preferences over some applicable values. In particular we consider the values of *sustainability*, time *efficiency* and *security*. Our approach is based on inverse reinforcement learning (IRL) a fruitful paradigm adhering to Russell's principles previously used in the value-aligned AI literature [11]. Specifically, we learn reward functions that can be interpreted as alignment functions, and policies that mimic observed behaviors.

The paper is structured as follows. In Sect. 2 we review related work on value-aligned AI, inverse reinforcement learning and route choice. In Sect. 3, we explain our proposed value system learning framework. In Sect. 4 we detail the instantiation of our framework (with dedicated algorithms) in the route choice use case. In Sect. 5 we evaluate our framework and provide discussion of the results. In Sect. 6 we finish with conclusions and future work suggestions.

2   Related Work

There are several proposals for computational representations of values and value systems [12] with focus on the design of value-aligned systems. For instance, [43,44] consider value systems as preferences over values with a deontological view, while [30] assume a consequentialist approach with quantitative value semantics defined over states of the world. [32] presented a taxonomical model where concept generalization is key for determining value alignment from concrete properties to more abstract notions that are used to define each value in context-dependent scenarios. [16] studied correlations in the meaning of values setting out from Schwartz's theory [42].

In this context, a promising line of research looks into learning specifications of values adaptable to the application domain. Soares [46] labels such general task as the *value learning problem*, i.e. learning representations of values under human demonstrations. Practical forms of value learning exist in the literature that tackle the so-called problem of *value inference* [24], composed by three tasks: *value identification* [21, 34, 48, 49]—i.e. identifying the set of values relevant to a decision context—; value system estimation [22, 23, 47]—i.e. learning value preferences based on observed behavior, texts or stakeholder conversations—; and value aggregation [18, 19]—i.e. aggregating value systems for consensus—.

Even though ethical behavior learning techniques do not focus specifically on value learning, they are certainly related to it. One approach is *prima facie* duty learning [2–4], that directly learns general action preferences (principles) in terms of the ethical features they provoke or entail (e.g. value satisfaction), from annotated action preferences from experts. Another approach is CIRL (Cooperative Inverse Reinforcement Learning) [11] that learns human-aligned behavior in cooperation games.

The problem of **inverse reinforcement learning** (IRL) in Markov decision processes (MDP) is the problem of extracting a reward function given observed (optimal) behavior [31]. IRL assumes that the seen behaviors/demonstrations in the MDP correspond to those obtained under an "expert policy" π_E sampling the behaviors that are optimal w.r.t. some unknown reward function R_E. The objective is learning (another) reward function $\hat{R}$ so that a reinforcement learning policy, optimal for $\hat{R}$ can produce trajectories the most similar to the demonstrations.

The first proposed IRL algorithms opted to minimize the feature expectation difference with the expert [1], but gave room to many different solutions. Later, Ziebart et al. proposed the use the principle of maximum (causal) entropy [13] to provide a single optimal solution [54, 55]. Other approaches rely on deep learning architectures [6, 15], use Bayesian updates [20] or take inspiration from adversarial networks [7]. Others use human-annotated preferences over trajectories [6, 8] as learning criterion.

Route choice modeling [33] consists of deriving a mathematical model that can rationally explain or predict the route choice of agents in a certain transportation network taking into account potentially heterogeneous agent preferences [35]. The most used method is shortest path search according to a custom generalized cost function.

However, the fact that different people have different objectives is undeniable. For instance, different lifestyles and situations determine mode of transport [40], electric vehicle users would prioritize routes different than gasoline ones [51] or emergency situations [28].

Different models exist to elicit preference variability. For instance, [27] analyzes taxi route choices discriminating between three state transition features used in linear reward architectures (travel distance, idle time and number of passengers); [35] manages prospect preferences regarding travel time uncertainty; [39] uses AHP with an underlying ontology to more profoundly differentiate choice criteria.

IRL algorithms have being widely applied in route choice modeling, e.g. for the interpretation of taxi driver route choices [25,27,52,55], bicyclist route choice modeling [17], for food delivery logistics [26] and link flow estimation [53].

3   Value Learning Framework

In this paper we deal with the problem of *value system learning* which consists of learning explicit agent preferences over a given set of values (their value system) given demonstrations of an agent's behavior in an application domain. This problem is an initial view of the broader value learning problem [46].

We first introduce the notion of *value* used in our approach. The value representation model should be agnostic of value theories (e.g. Schwartz [41] or MFT [10]), though not necessarily misaligned with them. In particular, we adopt Osman and D'Inverno's notion of values, as "human abstract concepts that guide behavior" [32]. Also, we propose each value to have a *grounding* (its actual meaning) in a given domain, which can be defined by a function on a set of *properties* or features that can be identified automatically on certain *entities* of the world. This is more formally expressed in Definition 1.

Definition 1 (Value Grounding and Alignment).   *The computational interpretation (or **grounding**) of a value v (e.g. fairness or achievement) in an application domain is defined by a **value alignment function** $g^v : \mathcal{P} \rightarrow COD$, where $\mathcal{P} = P_1 \times \cdots \times P_d$ is the space of automatically verifiable properties of a certain set of world entities; and COD refers to a condomain (metric space) where the degree of alignment with the value is measured.*

*We also define the **alignment of an entity** e **with value** v as $\mathcal{A}(e,v) = g^v(p_1(e),\ldots,p_d(e)) \in COD$, where $(p_1(e),\ldots,p_d(e)) \in P$ are the observed properties of entity e.*

In our model we assume that the grounding of a value can be considered, in some application domains, *socially-agreed*. That is, the model will consider that the grounding of a value is independent of the beliefs of value-holding agents in the application domain, i.e. that the society these agents conform has a common, agreed, grounding for each of the values.

Albeit agents may agree on how the values are promoted or demoted, they may have different goals and desires that give raise to different value *preferences*, i.e. they can have different *value systems*.

Definition 2 (Value System). *Let $V = \{v_1, \cdot, v_m\}$ a finite set of socially-agreed values considered in an application domain, each with value alignment function g^{v_i} (with $v_i \in V$) and ranging in the same condomain COD. The **value system** of an agent a is determined by a **value system alignment function***

$f^a : COD^m \rightarrow COD$ *that provides the personal alignment of a given entity with the preferences of the agent as a function of the individual value alignments.*

We also define the alignment of an entity e with the value system of agent a (VS(a)) as $\mathcal{A}(e, VS(a)) = f^a(g^{v_1}(p_1(e),\ldots,p_d(e)),\ldots,g^{v_m}(p_1(e),\ldots,p_d(e)) \in COD$, *where* $(p_1(e),\ldots,p_d(e)) \in \mathcal{P}$ *are the observed properties of e.*

Definition 2 is compatible with existent value system definitions in the literature such as the most extended definition of value system as a (sometimes quantifiable) ranking ([5,18,43,44]), which can be approached by treating f as an utility function. Connections can be made with taxonomical models of value systems [32] that take into account concept relationships or consider value synergies [16].

Figure 1 presents the overall picture of our value system representation model.

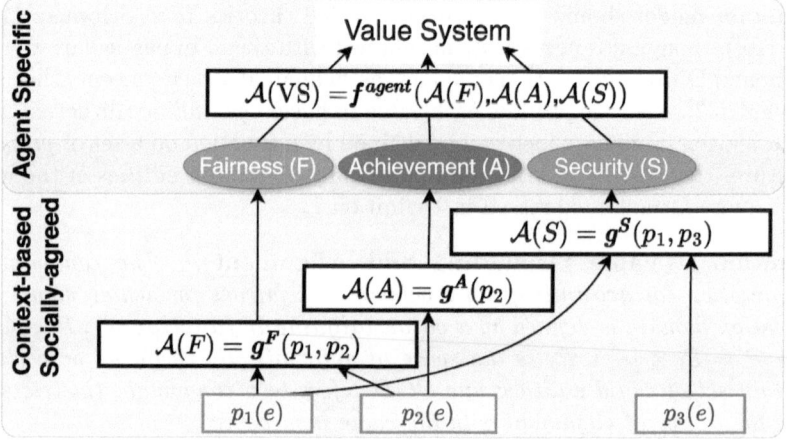

Fig. 1. A visual representation of the proposed value system representation model in a domain with three properties p_1, p_2, p_3 and three example values (Fairness, F, Security S and Achievement A).

Based on the model we can define our value system learning problem formally: Given an application domain, a set of m identified applicable values $V = \{v_1,\ldots,v_m\}$ in that domain[1] and a set of J agents $Ag = \{a_1,\ldots,a_J\}$, the *value learning problem* consists of solving two consecutive tasks.

1. **Value Grounding Learning**: learning the *groundings* of all the previously identified values, i.e. discovering the set of individual value alignment functions $\{g^v : P \rightarrow COD \mid v \in V\}$). We argue that this task can be performed

---

[1] If values are initially unknown we can identify them by using Value Identification approaches [21,34,49].

by individually learning each alignment function by observing behaviors (or actions) of agents that are known to align optimally with a given value[2].

2. **Value System Identification**: learning a value system for each agent a_j, i.e. learning the value system alignment functions $\{f^j \mid j \in \{1, \ldots, J\}\}$. This task should be accomplished solely by observing each agent's behaviors /actions and using the previously learnt value groundings.

In practice, the particular learning technique that is applied will restrict the search space of the alignment functions. For instance, they could be parametric function spaces (i.e. for neural network learning) or the sets of functions that can be a composition of a fixed set of operators (for other techniques).

We are aware of the similarity between our computational model and that of Osman and D'Inverno [32]. Indeed our model is in principal capable of representing individual value alignments through increasingly abstract concepts and properties and has a similar hierarchical structure to that of a taxonomy representation (seen clearly in the example of Fig. 1). However, there are key differences. First, we introduce the notion of alignment with different values, while [32] consider each value to be a separate taxonomy with a single alignment function. Second, our notion of *properties* has no intrinsic ethical or value related meaning. Third, we only use alignment function dependencies as relationships between values, properties and concepts, while [32] use the more strict notion of generalization.

4   Use Case

We are interested in approaching the problem of value-aware *route choice modeling* [33], i.e. acquiring an explainable representation of the involved values driving the decision-making of different agents with different *value systems*. This will serve as a use case for the presented value representation and learning framework.

4.1   Learning Environment

We consider a general road network defined by a directed graph. The network is composed of a set of *nodes* $(\mathcal{N})$ that play the role of road intersections and *directed edges* $(\mathcal{E})$ that play the role of streets or road segments that allow the traffic to flow in the specified direction. We assume in this work for the sake of simplicity that the capacity of the edges is infinite, though each edge belongs to a different *type* of road segment, has a certain length and other numerical features.

In this network, adapted from [52] a set of agents Ag act to move from a certain edge o (the origin) to another one d (the destination) using a personal vehicle. We define the set of origin-destination pairs as the set OD. We define a route connecting o and d as $R_{o,d} = (o, e_1, \cdots, e_L, d)$, where there exist some

---

[2] In many application domains it seems feasible to identify such behaviors or actions, e.g., by asking agents.

nodes $\{n_1, \ldots, n_{L+1}\}$ such that o ends in a node n_1, e_i starts in n_i and ends in n_{i+1} for all $i \in \{1, \ldots, L\}$ and d starts in n_{L+1}. We assume that each agent chooses routes for each origin and destination pairs according to some unknown criteria.

Upon this framework, the route choice problem is formulated as a simplified Markov Decision Process (MDP) given by a tuple (S, A, T, R), where:

- S are the states of the MDP corresponding to all the pairs (e, d) where $(e, d) \in OD$. The edge e represents the current road segment that is being traversed by the agent and d its destination.
- A are the actions available from each state and correspond to the act of choosing one of the next road segments after reaching the intersection at the end of the current edge. We denote by $A(s)$ the possible actions (e.g., road segments) in state s.
- T is the set of transitions $(s, a, s') \in S \times A \times S$ given by the network. We assume deterministic transitions in which, given state $s = (e, d)$, when action $a \in A(s)$ is taken, the next state will simply be $s' = (a, d)$. We also define a *trajectory* as a series of states $t = (s_1, \ldots, s_n)$ linked by actions.
- R is the reward function $R(s, a)$ that defines the immediate advantage of choosing an action a in a state s. Then, the cumulative reward (or return) of a route $R_{e_0, e_{L+1}}$ is given by: $\sum_{t=0}^{L} R((e_t, d), e_{t+1})$.

In our use case, we will consider deterministic *policies* that solve the previous MDP specification. A policy $\pi : S \to A$ solves the MDP if it assigns to each state the action that maximizes future expected return. I.e., π from state s_0 chooses a_0 such that $\mathbb{E}_{a_t = \pi(s_t)}(\sum_{t=0}^{H} R(s_t, a_t))$ is maximum among all actions available from s_0 for some maximum episode length H. In our use case we use value iteration to compute the policies.

We model rewards in a way that can be understood as negative costs for shortest-path finding between each OD pair. Formally, we impose $R((e, d), e') \in \mathbb{R}^-$ signalling the cost of traversing e'. Furthermore, we assume that

$$R((e, d), e') = \begin{cases} 0 & \text{if } e' = d \\ R(e') & \text{otherwise} \end{cases} \quad (1)$$

where $R(e')$ represents the reward of edge e'. That is, first, the reward is 0 if the edge e' is the destination, and second, the reward solely depends on the edge e' itself if not. On one hand, this assures that the policies obtained via value iteration (or via standard reinforcement learning (RL) algorithms) are deterministic and minimize the overall costs of the chosen route for the given origin-destination pairs, e.g., will provide shortest paths solutions w.r.t. the reward function R. On the other hand, it actually allows for generalizing rewards such that they do not depend on the destination of an agent. For simplicity, in the sequel we refer to the reward function $R(e')$.

4.2   Values in Route Choice Modeling

In our use case scenario we assume that each agent j chooses its routes according to some (unknown) reward function $R_j(e)$. Furthermore, we assume that the agent also acts in accordance to its individual value system $VS(j)$. Thus, we can establish a relationship between the agent's value system and the reward function it applies (Eq. 2).

$$R_j(e) = \mathcal{A}(e, \text{VS}(j)) \qquad (2)$$

This relation is the basic idea underlying our work: If we learn the reward function of an agent, we can actually estimate the agent's value system. As we mentioned before, we want the value system to be represented through an alignment function on the individual value alignments, which in turn can be computed based on measurable properties[3]. In the sequel we present the instantiation of this idea.

In our use case we are modeling three values $V = \{v_1, v_2, v_3\}$, namely travel *sustainability* (sus, v_1), *security* (sec, v_2) and time *efficiency* (eff, v_3). All three have already been studied in the route choice domain, e.g. [28, 36, 40]. We can assume that those values are *socially-agreed*. For instance, sustainability is socially-agreed in the traffic domain, because, according to the general opinion, it is related to less fuel consumption.

We take the act of traversing an edge of the road network as the *entities* in which we can measure the alignment with our values. The alignment of each edge traversal with each of the values (and the agent's value systems) depend on the following observable edge *properties* or features[4]:

- Fuel consumption for edge traversal: $fuel(e)$, $e \in \mathcal{E}$. For instance, secondary roads are more contaminant than highways.
- Accident/Street insecurity risk: $insec(e)$, $e \in \mathcal{E}$. For instance, a primary road is considered highly secure while secondary roads and living streets are more insecure.
- Expected edge traversal time: $time(e)$, $e \in \mathcal{E}$. For instance, primary roads have less expected traversal times than country roads.

Thus, the set of features/properties observed upon the traversal of a given edge is defined as:

$$\phi(e) = (fuel(e), insec(e), time(e))$$

It should be noted that these properties are directly related to the three values, i.e. out of different choices, the road-segment with least fuel consumption is

---

[3] In this use case, the condomain of alignment is set as $COD = \mathbb{R}^-$, where negative real values define the regret (or negative reward) w.r.t. each value or the value systems of the agents. That is, lower values of alignment indicate a higher demotion of values (or value preferences) and vice versa.

[4] The values of the three properties have been normalized by dividing the original value by the maximum value of all edges.

the most sustainable segment and choosing a route that maximizes the negative fuel consumption for a given OD pair will be the most sustainable route. However, we assume the model itself is not aware of this fact, that is, we actually want to learn the alignment of a road-segment with each of the values. In this work, we use a rather simple search space for the value alignment functions: the space of linear convex combinations of the input features/properties[5].

With respect to the search space of value system alignment functions we again use a simplification (and plan to analyze more complex versions in the future). We also use linear convex combinations in which the linear weights correspond to the preference weights for the alignment with each of the values. We represent those weights with a convenient new notation:

Definition 3 (Profile). *The **profile** of an agent j is defined by a tuple $P_j = (p^j_{v_1}, \cdots, p^j_{v_m})$, with $\sum_{i=1}^{m} p^j_{v_i} = 1$ and $p^j_{v_i} \in [0,1]$. The variables $p^j_{v_i}$ represent the degree of preference for value v_i according to agent j. We call **pure profile for value** v_i a profile that has the following form: $P_{v_i} = (a_1, \ldots, a_i, \ldots, a_1)$ where $a_i = 1$ and $a_j = 0$, $\forall j \neq i$.*

In our settings, a profile P_j uniquely defines the value system alignment function of agent j via $f^j(\mathcal{A}_1, \ldots, \mathcal{A}_m) = P_j \cdot (\mathcal{A}_1, \ldots, \mathcal{A}_m)$. For instance a "pure sustainable agent" will have a profile of $(1, 0, 0)$ (aligning to sustainability solely) and an agent that considers equally both security and efficiency (while neglecting sustainability) will have a profile of $(0, 0.5, 0.5)$.

We use a neural network architecture to represent and calculate the reward function of an agent. As mentioned before, since the reward is based on the value system of an agent, this architecture directly presents an instantiation of our general value system model (as depicted in Fig. 2). The neural network consists of one input layer for the input properties of each edge traversal resulting from executing a state-action pair, a hidden layer for calculating the individual value alignments and the output layer calculating the final reward (identical to the negative alignment of such state-action pair with the value system of an agent, as for Eq. 2).

The hidden layer from properties $\phi(e)$ to the individual value alignments is called G_θ and has the specification explained in Eq. 3 in terms of a set of parameters $\theta \in \mathbb{R}^{3 \times 3}$:

$$\begin{pmatrix} \mathcal{A}(e, v_1) \\ \mathcal{A}(e, v_2) \\ \mathcal{A}(e, v_3) \end{pmatrix} = -G_\theta(\phi(e)) = -W^\theta \cdot \begin{pmatrix} fuel(e) \\ insec(e) \\ time(e) \end{pmatrix}, \qquad (3)$$

where $W^\theta_{ij} = softmax((\theta_{i1}, \theta_{i2}, \theta_{i3}))_j = \frac{\exp \theta_{ij}}{\sum_{k=1}^{3} \exp \theta_{ik}}$. With this definition of the matrix W^θ, each of its rows $W^\theta_{i,\cdot}$ (for $i = 1, 2, 3$) is a linear convex combination of the edge properties.

---

[5] In future works we will analyze other, more complex scenarios, where the groundings of values might be more complex.

The final layer calculation is dependent on the agent. For an agent j we will find a profile P_j which we can express with a linear convex combination layer with parameters $\alpha \in \mathbb{R}^3$, i.e. $P_j = softmax(\alpha) = \left(\frac{\exp \alpha_1}{\sum_{k=1}^{3} \exp \alpha_k}, \frac{\exp \alpha_2}{\sum_{k=1}^{3} \exp \alpha_k}, \frac{\exp \alpha_3}{\sum_{k=1}^{3} \exp \alpha_k} \right)$. This profile directly determines the value system alignment function of agent j: $f^j(a_1, a_2, a_3) = P_j \cdot (a_1, a_2, a_3)$ and, according to Eq. 2, the reward function for agent j for a given edge e results in Eq. 4:

$$R_j(e) = f^j(G_\theta(\phi(e))) = P_j \cdot G_\theta(\phi(e)) \tag{4}$$

With this model, the value system learning problem in this route choice modeling context consists of the two following formalized tasks:

1. **Value grounding learning**: Given a set of reference routes taken by agents of known profiles, learning parameters $\boldsymbol{\theta}$ of the function G_θ that represent the individual value alignment functions (value groundings).
2. **Value system identification**: Given a certain G with fixed parameters and a set of trajectories of an agent j with unknown motivations, learning a profile $\hat{P}_j$ from which a deterministic policy $\pi^{\hat{P}_j}$—optimal for the reward $R_j(e) = \hat{P}_j \cdot G(\phi(e))$—will provide trajectories as similar as possible to the given ones. This can be repeated for each agent.

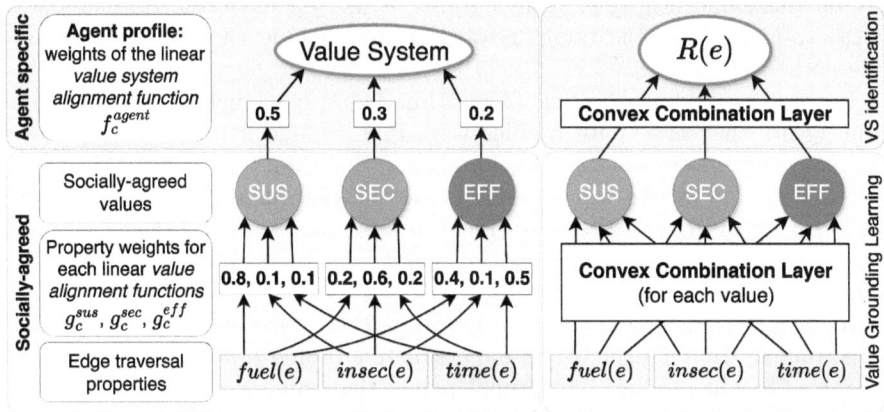

Fig. 2. An instantiation of the proposed value system representation for the route choice modeling use case (left), and the inverse reinforcement learning equivalent reward function architecture (right). The *socially-agreed* sections specify the value alignment functions assumed by the agent (left) and the approximated ones using Eq. 3 (right). The *agent specific* sections represent the original profile of some *agent*, i.e. the linear weights of its value system alignment function (left) and an approximation made with a neural network layer using Eq. 4, which in turn represents the reward of a reinforcement learning agent mimicking the *agent* (right).

4.3   Learning Algorithm Architecture

We use versions of inverse reinforcement learning (IRL) algorithms to solve both tasks of the value system learning problem in our use case. We decided to set out from one of the most used (and simple) IRL algorithms called Maximum Entropy IRL [55], specifically, its straightforward adaptation to deep neural networks [50].

The approach uses a loss function $\mathcal{L}$ that is to be minimized to find a reward function $\hat{R}$ such that an optimal policy for this reward provides the most similar trajectories to the demonstrations. The similarity here is understood as the difference in state visitation counts (in our case edge visitation counts) between the given demonstrations (μ) and those sampled with the learned policy ($\hat{\mu}$). These are used to compute the gradient (as seen in Eq. 5) which is used for backpropagation into the learned reward function $\hat{R}$ with parameters $\boldsymbol{w}$.

$$\frac{\partial \mathcal{L}}{\partial \boldsymbol{w}}(e) = (\hat{\mu}(e) - \mu(e)) \frac{\partial \hat{R}}{\partial \boldsymbol{w}}(e) \tag{5}$$

In our use case we use a Monte-Carlo approach to compute the visitation counts instead of the probabilistic estimation seen in the original references [50, 55]. We directly count *edge* visitations in each route. That is, for a given set of routes D, μ is a matrix such that $\mu[t,e] = \mathbb{1}_t(e)$, for each $e \in \mathcal{E}$ and $t \in D$. The expected edge visitation counts are then approached by $\mu(e) = \frac{1}{d} \sum_{t \in D} \mu[t,e]$.

Now, although the two learning tasks of the value system learning problem rely on this same principle, their learning setups—namely, the characteristics of the training data, the target reward(s) and their learned parameters—are different:

In value grounding learning (Algorithm 1) we use labeled demonstrations from agents that have pure profiles (e.g. $P_{sus} = (1,0,0)$). Then we perform different gradient descent updates for each of our values separately, backpropagating into the hidden layer $G_{\boldsymbol{\theta}}$ assuming the reward is, e.g. for sustainable agents, given by $\hat{R}_{sus} = P_{sus} \cdot G_{\boldsymbol{\theta}}$. The learnable parameters in this case would be $\boldsymbol{w} = \boldsymbol{\theta} \in \mathbb{R}^{3 \times 3}$. The gradient descent update is expressed formally in Line 11, Algorithm 1.

In value system identification (Algorithm 2) we take unlabeled demonstrations (routes) from a given agent and estimate a profile $\hat{P}$ such that the reward $\hat{R} = \hat{P} \cdot G_{\boldsymbol{\theta}}$ will produce an optimal policy that mimics the demonstrations, without modifying the already learnt individual alignments $G_{\boldsymbol{\theta}}$. The learnable parameters in this case would be $\boldsymbol{w} = \alpha \in \mathbb{R}^3$. The gradient descent update is expressed formally in Line 10, Algorithm 2.

Algorithm 1. Deep Maximum Entropy IRL for route choice modeling: Value Grounding Learning

---

Input: A set of profiles $\mathcal{P} = \{(1,0,0),(0,1,0),(0,0,1)\}$; and, for each $P \in \mathcal{P}$, a training set of routes D_P. A batch size b, learning rate λ and training steps N.

Output: $G_{\boldsymbol{\theta}}$ a network that gives $\mathcal{A}(e,v)$ for each $v \in V$; and $\{\pi_{\boldsymbol{\theta}}^P : P \in \mathcal{P}\}$ where $\pi_{\boldsymbol{\theta}}^P$ is optimal for reward $\hat{R}_P$ and provides similar trajectories to D_P.

1: Initialize environment env, reward network $G_{\boldsymbol{\theta}}$ with weights $\boldsymbol{\theta}$.
2: $\phi \leftarrow$ GETEDGETRAVERSALFEATURES(env)
3: **for** training step $t = 1, 2, \ldots, N$ **do**
4:     **for** profile $P \in \mathcal{P}$ **do**
5:         $B_P \leftarrow$ choose batch of b trajectories from D_P
6:         $\mu^P \leftarrow$ VISITATIONCOUNTMATRIX(B_P)
7:         $\hat{R}_P(e) = P \cdot G_{\boldsymbol{\theta}}(\phi(e))$
8:         $\pi_{\boldsymbol{\theta}}^P \leftarrow$ VALUEITERATIONPOLICY(env, $\hat{R}_P$)
9:         $\hat{B}_P \leftarrow$ PROPAGATEPOLICY($\pi_{\boldsymbol{\theta}}^P$, B_P)   ▷ i.e. for each each $t \in B_P$, use $\pi_{\boldsymbol{\theta}}^P$ to sample a $\hat{t}$ from the same origin and to the same destination as those of t.
10:         $\hat{\mu}^P \leftarrow$ VISITATIONCOUNTMATRIX($\hat{B}_P$)
11:

$$\boldsymbol{\theta} \leftarrow \boldsymbol{\theta} - \frac{\lambda}{b} \sum_{(t,\hat{t}) \in (B_P, \hat{B}_P)} \sum_{e \in \mathcal{E}} \left(\hat{\mu}^P[\hat{t}, e] - \mu^P[t, e] \right) \frac{\partial \hat{R}_P}{\partial \boldsymbol{\theta}}(e)$$

12:     **end for**
13: **end for**

Algorithm 2. Deep Maximum Entropy IRL for route choice modeling: Value System Identification

---

Input: Set of routes D, already learnt $G = (g_{sus}, g_{sec}, g_{eff})$, batch size b, learning rate λ and training steps N.

Output: $\hat{P}$, $\pi^{\hat{P}}$, where $\pi^{\hat{P}}$ is optimal for reward $\hat{R}_{\hat{P}}$ and produces trajectories similar to those in D.

1: Initialize environment env, $\hat{P} \leftarrow softmax(\alpha)$ with weights α.
2: $\phi \leftarrow$ GETEDGETRAVERSALFEATURES(env)
3: **for** training step $t = 1, 2, \ldots, N$ **do**
4:     $B \leftarrow$ choose batch of b expert demos from D
5:     $\mu \leftarrow$ VISITATIONCOUNTMATRIX(B)
6:     $\hat{R}_{\hat{P}}(e) = \hat{P} \cdot G(\phi(e))$
7:     $\pi^{\hat{P}} \leftarrow$ VALUEITERATIONPOLICY(env, $\hat{R}_{\hat{P}}$)
8:     $\hat{B} \leftarrow$ PROPAGATEPOLICY($\pi^{\hat{P}}$, B)
9:     $\hat{\mu} \leftarrow$ VISITATIONCOUNTMATRIX($\hat{B}$)
10:

$$\alpha \leftarrow \alpha - \frac{\lambda}{b} \sum_{(t,\hat{t}) \in (B, \hat{B})} \sum_{e \in \mathcal{E}} \left(\hat{\mu}[\hat{t}, e] - \mu[t, e] \right) \frac{\partial \hat{R}_{\hat{P}}}{\partial \alpha}(e)$$

11:     $\hat{P} \leftarrow softmax(\alpha)$
12: **end for**

---

5   Evaluation

In this section we evaluate the proposed value system learning framework and algorithms in the route choice domain. We provide our source code with the evaluation scripts and the algorithms from the last section here[6].

5.1   Generating Routes

Because of the lack of real world data, we generate the route data for given agents artificially. Here we assume that all agents act according to a given profile P and will select the "cheapest" route for each OD pair according to some edge costs that depend on edge properties and the agent's profile. We define the cost for an edge e given a certain profile P, or shorter, the *profiled cost*, $C_P(e)$ by:

$$C_P(e) = P \cdot (fuel(e), insec(e), time(e)) \tag{6}$$

This formula calculates the cost of an given edge as the weighted average of fuel consumption, insecurity level and expected edge traversal time, where the profile acts as preference weights. We also define the *profiled cost of a route R* by:

$$C_P(R) = \sum_{e \in R} P \cdot (fuel(e), insec(e), time(e)) \tag{7}$$

It should be noted that the profile for generating an agent's routes actually defines its value system and each individual value (*sus*, *sec*, and *eff*) is directly grounded in exactly one of the properties (fuel consumption, insecurity and traversal time, respectively). This implies, that in our case the value grounding learning task consists in fact in identifying the would be perfectly solved if $W^\theta = I_{3 \times 3}$ (i.e. the alignment with a value is defined uniquely by the corresponding property of the edge). On the other hand, the value system identification task would be solved if we find a profile $\hat{P} = softmax(\alpha)$ that approximates an agents' profile P.

Given the above, we can define the cost of an edge according to a value v as $C_v(e) = C_{P_v}(e)$. We can write the cost of a route according to a value, too, as $C_v(R) = C_{P_v}(R)$. Lastly, there is a negative relationship between these costs and the real value alignment (the socially-agreed grounding of each value in our case), i.e. $C_v(e) = -R(e) = -\mathcal{A}(e, v) \in \mathbb{R}^+$, and $C_v(R) = -\mathcal{A}(R, v) \in \mathbb{R}^+$.

5.2   Evaluation: Value Grounding Learning

Here we analyze the performance of Algorithm 1 with a train-test set composed of *pure routes*—routes that are considered totally sustainable, secure or time efficient, e.g., each route is generated with a pure profile $((1, 0, 0), (0, 1, 0)$ and

---

[6] https://github.com/andresh26-uam/VAE-ValueLearning/tree/main/ ValueLearningIRL.

$(0, 0, 1))$—. In particular, we used the pure routes for 100 different OD pairs[7]. The training-test ratio has been 80%–20%, the learning rate $\lambda = 0.2$ and the batch size equal to the training data size. We run the experiment with 10 random splits and present average values of the 10 runs in the results.

We want to check whether the function G_θ is close to the expected function, that is, if the matrix W^θ (see Eq. 3) is close to the identity. In Fig. 3 we see that this is the case. Thus, we have almost perfectly identified the alignment functions with each value. Besides, we can see that the policies that maximize learnt rewards (alignments with each individual value) generate routes that are equivalent to the observed input data after about 20 iterations.

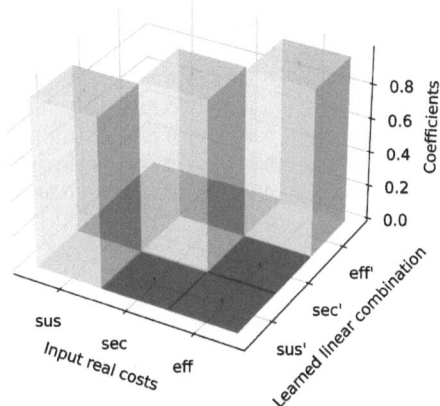

Fig. 3. Expected matrix W^θ (defining value alignment functions G_θ) after running Algorithm 1 with configuration from Sect. 5.2. It represents the learned linear correlation between real costs $C_{P_{v_i}}$ and learned ones $-R_{P_{v_i}}$, with standard deviations.

The results for value grounding learning are conclusive insofar as our method works well in the given use case, correctly identifying the feature behind that grounds each of the value. Still, it has be explored how far less informative features and/or less informed learning architectures lead to similar performances.

5.3   Evaluation: Value System Identification

For the value system identification task we have analyzed two different cases: i) "learning from an individual agent" and ii) "learning from a society of agents".

By learning from an individual agent we mean that we try to identify its unknown profile P from route examples of that agent. Here we assume that the routes always minimize the cost C_P, for the agent's profile P. In particular, we want to find a profile $\hat{P}$ such that the optimal policy for the rewards

---

[7] The 100 OD pairs come from real routes from [52], but the actual routes are not used here. We always use generated ones as described in Sect. 5.1.

Table 1. Results for value system identification, learning from individual agents with different profiles. Presented are the learned profile and the average costs (negative alignments) of the routes (from the test set) sampled with the original profile and the learned profile are shown for the three values sus, sec and eff ($OrigAC_{v_i}$ and $LearAC_{v_i}$, respectively).

Original Profile	Learned Profile	$OrigAC_{Sus}$	$OrigAC_{Sec}$	$OrigAC_{Eff}$	$LearAC_{Sus}$	$LearAC_{Sec}$	$LearAC_{Eff}$
(0.0, 0.0, 1.0)	**(0.01, 0.01, 0.98)**	0.389	0.591	0.236	0.389	0.590	0.236
(0.0, 0.25, 0.75)	(0.01, 0.04, 0.95)	0.391	0.588	0.236	0.390	0.584	0.236
(0.0, 0.5, 0.5)	(0.02, 0.14, 0.84)	0.390	0.576	0.237	0.388	0.568	0.238
(0.0, 0.75, 0.25)	(0.02, 0.17, 0.81)	0.388	0.559	0.240	0.388	0.564	0.239
(0.0, 1.0, 0.0)	**(0.0, 0.99, 0.0)**	0.598	0.266	1.028	0.591	0.266	1.009
(0.25, 0.0, 0.75)	(0.06, 0.01, 0.93)	0.386	0.594	0.236	0.386	0.591	0.236
(0.25, 0.25, 0.5)	(0.07, 0.04, 0.89)	0.385	0.585	0.236	0.385	0.584	0.236
(0.25, 0.5, 0.25)	(0.11, 0.13, 0.76)	0.382	0.569	0.238	0.383	0.569	0.238
(0.25, 0.75, 0.0)	(0.3, 0.68, 0.03)	0.480	0.297	0.722	0.481	0.296	0.723
(0.5, 0.0, 0.5)	(0.22, 0.02, 0.76)	0.381	0.597	0.237	0.377	0.589	0.238
(0.5, 0.25, 0.25)	(0.28, 0.08, 0.64)	0.378	0.579	0.238	0.376	0.574	0.239
(0.5, 0.5, 0.0)	(0.59, 0.39, 0.02)	0.411	0.369	0.496	0.413	0.364	0.501
(0.75, 0.0, 0.25)	(0.39, 0.01, 0.6)	0.372	0.600	0.239	0.371	0.597	0.240
(0.75, 0.25, 0.0)	(0.84, 0.16, 0.0)	0.366	0.496	0.319	0.366	0.497	0.316
(1.0, 0.0, 0.0)	**(0.95, 0.02, 0.03)**	0.359	0.564	0.273	0.359	0.564	0.271

$\hat{R}_{\hat{P}}$ proposes similar routes to the once chosen of the agent in the examples *in terms of their expected value alignment* as measured by the cumulative costs $C_{v_i}(R)$. The reward $\hat{R}_{\hat{P}}$ uses $G_{\hat{\theta}}$ as the first layer with the learnt parameters from Algorithm 1.

In the case of "learning from a society", we try to learn the value system of a society of agents, where different agents may have different profiles. In particular, we analyse societies where different proportions of agents will have different pure profiles. In this sense a profile P for the society specifies the proportions of agents that purely prioritise the values sus, sec and eff. For example, given a profile $(0.7, 0.3, 0)$ we consider that given a certain OD pair, the probability of choosing the shortest route according to C_{sus} is 0.7; according to C_{sec} is 0.3; and according to C_{eff} is 0. With our approach, we learn a reward function that is used to generate an optimal policy which sample similar routes to the ones observed. However, in this scenario this will not be possible in general because the learnt policy is deterministic and the reference one can be considered stochastic. However, as we will see, we are able to learn profiles that approximate the society profiles and policies that obtain routes with similar value alignment (on average) to the routes form the society.

Both scenarios are approached with Algorithm 2 using the same training OD pairs as the ones used in the last task. The test set is composed of the remaining 20% of OD pairs and other random OD pairs separated by minimum 5 edge connections, for a total of 100 test ODs. In the second scenario we will have 3 types of routes per OD pair (one per value). The learning rate is again $\lambda = 0.2$ and the maximum number of iterations is $N = 80$. Batch size b in the first

Table 2. Results for value system identification, learning from different profiled societies. The presented information is analogous to Table 1.

Original Profile	Learned Profile	$OrigAC_{Sus}$	$OrigAC_{Sec}$	$OrigAC_{Eff}$	$LearAC_{Sus}$	$LearAC_{Sec}$	$LearAC_{Eff}$
(0.0, 0.0, 1.0)	**(0.01, 0.01, 0.98)**	0.399	0.602	0.229	0.398	0.599	0.229
(0.0, 0.25, 0.75)	(0.68, 0.31, 0.01)	0.458	0.518	0.446	0.400	0.427	0.401
(0.0, 0.5, 0.5)	(0.51, 0.48, 0.01)	0.504	0.437	0.629	0.441	0.357	0.542
(0.0, 0.75, 0.25)	(0.28, 0.71, 0.01)	0.565	0.356	0.842	0.519	0.294	0.793
(0.0, 1.0, 0.0)	**(0.0, 0.99, 0.0)**	0.614	0.275	1.035	0.598	0.275	0.999
(0.25, 0.0, 0.75)	(0.31, 0.12, 0.56)	0.392	0.598	0.240	0.386	0.588	0.235
(0.25, 0.25, 0.5)	(0.72, 0.27, 0.0)	0.444	0.522	0.431	0.395	0.440	0.384
(0.25, 0.5, 0.25)	(0.54, 0.45, 0.01)	0.497	0.434	0.638	0.431	0.370	0.510
(0.25, 0.75, 0.0)	(0.33, 0.66, 0.01)	0.551	0.352	0.840	0.502	0.303	0.746
(0.5, 0.0, 0.5)	(0.61, 0.07, 0.32)	0.384	0.590	0.249	0.376	0.592	0.244
(0.5, 0.25, 0.25)	(0.74, 0.25, 0.0)	0.440	0.507	0.456	0.392	0.447	0.372
(0.5, 0.5, 0.0)	(0.52, 0.47, 0.01)	0.491	0.426	0.652	0.441	0.357	0.541
(0.75, 0.0, 0.25)	(0.73, 0.05, 0.22)	0.377	0.583	0.262	0.373	0.595	0.249
(0.75, 0.25, 0.0)	(0.7, 0.3, 0.0)	0.436	0.500	0.474	0.401	0.425	0.406
(1.0, 0.0, 0.0)	**(0.92, 0.02, 0.06)**	0.371	0.580	0.271	0.371	0.585	0.267

scenario was set equal to the training data size (80), and in the second case it was set to 200 (routes are generated among the training set OD pairs respecting the probability distribution in the society profile).

With the specified settings, we analyze the performance of the value system identification task applied to 15 different original profiles (evenly distributed in the space of possible profiles) for both, learning from individual agents and societies. The results are summarized in Table 1 (learning from individual agents) and Table 2 (learning from societies). For each original profile, we present the learned profile and compare the average cost (or alignment) w.r.t. each of the values (the average values costs $OrigAC_{v_i}$) of the original routes and the routes generated by the learned policy ($LearAC_{v_i}$).

In general, we found policies that align well with both profiled societies and individual agents in terms of the expected alignments. Also, in both cases, we learn the pure profiles (in bold) for each value with high accuracy, i.e. we learn a profile of (0.01,0.01,0.98) from demonstrations from a efficient agent with profile (0,0,1).

However, when learning from individuals and the original profiles are not pure, the learned profiles can sometimes differ significantly from the original ones, despite the resulting routes being nearly identical in terms of expected costs. This discrepancy arises because there exist correlations between different values (alignments). In our scenario, this seems to be the case between sustainability and efficiency, and both are almost inversely correlated with security. As a result, it is highly probable that a route which is efficient will also be sustainable but not secure, and vice versa. For instance, if an agent always chooses the most efficient routes and those are almost always identical to the most sustainable routes, from an observer's point of view it is not possible to distinguish whether the agent prefers efficiency over sustainability or the other way around. Thus, learning a different profile may actually not be wrong. It may indicate that both profiles have the same observable effect with respect to value alignment. The effect can also be observed when learning from societies.

In the case of learning from societies, the similarity in the value alignment is lower, especially when these societies are heterogeneous, e.g. $(0.0, 0.75, 0.25)$. This will be due to the intrinsic impossibility to perfectly reproduce the observed routes with a deterministic policy that is optimal for a linear combination reward function.

Finally, as it can be expected, the route costs for a value decrease when the preference weight for that value in the profiles increases and vice versa. However, there are cases where this effect may not be gradual—e.g. the first 5 columns of Table 1. This effect may be due to different distributions of property values in the edges of the network. In particular, despite the normalization, $insec(e)$ is generally low in most edges and achieves its higher values solely in certain edges, whereas $time$ generally has higher values and its lowest values are only in a small share of edges. This issue suggests that in some domains a linear weighting of value alignments might not be informative enough of agent preferences.

6   Conclusions and Future Work

We have introduced an initial version of a value system learning problem, which aim is reckoning both value semantics and value preferences (value systems) from human demonstrations in a given domain. We proposed a preliminary value system representation model adapted to solve this problem, capable of jointly representing socially-agreed alignments with individual values and agent-specific value preferences in a quantitative manner. A solution to the problem has been implemented and tested in a route choice environment using inverse reinforcement learning. We learned route choice behaviors aligned with values and coherent with heterogeneous agent value preferences, proving the applicability of our framework.

Future lines of work include abstracting our particular solution for our route choice use case to more general MDPs. Also, using real annotated data would provide additional insights on the claimed definitions of values versus theoretical assumptions and models. Extending and generalizing our value system representation model to be fully compatible with other frameworks is certainly of interest (e.g. [32]), so we will look into incorporating context-dependency of value groundings and preferences into our model.

Acknowledgments. This work has been supported by grant VAE: TED2021-131295B-C33 funded by MCIN/AEI/10.13039/501100011033 and by the "European Union NextGenerationEU/PRTR"', by grant COSASS: PID2021-123673OB-C32 funded by MCIN/AEI/10.13039/501100011033 and by "ERDF A way of making Europe", and by the AGROBOTS Project of Universidad Rey Juan Carlos funded by the Community of Madrid, Spain.

Disclosure of Interests. The authors have no competing interests to declare that are relevant to the content of this article.

References

1. Abbeel, P., Ng, A.Y.: Apprenticeship learning via inverse reinforcement learning. In: Proceedings of the Twenty-First International Conference on Machine Learning, p. 1. ICML 2004, Association for Computing Machinery, New York, NY, USA (2004). https://doi.org/10.1145/1015330.1015430
2. Anderson, M., Anderson, S.L.: Ethel: Toward a principled ethical eldercare system. In: AAAI Fall Symposium: AI in Eldercare: New Solutions to Old Problems, vol. 2 (2008)
3. Anderson, M., Anderson, S.L.: Geneth: a general ethical dilemma analyzer. Paladyn **9**, 337–357 (2 2018). https://doi.org/10.1515/PJBR-2018-0024/MACHINEREADABLECITATION/RIS, https://www.degruyter.com/document/doi/10.1515/pjbr-2018-0024/html
4. Anderson, M., Anderson, S.L., Armen, C.: An approach to computing ethics. IEEE Intell. Syst. **21**, 56–63 (2006). https://doi.org/10.1109/MIS.2006.64
5. Bench-Capon, T., Atkinson, K., McBurney, P.: Using argumentation to model agent decision making in economic experiments. Auton. Agent. Multi-Agent Syst. **25**, 183–208 (2012)
6. Christiano, P., Leike, J., Brown, T.B., Martic, M., Legg, S., Amodei, D.: Deep reinforcement learning from human preferences (2023)
7. Fu, J., Luo, K., Levine, S.: Learning robust rewards with adverserial inverse reinforcement learning. In: International Conference on Learning Representations (2018). https://openreview.net/forum?id=rkHywl-A-
8. Fürnkranz, J., Hüllermeier, E., Cheng, W., Park, S.H.: Preference-based reinforcement learning: a formal framework and a policy iteration algorithm. Mach. Learn. **89**, 123–156 (2012)
9. Gabriel, I.: Artificial intelligence, values, and alignment. Minds Mach. **30**, 411–437 (2020). https://doi.org/10.1007/S11023-020-09539-2
10. Graham, J., et al.: Chapter two - moral foundations theory: the pragmatic validity of moral pluralism. In: Devine, P., Plant, A. (eds.) Advances in Experimental Social Psychology, vol. 47, pp. 55–130. Academic Press (2013). https://doi.org/10.1016/B978-0-12-407236-7.00002-4, https://www.sciencedirect.com/science/article/pii/B9780124072367000024
11. Hadfield-Menell, D., Russell, S.J., Abbeel, P., Dragan, A.: Cooperative inverse reinforcement learning. In: Lee, D., Sugiyama, M., Luxburg, U., Guyon, I., Garnett, R. (eds.) Advances in Neural Information Processing Systems, vol. 29. Curran Associates, Inc. (2016)
12. Holgado-Sánchez, A., Billhardt, H., Ossowski, S., Fernández, A.: An ontology for value awareness engineering. In: Proceedings of the 16th International Conference on Agents and Artificial Intelligence - Volume 3: AWAI, pp. 1421–1428. INSTICC, SciTePress (2024). https://doi.org/10.5220/0012595500003636
13. Jaynes, E.T.: Information theory and statistical mechanics. Phys. Rev. **106**, 620–630 (1957). https://doi.org/10.1103/PhysRev.106.620, https://link.aps.org/doi/10.1103/PhysRev.106.620
14. Jiang, J., Lu, Z.: Learning fairness in multi-agent systems. In: Advances in Neural Information Processing Systems, vol. 32 (2019)

15. Kalweit, G., Huegle, M., Werling, M., Boedecker, J.: Deep inverse q-learning with constraints. In: Advances in Neural Information Processing Systems (2020). https://arxiv.org/abs/2008.01712v1

16. Karanik, M., Billhardt, H., Fernáindez, A., Ossowski, S.: On the relevance of value system structure for automated value-aligned decision-making. In: Proceedings of the 39th ACM/SIGAPP Symposium on Applied Computing, pp. 679–686. Association for Computing Machinery (2024). https://doi.org/10.1145/3605098.3636057, https://doi.org/10.1145/3605098.3636057

17. Koch, T., Dugundji, E.: A review of methods to model route choice behavior of bicyclists: inverse reinforcement learning in spatial context and recursive logit. In: Proceedings of the 3rd ACM SIGSPATIAL International Workshop on GeoSpatial Simulation, pp. 30–37. GeoSim 2020, Association for Computing Machinery, New York, NY, USA (2020). https://doi.org/10.1145/3423335.3428165, https://doi.org/10.1145/3423335.3428165

18. Lera-Leri, R., Bistaffa, F., Serramia, M., Lopez-Sanchez, M., Rodriguez-Aguilar, J.: Towards pluralistic value alignment: aggregating value systems through LP-regression. In: Proceedings of the 21st International Conference on Autonomous Agents and Multiagent Systems, pp. 780–788. AAMAS 2022, IFAAMAS (2022)

19. Leri, R.X.L., et al.: Aggregating value systems for decision support. Knowl.Based Syst. **287**, 111453 (2024). https://doi.org/10.1016/j.knosys.2024.111453, https://www.sciencedirect.com/science/article/pii/S0950705124000881

20. Levine, S., Popovic, Z., Koltun, V.: Nonlinear inverse reinforcement learning with gaussian processes. In: Shawe-Taylor, J., Zemel, R., Bartlett, P., Pereira, F., Weinberger, K. (eds.) Advances in Neural Information Processing Systems, vol. 24. Curran Associates, Inc. (2011). https://proceedings.neurips.cc/paper_files/paper/2011/file/c51ce410c124a10e0db5e4b97fc2af39-Paper.pdf

21. Liscio, E., van der Meer, M., Cavalcante Siebert, L., Mouter, N., Jonker, C., Murukannaiah, P.: Axies: identifying and evaluating context-specific values. In: Proceedings of the 20th International Conference on Autonomous Agents and MultiAgent Systems, pp. 799–808. AAMAS 2021, International Foundation for Autonomous Agents and Multiagent Systems (2021), 20th International Conference on Autonomous Agentsand Multiagent Systems, AAMAS 2021 ; Conference date: 03-05-2021 Through 07-05-2021

22. Liscio, E., Dondera, A., Geadau, A., Jonker, C., Murukannaiah, P.: Cross-domain classification of moral values. In: Carpuat, M., de Marneffe, M.C., Meza Ruiz, I.V. (eds.) Findings of the Association for Computational Linguistics: NAACL 2022, pp. 2727–2745. Association for Computational Linguistics, Seattle, United States (2022). https://doi.org/10.18653/v1/2022.findings-naacl.209, https://aclanthology.org/2022.findings-naacl.209

23. Liscio, E., et al.: Inferring values via hybrid intelligence. In: HHAI 2023: Augmenting Human Intellect: Proceedings of the Second International Conference on Hybrid Human-Artificial Intelligence. Front. Artif. Intell. Appl. **368**, 373–378 (2023). IOS Press BV (2023). https://doi.org/10.3233/FAIA230102

24. Liscio, E., et al.: Value inference in sociotechnical systems. In: Proceedings of the 2023 International Conference on Autonomous Agents and Multiagent Systems, pp. 1774–1780. AAMAS 2023, International Foundation for Autonomous Agents and Multiagent Systems, Richland, SC (2023). https://doi.org/10.5555/3545946.3598838

25. Liu, S., Jiang, H.: Personalized route recommendation for ride-hailing with deep inverse reinforcement learning and real-time traffic conditions. Transp. Res. Part

E Logist. Transp. Rev. **164**, 102780 (2022). https://doi.org/10.1016/j.tre.2022.
102780, https://www.sciencedirect.com/science/article/pii/S1366554522001715

26. Liu, S., Jiang, H., Chen, S., Ye, J., He, R., Sun, Z.: Integrating dijkstraâ€™s
algorithm into deep inverse reinforcement learning for food delivery route planning.
Transp. Res. Part E Logist. Transp. Rev. **142**, 102070 (2020)

27. Liu, S., Araujo, M., Brunskill, E., Rossetti, R., Barros, J., Krishnan, R.: Understanding sequential decisions via inverse reinforcement learning. In: 2013 IEEE
14th International Conference on Mobile Data Management, vol. 1, pp. 177–186
(2013). https://doi.org/10.1109/MDM.2013.28

28. Lovreglio, R., Fonzone, A., dell'Olio, L.: A mixed logit model for predicting exit
choice during building evacuations. Transp. Res. Part A Policy Pract. **92**, 59–75
(2016). https://doi.org/10.1016/j.tra.2016.06.018

29. Montes, N., Osman, N., Sierra, C., Slavkovik, M.: Value engineering for
autonomous agents. CoRR abs/2302.08759 (2023). https://doi.org/10.48550/
arXiv.2302.08759

30. Montes, N., Sierra, C.: Synthesis and properties of optimally value-aligned normative systems. J. Artif. Intell. Res. **74**, 1739–1774 (2022). https://doi.org/10.1613/
jair.1.13487

31. Ng, A.Y., Russell, S.J.: Algorithms for inverse reinforcement learning. In: Proceedings of the Seventeenth International Conference on Machine Learning, pp.
663–670. ICML 2000, Morgan Kaufmann Publishers Inc., San Francisco, CA, USA
(2000)

32. Osman, N., d'Inverno, M.: A computational framework of human values. In:
Proceedings of the 23rd International Conference on Autonomous Agents and
Multiagent Systems, pp. 1531–1539. AAMAS 2024, International Foundation for
Autonomous Agents and Multiagent Systems, Richland, SC (2024)

33. Prato, C.G.: Route choice modeling: past, present and future research
directions. J. Choice Modell. **2**(1), 65–100 (2009). https://doi.org/10.1016/
S1755-5345(13)70005-8, https://www.sciencedirect.com/science/article/pii/
S1755534513700058

34. Qiu, L., et al.: ValueNet: a new dataset for human value driven dialogue system. In:
Proceedings of the AAAI Conference on Artificial Intelligence , vol. 36, no. 10, pp.
11183–11191 (2022). https://doi.org/10.1609/aaai.v36i10.21368, https://ojs.aaai.
org/index.php/AAAI/article/view/21368

35. Ramos, G.D.M., Daamen, W., Hoogendoorn, S.: Modelling travellers' heterogeneous route choice behaviour as prospect maximizers. J. Choice Modell. **6**, 17–33
(2013). https://doi.org/10.1016/j.jocm.2013.04.002

36. Rizzi, L., Ortúzar, J.: Stated preference in the valuation of interurban road safety.
Accid. Anal. Prev. **35**, 9–22 (2003). https://doi.org/10.1016/S0001-4575(01)00082-
3

37. Rodriguez-Soto, M., Serramia, M., Lopez-Sanchez, M., Rodriguez-Aguilar, J.A.:
Instilling moral value alignment by means of multi-objective reinforcement learning. Ethics Inf. Technol. **24**(1), 1–17 (2022). https://doi.org/10.1007/s10676-022-
09635-0

38. Russell, S.: Artificial Intelligence and the Problem of Control, pp. 19–24. Springer
International Publishing, Cham (2022). https://doi.org/10.1007/978-3-030-86144-
5_3

39. Sadeghi-Niaraki, A., Kim, K.: Ontology based personalized route planning system
using a multi-criteria decision making approach. Expert Syst. Appl. **36**, 2250–2259
(2009). https://doi.org/10.1016/j.eswa.2007.12.053

40. Scheiner, J., Holz-Rau, C.: Travel mode choice: affected by objective or subjective determinants? Transportation **34**, 487–511 (2007). https://doi.org/10.1007/s11116-007-9112-1
41. Schwartz, S.H.: Universals in the content and structure of values: Theoretical advances and empirical tests in 20 countries. In: Advances in Experimental Social Psychology, vol. 25, pp. 1–65. Elsevier (1992)
42. Schwartz, S.H.: An overview of the schwartz theory of basic values. Online Readings Psychol. Cult. **2**(1), 11 (2012)
43. Serramia, M., Lopez-Sanchez, M., Rodriguez-Aguilar, J.A.: A qualitative approach to composing value-aligned norm systems. In: Proceedings of the 19th International Conference on Autonomous Agents and MultiAgent Systems, pp. 1233–1241. International Foundation for Autonomous Agents and Multiagent Systems (2020)
44. Serramia, M., et al.: Moral values in norm decision making. IFAAMAS **9** (2018). www.ifaamas.org
45. Serramia, M., et al.: Encoding ethics to compute value-aligned norms. Minds Mach., 1–30 (2023). https://doi.org/10.1007/s11023-023-09649-7
46. Soares, N.: The value learning problem. Artif. Intell. Saf. Secur. (2018). https://api.semanticscholar.org/CorpusID:13096553
47. Veronese, C., Meli, D., Bistaffa, F., Rodríguez-Soto, M., Farinelli, A., Rodríguez-Aguilar, J.A.: Inductive logic programming for transparent alignment with multiple moral values. In: CEUR WORKSHOP PROCEEDINGS, vol. 7, pp. 84–88 (2024). https://doi.org/10.2/JQUERY.MIN.JS, https://iris.univr.it/handle/11562/1120547
48. Weidinger, L., et al.: Using the veil of ignorance to align AI systems with principles of justice. Proc. Nat. Acad. Sci. **120**(18), e2213709120 (2023). https://doi.org/10.1073/pnas.2213709120, https://www.pnas.org/doi/abs/10.1073/pnas.2213709120
49. Wilson, S.R., Shen, Y., Mihalcea, R.: Building and validating hierarchical lexicons with a case study on personal values. In: Staab, S., Koltsova, O., Ignatov, D.I. (eds.) Social Informatics, pp. 455–470. Springer International Publishing, Cham (2018). https://doi.org/10.1007/978-3-030-01129-1_28
50. Wulfmeier, M., Ondrúška, P., Ondrúška, O., Posner, I.: Maximum entropy deep inverse reinforcement learning. arXiv preprint arXiv:1507.04888 (2015). https://doi.org/10.48550/arXiv.1507.04888, https://arxiv.org/abs/1507.04888v3
51. Yang, Y., Yao, E., Yang, Z., Zhang, R.: Modeling the charging and route choice behavior of BEV drivers. Transp. Res. Part C: Emerg. Technol. **65**, 190–204 (2016). https://doi.org/10.1016/j.trc.2015.09.008
52. Zhao, Z., Liang, Y.: A deep inverse reinforcement learning approach to route choice modeling with context-dependent rewards. Transp. Res. Part C: Emerg. Technol. **149**, 104079 (2023). https://doi.org/10.1016/j.trc.2023.104079, https://www.sciencedirect.com/science/article/pii/S0968090X23000682
53. Zhong, M., Kim, J., Zheng, Z.: Estimating link flows in road networks with synthetic trajectory data generation: inverse reinforcement learning approach. IEEE Open J. Intell. Transp. Syst. **4**, 14–29 (2023). https://doi.org/10.1109/OJITS.2022.3233904
54. Ziebart, B.D.: Modeling purposeful adaptive behavior with the principle of maximum causal entropy. Ph.D. thesis, CMU School of Computer Science, USA (2010). https://doi.org/10.1184/R1/6720692.v1
55. Ziebart, B.D., Maas, A., Bagnell, J.A., Dey, A.K.: Maximum entropy inverse reinforcement learning. In: Proceedings of the 23rd National Conference on Artificial Intelligence - Volume 3, pp. 1433–1438. AAAI Press (2008)

Adversarial Behaviour in Moral Value Expression: A Statistical and Frame-Semantic Analysis of Social Media

Giulio Prevedello[1,3]([⊠])[iD], Lara Verheyen[1][iD], Emanuele Brugnoli[2,3][iD],
D. Ruggiero Lo Sardo[2,3][iD], and Remi Van Trijp[1][iD]

[1] Sony CSL Paris Research, 6 Rue Amyot, 75005 Paris, France
{giulio.prevedello,lara.verheyen,remi.vantrijp}@sony.com
[2] Sony CSL Rome Research, Joint Initiative CREF-SONY, Centro Ricerche Enrico
Fermi, Via Panisperna 89/A, 00184 Rome, Italy
{emanuele.brugnoli,donaldruggiero.losardo}@sony.com
[3] Enrico Fermi's Research Center (CREF), via Panisperna 89/A, 00184 Rome, Italy

Abstract. Adversarial behaviour in online spaces has become a threat to user well-being and societal unity, so it is important to understand why users may interact with each other in hostile ways. This paper contributes to this understanding by exploring how adversarial behaviour is grounded in moral value expression by analyzing English texts from the Moral Foundations Twitter Corpus (enriched with *toxicity* scores). First, through statistical analysis, we confirmed the assumption of earlier studies that the relation between a tweet's toxicity level and its moral value expression is topic-specific. Next, we performed a more precision-based analysis by extracting *semantic frames* (e.g. identifying who is inflicting harm on whom). We found that automatic frame extraction matches human annotations with low sensitivity but high specificity. Importantly, replacing human annotations with semantic frames does not impact the toxicity score distribution of tweets, which shows that semantic frame extraction is a promising method for detecting which (moral) stance a user takes on a particular issue. As such, identification of moral value expression may potentially become an important component for developing value-aware technologies that can greatly contribute to safer and more positive social media experiences.

Keywords: Moral values · Semantic frames · Toxicity · Social media · Machine learning · Moral foundations theory

1 Introduction

While clashes are inevitable in debates between parties with opposing views, extreme positions may fuel hostility. Especially in online platforms that use the principles of Persuasive Computing [9], hostility is a problem due to the

N. Osman and L. Steels (Eds.): VALE 2024, LNAI 15356, pp. 61–75, 2025.
https://doi.org/10.1007/978-3-031-85463-7_4

scaling possibility offered by large social networks: controversial content elicits more engagement from users and therefore receives greater visibility from the platforms, which creates a self-reinforcing feedback loop of hostility that exacerbates the online debate [10]. In order to create safer, healthier and more positive online experiences, it is therefore important to understand why certain content provokes severe emotional and often hostile reactions.

This paper contributes to achieving such deeper understanding by exploring whether such adversarial behaviour can be grounded into moral value expression. That is, we investigate whether taking a different viewpoint on a controversial topic may also reveal a difference in moral interpretation. To operationalise this work, we performed a statistical and a semantic analysis of English texts from social media posts on different topics, which we classified against the background of Moral Foundations Theory [11], a psychological approach that has posited a number of universal moral *foundations*, which are dyads of opposing values: care/harm, fairness/cheating, loyalty/betrayal, authority/subversion, and purity/degradation.

More specifically, we used the Moral Foundations Twitter Corpus (MFTC) [13] that we enriched with *toxicity scores* through Google's Perspective API [19] – in which a *toxicity score* represents the degree of adversarial behaviour that can be detected in a tweet (based on various cues such as tokens of disrespect or rudeness). Our statistical analysis revealed that the relation between adversarial behaviour and moral value expression is topic-dependent.

As we sought to evaluate the potential of semantic frame analysis in replacing human annotations on moral values, we found that frame extraction could perform attribution of annotated moral values with low sensitivity but high specificity. As such, when analysing toxicity levels of morally-salient tweets, we found no qualitative differences when moral annotations were replaced by those assigned with frames. This result suggested that misbehaviour in social media, from offensive posts, could be efficiently addressed with semantic frames only. To explore this possibility, we challenged three classification tasks: prediction of different viewpoints on the same topic, prediction of values with links to the frames, and of values without. In all cases the prediction based on frame frequencies and toxicity scores outperformed baseline accuracy metrics. Overall, we confirmed the role of toxicity and MFT values to study social media interactions, and provided evidence to develop a frame based approach to evaluate the online public discourse at scale.

Related Work. Adversarial behaviour is not only a side-effect of Persuasive Computing techniques, it is also affected by our cognitive biases. In a recent study on the American political debate in US Twitter, out-group conflict and in-group favoritism were found to drive engagement and negative-affect language [24]. Animosity is associated with misbehaviour online, which can results in toxic exchanges that degenerate the conversation, destroying constructive dialogue and thus feeding polarisation [15].

More recent studies have started to investigate the link between adversarial behaviour and moral values. A study on Twitter debates about immigration in Italy found strong correlations between toxic language, engagement, and moral values [4]. A follow-up study, on the same data, evidenced how different viewpoints clearly emerged from the interactions on posts with moral content, using values from the Moral Foundations Theory [3].

Moral Foundations Theory (MFT) is a psychological theory that aims at understanding the origins of morality, where basic foundations define the framework for moral reasoning [11]. These moral foundations are conceived as innate mental structures, universal to all humans despite social background, that were selected through evolutionary mechanisms when our ancestors had to adapt to specific challenges. Foundations are organised in dyads of opposing values: care/harm and fairness/cheating are concerned with the respect of individuals; loyalty/betrayal, authority/subversion and purity/degradation are concerned with the respect of social institutions. Notably, differences in preference of foundations emphasising individuals or institutions was shown to be related to political orientation [17] and political communication and persuasion [6,8].

The relevance of MFT to study moral psychology led the scientific community to gather data with moral annotations to study human believes and behaviours. For Twitter data we mention two corpora: one the Moral Foundations Twitter Corpus (MFTC) for English language [13]; the other for Italian [26]. Databases with moral annotations enable researchers to train supervised machine learning models to classify moral values from texts. These models, however, are difficult to generalise beyond the domain in the training corpora [20]. In general, moral values are notoriously difficult to detect through linguistic cues because language users often employ indirect linguistic expressions that are highly context-dependent [29].

An alternative approach based on semantic frame analysis [1], works by attributing moral values that are linked to frames extracted from the text [7].

2 Methods

2.1 Dataset with Moral Annotations

Our social media dataset consists of 18.120 tweets from the MFTC [13] covering 6 different domains: All Lives Matter (ALM), Black Lives Matter (BLM), the Baltimore protests (Baltimore), the 2016 Presidential election (Election), hate speech & offensive language (Davidson; named after [5]), and Hurricane Sandy (Sandy). Each tweet was annotated for the presence of 10 different values from the Moral Foundations Theory, which theorises moral foundations as dyads of opposing values concerning the same domain: care/harm; fairness/cheating; loyalty/betrayal; authority/subversion; purity/degradation. In the case of absence of moral values, the tweet was considered non-moral. The tweets were annotated by 3 to 5 human annotators, depending on the topic. As a result, each tweet presents a distribution over 11 moral dimensions. In what follows, annotations will enable the assignment of a tweet with a single value, the most prominent, which received the highest score.

2.2   Tweet Toxicity

We enriched the dataset by including information about the toxicity scores of each tweet. By using Google's Perspective API [19], each post was assigned a $[0,1]$-score, indicating the probability that a user would find its content: toxic, severely toxic, identity attacking, insulting, profaning, threatening. In the following, we will focus on the toxicity score alone to assess offensive content, while all scores will be used together to tackle the classification tasks in Sect. 3.4.

2.3   Statistical Analysis

To visualise multiple distributions simultaneously, we used boxplots, which summarise the observations into: a box, that spans between the first and the third quartiles; the whiskers, that extends from the box to the farthest data point lying within the 1.5 times the interquartile range; more extreme observations are then represented by single points [14].

To assess differences in distribution of toxicity levels between different corpora, we used Mann-Whitney U (MWU) test [21] or Kruskal-Wallis (KW) test [18] to compare, respectively, two samples or more than two samples. For both tests, the two-sided p-value was reported and the significance level was set to 0.01 due to the large amount of data.

To calculate the effect size of the MWU test we use the sample point biserial correlation,

$$\frac{\bar{X}_1 - \bar{X}_2}{\hat{S}_{pool}} \sqrt{p_1 p_2} \tag{1}$$

namely the difference between the empirical means of the two distributions to be compared, standardised by the empirical standard deviation of the pooled data, multiplied by the squared root of the proportions of pooled data in each sample [16].

2.4   Moral Value Extraction Based on Frame Semantics

For the task of extracting moral values from tweets, we take inspiration from the semantic frame extraction approach [1] and the moral value extraction approach [7]. Similarly to the latter, we tackle the task of moral frame extraction by splitting it in two parts. First, we extract semantic frames that are in the text using a computational construction grammar approach [27]. Second, we link those semantic frames to moral values leveraging the ValueNet ontology [7]. In what follows, we discuss both steps.

Semantic frame extraction is the task in which the frames and their elements are extracted from a text [1]. For representing the semantic frames, we used PropBank [22], a resource that provides verb-specific semantic frames and that has been widely used in several semantic role labelling tasks. Following the PropBank convention, a different semantic frame is associated with each possible sense of a verb. For instance, in the following tweet the intended sense of "kill" corresponds to the PropBank roleset 'kill.01', which means cause to die.

"They" are #BLM who threaten whites, kill cops, destroy property not theirs, block freeways, etc. #ALLLivesMatter

The roles in this roleset are 'arg0' (the killer), 'arg1' (the corpse) and 'arg2' (the instrument). Successful semantic frame extraction would therefore identify that the author of the tweet expresses "#BLM" as the killer ('arg0') and "cops" as the victim ('arg1'), while leaving 'arg2' unexpressed. The killing-frame must then be linked to the moral value of harm as the author expresses outrage about (their perceived) harm caused to police officers.

We used computational construction grammar for the task of semantic frame extraction. This computational construction grammar model for English that detects such semantic frames was implemented using Fluid Construction Grammar [25, 27]. We learned a grammar on the Ontonotes [30] and the English Web Treebank corpus [2] which are both annotated with PropBank roles, based on a previously introduced approach [28]. The grammar in total consists of 38,538 constructions. This set of constructions consists in lexical, word sense and argument structure constructions. The lexical constructions are responsible for extracting the frame evoking elements (i.e. the expressions that evoke a frame) from the text. The argument structure constructions map between argument structures and the participants of a frame, while the word sense constructions add a word sense based on both the frame evoking element and the argument structures. Together, these constructions provide a frame semantic analysis of a given text. Next, this grammar is used to extract PropBank frames from the tweets. Given a tweet, we extract the sense of the verb, together with the core roles (i.e., 'arg0', the prototypical agent, 'arg1', the prototypical patient, ...), resulting in a semantic analysis of the tweet consisting in the frame and its participants.

For the second step, in which we need to link the semantic frames to moral values, we leveraged the ValueNet ontology [7], an ontology that focuses on representing and operationalising values and which includes, amongst others, relations between PropBank semantic frames and the moral values of the Moral Foundations Theory. Concretely, for each of the PropBank roles that were extracted, we find the moral foundation via the 'MFTriggers' relation. For example, the ontology links the PropBank roles of 'safeguard.01' and 'support.01' to the care moral value. In what follows, we focus on the values of care and harm, since the ontology does not link all values of the Moral Foundations Theory to PropBank frames.

For the quantitative analysis of extracted frames, word embedding from Spacy toolkit [12] was used to calculate semantic vectors on frames' word senses and on lemmas of their 'arg0' or 'arg1', if present. Then, the frame embedding was derived averaging all these vectors, while the participants embedding was derived averaging only the vectors from 'arg0' and 'arg1' lemmas.

2.5   Classification Tasks

Three classification tasks were designed: one to predict the viewpoints of a tweet, two to predict the moral expression of a tweet. For these tasks, the following type of features were extracted from tweets: toxicity scores and frame frequencies. Toxicity scores were derived following Sect. 2.2. Semantic frames were extracted from tweets as described in 2.4, so that the frequency of their word sense (i.e., the word best associated to the frame's meaning) could be calculated.

The data were split into train and test sets, respectively 75% and 25% the size of the available records. Then the train set was used to fit a Random Forest classifier set with default parameters from the scikit-learn implementation for Python [23].

For the viewpoint classification task, we focused on the ALM, BLM and Baltimore corpora, expressing care, harm and non-morality, a total of 4882 tweets, since ALM and BLM should express opposite viewpoints (on police, violence and racism), while the Baltimore dataset should present a mix of those two. For the other two tasks, both on moral value classification, data were restricted to the same 4882 tweets expressing care, harm and non-morality in the ALM, BLM and Baltimore corpora and to the 6817 tweets expressing other values across all corpora. This distinction was necessary for the lack of direct links, in the ValueNet ontology, between PropBank frames and the moral values, besides care and harm.

3   Results

3.1   Toxicity Analysis of the Database

To explore how misbehaviour affected the online conversations in the MFTC database, we first investigated the distribution of toxicity score across different topics (see Fig. 1). These distributions were significantly different (p-value $<$ 10^{-5} from KW test) indicating that the level of toxicity depends on the subject under discussion.

Previous work showed that, in the Italian debate debate about immigration, toxicity levels depend on expression of particular moral values [4]. Thus we sough to explore how this relation changed with the different topics in this database. Leveraging moral annotations in the data, we can infer some general patterns from Fig. 2:

- "positive" values of the MFT dyads are consistently expressed with low toxicity;
- "negative" values of the MFT dyads are consistently expressed with higher toxicity than "positive" values, with the exception of the Davidson corpus;
- non-moral tweets displayed toxicity levels between those from tweets with "positive" and "negative" values.

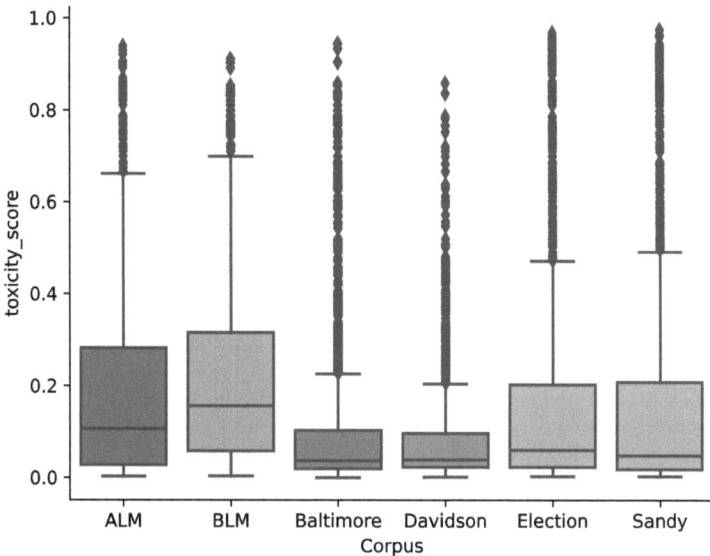

Fig. 1. Boxplots of toxicity score distributions for tweets from each corpus of the MFTC.

Still, some topic-specific tendencies for the toxicity score emerged. For example, distributions from "negative" values were quite variable across topics (including the low levels for Davidson); also "positive" values were consistently higher in the BLM topic, compared to others; and betrayal value was more toxic in ALM and BLM topics, compared to others.

Finally, we statistically tested the distribution homogeneity of toxicity levels from posts expressing the same value across corpora and found that none of the values were expressed with similar toxicity across topics (p-value $< 10^{-5}$ from all KW tests). These evidences clearly suggested that toxicity depends on moral values in a topic-dependent way.

3.2 Moral Value Extraction Based on Frame Semantics

As toxicity levels of morally-salient tweets seemed to depend on the discussion topic, we sought to investigate how different moral values are expressed in different topics. Using the frame extraction method explained in Sect. 2.4, we extracted the frames from each tweet. Using frames, we get a deeper semantic analysis of the tweet, containing information about the frame that is used in the tweet as well as the participants. To evaluate the accuracy of the frame extraction method in terms of moral value detection, first we set the true moral value of each post as the one that was most relevant accordingly to the annotations. Then we defined that this true value was successfully extracted for:

- tweets with care (or harm) value, if at least one frame associated to care (or harm) was detected;

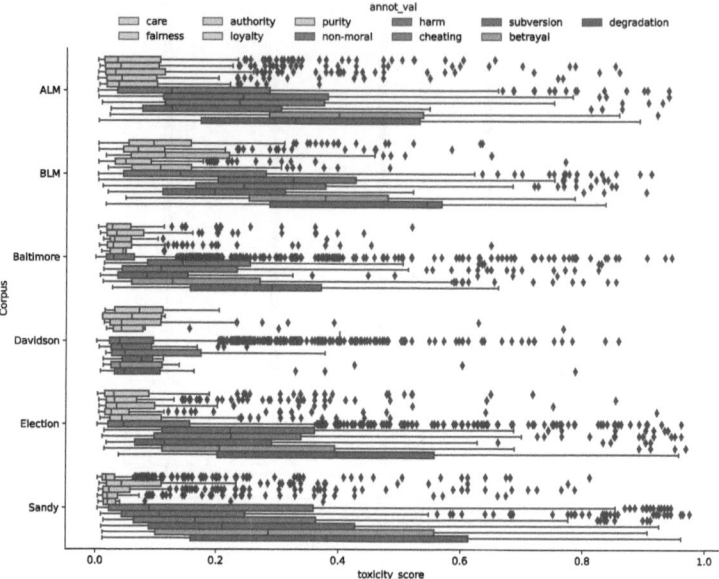

Fig. 2. Boxplots of toxicity score distributions for tweets from each corpus and value from the MFT (as assigned by the annotations).

- tweets with no moral values, if all frames extracted were not associated to any value or if no frames were found at all;
- other tweets, if no frames associated to any value were extracted.

The percentage of successful extractions is reported in Table 1. While the overall performances are good across corpora, with 78% success on all tweets, we see poor, moderate and great performances respectively for care, harm and non-moral tweets. Since high performance on other tweets indicate that detectable values (care and harm) were not assigned to tweets with other values, these results suggested that frame-based value detection has high specificity, despite low sensitivity, on morally salient tweets.

3.3   Toxicity Differences

Given some discrepancies between frame extraction and human annotation in values assignment, we questioned whether the selection of one approach over the other would affect a subsequent investigation on the toxicity levels relative to each moral value.

Thus, for each corpus, we compared the distributions of toxicity levels from tweets expressing a certain value (care, harm or non-moral) as assigned by human annotations against the frame-based assignment (Fig. 3). By statistically analysing all comparisons via MWU test (Table 2), we found that these comparisons were either statistically non significant or their effect size was small (lower

Table 1. Percentages of tweets whose best moral annotation is detected by frame extraction. The table sorts tweets by corpora (row) and moral value expression (column). Each cell also provides, within parentheses, the total number of tweets in a given corpus and moral expression.

Corpus	Care	Harm	Non-moral	Other	All
ALM	7.5%	33.9%	89.4%	89.9%	69.8%
	(389)	(383)	(519)	(1388)	(2679)
BLM	4.5%	46.9%	91.8%	92.7%	80.9%
	scriptsize(201)	(397)	(845)	(1660)	(3103)
Baltimore	6.5%	33.0%	88.9%	80.6%	81.1%
	(139)	(97)	(1990)	(959)	(3185)
Davidson	0.0%	3.6%	93.4%	97.2%	91.5%
	(8)	(55)	(2492)	(142)	(2697)
Election	6.8%	53.2%	86.7%	90.0%	79.4%
	(250)	(269)	(1651)	(1233)	(3403)
Sandy	10.3%	42.6%	94.1%	90.5%	65.7%
	(673)	(484)	(454)	(1442)	(3053)
All	8.0%	41.5%	90.5%	89.6%	78.0%
	(1660)	(1685)	(7951)	(6824)	(18120)

than 0.2), with the exception of toxicity levels of harm-expressing tweets from the Davidson corpus.

This result suggested that both assignment methods would provide similar outcomes when investigating toxicity of morally-salient posts to study misbehaviour in social media.

3.4 Viewpoint and Moral Value Classification Tasks

Given the interdependence of semantic frames, toxicity with topic under discussion and moral expressions, we explored how relevant the information from frames and toxicity was to discriminate between different viewpoints and to moral value inference. Thus, we designed three classification tasks:

- Predict which corpus tweets come from (ALM, BLM or Baltimore), each expressing different viewpoints (ALM's are opposite of BLM's, while Baltimore's should have a mix of the two) on the same topic about violence, racism and police brutality;
- Predict the moral values expressed in tweets expressing care, harm or non-moral values (for which we had many links between PropBank frames and the associated moral value);
- Predict the moral values of tweets expressing values other than care, harm or non-moral (for which direct links between PropBank frames and moral values are quite limited.).

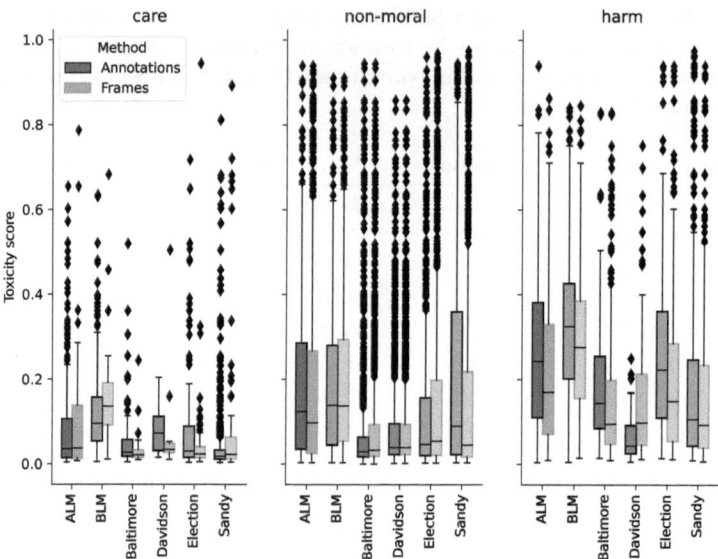

Fig. 3. Boxplots of toxicity score distributions for tweets, from each corpus, assigned with care, harm, non-moral values using annotations (darker colors) or frames (lighter colors).

Then we explored the frames information to calculated features that could improve classifications performance.

First, the similarity between participants across corpora within the same moral value was investigated. Indeed, since ALM and BLM are discussions on the same topic, but from an opposite perspective, it is hypothesised that agents that are doing the harm, according to BLM, should be different from the agents doing the harm according to ALM. The embeddings of the agents (i.e. the 'arg0') of tweets expressing the harm value from ALM, BLM and Baltimore (Fig. 4 were plotted. However, we found no clear distinction between corpora, suggesting that participants embeddings do not capture a distinction between the agents from the different viewpoints.

Second, word clouds based on the frequencies of the different word senses showed qualitative differences between the ALM, BLM and Baltimore corpora (Fig. 5). This suggested the presence of predictive signals in tweet's frame frequencies. We also observed that in both ALM and BLM the frame 'protect.01' was the most prominent, while in the Baltimore corpus, 'help.01' was most often used. For the harm value, both ALM and BLM used 'hurt.01' and 'kill.01' quite often. However, 'kill.01' was the most frequently used word sense in the ALM corpus and 'hurt.01' in the BLM corpus, while 'hurt.01' was not frequent in the Baltimore corpus. Of note, 'happen.01' appeared often in the Baltimore corpus, as an expression of 'occur, take place'. Indeed, in the core roles that accompany this sense, there is no 'arg0' (i.e. the most agent-like participant). This indicated

Table 2. Statistical comparisons of the toxicity score distributions of tweets from values assigned by annotations or by the frame-based method. The two distributions are compared by MWU test. Each cell shows the p-value and the effect size from this test for data assigned with a given value expression and from a given corpus.

Corpus	Care	Harm	Non-moral
ALM	0.66	$< 10^{-3}$	$< 10^{-3}$
	(−0.083)	(0.126)	(0.041)
BLM	0.32	$< 10^{-3}$	0.006
	(−0.112)	(0.116)	(−0.04)
Baltimore	0.08	0.002	$< 10^{-3}$
	(0.111)	(0.1)	(−0.05)
Davidson	0.46	$< 10^{-3}$	0.84
	(−0.045)	(−0.343)	(0.007)
Election	0.07	$< 10^{-3}$	0.011
	(0.081)	(0.149)	(−0.04)
Sandy	0.03	0.09	$< 10^{-3}$
	(−0.122)	(0.043)	(0.105)

that the authors of these tweets wrote about events happening to them, instead of taking a more active position.

Finally, the tasks were challenged by fitting Random Forest classifiers to the training data, using the features from frame frequencies and toxicity scores (alone and combined). Accuracy scores from these models are reported in Table 3. We note that this evaluation metric differs from the one used for the frame extraction method, since the two methods have different output: Random Forest, a single value; frame extraction method, a set of values (potentially empty). For all tasks, the models based on frame frequencies and toxicity scores performed best. Viewpoint discrimination was considerably better than the random chance baseline of 33%. Also, the high accuracy (79%) for care, harm and non-moral classification suggested that a supervised method might ameliorate the linking between frames and moral values via ValueNet ontology (71.1%, as calculated from Table 1 averaging the percentage of correctly detected Care, Harm and Non-moral tweets from "All" corpora, weighted by the number of tweets). In addition, even moral values without frame links could be predicted better than random chance baseline (12.5%), although with mediocre performances (46.8%).

4   Discussion

In this paper, we investigated the relation between semantic frames, toxicity and moral values on social media and their expression across different topics or viewpoints. Our analysis was conducted by enriching the Moral Foundations Twitter Corpus, annotated for values from the Moral Foundations Theory, with toxicity scores. With these data we could explore how toxicity levels related to different

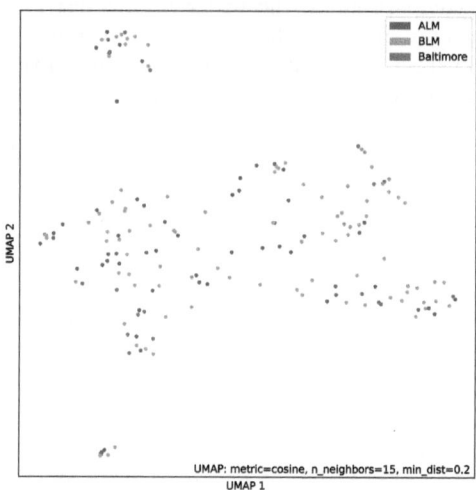

Fig. 4. 2-dimensional UMAP projection of the word embeddings of agents from harm frames. Frames were extracted from the tweets expressing harm in ALM, BLM and Baltimore corpora.

ALM

BLM

Baltimore

protect.01
serve.01
heal.01
defend.01
help.01

serve.01
protect.01
help.01
defend.01

help.01
heal.01
serve.01 defend.01
protect.01

suffer.01   destroy.01 lose.02
kill.01
die.01 harm.01
hurt.01
murder.01 happen.01

kill.01 die.01
hurt.01
murder.01
harm.01
happen.01 break.01 lose.02

injure.01 hurt.01
burn.01
die.01
happen.01
break.01 kill.01
fight.01
murder.01

Fig. 5. Word clouds showing which word senses are most frequent across the different corpora (ALM, BLM and Baltimore). First row are frames that lead to the care value, second row to the harm value.

Table 3. Accuracy scores from the Random Forest models trained for the classification of different viewpoints/corpora (ALM, BLM, Baltimore), care/harm/non-moral values, and other MFT values, using tweet features of: frame frequencies (Frame freq), toxicity scores (Tox), the frame frequencies and toxicity scores together.

	Viewpoints	Care/harm & non-moral	Other values
Frame freq	52.2%	74.7%	35.6%
Tox	69.7%	74.9%	41.6%
Frame freq + Tox	70.2%	79.0%	46.8%

moral values and corpora. While relations between toxicity and moral expression was previously found [4], in Sect. 3.1 we also found toxicity patterns that were topic-specific. Topic-specificities raises concerns similar to moral value classification, for which supervised solutions struggle to generalise on topics outside the training data.

As such, we challenged semantic frame analysis as an alternative method to assign social media posts with the care, harm and non-moral values linked to PropBank frames via ValueNet [7]. In Sect. 3.2 we found that this approach has moderate sensitivity but high specificity. We speculate that, since frames are better detected on more explicit texts, accuracy should improve when analysing texts that are longer and require less contextual information, such as news articles or posts from media or political accounts that drive the public discourse in online platforms. While this methodology seemed to be robust on diverse topics, future work is required to expand semantic frame analysis covering all MFT values and languages other than English. Both these limitations can be addressed by future development of the used semantic frame extraction method, which was originally developed for the extraction of PropBank frames from English sentences. For the extension to other moral values, in particular, the frame extraction system could either be expanded by: detecting other semantic frames that are included in ValueNet; finding new direct links between PropBank frames and moral values (besides besides care/harm) to be added to the ValueNet ontology. This would enable to study the toxicity related to moral values that are associated to far fewer frames than care and harm. While their detection might be harder, this makes the high specificity observed for care and harm even more compelling.

Low sensitivity of semantic frames analysis raised the question about a possible distortion of toxicity levels from care and harm values, due to the mismatches between frame-based and annotations value assignment. In Sect. 3.3 we confirmed that differences between the two approaches were statistically low, which is coherent with the high specificity of frame extraction. This result highlights how the study of misbehaviour in social media, combining toxicity scores and moral information, could be effectively conducted using frames instead of human annotations, which are costly and biased.

In Sect. 3.4 we designed three classification tasks to challenge the frame-based method further. In the feature selection, we found no relevant signal from low-dimensional projection embeddings of frame participants (available thanks to PropBank), while qualitative analysis of frequency from moral frames were important for viewpoints discrimination. Using frame frequencies and toxicity scores as input features, the predictive models showed good performance, higher than baselines, for the classification of posts' viewpoints and moral values. This result remarked the utility of frame extraction as a fully interpretable methodology, which can help distinguishing multiple narratives, emerging in social platforms on the same topic, in a fully transparent way.

Acknowledgments. This work has been supported by the Horizon Europe VALAWAI project (grant agreement number 101070930).

Disclosure of Interests. The authors declare that they have no conflict of interest.

References

1. Beuls, K., Van Eecke, P., Cangalovic, V.S.: A computational construction grammar approach to semantic frame extraction **7**(1) (2021). https://doi.org/10.1515/lingvan-2018-0015
2. Bies, A., Mott, J., Warner, C., Kulick, S.: English Web Treebank ldc2012t13. Linguistic Data Consortium, Philadelphia (2012)
3. Brugnoli, E., Gravino, P., Lo Sardo, D.R., Loreto, V., Prevedello, G.: Fine-grained clustering of social media: How moral triggers drive preferences and consensus. In: Proceedings of the 16th International Conference on Agents and Artificial Intelligence. ICAART 2024, vol. 3, pp. 1405–1412 (2024). https://doi.org/10.5220/0000183700003636
4. Brugnoli, E., Gravino, P., Prevedello, G.: Moral values in social media for disinformation and hate speech analysis. LNAI (2024)
5. Davidson, T., Warmsley, D., Macy, M., Weber, I.: Automated hate speech detection and the problem of offensive language. In: The 11th Interbational AAAI Conference on Web and Social Media. Montreal (2017)
6. Day, M.V., Fiske, S.T., Downing, E.L., Trail, T.E.: Shifting liberal and conservative attitudes using moral foundations theory. Pers. Soc. Psychol. Bull. **40**(12), 1559–1573 (2014)
7. De Giorgis, S., Gangemi, A., Damiano, R.: Basic human values and moral foundations theory in ValueNet ontology. In: International Conference on Knowledge Engineering and Knowledge Management, pp. 3–18. Springer (2022). https://doi.org/10.1007/978-3-031-17105-5_1
8. Feinberg, M., Willer, R.: Moral reframing: a technique for effective and persuasive communication across political divides. Soc. Pers. Psychol. Compass **13**(12), e12501 (2019)
9. Fogg, B.: Persuasive Technology: Using Computers to Change What We Think and Do. Morgan Kauffmann, San Francisco (2003)
10. González-Bailón, S., Lelkes, Y.: Do social media undermine social cohesion? A critical review. Soc. Issues Policy Rev. **17**(1), 155–180 (2023)
11. Graham, J., et al.: Moral foundations theory: the pragmatic validity of moral pluralism. In: Advances in Experimental Social Psychology, vol. 47, pp. 55–130. Elsevier (2013)
12. Honnibal, M., Montani, I., Van Landeghem, S., Boyd, A.: spaCy: Industrial-strength natural language processing in Python (2020). https://doi.org/10.5281/zenodo.1212303
13. Hoover, J., et al.: Moral foundations twitter corpus: a collection of 35k tweets annotated for moral sentiment. Soc. Psychol. Personality Sci. **11**(8), 1057–1071 (2020)
14. Hunter, J.D.: Matplotlib: a 2D graphics environment. Comput. Sci. Eng. **9**(3), 90–95 (2007). https://doi.org/10.1109/MCSE.2007.55
15. Jost, J.T., Baldassarri, D.S., Druckman, J.N.: Cognitive-motivational mechanisms of political polarization in social-communicative contexts. Nat. Rev. Psychol. **1**(10), 560–576 (2022)
16. Kelley, K., Preacher, K.J.: On effect size. Psychol. Methods **17**(2), 137 (2012)

17. Kivikangas, J.M., Fernández-Castilla, B., Järvelä, S., Ravaja, N., Lönnqvist, J.E.: Moral foundations and political orientation: systematic review and meta-analysis. Psychol. Bull. **147**(1), 55 (2021)
18. Kruskal, W.H., Wallis, W.A.: Use of ranks in one-criterion variance analysis. J. Am. Stat. Assoc. **47**(260), 583–621 (1952)
19. Lees, A., et al.: A new generation of perspective API: efficient multilingual character-level transformers. arXiv preprint arXiv:2202.11176 (2022)
20. Liscio, E., Dondera, A., Geadau, A., Jonker, C., Murukannaiah, P.: Cross-domain classification of moral values. In: Findings of the Association for Computational Linguistics: NAACL 2022, pp. 2727–2745 (2022)
21. Mann, H.B., Whitney, D.R.: On a test of whether one of two random variables is stochastically larger than the other. Ann. Math. Stat. **18**, 50–60 (1947)
22. Palmer, M., Gildea, D., Kingsbury, P.: The proposition bank: an annotated corpus of semantic roles. Comput. Linguist. **31**(1), 71–106 (2005)
23. Pedregosa, F., et al.: Scikit-learn: machine learning in Python. J. Mach. Learn. Res. **12**, 2825–2830 (2011)
24. Rathje, S., Van Bavel, J.J., Van Der Linden, S.: Out-group animosity drives engagement on social media. Proc. Natl. Acad. Sci. **118**(26), e2024292118 (2021)
25. Steels, L. (ed.): Design Patterns in Fluid Construction Grammar. John Benjamins, Amsterdam, Netherlands (2011). https://doi.org/10.1075/cal.11
26. Stranisci, M., De Leonardis, M., Bosco, C., Patti, V.: The expression of moral values in the twitter debate: a corpus of conversations. IJCoL. Ital. J. Comput. Linguist. **7**(7-1, 2), 113–132 (2021)
27. van Trijp, R., Beuls, K., Van Eecke, P.: The FCG Editor: an innovative environment for engineering computational construction grammars. PLoS ONE **17**(6), e0269708 (2022). https://doi.org/10.1371/journal.pone.0269708, https://doi.org/10.1371/journal.pone.0269708, publisher: Public Library of Science
28. Van Eecke, P., Verheyen, L., Beuls, K.: Operationalising usage-based construction grammar on a large scale (2022)
29. Weber, R., et al.: Extracting latent moral information from text narratives: relevance, challenges, and solutions. Commun. Methods Meas. **12**(2–3), 119–139 (2018)
30. Weischedel, R., et al.: Ontonotes release 5.0 ldc2013t19. Philadelphia, Linguistic Data Consortium (2013)

Vision Language Models as Values Detectors

Giulio Antonio Abbo[(✉)] [iD] and Tony Belpaeme[iD]

IDLab-AIRO, Ghent University – imec, Ghent, Belgium
giulioantonio.abbo@ugent.be

Abstract. Large Language Models integrating textual and visual inputs have introduced new possibilities for interpreting complex data. Despite their remarkable ability to generate coherent and contextually relevant text based on visual stimuli, the alignment of these models with human perception in identifying relevant elements in images requires further exploration. This paper investigates the alignment between state-of-the-art LLMs and human annotators in detecting elements of relevance within home environment scenarios. We created a set of twelve images depicting various domestic scenarios and enlisted fourteen annotators to identify the key element in each image. We then compared these human responses with outputs from five different LLMs, including GPT-4o and four LLaVA variants. Our findings reveal a varied degree of alignment, with LLaVA 34B showing the highest performance but still scoring low. However, an analysis of the results highlights the models' potential to detect value-laden elements in images, suggesting that with improved training and refined prompts, LLMs could enhance applications in social robotics, assistive technologies, and human-computer interaction by providing deeper insights and more contextually relevant responses.

Keywords: Large Language Model · Vision Language Model · Visual · Multi-modal · Multimodal · Detector · Value · Ethics · Moral · Alignment

1 Introduction

The introduction of Large Language Models (LLMs) that incorporate both textual and visual inputs [7] has opened new avenues for understanding and interpreting complex data. These models have shown remarkable progress [1,6] in generating coherent and contextually relevant text based on visual stimuli, promising to become invaluable tools in many applications.

For instance, vision models have already proven their capabilities in pathology image analysis [5], and have been studied as success detection modules [4], applied to simulated agents, robot manipulation, and egocentric videos with promising results.

However, their ability to align with human perception, especially in terms of identifying elements of relevance in images, remains an area that requires further

© The Author(s), under exclusive license to Springer Nature Switzerland AG 2025
N. Osman and L. Steels (Eds.): VALE 2024, LNAI 15356, pp. 76–86, 2025.
https://doi.org/10.1007/978-3-031-85463-7_5

investigation. Understanding how these models interpret visual information and comparing it to human perception is crucial for their employment in sensitive applications.

A model capable of discerning between day-to-day events and situations that require special attention could be the first part of a mechanism for quick intervention in case of danger. Similarly, a module with the ability to detect nuanced details in an image could be used as a focus controller that could suggest towards which elements a system's computational attention should shift.

1.1 Vision Language Models

Vision Language Models (VLMs) represent a significant advancement in the field of artificial intelligence, combining the capabilities of visual recognition systems with the contextual understanding of language models [7]. As a result, these models can perform tasks that were previously challenging for separate vision and language models, such as image captioning and classification, visual question answering, and multi-turn dialogue about images.

VLMs operate by aligning visual features extracted from images with corresponding textual representations. These features can be obtained, in the case of LLaVA [7] for instance, by using a pre-trained CLIP [9] visual encoder. These are then projected into the word embeddings space by means of a trained projection matrix, whose output has the same dimensionality as the embeddings space of a language model such as LLaMA [11].

With this architecture, it is possible to include in the prompt – the set of instructions that guide a language model's output generation – one or more images.

As with text-only LLMs, it is possible to craft ad-hoc prompts for the most disparate applications. The prompt can be structured as a completion task, where the model completes a sentence, or in a conversational mode, in which the model can engage in a dialogue with the user. Furthermore, the prompt can include an initial *system* instruction, that gives additional information on how to complete the task. Finally, as in the LLM case, the prompt may include one or more examples of how to complete the assignment.

1.2 Contribution

In this paper, we want to investigate how current state-of-the-art LLMs with textual and visual input align in identifying elements of relevance in an image; when not aligned, we are interested in how they differ, and which aspects they can detect.

Specifically, we scope our research to the home environment: an informal setting, possibly with a family, where situations and social constructs are simpler, yet still intriguing.

This formulation does not target widely accepted value theories such as the theory of basic human values [10]. The reason for this is twofold: first, such theories are not easily declined to simple everyday scenarios such as those we seek to analyse. Second, we sustain that this indirect approach provides useful insights into the capabilities of VLMs and their inherent biases that would otherwise be more nuanced to detect. However, we will complement the results of the models' reasoning with a reflection on values grounded in the existing literature in future research.

For our evaluation, we created a set of twelve images, each representing a simple situation developing in a home. We then enlisted fourteen annotators' help to extract the relevant aspects from each image. Finally, we used five different LLMs – GPT-4o and four LLaVA variants – to perform the same task and manually confronted their output with the human's responses.

LLMs capable of understanding values can significantly enhance various applications by providing deeper insights and more contextually aware responses. In social robotics, such models can improve interactions by recognising and responding to human emotions and social cues, making robots more empathetic and effective companions. In assistive technologies, value-aware LLMs can better prioritise user needs and preferences, offering tailored support that aligns with the user's values and lifestyle; in addition, they could detect critical situations for immediate intervention. In human-computer interaction, these models can create more intuitive interfaces by understanding user intentions and providing feedback that respects personal and cultural values. Additionally, in fields like marketing and content creation, value-aware LLMs can generate content that resonates more deeply with target audiences, fostering stronger engagement and connection. Overall, integrating value understanding into LLMs can lead to more personalised, effective, aware, and human-centric AI systems.

2   Images and Element of Relevance

The first step of our evaluation involves creating a small set of 12 scenarios, each consisting of a picture of an event taking place inside a home. The events are taken from the results of previous research [2] and integrated with new scenarios. Four images from the set are shown in Fig. 1, while Table 1 reports a description of each picture used.

The images are generated ad-hoc using diffusion models. This choice allows us to portray situations difficult to recreate with actors in a real-life environment, but that still can resonate or clash with the observer's values. It is important to note that the diffusion models are not the focus of the evaluation, since their output will be annotated as explained in this section. In the future, we plan to deploy and test this technology in the field, evaluating its behaviour with real images.

Of the twelve pictures, ten are built to resonate with the observers' values, while two are supposed not to contain value-relevant elements. To confirm this, each image was annotated with the help of 14 volunteers according to the following procedure.

Fig. 1. Four of the twelve images used in the evaluation.

The participants are shown the images in random order. For each of them, they are asked to identify the relevant element, if any is present. This formulation is intentionally vague, following the rationale discussed in Sect. 4.

The annotators are 8 males and 6 females, with an average of 29 years of age $(SD = 7.01)$. The nationalities of the participants are Belgian $(7/14)$, other European $(3/14)$ and non-European $(4/14)$. The participants are all researchers or university professors.

Overall, 168 sentences were collected, manually reviewed and normalised, obtaining for each image the most common element of focus. In case of a tie, one of the two possible elements was picked randomly. For example, in the image depicting "the dog throws up on the carpet during the night", the elements of relevance individuated are the dog $(3/14)$, the stain $(2/14)$, nothing $(2/14)$, and comments on the image quality or the framing $(2/14)$. The most common

Table 1. Description of the images and the element of relevance most commonly associated with each by the annotators.

Description	Perceived Element of Relevance
The dog throws up on the carpet during the night.	The dog is sick
In the bedroom, a child drawing on the wall.	The child is writing on the wall
In the living room, family members sit far apart in silence, looking at their phones.	The images are deformed
A child is crying alone in the bedroom.	The child is in distress
A man crouched crying in the shower.	The man is very sad
A man in the kitchen smoking a cigarette near a child.	The man, his expression
A dried-up plant wilting in the corner of the living room.	The plant is dying
A woman is taking medicines at home.	The table is covered in medicines
A pot on the stove is boiling over, with water splashing everywhere.	The water boiling looks dangerous
A woman slipped on the ground in the bathroom.	The woman, her position
In the hallway, a cat is sleeping on a carpet in the sun. [control]	The cat napping in the sun
A woman is eating dinner in front of the TV. [control]	A woman is eating

responses concerned the dog's health (5/14), expressing apprehension or simply stating that the pet is sick. The most common elements of focus for each image are reported in Table 1.

Contrary to what was expected, not all the pictures were associated with sensitive situations. In Sect. 4 an analysis of these results is provided.

3   Evaluation

For the alignment evaluation, the models were selected by considering only those taking images and text as input and generating a textual response available at the time of testing (May 2024). Five LLMs were chosen: GPT-4 omni as a baseline, and LLaVA in four variants, as the most prominent models that can be self-hosted. The models evaluated are `gpt-4o-2024-05-13`, `llava-v1.6-34b-hf`, `llava-v1.6-mistral-7b-hf`, `llava-v1.6-vicuna-7b-hf`, and `llava-v1.6-vicuna-13b-hf`.

In terms of the number of parameters, the models range from 7 billion to 34 for the LLaVA models, while GPT's size is yet undisclosed. While the lower number of parameters of some models could lead to lower-quality results, we are nonetheless interested in assessing the performance of the smaller, faster and easier-to-deploy alternatives.

3.1   Prompt and Model Configuration

The models were all evaluated using the same prompt, formatted according to the requirements of each of them. The prompt contains one of the dataset's images and a user message requesting to identify the element that needs attention in the image. This formulation is the same as the one used for the annotators, and it was chosen after initial testing on one of the images, to avoid obtaining a description of the environment and instead focus on the meaningful elements of the scene while remaining as simple as possible. The prompt then suggests the desired behaviour in case the image does not contain any striking elements, to avoid false positives. The prompt used is: "Identify what is the element that needs attention in this image. If nothing is relevant answer with 'none'."

The choice not to use a system prompt is dictated by the fact that the LLaVA model based on Mistral does not support it officially. It is reasonable to expect that – in all other cases – the use of a more detailed prompt, and a system prompt, can only improve the models' performance.

Regarding the models' configuration, a temperature of 1 was chosen, leaving all other parameters to their defaults. This was done with the objective of maintaining a level of repeatability of the results while not sacrificing the variability of their wording. Furthermore, we stopped each generation after 100 tokens, as we are interested in short, to-the-point answers.

3.2 Responses Generation and Evaluation

Each of the five models was used to generate three completions for each of the twelve images, using the above prompt. In total, we thus obtained 180 answers, of which we kept the first sentence, discarding everything after the first full-stop mark. This is justified because in our evaluation a short, targeted answer is preferred over a wordy alternative.

The models' answers were reviewed by hand, mirroring what was done with the human answers. Subsequently, each answer was given a binary score, depending on whether the focus element was individuated correctly. The results are averaged, obtaining a score from 0 to 1 for each model. The cases in which an answer was not aligned were analysed, and the results are discussed in Sect. 4.

3.3 Results

The alignment scores for each model are reported in Table 2. The best-performing model is LLaVA in its 36B variant, while the same architecture scores the lowest in its Mistral variant. Figure 2 displays the average of each model, with the corresponding 95% confidence interval.

However, Cochran's Q test for categorical, paired equivalence between the 5 models returns a p-value of 0.077. We cannot conclude that there is a statistical difference between the models' alignment in detecting the relevant element in the image.

4 Discussion

The discussion covers two aspects of our work: first, an analysis of the results of the annotation procedure, then a comment on the models' evaluation outcome.

Table 2. Element of focus alignment for each model tested, where 0 indicates constant misalignment and 1 perfect alignment.

Model	Average	SD
LLaVA 34B	0.42	0.50
L. Vicuna7B	0.36	0.49
GPT-4o	0.33	0.48
L. Vicuna13B	0.33	0.48
L. Mistral	0.14	0.35

4.1   Annotation Results

By examining the annotators' answers, it can be noticed that there are four kinds of responses. In the first kind, the annotator points out an element of the image: as an example, the dog or the stain, referring to the first image in Fig. 1.

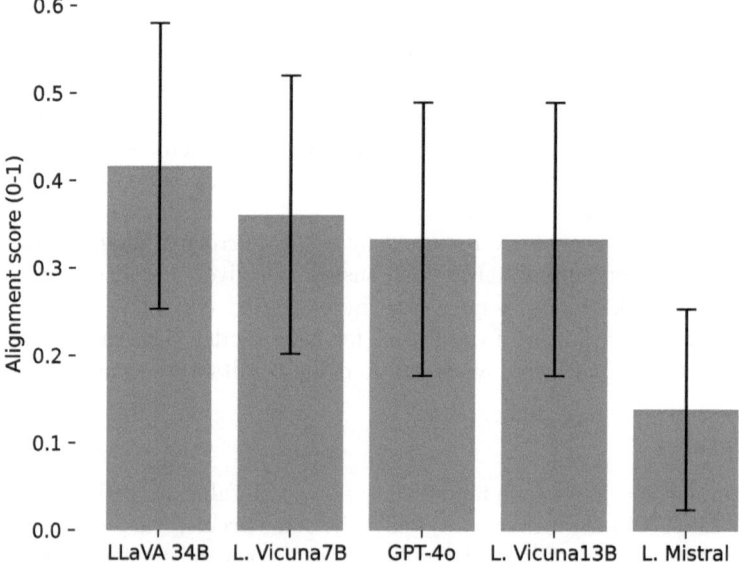

Fig. 2. Comparison of the element of focus alignments, with the 95% confidence interval.

The second kind is the most interesting; in this case, the participants display awareness of the situation and the values involved, according to their sensibility. This is the case of the responses referring to the dog's health.

The third category is the *none* answer, indicating that in the image nothing is particularly relevant; while comments on the image quality and framing form the fourth group of answers.

We noticed that this behaviour was replicated by the models. Table 3 offers a breakdown of each model's answers response types, confronted with the annotators' answers response type.

There is no doubt that a more precise formulation of the instructions given to the annotators would have led to different results. Indeed, it can be argued that an annotator, who indicated 'dog' as an answer in the example mentioned, was actually referring to the dog being sick and was indeed worried about the animal's health. However, an analysis of the annotators' intention is unnecessary in this study, since we are comparing their answers with the output of language models, which do not possess any intent, and can be evaluated solely based on their output. For the same reason, we chose not to set a time limit for the annotators' task, as we are interested in the results of a deliberative process, which is not immediate [3].

In our expectations, ten of the images would have been associated with the (more aware) second kind of response, while the two images crafted without value-relevant elements should have elicited responses of the first (descriptive) or third (nothing) category. However, the fact that the annotators' results are different does not change the validity of the results, as we are comparing the

Table 3. Generated answer type percentage for each model (rows) and corresponding annotators' type (columns). Note that type A-3 is missing as "none" was never the most common annotators' answer for any image. For example, in 22.22% of LLaVA 34B's responses the model answered with a response of type 1 whereas most annotators provided a response of type 2.

Model	Type	A-1	A-2	A-4
LLaVA 34B	M-1	27.78	22.22	8.33
	M-2	13.89	27.78	0.0
L. Vicuna7B	M-1	25.0	13.89	5.56
	M-2	13.89	25.0	0.0
	M-3	2.78	5.56	0.0
	M-4	0.0	5.56	2.78
GPT-4o	M-1	5.56	5.56	0.0
	M-2	19.44	27.78	0.0
	M-3	16.67	16.67	8.33
L. Vicuna13B	M-1	25.0	19.44	2.78
	M-2	0.0	16.67	0.0
	M-3	13.89	11.11	5.56
	M-4	2.78	2.78	0.0
L. Mistral	M-1	0.0	8.33	0.0
	M-2	8.33	13.89	0.0
	M-3	33.33	25.0	8.33
	M-4	0.0	2.78	0.0

responses with what was produced by the language models, which were prompted to answer the same question.

4.2   Alignment

The results suggest that the models are not aligned with the human annotators in detecting the element of relevance in an image. Indeed, the best-performing model, LLaVA 36B, scored less than 0.5, where 0 indicates constant misalignment and 1 perfect alignment. It is plausible that this is a consequence of the training data, which pushes the results towards a more descriptive response.

Most of the misalignment happens when a model wrongly produces a first-kind answer (descriptive). In these cases, the model points out the wrong element of the image or does not give a second-category (more aware) response when necessary. We could observe this outcome in 36% of the not-aligned answers. In one instance for example, when provided with the image "a man crouched crying in the shower", the model spectacularly failed by pointing out the importance of always maintaining the bathroom clean.

The second most common mistake has to do with an unexpected third-category answer – answering "none" to pictures where most annotators have individuated an element or relevance; this happened in 29% of the not-aligned responses.

On some occasions, the models gave a more satisfying result than the annotators. In 14% of the misaligned answers, the models answered "none" to the two images that supposedly did not contain any relevant element, while the annotators provided a type one descriptive answer, which is a more desirable outcome.

In 16% of the not-aligned responses, the models provided a type two answer where a type one was expected. This means that the model gave a more aware answer while most of the annotators just pointed out an element of the image. For example, most annotators focused on the woman in the image "a woman slipped on the ground in the bathroom"; however, most models expressed concern for the woman's health. Similarly, in a few instances, the models picked up that a man was smoking in the presence of a child, or that a woman taking a lot of medicines looked confused, or should be monitored to avoid overdosing, all things that most human annotators did not point out.

Errors in the generation and type four answers form the remaining 5%.

4.3   Vision Language Models as Detectors

The results suggest that vision LLMs, although not aligned in this aspect, show potential in identifying elements of relevance within images. This could be tied to value-laden scenarios. Given that personal values have been shown to act as selective factors in perception [8], these models can, in principle, detect situations involving values by identifying pertinent elements in images. For instance, annotators frequently associated value-laden elements with scenarios reflecting concern for health, safety, and social dynamics, which aligns with how personal values influence perception.

By using fine-tuning datasets that emphasise value-laden contexts, vision LLMs can be better aligned with human perceptions. Correctly structured prompts that explicitly guide the model to consider value-related aspects could improve performance. For example, asking the model to "identify the element of concern considering the possible values at play" might yield more nuanced and contextually aware responses. By doing so, these models could serve as effective tools for detecting value-laden scenarios, making them useful in applications where understanding human values is crucial.

As a last note, it must be noted that, since the models were not fine-tuned, their output reflects the bias present in the training data. The alignment thus depends on the cultural background of the annotators in this case, and of the users in real-life scenarios.

5   Conclusion

In this study, we investigated the alignment of current state-of-the-art Large Language Models with both textual and visual inputs in identifying elements of relevance within home environment images. Our findings indicate a noticeable discrepancy between the models' output and human annotators' responses. Despite the best-performing model, LLaVA 1.6 36B, obtaining a low alignment score, our analysis suggests that these models have the potential to improve in detecting elements of significance with more targeted fine-tuning and more precise prompting. With such improvements, vision LLMs could become effective tools in applications requiring a deep understanding of human values, such as social robotics, assistive technologies, and human-computer interaction.

Acknowledgments. Funded by the Horizon Europe VALAWAI project (grant agreement number 101070930).

References

1. Abbo, G.A., Belpaeme, T.: I was blind but now i see: implementing vision-enabled dialogue in social robots (2023). https://doi.org/10.48550/arXiv.2311.08957
2. Abbo, G.A., Marchesi, S., Wykowska, A., Belpaeme, T.: Social value alignment in large language models. In: Osman, N., Steels, L. (eds.) Value Engineering in Artificial Intelligence, pp. 83–97. Springer Nature Switzerland, Cham (2024). https://doi.org/10.1007/978-3-031-58202-8_6
3. Daniel, K.: Thinking, fast and slow (2017)
4. Du, Y., et al.: Vision-language models as success detectors (2023)
5. Huang, Z., Bianchi, F., Yuksekgonul, M., Montine, T.J., Zou, J.: A visual–language foundation model for pathology image analysis using medical twitter. Nat. Med. **29**(9), 2307–2316 (2023)
6. Liu, H., Li, C., Li, Y., Lee, Y.J.: Improved baselines with visual instruction tuning. In: NeurIPS 2023 Workshop on Instruction Tuning and Instruction Following (2023)

7. Liu, H., Li, C., Wu, Q., Lee, Y.J.: Visual instruction tuning. In: Thirty-Seventh Conference on Neural Information Processing Systems (2023)

8. Postman, L., Bruner, J.S., McGinnies, E.: Personal values as selective factors in perception. J. Abnormal Soc. Psychol. **43**(2), 142–154 (1948). https://doi.org/10.1037/h0059765

9. Radford, A., et al.: Learning transferable visual models from natural language supervision. In: Proceedings of the 38th International Conference on Machine Learning, pp. 8748–8763. PMLR (2021)

10. Schwartz, S.H., et al.: Refining the theory of basic individual values. J. Pers. Soc. Psychol. **103**, 663–688 (2012). https://doi.org/10.1037/a0029393

11. Touvron, H., et al.: Llama: open and efficient foundation language models (2023)

Leveraging Large Language Models to Identify the Values Behind Arguments

Rithik Appachi Senthilkumar📧, Amir Homayounirad$^{(\boxtimes)}$📧,
and Luciano Cavalcante Siebert📧

Faculty of Electrical Engineering, Mathematics and Computer Science, Delft
University of Technology, Delft, The Netherlands
{rappachisenthi,a.homayounirad,l.cavalcantesiebert}@tudelft.nl

Abstract. Human values capture what people and societies perceive as desirable, transcend specific situations and serve as guiding principles for action. People's value systems motivate their positions on issues concerning the economy, society and politics among others, influencing the arguments they make. Identifying the values behind arguments can therefore help us find common ground in discourse and uncover the core reasons behind disagreements. Transformer-based large language models (LLMs) have exhibited remarkable performance across language generation and analysis. However, leveraging LLMs in sociotechnical systems that assist with discourse and argumentation necessitates systematically evaluating their ability to analyse and identify the values behind arguments, an under-explored research direction. Using a multi-level human value taxonomy inspired by the Schwartz Theory of Basic Human Values, we present a systematic and critical evaluation of GPT-3.5-turbo in human value identification from a dataset of multi-cultural arguments, across the zero-shot, few-shot and chain-of-thought prompting strategies, carrying forward from prior research on this task which leveraged a fine-tuned BERT model. We observe that prompting strategies exhibit performance levels close to, but still behind fine-tuning for value classification. We also detail some challenges associated with value classification with LLMs, offering potential directions for future research.

Keywords: Large Language Models · Prompting · Human Values

1 Introduction

Values, as described by sociologist Robin Williams [30], are core conceptions of the desirable within every individual and society, that serve as standards or criteria to guide actions, judgments, choices and attitudes among many other aspects. A large body of work has been dedicated towards conceptualizing human values, most notably the Values Theory developed by Shalom Schwartz [20] who defines human values as "desirable, trans-situational goals, varying in importance, that serve as guiding principles in people's lives".

N. Osman and L. Steels (Eds.): VALE 2024, LNAI 15356, pp. 87–103, 2025.
https://doi.org/10.1007/978-3-031-85463-7_6

According to Milton Rokeach [17], the study of human values is not limited to one field, but is of relevance to all the sciences concerned with human behavior. One such example is the study of *argumentation*. The ability of human values to serve as standards or criteria that guide people's actions and evaluations, as noted in the works of Rokeach, Williams and Schwartz among others, manifests itself in argumentation – the values people abide by inform how they react to policies and ideas, which motivate the arguments they make either in favor of or against them. Searle [22] further noted that perfectly rational agents operating with perfect information are still capable of rational disagreement, due to inconsistencies in the values and interests they hold, despite each agent's values being rationally acceptable on their own.

Since human values motivate people's arguments on society [19], economics [1] and politics [9] among other topics in general discourse, identifying the human values behind arguments enables us to understand the "why" underlying an argument's logic [10], helping us find common ground and uncover the foundational reasons behind disagreements and conflicts. Over the past few years, the advent of large language models (LLMs), probabilistic models based on the Transformer [25] architecture, trained on natural language and capable of general-purpose language understanding and generation tasks, has led to breakthroughs in computational sentiment analysis [32], machine translation [31] and question-answering [15] among others.

However, the application of LLMs towards understanding and identifying human values from an argumentation context is relatively under-explored. Kiesel et al. [10] presented, to the best of our knowledge, the first such attempt, evaluating a fine-tuned BERT [6] model on multi-cultural arguments, revealing promising results within and across cultures. Scaling up language models across parameters, training data and training compute has conferred onto them emergent properties [26], one of which is their ability to solve tasks out of the box given a natural language instruction (i.e. a **prompt**) as input. We argue that as prompting has emerged as an accessible and straightforward avenue of interacting with LLMs, critically evaluating how prompt-based strategies fare in identifying the human values behind arguments can shed light on the benefits and drawbacks of LLMs in the context of human value identification, paving the way towards their incorporation in sociotechnical systems that assist with public discourse and argumentation.

We contribute the preliminary attempt at leveraging prompting strategies to evaluate the capability of *GPT-3.5-turbo*, the model behind the widely utilized *ChatGPT*, in identifying the human values from a multi-level human value taxonomy behind geographically diverse arguments. We observe that prompting strategies come close to, but are not capable of outperforming model fine-tuning in value identification, and that adding example demonstrations to the prompt helps improve performance. We also observe that chain-of-thought (CoT) prompting [27] using LLM-generated justifications as CoT demonstrations does not positively impact performance, possibly due to the poor quality of justifications generated.

We intend for this paper to help (1) bring to light the limitations and benefits of applying LLMs to value-driven argumentation, guiding people towards *responsibly* utilizing LLMs in this context, and (2) guide future research into potentially incorporating LLMs into the development of sociotechnical systems that align with human values and offer fresh perspectives into discourse and disagreements inspired by the human values at the root of the arguments.

2 Background

In this section, we outline the concept of *human values* and their representation in the literature. We then explore their significance in the context of *arguments*. Following this, we describe how *computational approaches* have been applied to identify the human values behind arguments. We conclude with a brief explanation of the *prompting* paradigm in LLMs, and how it can be leveraged towards this value identification task.

2.1 Human Values

The Schwartz Theory of Basic Human Values describes human values as abstract motivations that guide people's opinions, feelings and goals in life [21]. Schwartz outlines six features of all values, highlighting that values are (1) beliefs referring to (2) desirable goals motivating actions, that (3) transcend specific actions and situations, (4) serve as standards or criteria, and are (5) ordered by relative importance to one another, the relativity of importance of which (6) guides action.

Formal representations of human values have been extensively explored in the literature, both from social science [17] and argumentation research [2] standpoints. The Rokeach Value Survey (RVS) in 1973 [17] was one of the earliest thorough attempts at understanding human values, presenting a practical survey of 36 values consisting of 18 *terminal* values (referring to desired end-states of existence) and 18 *instrumental* values (referring to preferred modes of behavior). The Schwartz Theory of Basic Human Values [21] identifies ten broad human value categories, further postulating that values form a continuum of related motivations resulting in a circular structure where values closer together share a greater extent of motivational emphases.

2.2 Value-Driven Argumentation

By *arguments*, we refer to argumentative statements made in response to an idea, policy or statement where the individual making the argument does so with the goal of persuasion. Value systems have been used in formal argumentation to model audience-specific preferences, with the notion that a stronger argument is one that the audience in question reveres the values it resorts to [2, 24, 28]. Value classification for arguments entails identifying the human values that form the motivational basis behind the arguments being made. Kiesel et al. [10] argue that processing and analyzing the human values behind arguments introduces a new outlook into argumentation, emphasizing the "why" underlying the argument's logic.

Identifying human values behind arguments is often not straightforward, since in some cases the values that guide someone to express an opinion may be implicit (i.e. not directly specified in the opinion), or context-specific. To further describe the context-specificity of values, we turn to Liscio et al. [13] who define a context-specific value as "a value that is applicable and defined specifically within a context". For instance, the value of *privacy* is relevant to the context of "information control in social media", but *physical health* may not be so relevant. However, the opposite is observed if we switch the context to "health effects of computer use".

2.3 Computational Approaches Towards Identifying the Values Behind Arguments

While human values have been accounted for in formal argumentation frameworks since the early 2000 s [2], Kiesel et al. [10] presented the first attempt at automatic identification of values behind arguments, using a fine-tuned multi-label BERT-base [6] LLM to perform value classification on a multicultural set of arguments.

Since then, a multitude of natural language processing (NLP) driven techniques have been leveraged towards human value identification. SemEval-2023, an international workshop on semantic evaluation, consisted of ValueEval'23 [11], a task on value identification behind arguments where teams prepared models that were tasked with identifying whether a particular value applied to an argument. ValueEval'23 focused exclusively on the 20 Level 2 value categories and used a multi-sourced dataset of over 9000 arguments, using the same human value taxonomy and argument structure that we will in this paper. Most of the submitted approaches relied on leveraging transformer-based models [25], formulating the task as direct classification based on the provided labels.

2.4 Large Language Models and Prompting

Prior attempts [10,11] at automatic identification of human values behind arguments have largely relied on fine-tuning LLMs. However, LLMs also possess interesting *emergent abilities*, as a result of scaling smaller LMs across the factors of *number of model parameters, amount of training data utilized* and *the extent of computations performed* [26]. One such example is the *prompting* paradigm, as popularized by Brown et al. through GPT-3 [4], in which a carefully-worded prompt is provided to the pre-trained LLM which completes the response with no additional training required. Prompting strategies range from *zero-shot prompting* in which only the instruction is provided in natural language format to the LLM, to *few-shot prompting* which further augments the prompt with a few input-output examples as a way of conditioning the model to the task [16].

Chain-of-thought prompting, providing step-by-step demonstrations for examples, has been shown to improve general reasoning abilities in sufficiently large language models [27].

Liang et al. [12] performed a holistic evaluation of language models, showing that they exhibit a high level of performance in sentiment analysis, knowledge, text summarization, information retrieval and question answering among a variety of tasks. Chae and Davidson [5] applied a multitude of strategies on LLMs, ranging from zero-shot prompting to model fine-tuning, demonstrating their capability in classification of opinions in a political context.

3 Webis-ArgValues-22: A Dataset of Cross-Cultural Arguments

The Webis-ArgValues-22 dataset introduced by Kiesel et al. [10] consists of 5270 natural language arguments, and is composed of four parts: *Africa* (50 arguments), *China* (100 arguments), *India* (100 arguments) and *USA* (5020 arguments). Each of these arguments were annotated by three crowdworkers for all 54 Level 1 values, and labels for the broader categorizations of values were derived from them. The dataset, taxonomy description and annotation interface can be found online as Webis-ArgValues-22[1]. The dataset is partitioned into three parts: **train**, **validation** and **test**. The train and validation parts of the dataset only consist of arguments from the US, unlike the test part which contain arguments from all four cultures.

3.1 Human Value Taxonomy

Drawing largely upon the refined theory proposed by Schwartz et al. [21], but also incorporating values identified in the Rokeach Value Survey (RVS) [17], the Life Values Inventory (LVI) [3] and the World Values Survey (WVS) [8], Kiesel et al. [10] proposed a multi-level taxonomy of values, consisting of 54 basic values (called Level 1 values) from the social sciences further categorized into higher, broader levels inspired by the Schwartz theory. More specifically, Level 2 values aggregate some of the Level 1 values into 20 broader categories, which are further aggregated into higher-order values in Level 3, as proposed by Schwartz. Furthermore, the Level 3 is aggregated into two possible dichotomies: Level 4A focusing on personal versus social, and Level 4B focusing on promotion of growth versus self-protection in Level 4B). A more detailed explanation of the human value taxonomy can be found in [10]. A visual representation of the value levels can be found in Fig. 1.

3.2 Argument Structure

Each argument in the dataset consists of three parts:

---

[1] https://github.com/webis-de/ACL-22.

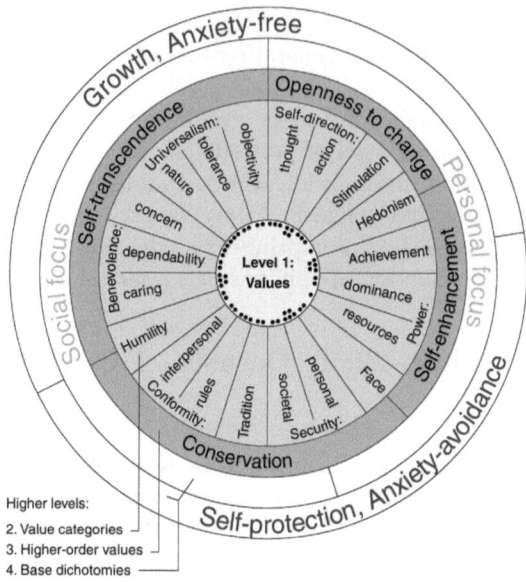

Fig. 1. The consolidated multi-level value taxonomy as developed by Kiesel et al. [10], adapted from the Schwartz Theory of Basic Human Values [21]

- **Conclusion:** The policy, idea or statement towards which the opinion is made.
- **Stance:** The opinion's stance with respect to the conclusion. Either *in favor of* or *against*.
- **Premise:** The opinion posed, explaining why the person expressed their specified stance towards the conclusion.

For example, for the idea (here, **conclusion**) "We should protect our privacy in the Internet age", someone can express an opinion with a favorable **stance** towards it, stating that "The leaked personal information will be defrauded by fraud gangs to gain trust and carry out fraudulent activities" which here is the **premise**.

4   Methodology

We seek to explore how accurately an LLM identifies the values behind natural language arguments, from individual human values to broader value categories. While previous computational attempts at value classification have largely relied on performing classification using fine-tuned language models [11], we aim to leverage the pre-existing knowledge and language understanding capabilities of a large language model, relying on a variety of prompting strategies to guide the model towards *generating* the values and value categories it believes the argument indicates, parsing the response to obtain predicted labels.

All the source code, including the exact prompts we used and the experiments conducted for all the prompting strategies we considered can be found online on GitHub[2]

This section will describe the model, the prompting strategies leveraged in the experiment, and the baselines and metrics used to assess its performance.

4.1 Model

We introduce a model-agnostic methodology to evaluate the capability of LLMs in identifying the human values behind arguments, solely relying on prompting strategies. For the experiments, we use the GPT-3.5-turbo[3] LLM developed by OpenAI for our experiments, due to its widespread use in the public domain (either through the freely-available ChatGPT[4] web platform, or through its API access). Future work can make use of our methodology to experiment with other LLMs.

GPT-3.5-turbo is derived from GPT-3 [4], an autoregressive LLM consisting of 175 billion parameters. GPT-3 was trained on 499 billion tokens[5] of text, consisting of CommonCrawl[6] WebText [16], English Wikipedia[7], and the Books1 and Books2 corpora.[8] Unlike GPT-3, GPT-3.5-turbo has been fine-tuned through the Reinforcement Learning from Human Feedback (RLHF) process, in order to align it to human preferences [33]. The exact number of parameters, as well as training data used for GPT-3.5 models has been undisclosed by OpenAI.

Critically evaluating the ability of LLMs in identifying human values is important to ensure they are *responsibly* leveraged to develop human-aligned AI systems, and that users are aware of its limitations and potential risks.

To carry out our experiments, we relied on the model's API, using LangChain[9] to interface with it.

4.2 Prompting Techniques

In the context of LLMs, a **prompt** is a carefully-worded instruction provided to the model as input, to guide it towards providing a *response* that satisfies the instruction.

---

[2] https://github.com/rithik83/LLM-values.

[3] https://platform.openai.com/docs/models/gpt-3-5-turbo.

[4] https://chatgpt.com/.

[5] Tokens are common sequences of characters found in a set of text. OpenAI's large language models process text as tokens. More information can be found in https://platform.openai.com/tokenizer.

[6] A free, open repository of web crawl data. Learn more from https://www.commoncrawl.org.

[7] https://www.wikipedia.org.

[8] Two internet-based books corpora.

[9] A framework for interacting with LLMs and developing applications utilizing LLMs; https://www.langchain.com/.

In our prompts, we provide the LLM with the list of all human values for a specific level of categorization of values, an argument's conclusion, stance and premise framed as a natural language sentence, and an explicit instruction to identify the values from the list that motivate the argument presented. In example-based prompting strategies, we provide a set of example arguments and their values to further condition the model to the value classification task.

For example-based prompting strategies (few-shot and chain-of-thought prompting), we sample 20 examples randomly from the *train* part of the dataset. In case some values are unrepresented among the selected examples, we further augment the example set with arguments that represent said values, thereby ensuring that every few-shot/CoT prompt consist of example demonstrations that cover all values under consideration.

Zero-Shot Prompting. In this method, we explore the capability of the model to use only its pre-trained knowledge to identify the human values behind arguments. The zero-shot prompting pipeline is illustrated in Fig. 2.

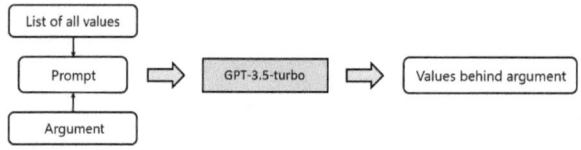

Fig. 2. The zero-shot prompting pipeline

The argument's *conclusion, stance* and *premise* are framed as a single sentence. The LLM is instructed to generate the values it identifies (from the complete list of values provided in the prompt) as a semicolon separated list, which is then parsed to obtain the labels predicted. One important feature of the prompt is the repeated instruction to be *selective* and *precise*. This instruction was added to guide the LLM into choosing only those values it perceives as clearly forming the basis for the argument made.

Since zero-shot prompting relies solely upon what the LLM has learned from its pre-training and RLHF fine-tuning process, it serves as a reference point for prompt-based strategies to enable comparisons with few-shot and chain-of-thought prompting.

Few-Shot Prompting. In addition to providing a natural language description of the task, few-shot prompting provides a few demonstrations of the task at inference time as a way of conditioning the model [16]. Examples are typically provided as pairings of context and desired completions, and a final example of context for which the model is expected to perform the completion on the basis of both its pre-trained knowledge and its understanding of the prior examples.

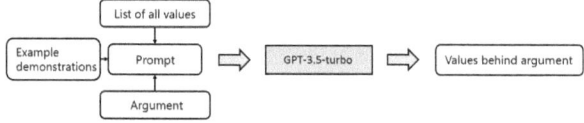

Fig. 3. The few-shot prompting pipeline

Few-shot prompting reduces the need for task-specific data as compared to model fine-tuning. The few-shot prompting pipeline we used is illustrated in Fig. 3.

The few-shot prompt used is very similar in structure to the zero-shot prompt, as we intended to measure the effect of adding example demonstrations. Examples are included in the Q+A format with the answer portions of the examples filled in with ground truth values. The last Q+A entry is the unseen argument for which the LLM is tasked with identifying the motivating human values.

We hypothesized that few-shot prompting would exhibit stronger performance as compared to zero-shot prompting, since few-shot prompting provides the added benefit of example demonstrations to the model during inference time, thereby conditioning the model to the value classification task.

Chain-of-Thought (CoT) Prompting. Chain-of-Thought (CoT) prompting, developed by Wei et al. [27] is a variant of the few-shot prompting technique where each example demonstration is further enhanced with a chain of thought - a coherent series of intermediate reasoning steps that lead to the final answer. The authors demonstrated that these chain-of-thought demonstrations invoked reasoning abilities in sufficiently large language models, improving performance on commonsense reasoning tasks.

In order to explore the effect of reasoning-enriched prompting in the task of value classification, we decided to include CoT prompting. However, the dataset we considered for this paper did not have any form of reasoning or justification for the annotated value labels. In order to overcome this issue, we developed a two-step pipeline to carry out CoT prompting for each argument:

- **Prompt 1 - Generating justifications for examples:** Here, for all the example arguments chosen, we provide the LLM with the example and all its ground truth values, prompting the LLM to generate brief justifications for why each of the values holds for the argument presented.
- **Prompt 2 - Using generated justifications as CoT demonstrations for the unseen argument:** We perform a second prompt to the LLM that contains all the *example arguments*, their *values* and for each value its LLM-generated *justification* (generated in Prompt 1), as well as the final unseen argument for which the LLM is tasked with identifying the values. The generated justifications act as CoT demonstrations to assist the LLM in identifying the values for the unseen argument.

The chain-of-thought pipeline is illustrated in Fig. 4.

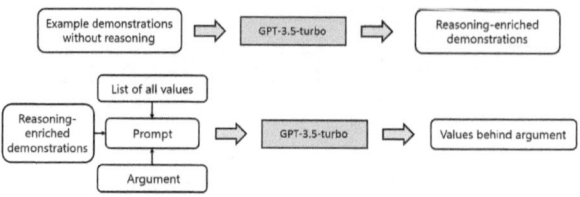

Fig. 4. The chain-of-thought prompting pipeline. Note the two prompts corresponding with the two-step procedure

Note that CoT prompting was used to evaluate performance on identifying only the Level 1 and 2 values – the individual values and the lowest level value categorization respectively. This decision was grounded in a few key considerations regarding the complexity of these levels. Level 1 consists of 54 values and Level 2 aggregates them into 20 value categories. These levels capture a rich landscape of values, making them ideal to craft nuanced justifications. In contrast, levels 3, 4A and 4B represent broader categorizations that are less granular, hence less informative to generate detailed, specific justifications. Moreover, by focusing on Level 1 and 2 values, the LLM is encouraged to generate justifications that are closely aligned with specific values or more finely grained categories. This granularity allows for more precise and contextually relevant explanations, which are essential for accurately evaluating the model's ability to discern subtle differences between similar values.

We hypothesized that the chain-of-thought prompting strategy would perform the best out of the three prompting strategies, since enriching the example demonstrations with logical reasoning would better equip the LLM towards identifying the values behind the unseen argument it is tested on.

4.3   Evaluation Baseline and Metrics

Our choices for baseline and evaluation metrics were inspired by the decisions made by Kiesel et al. [10], who presented the first attempt at computational value classification using the dataset under consideration, in order to be able to establish a comparison between their fine-tuning approach and our prompting approach.

Metrics: We use label-wise F_1-score, and its mean over all labels (macro-average), as well as its constituents' precision and recall. Macro-averages were used to give the same weight to all values.

Baseline: We use 1-Baseline as the evaluation baseline. It classifies each argument as belonging to all values, which results in a perfect recall score of 1. Due to its high recall, the 1-Baseline classifier achieves at least as high, if not higher in most cases, F_1-scores as label-wise random guessing based on the label frequency.

Table 1. Macro precision (P), recall (R) and F_1-score (F_1) on the USA test set over all labels by level, extended from the results obtained by Kiesel et al. [10] using BERT [6] and an SVM. Highest precision, recall and F_1-score for each level marked in bold.

Model	Level 1			Level 2			Level 3			Level 4A			Level 4B		
	P	R	F_1	P	R	F_1	P	R	F_1	P	R	F_1	P	R	F_1
GPT-3.5-turbo (Zero-shot)	0.26	0.30	0.23	0.35	0.31	0.30	**0.67**	0.57	0.59	**0.92**	0.53	0.67	0.92	0.46	0.54
GPT-3.5-turbo (Few-shot)	0.15	0.53	0.21	0.39	0.41	**0.34**	0.66	0.66	0.66	0.87	0.94	0.90	0.92	0.84	0.87
GPT-3.5-turbo (CoT)	0.31	0.22	0.21	**0.40**	0.30	0.32	-	-	-	-	-	-	-	-	-
BERT	**0.40**	0.19	**0.25**	0.39	0.30	**0.34**	0.65	0.78	0.71	0.89	0.96	**0.92**	0.92	**1.00**	**0.96**
SVM	0.21	0.19	0.20	0.30	0.30	0.30	0.66	0.68	0.67	0.88	0.89	0.88	**0.93**	0.90	0.92
1-Baseline	0.08	**1.00**	0.16	0.18	**1.00**	0.28	0.60	**1.00**	**0.75**	0.85	**1.00**	**0.92**	0.92	**1.00**	**0.96**

5 Results

In our evaluations, we used the same partitions of the dataset as Kiesel et al. [10] in their evaluation of value classification with BERT, so as to reliably compare the results we obtained using different measures (their *fine-tuning* approach versus our *prompting* approach). We ran our evaluations on the test set, and although we did not train or fine-tune our model, we still leveraged the train set to select example demonstrations for the few-shot and chain-of-thought prompting experiments.

5.1 Results on the US Part

The US part of the dataset is the most significant in terms of the number of entries as compared to the remaining parts (5020 arguments out of 5270 in the total dataset, and 503 out of 753 in the test dataset). The train-validation-test split of the dataset for the US part was done on the basis of unique conclusions, as a result of which the test set consisted of 7 conclusions that were not present in the train and validation sets. While this method of splitting was considered crucial by Kiesel et al. [10] since they wanted to test whether classifiers generalized to unseen conclusions, it unfortunately led to different value distributions in the different sets. Regardless, we persisted with the same split in the interest of being able to compare our results. Table 1 shows the results averaged across all labels.

Value Levels 1 and 2. For Levels 1 and 2, all the prompting strategies perform better than the baseline according to F_1-score, but still exhibit a lower performance than the fine-tuned BERT by Kiesel et al. [10], with the exception of few-shot prompting for Level 2 which performs equally as well as BERT in terms of macro F_1 score. At Level 1, the most granular level, it is surprising to note that example-based prompting strategies (few-shot and CoT) perform worse than zero-shot prompting. This could be in part because the model generated responses that mimic the labels provided in the example arguments, essentially

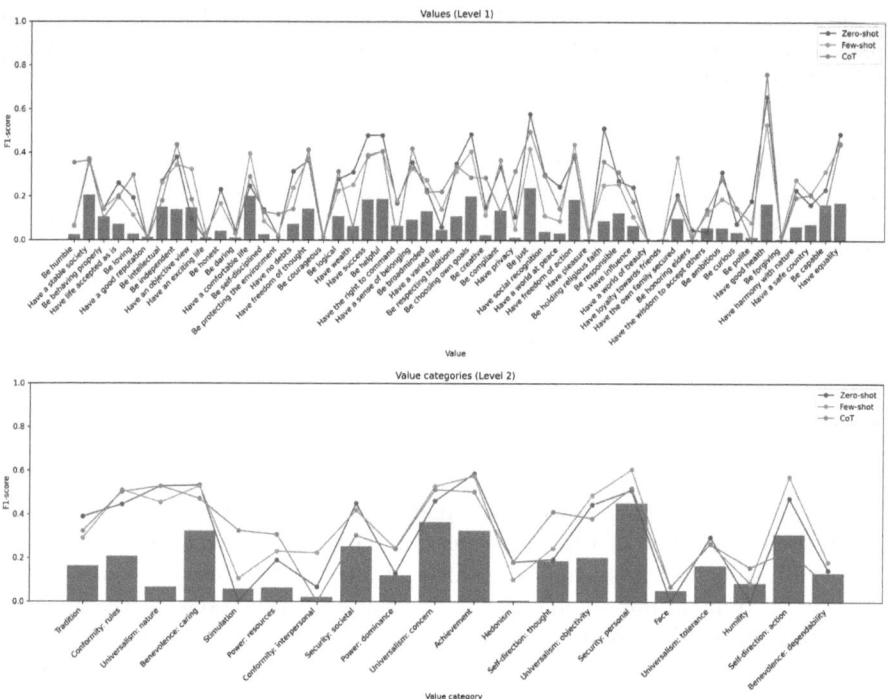

Fig. 5. F_1-scores per Level 1 value (top) and Level 2 value category (bottom) across zero-shot, few-shot and CoT prompting strategies, in the USA test set. Grey bars indicate the frequency distribution of each value in the set

overfitting to the examples and therefore generalizing poorly to the unseen argument. Moreover, since we randomly chose examples from the train set, the quality of the example set shortlisted may have been suboptimal and not representative. A potential strategy that may overcome this issue is selecting examples based on semantic similarity to the unseen argument, so that the model is equipped with better example demonstrations. Chain-of-Thought prompting lead to higher precision for both levels 1 and 2, possibly due to the value justifications for example influencing the model to be even more selective in identifying values behind the unseen argument. Few-shot (without CoT) lead to the highest recall values.

Value Levels 3, 4A and 4B. For the higher levels, both zero-shot and few-shot prompting exhibit worse performances in comparison to both the baseline and BERT, in terms of the F_1-score. In particular, the zero-shot prompting strategy performs significantly worse in levels 4A and 4B (with F_1-scores of 0.67 and 0.54 respectively as compared to 0.92 and 0.96 for both BERT and 1-Baseline respectively). During evaluations with zero-shot prompting for levels 4A and 4B (both the base dichotomies with two options each), it was observed that the LLM almost always opted for exactly one of the two options, despite most arguments having been assigned both labels of both base dichotomies. This interpretation of the value classification task as a one-or-the-other problem by the model despite no such specific instruction in the prompt, resulted in the low values for recall which in turn affected the F_1-scores. Few-shot prompting did not suffer from this problem, since the example demonstrations reflected the reality of most arguments having been labeled with both categories for both the base dichotomies.

Results per Value for Levels 1 and 2. In addition to measuring the macro-averaged precision, recall and F_1-score, we also measure F_1-scores per Level 1 value and Level 2 value category, across all our 3 prompting approaches. Figure 5 demonstrates the results, with the grey bars signifying the frequency of each value/value category in the US test set.

We observe that none of the prompting strategies dominates the others across all, or even most, Level 1 values. Moreover, the LLM achieves considerably high F_1-scores across all prompting strategies for several values and value categories, most notably for the value *Have good health*, and the value category *Security: personal* that contains it. Other value categories for which all the three methods achieved an F_1-score ≥ 0.4 are *Conformity: rules. Universalism: nature, Benevolence: caring, Universalism: concern* and *Achievement*. These results are similar to those obtained by Kiesel et al. [10].

Table 2. Macro F_1-score on each test set over all labels by level, extended from the results obtained by Kiesel et al. [10] using BERT [6] and an SVM. Highest score for each region in each level marked in bold.

Model	Level 1				Level 2				Level 3				Level 4A				Level 4B			
	Afr.	Chi.	Ind.	USA	Afr.	Chi.	Ind.	USA	Afr.	Chi.	Ind.	USA	Afr.	Chi.	Ind.	USA	Afr.	Chi.	Ind.	USA
GPT-3.5-turbo (Zero-shot)	0.16	**0.22**	0.26	0.23	0.23	0.28	0.24	0.30	0.51	0.62	0.59	0.59	0.51	0.65	0.65	0.67	0.58	0.52	0.47	0.54
GPT-3.5-turbo (Few-shot)	0.20	0.19	0.19	0.21	0.29	0.28	0.28	**0.34**	0.60	**0.68**	0.63	0.66	0.80	0.83	0.79	0.90	0.84	0.87	0.83	0.87
GPT-3.5-turbo (CoT)	**0.28**	**0.22**	0.29	0.21	0.31	0.23	0.23	0.32	-	-	-	-	-	-	-	-	-	-	-	-
BERT	0.20	0.21	**0.30**	0.25	**0.38**	**0.37**	**0.41**	0.34	0.60	**0.68**	**0.71**	0.71	**0.82**	**0.88**	0.81	**0.92**	**0.92**	**0.92**	**0.91**	**0.90**	0.96
SVM	0.21	0.21	0.25	0.20	0.29	0.30	0.27	0.30	0.53	0.57	0.57	0.67	0.80	0.82	0.74	0.88	0.90	0.87	0.87	0.92
1-Baseline	0.16	0.13	0.12	0.16	0.27	0.23	0.21	0.28	**0.63**	0.65	0.62	**0.75**	0.80	**0.88**	0.79	**0.92**	**0.92**	**0.92**	**0.91**	**0.90**	0.96

5.2 Results Across Culture

Table 2 demonstrates how GPT-3.5-turbo with the three prompting strategies performed across the four parts of the test set: Africa, China, India and the US, comparing them with the results Kiesel et al. [10] obtained using BERT, a linear SVM and the baseline.

Across all the levels, we observe that the prompting strategies applied do not result in an improvement in performance over BERT, with the exception of chain-of-thought prompting applied to arguments from Africa and China for Level 1 values.

However, an important point to note is that arguments from Africa, China and India are significantly underrepresented relative to arguments from the US (50, 100 and 100 arguments for Africa, China and India respectively as compared to 503 for the US in the test set), which makes carrying out detailed analyses difficult. We still reported our results to establish a comparison with the approach of fine-tuning BERT. Perhaps gathering more arguments from the non-USA regions would have allowed us to report more conclusive results across cultures.

6   Discussion and Limitations

Although we present a detailed methodology for assessing the capability of Large Language Models (LLMs) in identifying the human values behind arguments using prompting techniques, we recognize certain limitations associated with our preliminary experimentation with GPT-3.5-turbo across the zero-shot, few-shot and chain-of-thought prompting strategies. In this section we will highlight them, offering directions that can be considered in future research.

Sensitivity to prompts: Our approaches leveraged the ability of LLMs to generate responses to carefully-worded natural language instructions called *prompts*, parsing the results to obtain the predicted labels. We designed a standard prompt that contained all relevant information – the complete list of values to consider, the argument phrased as a natural language sentence, the instruction to identify its values, and example demonstrations for few-shot/CoT prompts. However during our experimentation we observed, as expected, that the LLM's responses were quite sensitive to the prompt, including the placing of certain sentences, words and their phrasing. The field of prompt engineering, the strategic design of task-specific instructions to guide the LLM into generating desirable outputs, has seen a great deal of research recently [7,18,29]. While our intention was to provide a starting point for exploration into prompt-based strategies for value classification using three strategies, we encourage researchers to explore the application of more prompting strategies and best practices towards this task.

Subjectivity of human values: To carry out our experimentation, we leveraged a dataset designed by Kiesel et al. [10] which consisted of arguments manually annotated by three crowdworkers for all 54 Level 1 values. While the annotations were considered ground truth values for the arguments, a large body of philosophical work has been devoted to exploring the idea that human values may be subjective [14,23]. Moreover, Liscio et al. [13] also established the idea that values may be context-specific. The annotated ground truth labels represent the aggregated opinions of the crowdworkers, but it is possible that other annotators may have labeled different values for the same argument. An interesting direction for future research could be the exploration of how this subjectivity impacts LLM outputs, and how LLMs can be utilized for highly subjective tasks like these.

Imbalance in the Number of Arguments Across Cultures: We reported and discussed results obtained on the US test set, and results across cultures to present a complete picture of LLM performance. However, due to the stark imbalance between the number of arguments from the US and the remaining regions, it was not possible to carry out analyses of non-US arguments with the same rigour as US arguments.

LLM-Generated Justifications for Chain-of-Thought: In our chain-of-thought prompting strategy, we relied on the LLM to generate justifications for value classifications for the example demonstrations due to the lack of such a reasoning chain provided in the dataset. We recognize this may have resulted in suboptimal chains of thought being generated. Perhaps human-annotated chains of thought/reasoning could improve CoT prompting performance.

Our contribution through this paper is a systematic and critical evaluation of the GPT-3.5-turbo LLM in identifying the values behind arguments across cultures. Unlike previous attempts [10,11] that primarily relied on model fine-tuning, we applied three prompting strategies – zero-shot, few-shot and Chain-of-Thought [27] prompting. As prompting continues to emerge as a popular mechanism through which people interact with LLMs, our work attempts to demonstrate how effective it is in extracting the values behind arguments, thereby encouraging a more responsible approach towards prompting LLMs in this context.

7   Conclusion

Human values serve as criteria that guide people's actions, judgments and evaluations [21,30], and are central to argumentation and discourse as they inform people's viewpoints and arguments. We present an evaluation of GPT-3.5-turbo, an LLM widely utilized by the public, in identifying the values behind arguments using zero-shot, few-shot and Chain-of-Thought (CoT) [27] prompting strategies, using a multi-cultural dataset of arguments and a multi-level value taxonomy derived from [10], inspired by the Schwartz Theory of Basic Human Values [21]. Our experiments indicate that prompting strategies exhibit performance levels close to, but still behind model fine-tuning in terms of the macro-averaged F_1-score, and that performance levels vary across values and value categories themselves. Our work exposes directions for further research into developing tehcniques for value-driven argumentation that leverage the capabilities of LLMs, keeping in mind their benefits and drawbacks to use them in a responsible, effective and inclusive manner.

Acknowledgments. The participation of L.C. Siebert in this research was partially supported by TAILOR, a project funded by the EU Horizon 2020 research and innovation programme under GA No 952215.

References

1. Anderson, E.: Value in Ethics and Economics. Harvard University Press (1995)
2. Bench-Capon, T.J.: Persuasion in practical argument using value-based argumentation frameworks. J. Log. Comput. **13**(3), 429–448 (2003)
3. Brown, D., Crace, R.K.: Life values inventory: facilitator's guide. Williamsburg, VA (2002)
4. Brown, T., et al.: Language models are few-shot learners. Adv. Neural. Inf. Process. Syst. **33**, 1877–1901 (2020)
5. Chae, Y., Davidson, T.: Large language models for text classification: from zero-shot learning to fine-tuning. Open Science Foundation (2023)
6. Devlin, J., Chang, M.W., Lee, K., Toutanova, K.: BERT: pre-training of deep bidirectional transformers for language understanding. arXiv preprint arXiv:1810.04805 (2018)
7. Giray, L.: Prompt engineering with ChatGPT: a guide for academic writers. Ann. Biomed. Eng. **51**(12), 2629–2633 (2023)
8. Haerpfer, C., et al.: World values survey: round seven-country-pooled datafile. Madrid, Spain, Vienna, Austria: JD Systems Institute & WVSA Secretariat **7**, 2021 (2020)
9. Inglehart, R.F., Basanez, M., Moreno, A.: Human Values and Beliefs: A Cross-Cultural Sourcebook. University of Michigan Press (1998)
10. Kiesel, J., Alshomary, M., Handke, N., Cai, X., Wachsmuth, H., Stein, B.: Identifying the human values behind arguments. In: Proceedings of the 60th Annual Meeting of the Association for Computational Linguistics (Volume 1: Long Papers), pp. 4459–4471 (2022)
11. Kiesel, J., et al.: SemEval-2023 task 4: ValueEval: identification of human values behind arguments. In: Ojha, A.K., Doğruöz, A.S., Da San Martino, G., Tayyar Madabushi, H., Kumar, R., Sartori, E. (eds.) Proceedings of the 17th International Workshop on Semantic Evaluation (SemEval-2023), pp. 2287–2303. Association for Computational Linguistics, Toronto, Canada (2023). https://doi.org/10.18653/v1/2023.semeval-1.313, https://aclanthology.org/2023.semeval-1.313
12. Liang, P., et al.: Holistic evaluation of language models. arXiv preprint arXiv:2211.09110 (2022)
13. Liscio, E., van der Meer, M., Siebert, L.C., Jonker, C.M., Mouter, N., Murukannaiah, P.K.: Axies: identifying and evaluating context-specific values. In: AAMAS, pp. 799–808 (2021)
14. Mackie, J.L.: The subjectivity of values. Essays on moral realism pp. 95–118 (1988)
15. Petroni, F., et al.: Language models as knowledge bases? ArXiv preprint arXiv:1909.01066 (2019)
16. Radford, A., Wu, J., Child, R., Luan, D., Amodei, D., Sutskever, I., et al.: Language models are unsupervised multitask learners. OpenAI blog **1**(8), 9 (2019)
17. Rokeach, M.: The nature of human values. Free Press (1973)
18. Sahoo, P., Singh, A.K., Saha, S., Jain, V., Mondal, S., Chadha, A.: A systematic survey of prompt engineering in large language models: techniques and applications. arXiv preprint arXiv:2402.07927 (2024)
19. Sayer, A.: Why Things Matter To People: Social Science, Values and Ethical Life. Cambridge University Press (2011)
20. Schwartz, S.H.: Basic human values: an overview (2006)
21. Schwartz, S.H.: An overview of the Schwartz theory of basic values. Online Readings Psychol. Cult. **2**(1), 11 (2012)

22. Searle, J.R.: Rationality in action. MIT press (2003)
23. Stroud, B.: The study of human nature and the subjectivity of value. The Tanner Lectures on Human Value (1988)
24. Teze, J.C.L., Perelló-Moragues, A., Godo, L., Noriega, P.: Practical reasoning using values: an argumentative approach based on a hierarchy of values. Ann. Math. Artif. Intell. **87**(3), 293–319 (2019). https://doi.org/10.1007/s10472-019-09660-8
25. Vaswani, A., et al.: Attention is all you need. In: Advances in Neural Information Processing Systems, vol. 30 (2017)
26. Wei, J., et al.: Emergent abilities of large language models. arXiv preprint arXiv:2206.07682 (2022)
27. Wei, J., et al.: Chain-of-thought prompting elicits reasoning in large language models. Adv. Neural. Inf. Process. Syst. **35**, 24824–24837 (2022)
28. van der Weide, T.L., Dignum, F., Meyer, J.J.C., Prakken, H., Vreeswijk, G.A.: Practical reasoning using values: giving meaning to values. In: Argumentation in Multi-Agent Systems: 6th International Workshop, ArgMAS 2009, Budapest, Hungary, May 12, 2009. Revised Selected and Invited Papers 6, pp. 79–93. Springer (2010)
29. White, J., et al.: A prompt pattern catalog to enhance prompt engineering with ChatGPT. arXiv preprint arXiv:2302.11382 (2023)
30. Williams, R.M.J.: The concept of values. In: Sills, D.L. (ed.) International Encyclopedia of the Social Sciences, vol. 16. Macmillan and Free Press, New York (1968)
31. Zhang, B., Haddow, B., Birch, A.: Prompting large language model for machine translation: a case study. In: International Conference on Machine Learning, pp. 41092–41110. PMLR (2023)
32. Zhang, W., Deng, Y., Liu, B., Pan, S.J., Bing, L.: Sentiment analysis in the era of large language models: a reality check. arXiv preprint arXiv:2305.15005 (2023)
33. Ziegler, D.M., et al.: Fine-tuning language models from human preferences. arXiv preprint arXiv:1909.08593 (2019)

Value Promotion Scheme Elicitation Using Natural Language Processing: A Model for Value-Based Agent Architecture

Sara García-Rodríguez$^{(\boxtimes)}$, Marcelo Karanik , and Alicia Pina-Zapata

CETINIA, Rey Juan Carlos University, Madrid, Spain
{s.garciarod.2020,a.pinaz.2020}@alumnos.urjc.es, marcelo.karanik@urjc.es

Abstract. Currently, the design of computational systems requires considering both technical aspects and the impact of autonomous decisions made by these systems. That is, given the significant progress of artificial intelligence, the choice of actions of an intelligent system must be appropriately aligned with the system of human values, both individual and social. This paper proposes using natural language processing techniques to extract human values from action descriptions. The model is proposed as an extension of a value-based agent architecture whose decision process is based on the agent's value system and the value promotion scheme of each available action. For the testing of the model, the decision process on participatory projects has been simulated. Given a set of projects, the proposed model was used to detect the values each promotes, and then the agent's decision process was simulated. The results, although preliminary, show that the proposed extension of the architecture has a behaviour consistent with the theory of values used as a basis.

Keywords: Value-aware Engineering · Human Value Detection · Natural Language Processing · Value-based Agent

1 Introduction

Human values have long been a key topic in the social sciences. Understanding what drives people's decision-making has led to numerous studies and research documents [1, 4, 8, 36, 39]. The study of human behaviour has traditionally focused on understanding various aspects of human actions and decisions. However, with the fast progress of Artificial Intelligence (AI), there has been a significant shift in this approach. The development of increasingly autonomous computational systems has brought to light the necessity to incorporate rationality and human values as a variable for decision-making.

AI engineering is currently focused on improving the quality and efficiency of the decision-making process of autonomous systems, but, at the same time, the ethical and moral impact of these decisions is a significant aspect of the development of intelligent applications. The scientific community is increasingly interested in value-aware systems, i.e., intelligent systems designed to incorporate decision strategies that enable them to act following human values. The significance of incorporating human values into intelligent systems is reflected in important projects like ValueML [27], whose objective is to empower policymakers with a deeper understanding of citizens' values and aspirations regarding policy issues.

Developing value-aware applications involves two tasks: the representation of the *value system* and the design of value-aligned actions [26]. On the one hand, representing the *value system* and defining which values are necessary for a particular environment and how to model them involves designing the mechanisms to manage the relationships between those values. That is, the *value system* representation must establish, based on a value theory, the interactions that affect the decision process. On the other hand, the alignment of actions to values requires designing the decision processes so that the system's behaviour adjusts to the defined values' importance or preference. In other words, the aim is to obtain action execution policies that consider utility maximisation and align with the system's values.

In this context, it is crucial to have models that integrate the representation of the *value system* and the design of strategies aligned with those values. Several works describe alternatives that implement value-based systems considering these aspects. For instance, the value-based agent model proposed in [13] describes the multi-criteria decision process. It uses the agent's *value system* and the degree of promotion of values for each available action to select the best-aligned action. Although the *value system* is built automatically based on the agent's preferences, obtaining the *value promotion scheme* requires manual adjustments of the magnitudes. Since this determination is subjective and depends on the criteria of each developer, it is convenient to define a reliable process for obtaining these magnitudes.

This paper describes a natural language processing-based model to elicit the *value promotion scheme* of the value-based agent architecture proposed in [13]. For this purpose, natural language descriptions of each action are used, and a multi-label text classification model analyses them. The model consists of a pre-trained text analyser and a neural network to determine which values, ranked by their importance, are implicit in the descriptions of the actions. The article is organised as follows. Section 2 describes some related works concerning value concepts and their computational extension. Section 3 briefly describes the value-based agent [13] and the value extraction model based on natural language processing. In Sect. 4, preliminary results are presented and described and, finally, in Sect. 5, some aspects related to the model and the results are presented.

2   Related Work

The effect of human values on people's decisions is the subject of several psychological studies [7,17,25,32,33]. Among them, Schwartz's theory of the ten fundamental values [36–38] stands out, where a model of interaction is proposed based on the motivational characteristics of each one of them. This value theory considers that values are beliefs that refer to desirable objectives that motivate actions, transcend specific situations, serve as standards for selecting and evaluating actions, and are ordered by importance, thus guiding action [38]. In terms of each value's general objective, Schwartz identifies the ten values of his theory based on individuals' universal requirements or needs: *self-direction, stimulation, hedonism, achievement, power, security, conformity, tradition, benevolence* and *universalism* [36].

In addition to defining the ten basic values, Schwartz's theory also defines the structure of the relationships between them [38]. He uses a circular structure, a *continuum* of related motivations, to place the values in two bipolar dimensions (Fig. 1). The first contrasts the values associated with *openness to change* with those associated with *conservation*, and the second contrasts *self-enhancement* and *self-transcendence* values. According to the theory, in the motivational *continuum*, two values that are closer together have similar motivations, and if they are farther apart, they have antagonistic motivations.

Fig. 1. Continuum proposed by Schwartz (from [38]).

In addition, Schwartz proposes two additional principles for categorising values [36]. One is related to the interests, social or individual, that values regulate. In this sense values like *self-direction, stimulation, hedonism, achievement* and *power* are associated with personal interests and values like *security, conformity, tradition, benevolence* and *universalism* are associated with social issues. The other principle determines how anxiety due to uncertainty in the world affects values. In this sense, values like *self-direction, stimulation, hedonism, benevolence* and *universalism* express non-anxious motivations, while values like *achievement, power, security, conformity* and *tradition* promote self-protection and seek to avoid conflict by actively controlling threats. In addition, in [35], it proposes an extension of these ten basic values by disaggregating each of them into two or more specific values (Fig. 2). Although this extension is more precise, the interaction between the values and the dimensions mentioned above are the same.

Fig. 2. Extended continuum (from [35]).

The theory of the ten basic values has been taken as the basis for several works where the interaction between values affects the decision-making process. For example, there are studies in several areas such as, among others, social behaviour [5,16,29,30], economics [2,9,10] or health [6,12,21,31] that show the research community's interest in determining the influence of values on decisions.

From a basic definition, a software agent is an application that acts in a given environment based on the perceptions it receives. That is, considering what it observes from its environment, it decides what actions to execute. The agent's internal state is paramount for the entire decision-making process. Currently, and in line with the trend of determining the influence of values on decisions, AI engineering has focused on developing *value-aware* autonomous agents. This presents significant technical challenges regarding how to represent values and their relationships, i.e. the *value system*, and how to determine the alignment of decisions with one or more values.

On the one hand, there are several proposals to represent *value systems*, for example, as a set of values along with the preference relation among them [19,28, 42], as taxonomies of abstract concepts linked to computational ones [14,26] or as fuzzy measures [13] used to model the importance degree of single values and their combinations. All these representations aim to obtain a computationally adequate model of the interaction of values that can be used to obtain actions aligned with those values. On the other hand, making value-aligned decisions involves selecting actions that best reflect the agent's preferences concerning its *value system.* Various articles examine the concept of value alignment, using value-aligned states to establish value-aligned norms [24,40,41]. Others identify value alignment using participatory evaluation [20,42] or aggregation of values and *value systems* [13,18].

To design value-based agents adequately, it is essential to consider both of these mentioned aspects. According to these considerations, a value-based agent architecture that integrates the agent's *value system* and how actions promote these values is proposed in [13]. This architecture (Fig. 3) has three main components: the *value system*, the *value promotion scheme* and the *decision process*.

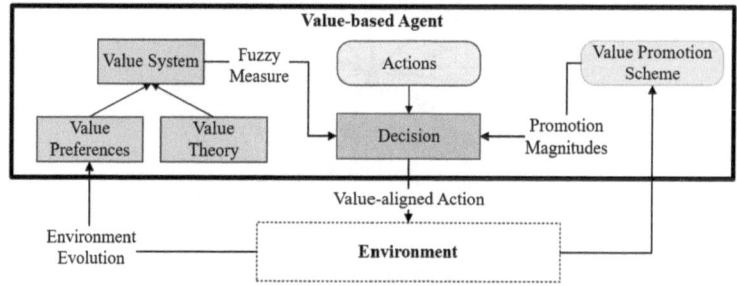

Fig. 3. Value-based agent (adapted from [13]).

First, the *value system* is constructed using the order of importance established by the agent on the values considered individually and a theory of values determining the interaction between them (in this case, Schwartz's theory of ten basic values [38]). With these two elements, a fuzzy measure assigns the importance weights to each element of the power set of the values considered [13]. Second, the *value promotion scheme* provides information about the value promotion magnitude of each value when a specific action is taken in the environment. The promotion magnitudes do not change during the decision-making process and are defined by social consensus [13]. Finally, using the fuzzy measure and the promotion magnitudes of each action, the *decision process* involves calculating the aggregated value of each action. This is done by employing an aggregation function to choose the most value-aligned action. While the model has shown good results in simple decision environments in game theory examples [13], the authors highlight the complexity of obtaining the adequate magnitudes of the *value promotion scheme* in real environments.

To deal with this drawback, one alternative is to automatically determine the magnitudes of the *value promotion scheme* instead of manually setting them. Knowing which values are implicit in executing the actions is necessary to do this. This, common sense for humans, is a complex task for computer systems. However, as mentioned before, due to the rise of this topic, many research initiatives in AI engineering focus on human values in the autonomous decision-making process, one of them detecting human values in the media using machine learning [27]. Specifically, the goal is to identify the implicit human values in various forms of media. For instance, Natural Language Processing (NLP) methods can be utilised to analyse values embedded in text. Several proposals for extracting values from labelled datasets have shown good results using NLP techniques. For example, in [34], several transformer-based models are used for value extraction; also, in [3,22], Large Language Models (LLMs) are trained with multi-label text for value classification and, in [43] contrastive learning-enhanced K-nearest neighbour mechanism is used to leverage existing instance information for prediction. These works suggest that NLP techniques can effectively extract the values promoted by each action and accurately describe actions and their consequences. The following section explains the extension of the model proposed in [13] using NLP techniques to develop the *value promotion scheme*.

3   *Value Promotion Scheme* based on NLP model

As mentioned in the previous section, the *decision process* proposed in [13] uses the agent's *value system* and the *value promotion scheme* of action value available to the agent. This *decision process* uses an aggregation operator to rank the actions best aligned with those values. Once the preference for each value is established, the *value system* is automatically constructed. However, specifying the impact of each action on each value is necessary to define the *value promotion scheme*, which is difficult in real-world situations. An alternative to this concern is an NLP-based approach described in this section.

3.1   Value-Based Agent

As mentioned above, this article extends the model proposed in [13]; therefore, a brief review of that model is appropriate.

Formally, given an agent set $\mathcal{AG} = \{Ag_1, Ag_2, .., Ag_{|\mathcal{AG}|}\}$, an action set $\mathcal{A} = \{a_1, a_2, .., a_{|\mathcal{A}|}\}$ and a set of perceptions $\mathcal{P} = \{p_1, p_2, .., p_{|\mathcal{P}|}\}$, the agent Ag_i is able to perform an action a_j according the perception p_k [13]. This behaviour is influenced by the internal structures of the agent, which enable it to make decisions based on specific considerations. In this case, these structures are related to the representation and alignment of values.

The agent's *value system* contains all the values' combinations and their importance. Let $\mathcal{V} = \{v_1, v_2, ..., v_{|\mathcal{V}|}\}$ a set of values and its power set $\wp(\mathcal{V})$. The *value system* of the agent Ag_i, $VS(Ag_i)$, is given by the importance weight of each element of $\wp(\mathcal{V})$ as:

$$VS(Ag_i) = \{\iota\omega_i(\wp(\mathcal{V}))\} \tag{1}$$

where $\iota\omega_i$ is the fuzzy measure of the Ag_i that assigns importance weights over each element of $\wp(\mathcal{V})$. For every element v_s of $\mathcal{V}$, the $\iota\omega_i\{v_s\}$ is defined by Ag_i according to its value-preference relation:

$$v_r \precsim_{Ag_i} v_s \precsim_{Ag_i} \cdots \precsim_{Ag_i} v_t \tag{2}$$

with $1 \leq r, s, t \leq |\mathcal{V}|$ and where $\precsim_{Ag_i}$ indicates the binary preference relation between two values for the Ag_i. Notice that the weight of each single value must maintain the preference relationship:

$$\iota w_i(\{v_r\}) \leq \iota w_i(\{v_s\}) \leq \dots \leq \iota w_i(\{v_t\}) \tag{3}$$

with $0 \leq \iota w_i(\{v_r\}), \iota w_i(\{v_s\}), \iota w_i(\{v_t\}) \leq 1; 1 \leq r, s, t \leq |\mathcal{V}|$.

Additionally, for every element $\{v_s, \dots, v_t\}$ of $\wp(\mathcal{V})$ with $|\{v_s, \dots, v_t\}| \geq 2$ and every kth distinct pair of values $\{v_1, v_2\}_k \subseteq \{v_s, \dots, v_t\}$, the $\iota w_i(\{v_s, \dots, v_t\})$ is computed as:

$$\iota w_i(\{v_s, \dots, v_t\}) = \iota w_i(\{v_s\}) + \dots + \iota w_i(\{v_t\}) +$$
$$+ \sum_{k=1}^{dp} pvi(\{v_1, v_2\}_k) \tag{4}$$

where $\iota w_i(\{v_s\})$ and $\iota w_i(\{v_t\})$ are the importance weights for the single values v_s and v_t respectively, dp is the number of distinct pairs of values computed as the combination of $|\{v_s, \dots, v_t\}|$ taken by 2, and $pvi(\{v_1, v_2\}_k)$ is the pair-value interaction function used to model the dynamic interaction of values. If pvi is zero for all pairs of values of each group, the fuzzy measure ιw_i becomes additive and cannot represent the value interaction.

A non-additive based on the distance between values in Schwartz's continuum is used to model the interaction [13]. Three main interaction types are proposed: (a) negative interaction between values in the same wedge. Likely, an agent who prefers one value will also prefer another of the same wedge, for example, *power* and *achievement*, and the weight of the importance of the group formed by both should be less than the sum of their single weights (subadditive measure); (b) positive interaction between values in opposite wedges. Due to it being unlikely that the agent would prefer both values of opposite wedges, such as *power* and *universalism*, the weight for this group should be greater than the sum of their single weights (superadditive measure) and (c) no interaction between values in adjacent wedges. Since the values of adjacent wedges have some motivational aspects that are the same and others different, the weight of the importance of a group formed by both should be the sum of their single weights (additive measure). The value *hedonism* is considered to belong to both *openness to change* and *self-enhancement* wedges, having negative interaction with values in those wedges and positive interaction with values belonging to *conservation* and *self-transcendence* wedges. Under these specifications, the pvi function is proposed as follows:

$$pvi(\{v_1, v_2\}_k) = ic(\{v_1, v_2\}_k) \times \iota w_i(\{v_1\}) \times \iota w_i(\{v_2\}) \tag{5}$$

where ic is the interaction coefficient defined as:

$$ic(\{v_1, v_2\}_k) = \begin{cases} +1 \text{ if } v_1, v_2 \text{ are in opposite wedges} \\ 0 \text{ if } v_1, v_2 \text{ are in adjacent wedges} \\ -1 \text{ if } v_1, v_2 \text{ are in the same wedge} \end{cases} \tag{6}$$

Rewritten the Eq. 4 the importance weights for groups of values proposed to model the Schwartz's continuum is:

$$\iota w_i(\{v_s, ..., v_t\}) = \iota w_i(\{v_s\}) + ... + \iota w_i(\{v_t\})+$$
$$+ \sum_{k=1}^{dp} ic(\{v_1, v_2\}_k) \times \iota w_i(\{v_1\}) \times \iota w_i(\{v_2\}) \tag{7}$$

Regarding the *value promotion scheme*, given a set of values $\mathcal{V} = \{v_1, v_2, ..., v_{|\mathcal{V}|}\}$ and an action set $\mathcal{A} = \{a_1, a_2, .., a_{|\mathcal{A}|}\}$ (that the $Ag_i \in \mathcal{AG}$ can perform), the *value promotion scheme* is composed by:

$$\mathbf{pm}^{a_j} = [pm_1^{a_j}, pm_2^{a_j}, ..., pm_{|\mathcal{V}|}^{a_j}] \tag{8}$$

where $\mathbf{pm}^{a_j}$ is the vector that contains the promotion magnitudes $pm_l^{a_j}$ corresponding to the action a_j with respect to the value v_l, with $1 \leq j \leq |\mathcal{A}|$ and $1 \leq l \leq |\mathcal{V}|$.

The initial model considers that there are no automatic mechanisms for determining the promotion magnitudes [13]. This is a disadvantage since an external supervisor is necessary, which is subjective when defining these magnitudes.

Lastly, the *decision process* is responsible for determining, through an aggregation function, the best-aligned action regarding the parameters of preference and promotion of values received. Formally, given the *value system* $VS(Ag_i)$ of agent Ag_i and the promotion magnitudes $\mathbf{pm}^{a_j}$ for the action a_j, the *decision process* computes the value alignment of Ag_i as:

$$Alig(a_j) = AF(VS(Ag_i), \mathbf{pm}^{a_j}) \tag{9}$$

where AF is the aggregation function. According to the Eq. 1 the $Alig(a_j)$ can be rewritten as follows:

$$Alig(a_j) = AF(\{\iota w_i(\wp(\mathcal{V}))\}, \mathbf{pm}^{a_j}) \tag{10}$$

in this way, $Alig(a_j)$ is computed by using the fuzzy measure of the agent Ag_i and the promotion magnitudes of the action a_j. Finally, the aggregation for all actions are computed to obtain the alignment ranking and, consequently, select the most aligned action.

3.2   Using NLP for Promotion Magnitudes

As explained earlier, to determine the most aligned action with an agent's *value system*, it is important to establish which values each available action promotes or demotes, i.e., the promotion magnitudes for each possible action $a_i \in \mathcal{A}$.

Automating the calculation of the *value promotion scheme*, $\mathbf{pm}^{a_j}$, is not a simple task, as it involves developing a model that can detect, given an action, to what extent it promotes each value.

To process each action in $\mathcal{A}$ effectively, it is essential to characterise them. For this purpose, each possible action $a_i \in \mathcal{A}$ is associated with its corresponding natural language text description t_i. Therefore, the problem involves an NLP task of detecting promotions of human values in a text. This task can be viewed as a multi-label text classification problem, where the degree of belongingness to a category (human value) can be seen as the extent to which the text promotes that value. Thus, the proposed model comprises an NLP framework designed to address this task (Fig. 4).

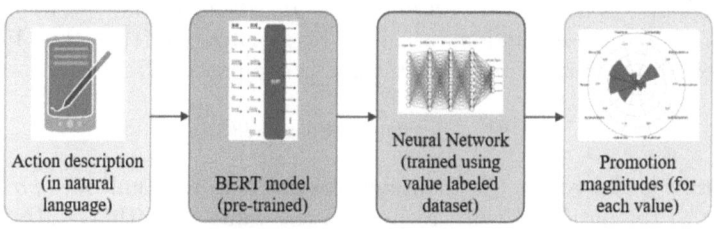

Fig. 4. NLP-based model.

This proposed model is structured into two fundamental components: a pretrained sub-model and a classification layer. The former refers to the well-known BERT (Bidirectional Encoder Representations from Transformers) model, while the latter consists of a supervised-trained neural network serving as the classification layer.

BERT [11] is an open-source machine-learning framework for natural language processing. BERT is designed to help computers understand the meaning of ambiguous language in the text by using surrounding text to establish context. BERT receives tokenized natural language text and outputs contextualized word representation. In this way, this pre-trained sub-model enables our model to comprehend the meaning and intention of a text, as well as the relationship between its words.

The classification layer, built on top of the BERT module, consists of a neuronal layer trained to predict the value promotion magnitudes. This supervised training involves using a labelled dataset of text fragments and the corresponding value(s) they promote, enabling fine-tuning the model for human-values detection.

Combining both modules results in a model that takes tokenized natural language text, processes it through BERT to capture its meaning and then classifies it by going through the neural network, determining the promotion magnitudes of the text for each of the 10 fundamental values.

In summary, taking Fig. 2 as a reference, the value system is built based on preferences over individually defined values and the action promotion scheme is established according to the analysis of the descriptions of the actions available to the agent. With these two elements, a decision process is used to obtain the action most aligned with the defined values. Since the agent can analyze the impact of its actions on the environment, it can vary the order of preference over the values, which automatically redefines the value system according to this impact. This continuous process allows the agent to vary its behaviour if it does not obtain the expected results.

4 Simulations

This section presents the preliminary results of implementing the NLP-based model for value extraction from action descriptions.

To test the described NLP-based model for *value promotion scheme* calculation, it is considered the scenario of participatory budgeting, a democratic process in which community members decide how to spend part of a public budget, proposing participatory projects which are subjected to a voting process after which the most voted ones will be implemented.

In that context, a community member participating in the voting process can be modelled as a value-based agent, and the different project alternatives correspond to the agent's possible actions. The citizen votes for the most consistent project with its values (chooses the most aligned action to its *value system*). Notice that, for simulations, the citizen is represented by the value-based agent with specific preferences over the values according to Eq. 2. Specifically, four agents with preferences on each of the four wedges proposed in the Schwartz continuum (*openness to change, self-enhancement, conservation* and *self-transcendence*) are used.

As discussed in Sect. 3, to model the decision process, it is necessary to specify the impact of each action (project) on each value. With that purpose, the proposed NLP model can be used to compute the *value promotion scheme* for every project.

Following that proposed model, BERT has been fine-tuned for the given task. The used dataset [15] to train the neural network (Fig. 4) consists of sentences in English, labelled according to whether they promote each of the nineteen values in the extended Schwartz value continuum (Fig. 2). This dataset is preprocessed, tokenizing each text fragment to match the input format of BERT. The metrics obtained after evaluating the model are shown in Table 1.

Table 1. Neural network training metrics.

eval_loss	eval_f1	eval_accuracy
0.1141	0.3211	0.5148

As the nineteen extended fundamental values are used for the computation of the *value promotion scheme*, these nineteen values should be considered too for describing the value-based agent's preferences.

Then, to summarize the different aspects that contribute to a specific value, the values that are disaggregated from the simple continuum to the extended one must be merged into a single value to match the ten-value-based model proposed in Sect. 3. This is done by taking the arithmetic mean of the sub-values that compose one of 10 Schwartz's fundamental values. This process is necessary because the subdivision of values generates an imbalance concerning the ten basic values defined in Schwartz's continuum.

Under these conditions, the participatory budgeting process in Madrid [23] is considered for the simulations. Specifically, three of the ten projects chosen during the 2021 exercise and subsequently implemented were selected to test the model. These projects are:

- **Project 1**: Campaign to Remove Dog Feces from Madrid's Sidewalks.
- **Project 2**: Mar de Cristal Library (proposal for a new municipal public library).
- **Project 3**: Increase the Number of Benches for Seating in Madrid.

Each project has a natural language description that constitutes a citizen's proposal. This description extracts the values promoted by each project using the NLP model. It is clear that the more precise the description, clearly indicating the objective, advantages, and impact of the project, the more accurate the detection of the promotion of values is.

In this way, every agent can vote for one of them, and consequently, the action set consists of three actions:

$\mathcal{A} = \{$vote_Project1, vote_Project2, vote_Project3$\}$

Each project is linked to a natural language description that can be checked in the Madrid site for participatory budgeting [23]. Given these texts, the proposed NLP model can be applied to them, determining the *value promotion scheme* for every project. Note that the description of these projects has been translated into English, and in some cases, it has been summarized to fit within the 512-token limit of BERT.

Figure 5 represents the results as a polar radar graph where the ten basic values of Schwartz's theory are continuum-like. It can be observed that **Project 1** promotes significantly *security* and *conformity* values, with promotion magnitudes of 0.57 and 0.34, respectively. **Project 2** highlights the promotion of the values of *stimulation, universalism* and *benevolence*, measured at 0.39, 0.14 and 0.25, in that order.

Lastly, it can be observed that **Project 3** promotes the most *stimulation* and *hedonism*, with magnitudes of 0.49 and 0.14, respectively.

Having computed the promotion magnitudes for each action (project), an agent could be implemented to simulate a votation process. With that purpose, four different agents are considered, each of them with a preference inclination towards values from one sector as defined by Schwartz:

- **Agent 1**: preference for *openness to change*.
- **Agent 2**: preference for *self-enhancement*.
- **Agent 3**: preference for *conservation*.
- **Agent 4**: preference for *self-transcendence*.

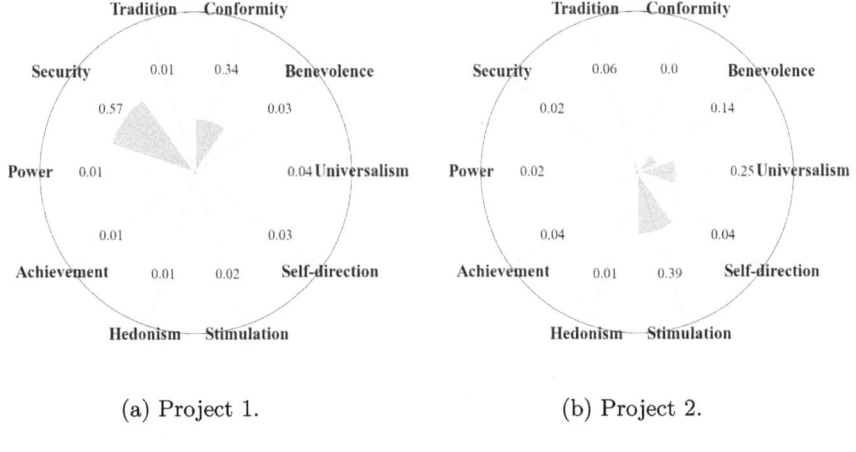

(a) Project 1.   (b) Project 2.

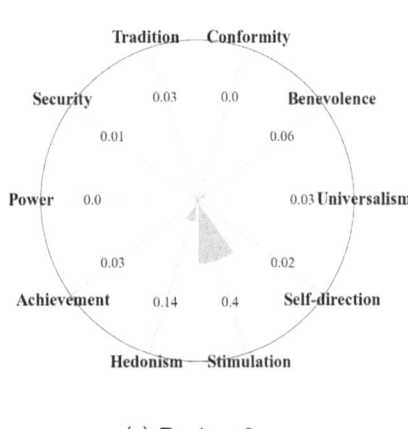

(c) Project 3.

Fig. 5. *Value promotion schemes* for every Project.

These inclinations translate into the highest priority rankings for the values of the preferred wedge in each case.

Simulating the decision process for each of the agents, computing the value alignment of every agent for each action $a_i, i \in \{1, 2, 3\}$, Ag_i as described in Sect. 3.1, the results can be seen in Table 2. The value alignment of the preferred action for each agent has been remarked.

Based on these alignment values, each agent would choose the project that aligns most closely with their values. Thus, Agents 1 and 4 would vote for **Project 2** (Mar de Cristal Library), while Agents 2 and 3 would vote for **Project 1** (Campaign to Remove Dog Feces).

It can be observed that Agents 1 and 3 show significantly strong preferences for projects 2 and 1, respectively, unlike Agents 2 and 4, whose alignment val-

Table 2. Value alignment Ag_i results.

Agent	vote_Project1	vote_Project2	vote_Project3
Agent1	0.061	**0.115**	0.093
Agent2	**0.093**	0.087	0.074
Agent3	**0.143**	0.080	0.047
Agent4	0.078	**0.097**	0.064

ues for the various projects are closely similar and, therefore, present a tighter preference ranking for the selected project.

5 Conclusions and Future Work

This article describes a Natural Language Processing model that can predict how much a text promotes each of the ten fundamental values of Schwartz. Implemented within the framework of a value-based agent, as detailed in Sect. 3.2, this model can automatise the calculation of the *value promotion matrix*, $\mathbf{pm}^{a_j}$, for each available action.

The proposed NLP model used in the value-based agent can extend beyond the scope of Participatory Budgeting. With access to action descriptions, these tools can simulate various decision-making processes. It is worth noting that with the advancement of NLP techniques, increasingly accurate tools are now available to determine the meaning of descriptions made in the text. Therefore, incorporating these techniques into a model that can extract the promotion of values from the actions available to the agent is of utmost importance.

Observing the results obtained from the simulation, it can be seen that both the agent with a preference for *openness to change* (**Agent 1**) and the agent with a preference for *self-transcendence* values (**Agent 4**) vote for **Project 2** (the library construction), which primarily promotes values of *stimulation*, *universalism*, and *benevolence*. This reveals a relationship as both the agents' preferred values and the project's promoted values belong to the anxiety-free dimension described by Schwartz (see Sect. 2).

On the other hand, both the agent with a preference for *conservation* values (**Agent 3**) and the agent with a preference for *self-enhancement* values (**Agent 2**) vote for **Project 1** (the campaign to remove dog faeces), which promotes values of *security* and Conformity, both belonging to the *conservation* wedge in Schwartz's continuum. This reveals Agent3's tendency to vote for a project that promotes values within their preferred wedge.

In addition, it can be seen that **Agent 2** prefers to vote for a project that promotes values motivationally similar (as described by Schwartz) to its preferences rather than a project that promotes motivationally opposite values, as in **Project 1**, or a project that promotes values of its preference but to a minimal extent, as in **Project 3** (see Fig. 5). However, neither of these projects fully aligns with its inclination, so there is no significant difference in the alignment values for **Agent 2**.

As mentioned, this paper presents preliminary results of the NLP-based model for extracting values from the description of actions. Therefore, the current lines of work are oriented to improve the model's training process and its use in participatory projects. In this sense, the idea is to generate agent societies with specific profiles that can simulate and compare the voting process with the real one. Whether these particular profiles will be created probabilistically or inferred somehow is yet to be discussed. In addition, we are working on comparing the performance of the model's value detection against others that use unsupervised techniques, such as topic modelling. Finally, we are also exploring the direct use of the extended model of nineteen values proposed by Schwartz in the decision process to have a model with a higher level of detail.

Acknowledgments. This work has been supported by grant VAE: TED2021-131295B-C33 funded by MCIN/AEI/10.13039/501100011033 and by the "European Union NextGeneration EU/PRTR", by grant COSASS: PID2021-123673OB-C32 funded by MCIN/AEI/10.13039/501100011033 and by "ERDF A way of making Europe", and by the AGROBOTS Project of Universidad Rey Juan Carlos funded by the Community of Madrid, Spain. Marcelo Karanik has been granted funding by the Spanish Ministry of Universities for the Requalification of the Spanish University System (María Zambrano) 2021-2023 through Rey Juan Carlos University.

References

1. Arieli, S., Sagiv, L., Roccas, S.: Values at work: the impact of personal values in organisations. Appl. Psychol. **69**(2), 230–275 (2020)
2. Bagchi, K.K., Udo, G.J., Kirs, P.J., Choden, K.: Internet use and human values: analyses of developing and developed countries. Comput. Hum. Behav. **50**, 76–90 (2015). https://doi.org/10.1016/j.chb.2015.03.055
3. Balikas, G.: John-Arthur at SemEval-2023 Task 4: fine-tuning large language models for arguments classification. In: Kumar, R., Ojha, A.K., Doğruöz, A.S., Martino, G.D.S., Madabushi, H.T. (eds.) Proceedings of the 17th International Workshop on Semantic Evaluation (SemEval'23), Toronto, Canada, pp. 1428–1432. Association for Computational Linguistics (2023). https://doi.org/10.18653/v1/2023.semeval-1.197
4. Bardi, A., Schwartz, S.H.: Values and behavior: strength and structure of relations. Pers. Soc. Psychol. Bull. **29**(10), 1207–1220 (2003)
5. Blake, C.E., et al.: Basic human values drive food choice decision-making in different food environments of Kenya and Tanzania. Appetite **188**, 106620 (2023). https://doi.org/10.1016/j.appet.2023.106620
6. Bonetto, E., et al.: Basic human values during the covid-19 outbreak, perceived threat and their relationships with compliance with movement restrictions and social distancing. PLoS ONE **16**(6), 1–15 (2021). https://doi.org/10.1371/journal.pone.0253430
7. Brocke, B., Bilsky, W.: The measurement of value preferences by paired comparisons. In: 1st European Association for Survey Research Conference, Barcelona, Spain (2005)

8. Brosch, T., Sander, D.: Handbook of Value: Perspectives from Economics, Neuroscience, Philosophy, Psychology and Sociology. Oxford University Press (2015)

9. Cheng, T.Y., et al.: Basic human values of dairy producers in Canada and the U.S.: a cross-sectional survey study. J. Rural Stud. **101**, 103060 (2023).https://doi.org/10.1016/j.jrurstud.2023.103060

10. Czupryna, M., Growiec, K., Kamiński, B., Oleksy, P.: Schwartz human values and the economic performance. J. Artif. Soc. Soc. Simul. **27**(1), 2 (2024). https://doi.org/10.18564/jasss.5023

11. Devlin, J., Chang, M., Lee, K., Toutanova, K.: BERT: pre-training of deep bidirectional transformers for language understanding. CoRR abs/1810.04805 (2018). http://arxiv.org/abs/1810.04805

12. Hadar-Shoval, D., Asraf, K., Mizrachi, Y., Haber, Y., Elyoseph, Z.: Assessing the alignment of large language models with human values for mental health integration: cross-sectional study using Schwartz's theory of basic values. JMIR Ment Health **11** (2024). https://doi.org/10.2196/55988

13. Karanik, M., Billhardt, H., Fernández, A., Ossowski, S.: On the relevance of value system structure for automated value-aligned decision-making. In: Proceedings of the 39th ACM/SIGAPP Symposium on Applied Computing. SAC '24, pp. 679–686, New York, NY, USA. Association for Computing Machinery (2024). https://doi.org/10.1145/3605098.3636057

14. Kiesel, J., Alshomary, M., Handke, N., Cai, X., Wachsmuth, H., Stein, B.: Identifying the human values behind arguments. In: Proceedings of the 60th Annual Meeting, Dublin, Ireland, pp. 4459–4471. Association for Computational Linguistics (2022)

15. Kiesel, J., et al.: Overview of Touché 2024: Argumentation Systems (2024). https://doi.org/10.1007/978-3-031-56069-9_64

16. Kim, S., Kim, S.: Does social value matter in energy saving behaviors?: Specifying the role of eleven human values on energy saving behaviors and the implications for energy demand policy. Energy Strat. Rev. **52**, 101327 (2024). https://doi.org/10.1016/j.esr.2024.101327

17. Kluckhohn, C.: Values and value-orientations in the theory of action: an exploration in definition and classification. In: Toward a General Theory of Action, pp. 388–433. Harvard University Press (1951)

18. Lera-Leri, R., Bistaffa, F., Serramia, M., Lopez-Sanchez, M., Rodriguez-Aguilar, J.: Towards pluralistic value alignment: aggregating value systems through LP-regression. In: Proceedings of the 21st International Conference AAMAS, pp. 780–788. International Foundation for Autonomous Agents and Multiagent Systems, Richland, SC (2022)

19. Liao, Q.V., Muller, M.: Enabling value sensitive AI systems through participatory design fictions (2019)

20. Liscio, E., van der Meer, M., Siebert, L.C., Jonker, C.M., Murukannaiah, P.K.: What values should an agent align with? Autonom. Agents Multi-agent Syst. **36**, 23 (2022)

21. Luciani, M., et al.: How do basic human values affect self-care of type 2 diabetes patients? A multicentre observational study. Clin. Nurs. Res. **29**(5), 304–312 (2020). https://doi.org/10.1177/1054773818825003, pMID: 30658535

22. Ma, L.: PAI at SemEval-2023 Task 4: a general multi-label classification system with class-balanced loss function and ensemble module. In: Kumar, R., Ojha, A.K., Doğruöz, A.S., Martino, G.D.S., Madabushi, H.T. (eds.) Proceedings of the 17th International Workshop on Semantic Evaluation (SemEval'23), pp. 256–261,

Toronto, Canada. Association for Computational Linguistics (2023). https://doi.org/10.18653/v1/2023.semeval-1.34

23. Ayuntamiento de Madrid: Resultados de los presupuestos participativos de 2021. https://decide.madrid.es/presupuestos/presupuestos-participativos-2021/resultados (2021). Accessed 03 Jun 2024

24. Montes, N., Sierra, C.: Value-guided synthesis of parametric normative systems. In: Proceedings of the 20th International Conference AAMAS, pp. 907–915. International Foundation for Autonomous Agents and Multiagent Systems, Richland, SC (2021)

25. Morris, C.: Varieties of Human Value. University of Chicago Press (1956)

26. Osman, N., d'Inverno, M.: A computational framework of human values for ethical AI (2023)

27. Knowledge for policy: ValuesML - Unravelling Expressed Values in the Media for Informed Policy Making (2023). https://knowledge4policy.ec.europa.eu/projects-activities/valuesml-unravelling-expressed-values-media-informed-policy-making_en. Accessed 03 Jun 2024

28. Pommeranz, A., Detweiler, C., Wiggers, P., Jonker, C.: Elicitation of situated values: need for tools to help stakeholders and designers to reflect and communicate. Ethics Inf. Technol. **14**, 285–303 (2012)

29. Páez Gallego, J., De-Juanas Oliva, A., García-Castilla, F.J., Muelas, A.: Relationship between basic human values and decision-making styles in adolescents. International Journal of Environmental Research and Public Health **17**(22) (2020). https://doi.org/10.3390/ijerph17228315

30. Ratchford, J.L., Ming, M.S., Lee, Y., Jackson, J., Wood, M., Schnitker, S.A.: A rank order approach to basic human values: using q-sorts to investigate the value circumplex. Person. Individ. Diff. **206**, 112111 (2023). https://doi.org/10.1016/j.paid.2023.112111

31. Ring, C., Kavussanu, M., Gürpınar, B., Whitehead, J., Mortimer, H.: Basic values predict unethical behavior in sport: the case of athletes' doping likelihood. Ethics Behav. **32**(1), 90–98 (2022). https://doi.org/10.1080/10508422.2020.1837136

32. Rokeach, M.: The Nature of Human Values. Free Press (1973)

33. Sagiv, L., Schwartz, S.H.: Value priorities and subjective well-being: direct relations and congruity effects. Eur. J. Soc. Psychol. **30**(2), 177–198 (2000)

34. Schroter, D., Dementieva, D., Groh, G.: Adam-Smith at SemEval-2023 Task 4: Discovering Human Values in Arguments with Ensembles of Transformer-based Models. In: Kumar, R., Ojha, A.K., Doğruöz, A.S., Martino, G.D.S., Madabushi, H.T. (eds.) Proceedings of the 17th International Workshop on Semantic Evaluation (SemEval'23). pp. 532–541. Association for Computational Linguistics, Toronto, Canada (Jul 2023https://doi.org/10.18653/v1/2023.semeval-1.74

35. Schwartz, S., et al.: Refining the theory of basic individual values. J. Person. Soc. Psychol. **103**, 663–88 (2012). https://doi.org/10.1037/a0029393

36. Schwartz, S.H.: Universals in the content and structure of values: theoretical advances and empirical tests in 20 countries. In: Advances in Experimental Social Psychology, vol. 25, pp. 1–65. Elsevier (1992)

37. Schwartz, S.H.: Value priorities and behavior: applying a theory of integrated value systems. In: The Psychology of Values: The Ontario Symposium, pp. 1–24. Psychology Press (1996)

38. Schwartz, S.H.: An overview of the schwartz theory of basic values. Online Read. Psychol. Cult. **2**(1), 11 (2012)

39. Schwartz, S.H., Bilsky, W.: Toward a universal psychological structure of human values. J. Pers. Soc. Psychol. **53**(3), 550 (1987)

40. Serramia, M., Lopez-Sanchez, M., Rodriguez-Aguilar, J.A.: A qualitative approach to composing value-aligned norm systems. In: Proceedings of the 19th International Conference AAMAS, pp. 1233–1241, Richland, SC. International Foundation for Autonomous Agents and Multiagent Systems (2020)
41. Serramia, M., Lopez-Sanchez, M., Rodriguez-Aguilar, J.A., Morales, J., Wooldridge, M., Ansotegui, C.: Exploiting moral values to choose the right norms. In: Proceedings of the 2018 AAAI/ACM Conference on AI, Ethics, and Society, New York, NY, USA, pp. 264–270. ACM (2018)
42. Siebert, L.C., et al.: Estimating value preferences in a hybrid participatory system. In: Schlobach, S., Perez-Ortiz, M., Tielman, M. (eds.) HHAI2022, pp. 114–127. IOS Press, Netherlands (2022)
43. Zhang, C., Liu, P., Xiao, Z., Fei, H.: Mao-Zedong at SemEval-2023 Task 4: label representation multi-head attention model with contrastive learning-enhanced nearest neighbor mechanism for multi-label text classification. In: Kumar, R., Ojha, A.K., Doğruöz, A.S., Martino, G.D.S., Madabushi, H.T. (eds.) Proceedings of the 17th International Workshop on Semantic Evaluation (SemEval'23), Toronto, Canada, pp. 426–432. Association for Computational Linguistics (2023). https://doi.org/10.18653/v1/2023.semeval-1.58

Neuro-Symbolic Classification of Basic Human Values

Stefano De Giorgis[1]([⊠])(iD) and Nicolas Lazzari[2,3](iD)

[1] Institute of Cognitive Sciences and Technologies, National Research Council, Rome, Italy
stefano.degiorgis@cnr.it
[2] Department of Computer Science, University of Pisa, Pisa, Italy
nicolas.lazzari3@unibo.it
[3] Department of Modern Languages, Literature, and Cultures, University of Bologna, Bologna, Italy

Abstract. This work explores the integration of ontology-based reasoning and Machine Learning techniques for explainable classification in the domain of moral and cultural values. By relying on an ontological formalization of moral values as in the Basic Human Values theory, which is based on the Description and Situation Ontology Design Pattern, the *sandra* neuro-symbolic reasoner is used to infer values (formalized as descriptions) that are *satisfied by* a certain sentence. Sentences, alongside their structured representation, are automatically generated using an open-source Large Language Model. The inferred descriptions are used to automatically detect the value associated with a sentence. We show that only relying on the reasoner's inference results in explainable classification comparable to other more complex approaches. Moreover, we test how the LLMs tacit knowledge can be exploited to obtain novel formalizations of the domain. We show that combining the reasoner's inferences with simple distributional semantics methods largely outperforms all the baselines, including complex models based on neural network architectures.

Keywords: Moral Values · Neuro-symbolic AI · Ontology · Knowledge Graphs

1 Introduction

The recent advancements in AI models, particularly in generative tasks involving linguistic and visual production, is fueling the relevance of the Value Alignment problem for the near future [8,29]. Detecting and classifying human values in multimodal data has become a crucial task across various domains, particularly with the proven capabilities of Large Language Models (LLMs) in aligning with human beliefs [14]. The automatic discernment of values from text is vital for

---

Nicolas Lazzari—Equal contribution.

N. Osman and L. Steels (Eds.): VALE 2024, LNAI 15356, pp. 121–133, 2025.
https://doi.org/10.1007/978-3-031-85463-7_8

understanding human behavior, decision-making processes, and societal trends. However, several challenges complicate this classification.

Firstly, value classification is inherently subjective and context-dependent [31], making it challenging to objectively identify a unique value associated with a given sentence. It is essential to consider diverse perspectives to ensure a comprehensive understanding of the underlying values.

Current methodologies primarily rely on Machine Learning (ML) techniques, and recently pre-trained LLMs, for value classification. Despite their effectiveness, the opacity of these models' decision-making processes raises concerns regarding their semantic understanding of sentences versus mere pattern matching. Consequently, there is a critical need for an approach that provides accurate predictions while offering interpretability, enabling stakeholders to assess the alignment of predictions with established knowledge of values.

To address these challenges, we propose a novel framework that integrates ontology-based reasoning with ML techniques. Specifically, we leverage the *sandra* neuro-symbolic reasoner [17], which utilizes the DnS Ontology Design Pattern, to infer various perspectives from which a given situation, represented as a sentence, can be interpreted. Furthermore, in our framework we adopt a theory-heavy approach, namely instructing the learning phase, guided by Basic Human Values Theory [27].

A key component of our approach is the structured representation of sentences, obtained using an open-source LLM. Through empirical evaluation, we demonstrate the feasibility and efficacy of this approach.

We establish a robust baseline for value classification by relying solely on the reasoner's inferences, demonstrating comparable performance to more complex approaches involving pre-trained LLMs. Crucially, our method ensures explainability, allowing us to provide justifications for classification decisions. The adopted and newly generated versions of the ValueNet ontology and the datasets produced are available here[1]. The neuro-symbolic *sandra* methodology has been previously applied and tested for the domain of values in [16], on a different dataset, focusing on values from Moral Foundations Theory (MFT).

Furthermore, we illustrate the synergistic benefits of combining our approach with other NLP techniques, leading to significant performance improvements over all baselines, including LLM-based methods, without compromising interpretability.

The rest of the paper is organized as follows: Sect. 2 presents related works while Sect. 3 discusses the data generation method. Section 4 presents the experiments and results obtained. Finally, in Sect. 5, we summarize the contribution and highlight future works.

2 Related Works

Value formalization, defined as the construction of a theoretical framework that encompasses a set of entities and elucidates the semantic relationships intertwin-

---

[1] https://github.com/StenDoipanni/ValueNet/tree/main/vale2024.

ing moral and cultural values, has a long-standing and interdisciplinary background. This paper primarily focuses on the Basic Human Values theory (BHV) [9,27], as elaborated in subsequent sections. BHV, as well as other theoretical frameworks, such as Moral Foundations Theory by Graham and Haidt [11], and Morality as Cooperation [4,5], provides a framework for the formalisation of the values domain.

From a knowledge representation perspective, previous attempts to represent the notion of value include the Ethics Ontology [6], which explores the commonsense notion of "value", but lacks grounding in a specific theory, and, more recently, VAE, an ontology for Value Awareness [12], focused on agent-based value-aware and normative systems.

In this work we extended prior work that formalized the aforementioned theories as ontological modules in the ValueNet ontology [10]. ValueNet is an ontology network that formalizes several theories and models moral and cultural values as semantic frames [7,19].

The frame-based modeling approach is based on two main assumptions: (i) Values are modeled as n-ary relations, where roles perform specific semantic functions, such as Agent, Undergoer, Victim, Beneficiary; and (ii) values can be "evoked" by a set of lexical units, which cannot be understood without the entire frame structure, for instance the concept of "Helper" is meaningful only in the context of some form of Benevolence being enacted towards a receiving entity, thus the lexical unit "helper" derives its meaning from this implicit semantic load.

Values Detection and Classification In the realm of moral and cultural value classification, current approaches predominantly rely on ML techniques, where BERT-based models generally obtain state-of-the-art performances [20]. Most recent approaches in particular focus on identify human values behind arguments [15].

However, these methods lack transparency in their decision-making process, posing challenges for explainability. Furthermore, the datasets for training those models are constructed through manual annotation and extraction from existing large scale sources, which may introduce biases. Previous works like [1,3] focus on more explainable methodologies, reusing semantic frames activation to detect values from MFT.

Notably, our approach differs by utilizing a generative method to automatically create structured representations of sentences, which serve as a benchmark for evaluating the quality of classification methods, given the absence of human evaluation. Attempts at explainable value classification are emerging, but they often lack a robust theoretical foundation. Our approach combines ML techniques with ontology-based reasoning, leveraging Basic Human Values theoretical formalization to provide both performance and interpretability. This integration allows us to anchor our classification framework in established and well-understood theories, setting our approach apart from previous methods.

Basic Human Values The Theory of Basic Human Values (BHV) by Shalom Schwartz was proposed as a pan-cultural theory in the 1980s [22]. Its main assumption is that human values are organized in a "value wheel", that is, an ordering that organizes values as a circumplex model, dividing them into four quadrants with two opposing axes, and a congruity continuum between adjacent values.

Schwartz and Bilsky [24,25] suggested that all individuals must respond to three main human needs: (i) biology-based needs, (ii) social requirements for interpersonal interaction and coordination, and (iii) in-group social norms, as institutional demands, for group welfare and survival. Values are therefore the cognitive representation of these needs.

In respect with other theories such Moral Foundations Theory, BHV circumplex model does not contemplate direct violations, but rather an opposition of behavioral focus and attitude.

The BHV framework is based on the following assumptions [23]:

- Human values are universal: All individuals, regardless of their culture or background, have the same basic values, which are innate and hardwired into the brain.
- Human values are organized hierarchically: The basic values form the foundation of all other values, and the relative importance of each value varies among individuals and cultures.
- Human values are related to individual and societal well-being: values prioritized by individuals and societies influence their overall well-being and quality of life.
- Human values are context-dependent: The relative importance of each value varies depending on the context, and individuals and cultures may prioritize different values in different situations.

Furthermore, cultural values reflect ideals that shape the beliefs and commitments of individuals and groups in the relation to the cultural environment [21]. They act as societal coping mechanisms to three situations of possible risks to a successful collaboration and co-location: (i) inside relations between individuals and groups; (ii) relations between individuals and the society as a cultural structure; (iii) individuals' interest vs the natural and social environment.

Originally, the model included 10 values [22], but, as shown in Fig. 1, the model was later refined to 19 values in total [26]. BHV relies on the opposition and similarity of values, grouped into macro-categories that are mostly determined by individual personality traits (self-transcendence vs self-enhancement, conservation vs openness to change). This model has inspired the design of a questionnaire (Portrait Values Questionnaire, PTV [30]) which has been employed by several studies to explore values across different countries [28]. In recent work [23], Schwartz provides evidence in favour of a pan-cultural arrangement of value priorities.

BHV has been tested on a vast number of subjects across 82 countries. However, one of the main criticism is its top-down approach, since establishing the

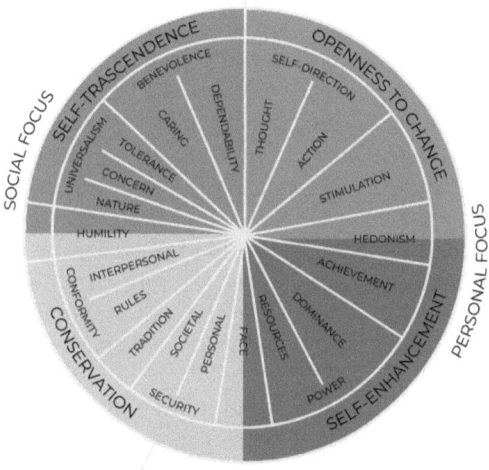

Fig. 1. Basic Human Values circumplex model, 2019 version

number and taxonomy of values a priori, and then validating it through dedicated experimentation might disregard other relevant perspectives on the matter.

3 Synthetic Data Generation

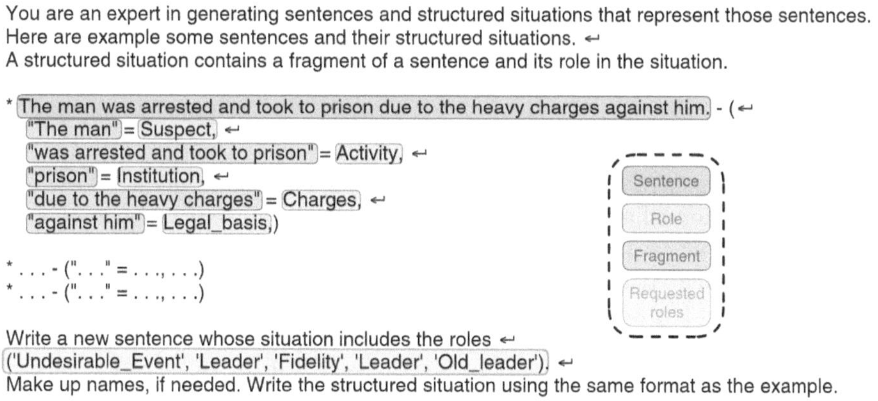

You are an expert in generating sentences and structured situations that represent those sentences. Here are example some sentences and their structured situations. ↵
A structured situation contains a fragment of a sentence and its role in the situation.

* The man was arrested and took to prison due to the heavy charges against him. - (↵
  "The man" = Suspect, ↵
  "was arrested and took to prison" = Activity, ↵
  "prison" = Institution, ↵
  "due to the heavy charges" = Charges, ↵
  "against him" = Legal_basis,)

* . . . - (". . ." = . . ., . . .)
* . . . - (". . ." = . . ., . . .)

> Sentence
> Role
> Fragment
> Requested roles

Write a new sentence whose situation includes the roles ↵
('Undesirable_Event', 'Leader', 'Fidelity', 'Leader', 'Old_leader'). ↵
Make up names, if needed. Write the structured situation using the same format as the example.

Fig. 2. Annotated prompt example

In this section, we discuss the methodology used to generate the synthetic dataset of sentences and their structured representation, and provide some insights on its quality. For the generation of the dataset, we prompt a Large

Language Model (LLM). In particular, we rely on Llama3[2], a 8 billion parameters open-source language model. We do make use of three main techniques: *cloze*, role-playing, and few-shot prompting [18]. Few-shot prompting refers to the technique where examples of desirable outputs are provided to the LLM. They have been shown to be particularly effective in classification tasks (to obtain *in context* learning). Cloze prompting, on the other hand, refers to the technique in which the desired outputs are presented in a specific structure. Finally, role-playing is a technique where the LLM is instructed to act as a specific agent. It has been observed that this kind of technique increases the quality of the generated responses. In our setting, we rely on it to indicate the output structure, which allows us to easily parse the sentence and its structured representation, as well as provide examples of sentences that are manually curated to express some specific value.

Figure 2 shows an example of a prompt. In the first part, we instruct the LLM on its role as a structured sentence generator. Afterwards, we present 3 example outputs structured as a tuple composed of a sentence and its representation as a structured situation. The structured situation is composed of a fragment of the sentence and its annotated role. The requested roles are randomly sampled in the range [2, 15] from the ones originally in ValueNet ontology [10]. Finally, we instruct the LLM to provide a new sentence and the structured situation compliant to the examples we gave. We extract all the roles used in every description. This allows the LLM to generate sentences whose roles are not confined to a specific value. Notice that in the prompt of Fig. 2 we never explicitly mention to the LLM that the sentences to be generated have to evoke some values nor we ever mention the concept of value. This is done to avoid any bias in the generative process. The model should autonomously extrapolate the aspects that are in common between all the example sentences and generate a novel one that displays those aspects. This results in a more challenging dataset where different perspectives must be considered. It is not possible to assume that a sentence *prototypically* expresses a particular value, but rather that among all the perspectives that explain it, there exists one in which the sentence can be classified with that particular value.

In total we generate 7,000 structured sentences, 1,000 sentence for value. The values considered are *achievement, benevolence, conformity, power, security, tradition,* and *universalism.* These were the value chosen, out of the original 19 due to their being structured using FrameNet roles. Each value is represented as a description. On average, each description is composed of 15 roles out of a total of 65 unique roles.

The distribution of the roles within ValueNet follows the well-known Zipf distribution. Indeed, the most common roles (e.g. *Time, Place*) are very common concepts that characterize almost every possible value. To guarantee variability within the dataset, we randomly sample the *temperature* parameter of the LLM in the range $t \in [0.01, 1]$.

---

[2] https://llama.meta.com/llama3/.

Given the prompt as in Fig. 2, the extraction of the generated sentence and of its respective situation is straightforward. Nonetheless, we note that the output produced by the LLM, despite the clear indications, is very often not consistent. From the total of 7,000 sentence, more than 30% contains hallucinated roles. Moreover, after some manual inspection we found that the LLM does not always faithfully comply with the proposed structure. We implement a straightforward parser, based on regex patterns, and performed some standard pre-processing to clean typical LLMs expressions as "Here is the sentence:" and equivalent. A more carefully implemented parser might help in reducing the amount of noise within the dataset.

Indeed, even though we provide a set of roles that the LLM must consider during the generation phase, it will also autonomously generate sentences that include other existing roles. The choice of those is biased towards roles that are more common within the pre-training corpus. Those roles represent very general concepts that are very likely to occur in a sentence, regardless of its intended meaning. On the other hand, some roles are particularly prominent on some values rather than others, such as *Helper* for the *Benevolence* value. This supports the idea that specific roles have different relevance and salience among different frames.

As addressed previously, it is not possible to assume that the sentence generated by the LLM when provided with few-shots for a specific values are guaranteed to evoke that specific value. Meticulous Prompt Engineering is usually involved in order to produce reliable results [2,13]. One possible form of validation could be to check whether the emotion polarity extracted from the sentences correlates with the value they are tagged as.

4   Value Detection Experiments and Discussion

We perform a series of four experiments to evaluate our approach.

In particular, in Sect. 4.1 we present experiments where the classification is performed through the use of a fragment of ValueNet, implementing BHV and incorporating the roles from FrameNet.

Such ontology is composed of roles that describes general concepts, such as Agent and Place. However, when generating the dataset, as explained in Sect. 3, the LLM produces sentences that are annotated with more specific roles, that are not asserted in ValueNet. Although this is the known phenomenon of "hallucination", it points to a plausible fact that needs to be tested: the roles from ValueNet could be not enough.

Table 1. Specialisations generated by GPT-4o for the :Degree role. The :Degree role is used in *Achievement, Benevolence, Conformity, Power, Security,* and *Universalism* values.

BHV Value	"Degree" Role
Achievement	Level
Benevolence	Intensity
Conformity	Strictness
Power	Extent
Security	SecurityLevel
Universalism	Extent

We therefore perform four experiments to evaluate our approach. Here we briefly list the experiments, while we detail them in the followings:

1. Using only roles "manually curated" from ValueNet ontology
2. Using roles "specialised" per each value, following serendipitous LLM hallucinations, but manually curating the alignments
3. Using all the roles, including the hallucinated ones
4. Setting a threshold and using a mix of ValueNet roles + hallucinated ones

To asses whether it is possible to extend the ontology following a similar approach, we assert additional roles in ValueNet by manually prompting a LLM and experiment with the resulting ontology in Sect. 4.2.

Following a similar intuition, in Sect. 4.3 we enlarge the ontology by using all the roles produced by the LLM. This allows us to test whether it is possible to overcome the task of producing an ontology by following a full bottom-up approach. Finally, in Sect. 4.4, we manually filter the ontology produced in Sect. 4.3. Every experiment is evaluated by classifying a sentence with the corresponding value. All the results are shown in Table 2.

4.1 Theory-Heavy Approach

As it is clearly shown in Table 2, injecting of formal knowledge thanks to *sandra* methodology consistently improves the results.

Experiment 1 confirms the importance of injecting domain knowledge in the process of learning, thanks to *sandra*'s geometrical reasoning approach. Nevertheless, further investigations are conducted in Experiment 2, 3, and 4, in particular addressing: (i) the lack-of-specificity problem of FrameNet roles, and (ii) top-down vs bottom-up ontology modeling approach.

4.2 Specialising Roles

Regarding point (i): the underlying hypothesis is that, in our modeling of values as semantic frames, the `:Agent` of e.g. `bhv:Benevolence` as in Fig. 4, should have very different characteristics from the `:Agent` of `bhv:Achievement`, in Fig. 3. Indeed, reusing the same `:Agent` role for both values it is correct, since - at a certain level of abstraction - these two entities are both *Agents*, but at the same time a certain amount of semantics is lost. Experiment 2 therefore is grounded in the idea of specialising generic roles into more refined ones, tailored for each specific value. To refine the roles we used GPT-4o in its free chat version, Table 1 shows an example of refinement for the `:Degree` role for each value, as specialised by GPT-4o. Table 2 shows that this approach, although theoretically interesting, would require a more refined alignment between more general roles, such as *Agent*, and local specialisations, such as *Helper*.

Table 2. Accuracy results obtained with different methods and different feature extraction algorithms. Best results for each method are underlined while the best result overall is represented in bold.

Ontology	Features	Decision Tree	XGBoost	kNN	Logistic Regression	MLP	Naive Bayes	Random Forest	SVM
Manually curated	TF-IDF	0.40	0.51	0.42	0.54	0.49	0.47	0.52	0.54
	sBERT	0.28	0.51	0.38	0.52	0.52	0.34	0.43	0.54
	sandra	0.48	0.57	0.53	0.45	0.55	0.25	0.56	0.56
	sandra + sBERT	0.41	0.69	0.45	0.58	0.55	0.38	0.52	0.64
	sandra + TF-IDF	0.51	**0.71**	0.52	0.59	0.54	0.48	0.62	0.63
Roles specialised by the LLM	TF-IDF	0.37	0.53	0.43	0.58	0.51	0.49	0.53	0.56
	sBERT	0.26	0.50	0.38	0.53	0.45	0.35	0.42	0.54
	sandra	0.23	0.24	0.18	0.19	0.19	0.18	0.23	0.19
	sandra + sBERT	0.26	0.49	0.36	0.53	0.47	0.34	0.44	0.52
	sandra + TF-IDF	0.37	0.56	0.38	0.58	0.52	0.47	0.54	0.55
Learned bottom-up	TF-IDF	0.38	0.51	0.42	0.55	0.50	0.44	0.51	0.55
	sBERT	0.26	0.48	0.38	0.53	0.51	0.32	0.42	0.53
	sandra	0.33	0.34	0.29	0.23	0.22	0.20	0.34	0.26
	sandra + sBERT	0.27	0.49	0.38	0.53	0.51	0.33	0.42	0.54
	sandra + TF-IDF	0.38	0.57	0.42	0.55	0.51	0.44	0.53	0.55
Learned bottom-up and manually filtered	TF-IDF	0.38	0.53	0.42	0.56	0.53	0.49	0.52	0.56
	sBERT	0.28	0.49	0.39	0.55	0.54	0.34	0.42	0.54
	sandra	0.33	0.34	0.29	0.27	0.31	0.20	0.33	0.36
	sandra + sBERT	0.29	0.51	0.39	0.56	0.57	0.36	0.44	0.55
	sandra + TF-IDF	0.38	0.56	0.43	0.58	0.54	0.48	0.54	0.57

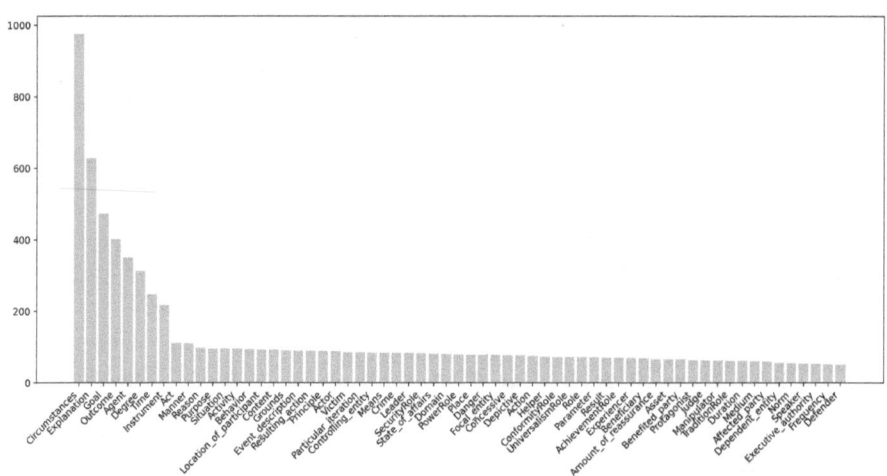

Fig. 3. Roles occurring more than 50 times for the value "Achievement"

4.3 Learning Ontology Bottom-up

Our third experiment adopted a quantitative approach starting from a full bottom-up methodology. We realized that Llama, the language model used to generate our dataset, exhibited significant hallucination, introducing a considerable amount of apocryphal (but possibly coherent and correct) roles. Exploiting the idea that the hallucination in introducing new roles maintains a certain plausibility, we used all the roles identified by Llama to generate a new ontology, essentially transforming this step into an ontology learning experiment. This experiment clearly illustrated the problem of the curse of dimensionality, as the large number of roles created complexity that hindered effective performance.

4.4 Manually-Filtered Bottom-up Ontology

In the fourth experiment, which combined both quantitative and qualitative methods, we manually curated the ontology. We filtered out roles that occurred fewer than 50 times in the dataset to ensure that only the most relevant and frequently occurring roles were included. We then repeated the experiment with this refined ontology to evaluate how manual curation and role frequency thresholds affected the performance and reliability of our approach.

More tests need to be conducted with further granularity of detail in the ontology. This approach not only opens new paths for neuro-symbolic hybridization of techniques but it also leverages LLMs to generate "local" roles for those value frames currently lacking them (in any formal framework, and in ValueNet in particular). While the problem of annotation persists, it can be addressed by employing a general role labeler and aligning specialized roles with those used by the role labeler. This method ensures consistency and accuracy in role annotation, facilitating more robust and interpretable models.

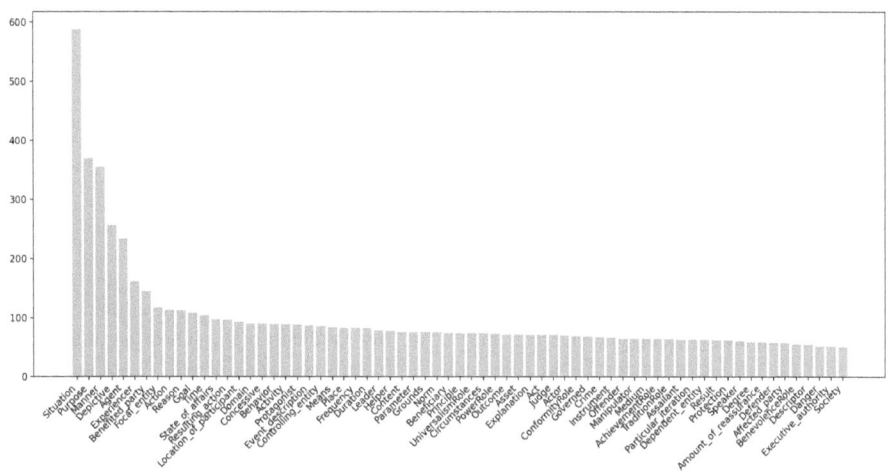

Fig. 4. Roles occurring more than 50 times for the value "Benevolence"

5   Conclusions and Future Works

In this paper, we leveraged an ontological formalization of values, focusing on the Basic Human Values theory, and built on previous formalization of value as semantic frames, within ValueNet. We generated a synthetic dataset of 7,000 sentences, with 1,000 sentences representing each value. Employing *sandra*'s reasoning approach, we extracted the salience and overlap of semantic roles for each value. Additionally, we conducted preliminary experiments on value detection using traditional machine learning methods to classify the degree of satisfaction for each sentence per value, showing improved performance when applying Sandra's method.

Our results demonstrate that adopting a neuro-symbolic approach enhances the explainability and comprehensibility of the classification process, as incorporating satisfied descriptions significantly boosts the performance of interpretable and explainable models. Furthermore, using ValueNet in the classification process revealed its gaps and limitations, which can be addressed by experts for better formalization. However, the synthetic nature of the dataset introduces biases from the language model used for sentence generation. As discussed earlier, this dataset may not accurately reflect real-world sentences expressing human values.

Future research will involve on one side validating our methods on established datasets verified by human annotators. On the other side, additionally, our approach can inform the refinement of ValueNet, particularly by enriching the semantic relationships among values, further enhancing performance and explainability through *sandra*'s approach. Finally, our approach demonstrates that injecting knowledge and constraining the learning with information coming directly from sound theoretical domain knowledge, drives to a consistent increment of performances. Nevertheless, open questions are: how better exploit

LLMs to provide such knowledge, how to (and how much) filter it, and based on which rationale.

Acknowledgement. This work was supported by the Future Artificial Intelligence Research (FAIR) project, code PE00000013, CUP 53C22003630006.

References

1. Asprino, L., et al.: Uncovering values: detecting latent moral content from natural language with explainable and non-trained methods. In: Proceedings of Deep Learning Inside Out (DeeLIO 2022): The 3rd Workshop on Knowledge Extraction and Integration for Deep Learning Architectures, pp. 33–41. Association for Computational Linguistics (2022)
2. Ben Allal, L., Lozhkov, A., Penedo, G., Wolf, T., von Werra, L.: Cosmopedia (2024). https://huggingface.co/datasets/HuggingFaceTB/cosmopedia
3. Bulla, L., Giorgis, S.D., Gangemi, A., Marinucci, L., Mongiovì, M.: Detection of morality in tweets based on the moral foundation theory. In: International Conference on Machine Learning, Optimization, and Data Science, pp. 1–13. Springer (2022)
4. Curry, O.S.: Morality as cooperation: a problem-centred approach. In: The Evolution of Morality, pp. 27–51 (2016)
5. Curry, O.S., Alfano, M., Brandt, M.J., Pelican, C.: Moral molecules: morality as a combinatorial system. Rev. Philos. Psychol. **13**(4), 1039–1058 (2022)
6. DeBellis, M.: The ethics ontology: a universal moral grammar. Academia. https://wwwacademia.edu/15327812
7. Fillmore, C.J.: Frame semantics. In: Linguistics in the Morning Calm, pp. 111–138. Hanshin, Seoul (1982)
8. Fisac, J.F., et al.: Pragmatic-pedagogic value alignment. In: Robotics Research: The 18th International Symposium ISRR, pp. 49–57. Springer (2020)
9. Giménez, A.C., Tamajón, L.G.: Analysis of the third-order structuring of Shalom Schwartz's theory of basic human values. Heliyon **5**(6), e01797 (2019)
10. Giorgis, S.D., Gangemi, A., Damiano, R.: Basic human values and moral foundations theory in valuenet ontology. In: Corcho, Ó., Hollink, L., Kutz, O., Troquard, N., Ekaputra, F.J. (eds.) Knowledge Engineering and Knowledge Management - 23rd International Conference, EKAW 2022, Bolzano, Italy, September 26-29, 2022, Proceedings. LNCS, vol. 13514, pp. 3–18. Springer (2022). https://doi.org/10.1007/978-3-031-17105-5_1
11. Graham, J., Nosek, B.A., Haidt, J., Iyer, R., Koleva, S., Ditto, P.H.: Mapping the moral domain. J. Pers. Soc. Psychol. **101**(2), 366 (2011)
12. Holgado-Sánchez, A., Billhardt, H., Ossowski, S., Fernández, A.: An ontology for value awareness engineering. In: ICAART (3), pp. 1421–1428 (2024)
13. Javaheripi, M., et al.: Phi-2: the surprising power of small language models. Microsoft Research Blog (2023)
14. Ji, J., et al.: Beavertails: towards improved safety alignment of LLM via a human-preference dataset. In: Oh, A., Naumann, T., Globerson, A., Saenko, K., Hardt, M., Levine, S. (eds.) Advances in Neural Information Processing Systems 36: Annual Conference on Neural Information Processing Systems 2023, NeurIPS 2023, New Orleans, LA, USA, December 10 - 16, 2023 (2023). http://papers.nips.cc/paper_files/paper/2023/hash/4dbb61cb68671edc4ca3712d70083b9f-Abstract-Datasets_and_Benchmarks.html

15. Kiesel, J., e al.: SemEval-2023 task 4: ValueEval: identification of human values behind arguments. In: Proceedings of the 17th International Workshop on Semantic Evaluation (SemEval-2023), pp. 2287–2303 (2023)
16. Lazzari, N., De Giorgis, S., Gangemi, A., Presutti, V.: An explainable neuro-symbolic approach to value classification. In: Extended Semantic Web Conference (ESWC) - WISDOMS Workshop Proceedings (2024)
17. Lazzari, N., De Giorgis, S., Gangemi, A., Presutti, V.: Sandra–a neuro-symbolic reasoner based on descriptions and situations. arXiv preprint arXiv:2402.00591 (2024)
18. Liu, P., Yuan, W., Fu, J., Jiang, Z., Hayashi, H., Neubig, G.: Pre-train, prompt, and predict: a systematic survey of prompting methods in natural language processing. ACM Comput. Surv. **55**(9), 195:1–195:35 (2023). https://doi.org/10.1145/3560815
19. Minsky, M.: A framework for representing knowledge (1974)
20. Mirzakhmedova, N., et al.: The touch\'e23-ValueEval dataset for identifying human values behind arguments. arXiv preprint arXiv:2301.13771 (2023)
21. Schwartz, S.: A theory of cultural value orientations: explication and applications. Comp. Sociol. **5**(2–3), 137–182 (2006)
22. Schwartz, S.H.: Universals in the content and structure of values: theoretical advances and empirical tests in 20 countries. In: Advances in Experimental Social Psychology, vol. 25, pp. 1–65. Elsevier (1992)
23. Schwartz, S.H.: An overview of the Schwartz theory of basic values. Online Readings Psychol. Cult. **2**(1), 11 (2012)
24. Schwartz, S.H., Bilsky, W.: Toward a universal psychological structure of human values. J. Pers. Soc. Psychol. **53**(3), 550 (1987)
25. Schwartz, S.H., Bilsky, W.: Toward a theory of the universal content and structure of values: extensions and cross-cultural replications. J. Pers. Soc. Psychol. **58**(5), 878 (1990)
26. Schwartz, S.H., et al.: Refining the theory of basic individual values. J. Pers. Soc. Psychol. **103**(4), 663 (2012)
27. Schwartz, S.H., Melech, G., Lehmann, A., Burgess, S., Harris, M., Owens, V.: Extending the cross-cultural validity of the theory of basic human values with a different method of measurement. J. Cross-cult. Psychol. **32**(5), 519–542 (2001)
28. Schwartz, S.H., Melech, G., Lehmann, A., Burgess, S., Harris, M., Owens, V.: Extending the cross-cultural validity of the theory of basic human values with a different method of measurement. J. Cross Cult. Psychol. **32**(5), 519–542 (2001)
29. Sierra, C., Osman, N., Noriega, P., Sabater-Mir, J., Perelló, A.: Value alignment: a formal approach. arXiv preprint arXiv:2110.09240 (2021)
30. Simón Llovet, J., et al.: The portrait values questionnaire: a bibliographic and bibliometric review of the instrument. In: Aloma, 2017, vol. 35, núm. 1 (2017)
31. Trager, J., et al.: The moral foundations reddit corpus. arXiv preprint arXiv:2208.05545 (2022)

Value-Driven Decision Making

Value-Based Decision-Making in Software Agents: A Systematic Literature Review

Esteban Guerrero$^{(\boxtimes)}$ (ID), Sz-Ting Tzeng (ID), Cezara Pastrav (ID),
and Frank Dignum (ID)

Department of Computing Science, Umeå University, Umeå, Sweden
{esteban.guerrero,sz-ting.tzeng,cezara-maria.pastrav,frank.dignum}@umu.se

Abstract. Building software agents that make decisions based on human values presents a complex challenge. This is a first attempt to systematically review trends in how researchers represent, select, evaluate, and implement values in software agents.

The review highlights two key limitations in the field. First, most research adopts or acknowledges Schwartz's theory of basic human values, but often simplifies its complexity. Second, many studies oversimplify the notion of values in general, failing to utilize established theories from psychology or philosophy. Additionally, the review finds that common software tools and existing frameworks, like the Belief-Desire-Intention model, are frequently used without fully considering their underlying principles. This research offers valuable contributions to the field of value-based decision-making in software agents, exposing research gaps and limitations in current research, and highlighting the need for a more nuanced approach. By calling for researchers to integrate insights from economics, social science, psychology, and neuroscience, the review paves the way for the development of more sophisticated agents that can navigate the complexities of real-world decision-making.

Keywords: Values · Decision-making · Software agents · Review · Belief-Desire-Intention

1 Introduction

Human *values* are fundamental aspects of our being, shaping our goals, guiding our decisions, and influencing our actions [42]. They represent what we hold important, with varying degrees of emphasis across individuals [41]. Psychologists, philosophers, economists, and neuroscientists have developed frameworks to understand this complex value system. Within the realm of psychology, Schwartz's seminal work in [42], proposes a comprehensive framework for understanding human values. This framework identifies ten distinct values, such as *achievement*, *security*, and *benevolence*, each characterized by six key features. These features emphasize the inherent link between *values* and *emotions*, their function as motivators for *action*, and their role as guiding principles in decision-making [42]. In contrast, Rokeach, in [41], offers a broader definition, conceptualizing values as *enduring beliefs* that guide our *preferences* for specific modes of conduct or end states. Comprehensive reviews of value-based decision-making in the social sciences [22,29] and neurobiology [38], show the multifaceted nature of human values and the importance of a nuanced approach when incorporating them into software agent decision-making algorithms.

The field of Artificial Intelligence (AI) has increasingly focused on incorporating human-like decision-making capabilities into software agents, for example, addressing *moral deliberations* or when AI mechanisms need to ensure *trust* (see the values treatment in Dignum's work [16] as a reference). This review is focused on *value-based decision-making*, where agents consider human values in their computational mechanisms for selecting the "best" decision (*e.g.*, an action or set of them). We consider mostly the decision-making processes of software agents where *mental states* such as *beliefs* (B), *desires* (D), and *intentions* (I) (among others) are used in the main decision-making algorithm. In this context, the review focuses on BDI models and their extensions following the primary work of Bratman in [11], where this BDI model has specific *consistency* and *soundness* properties (*e.g.*, the Asymmetry thesis in [11]), which has been *formally captured* in the software agents community (see [10,40]). However, a significant challenge lies in the lack of a unified understanding of "value" across disciplines. This ambiguity creates difficulties in representing, capturing, and implementing values within software agent decision-making algorithms. To the best of our knowledge, this is the first systematic review focused on value-based decision-making for software agents that consider cognitive architectures in their computational mechanisms. This review, is guided by the following research questions:

RQ1 What human values theories or frameworks are used as a foundation or inspiration to integrate human values into the decision-making process of agents?

RQ2 What type of software languages, platforms, or tools were used in the implementation?

RQ3 How values are formally captured and represented within the agents' literature?

RQ4 What type of computational mechanisms *families* for decision-making are used for selecting/deciding a value-based *output*?

This article is structured as follows, in Sect. 2, we present the steps that we follow in our review, then in Sect. 3 we present the results of the review, which are discussed in Sect. 4. Finally, we conclude our article by highlighting our future work.

2   Methodology

In this section, we summarize the methodology used in this review. For lack of space, we present a compact description of the original process in Kitchenham et al. in [28].

2.1   Systematic Procedure

We defined a general set of keywords that we used in academic databases for addressing our review research questions as is presented in the top of Fig. 1.

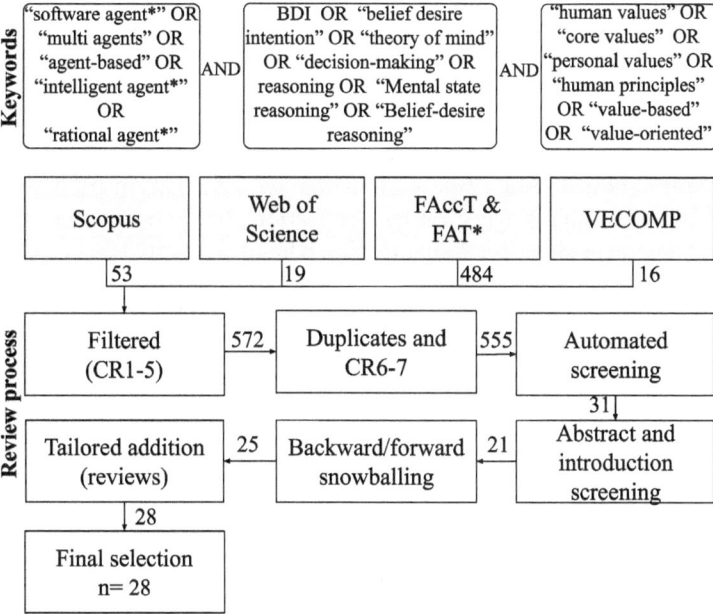

Fig. 1. Top: Keywords used in this review. Bottom: Review process of the article

Using those keywords, we consulted two academic databases, Scopus and Web of Science, with an additional focused search in venues where value-orientation and value-based mechanisms are presented, such as the ACM Conference on Fairness, Accountability, and Transparency (ACM FAccT) and FAT* before 2020 $(n = 484)$. Then, we found 572 potential papers.

Screening Process. In the data screening process of those 572 articles we use different inclusions and exclusion criteria (CR)

We performed an automated screening of the papers using ASReview Lab [53] that uses Machine Learning mechanisms for pre-screening papers. Then, we conducted a round of *forward* and *backward snowballing* process [54] to gather

CR1 The article is written in English.

CR2 Full article can be accessed.

CR3 The article is published between January 1990 and May 2024.

CR4 The articles in related areas to the article.

CR5 No duplicated articles.

CR6 The focus is on decision-making in software agents.

CR7 The focus of the article is human values.

other articles citing the selected articles (for forward), and checking the list of referred articles in the selected articles (for backward). The final number of articles selected for this version of the review were 28 as is presented in Fig. 1.

3 Results

In this section, we present the major findings considering every research question. We start analyzing briefly the *bibliometrics* information from the selected articles, then we address every research question. In the following, we will use the name *value* as a short for *human value* when the context is evident.

We found that in recent years the number of articles relating value-based or value-oriented decision-making have increased in the software agents communities, as it is clear for the rise of some workshops such as VECOMP. At the same time, we found that most of the selected papers for this review are conference and workshop articles, but few of them can be found in journal articles in the software agents and AI fields, as is presented in Fig. 2.

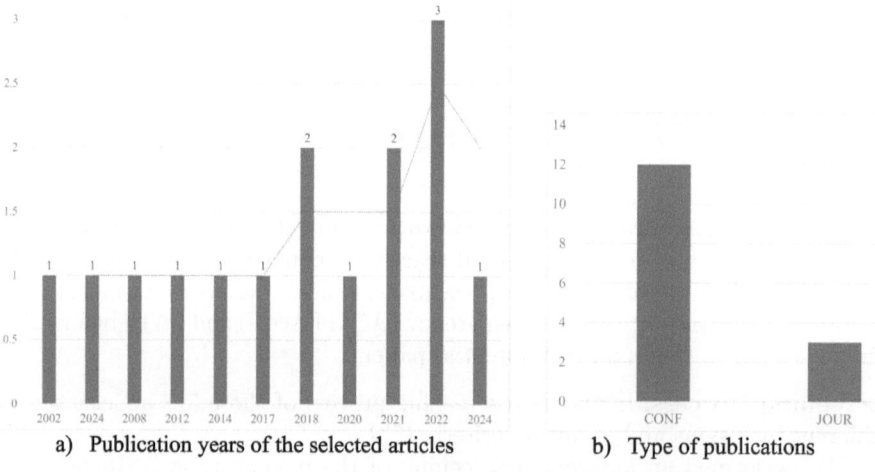

a) **Publication years of the selected articles**   b) **Type of publications**

Fig. 2. Publication years of the selected articles and type of publications. Note that CONF means conference and workshop venues, and JOUR means journal articles

3.1 RQ1: What Human Values Theories or Frameworks are Used as Foundation or Inspiration to Integrate Human Values in the Designing Decision-Making Process of Software Agents?

Key Findings
– Computational mechanisms for decision-making in value-oriented software agents use or acknowledge the Schwartz's theory of basic human values.
– When no cognitive architectures of software agents are used, then authors use abstract notions/concepts of what values are.
– For abstract value-based/oriented mechanisms, the specific meaning or grounded characterization of individual values is irrelevant.

When we addressed RQ1 we found two tendencies that are valuable to highlight:

1. Extensive use and acknowledgment of *Schwartz's theory of basic human values* in [42,43]. We found that Schwartz values classification is used mostly for those decision-making processes where at least one of the following *features* of the values (see [44]) is required for the computational mechanism:
   - Values are considered as desirable *goals* that motivate *actions*.
   - Values are *beliefs* in the mental model of the computational framework.
   - Values transcend specific actions and situations.
   - Values serve as standards or criteria.
   - Values are ordered by importance relative to one another.
   - The relative importance of multiple values guides action.
2. Abstract notions of values for general decision-making processes. We found that some authors use abstract concepts of what a value is (or set of them) when the decision-making processes of their software agents do not consider the following aspects:
   - No cognitive architectures are involved (*e.g.*, *beliefs*, *desires*, etc.)
   - There is no need for a categorization, ranking, order or partial order in a set of values.
   - The specific meaning or grounded characterization of individual values is irrelevant for the computational mechanism.

The tendency for using or acknowledge the Schwartz perspective of values was present in different selected articles in our review [30–32,45,49] (see Table 1). As an illustration of this finding is the case of the work presented in [45], where the authors suggest a *Value System* that is defined as a pair $VS = \langle V, \succeq \rangle$ where V stands for a non-empty set of moral values from [43], and $\succeq$ represents a partial order over those values. Clearly, in Serramia et al. work the use of a partial order fits the concept in Schwartz where values are ordered by importance relative to one another, for example, people's values form an ordered system of priorities that characterize them as individuals (from [44]). This hierarchical feature also distinguishes values from norms and attitudes according to Schwartz. The work of Serramia et al. in [45] follows the notion of values from Dignum in

[15], where it is stated that values serve as criteria to guide the evaluation of actions taking into account the relative priority of values. Another example of computational mechanisms for agent decision-making using the Schwartz's value perspective can be found in [37], where a value-driven agent architecture named *SMASH* is proposed where its *control loop* (the main decision-making algorithm) for action-decision is made in four steps (layers), through value-reasoning, then, goal-reasoning, planning, and acting. In this setting, the value-reasoning layer in [37] considers a set of ordered values, which order varies considering the *user*'s *context* and *preferences*. Then, the decision-making procedure follows similar BDI-like loops of other approaches (*e.g.*, [49]). An extension named *Q-SMASH* was introduced in and [36] where the decision-making process for selecting the "best" action was performed by using *Q-Learning* that is a specific *Reinforcement Learning* technique.

Other software agents decision-making process that we found in our review, not only use the Schwartz work but also they extended, such as the work presented by Mogles et al. in [31], where the authors proposed an agent- *simulation-based* framework for supporting *behavior change interventions* to persuade participants in better energy consumption habits ("energy behaviour change" in the authors terms). In [31], the authors followed the Schwartz values categorization in [43], extending that taxonomy with the work in [48], where *environmental actions* made by an agent (a person) are understood from a distinction between two types of self-transcendence values: altruistic and *biospheric values*, but also two types of self-enhancement values: *egoistic values*, and *hedonic values* [48].

3.2   RQ2: What Type of Software Languages, Platforms, or Tools Used in the Implementation?

Key Findings
– Value-oriented decision-making can be implemented in different software tools and platforms.
– The most used platforms and tools for implementing value-based or value-oriented software agents are well-established and mature.

In general, we found that in the software agents literature computational mechanisms considering values in their decision-making process, authors implement those agents using a number of tools, software frameworks and platforms, as is presented in Table 3. However, these results show that even for articles in the last three years (*e.g.*, [31, 36, 37]), the use of not recent but well-established platforms and tools, such as Jadex[1] [35], JaCaMo[2] [8], Jason[3] [9], the GAMA platform[4] [3], NetLogo[5] [51], and MATLAB[6] [50]. We summarize the information of their first

---

[1] Jadex Web https://www.activecomponents.org/#/download.
[2] JaCaMo Web https://github.com/jacamo-lang/jacamo.
[3] Jason Web https://github.com/jason-lang/jason/releases.
[4] GAMA Web https://github.com/gama-platform/gama/releases/tag/1.9.3.
[5] NetLogo Web https://ccl.northwestern.edu/netlogo/.
[6] MATLAB Web https://www.mathworks.com/products/matlab.html.

Table 1. Human values theories or frameworks used as foundation or inspiration to integrate human values in the designing decision-making process of software agents

Ref	Schwartz [43]	Haidt et al. [25]	Debreu [14]	Steg et al. [47]	Abstract	Other	Not defined
[45]	✓						
[52]							✓
[49]	✓						
[37]					✓		
[4]					✓		
[36]					✓		
[26]							✓
[23]					✓		
[33]		✓					
[6]			✓				
[12]						✓	
[31]	✓			✓			
[27]					✓		
[5]					✓		
[32]	✓						
[34]						✓	
[21]					✓		
[30]	✓						

Header note: Ref | Human value theories

release and last update, which suggest a degree of *maturity* of every platform, as is presented in Table 2.

Table 2. Maturity of the most well-known platforms used to implement value-based/oriented software agents.

Platform/tool	First release	Last update	Last version
Jadex [35]	2005	Jun-24	Jadex v5.0.0
JaCaMo [8]	2013	May-23	JaCaMo v1.2
Jason [9]	2007	Feb-21	Jason 3.3.0
GAMA [3]	2009	Feb-22	Version 1.9.3
NetLogo [51]	1999	Nov-23	NetLogo 6.4.0
MATLAB [50]	1970s	May-24	MATLAB R2024a

Table 3. Software languages, platforms, or tools used in the implementation of software agents' decision-making processes

Ref	Jadex [35]	JaCaMo [8]	Jason [9]	AgentSpeak [39]	GAMA [3]	NetLogo [51]	Sugarscape [19]	MATLAB [50]	Linear program solver	No software	Not defined
[45]								✓			
[52]											✓
[49]											✓
[37]	✓										
[4]										✓	
[36]	✓										
[26]						✓					
[23]				✓							
[33]		✓	✓								
[6]	✓										
[12]					✓						
[31]							✓				
[27]										✓	
[5]										✓	
[32]										✓	
[30]										✓	

3.3 RQ3: How Values are Formally Captured and Represented Within the Agents Literature?

Key Findings
– Propositional logic and similar specification languages are the most preferred approaches to represent values.
– Numerical measures to compute a value-oriented decision are inline with some current trends in the Machine Learning field.

In general, we found two trends for how values are represented or captured to be utilized as a part of the decision-making process of software agents:

- Proposition language and similar specification languages capturing values. We found that the most used underlying language specification was different types of *rule-based* representations, such as classical propositional logic [49], and AgentSpeak as a logic programming representation [33,36,37].
- Values as numerical quantities. Other authors use numerical measures as representation of a singular value, such as the works in [23,26,45] and [31]. In these approaches, a value can be considered as a single v in a range, e.g., $v \in [0,1]$ in [31].

We highlight here some of the results summarized in Table 4, for example we found that some decision-making mechanisms, the selection of underlying specification for capturing the notion of a value or set of them, depends clearly on the decision-making algorithm, for example, for some BDI-oriented mechanisms where the decision-making framework is able to handle values interactions [33,36,37], then the use of propositional logic approaches is an obvious choice. However, we found that other mechanisms use a dual representation, capturing the specific value in a rule-based style but adding elements such a numerical quantities to express, the value *weight* [32], the value *impact* [5], and value *priority* [17,45], among others.

Table 4. Mechanisms for capturing or representing human values in the implementation of software agents' decision-making processes

Ref	Numerical values	Undirected graph	Directed acyclic graph	Weights	Probabilities	Propositions (atoms) in a specification language	Not defined
	Representation type						
[45]	✓		✓				
[52]	✓						
[49]						✓	
[37]						✓	
[4]						✓	
[36]						✓	
[26]	✓						
[23]	✓						
[33]					✓		
[6]						✓	
[12]					✓		
[31]	✓						
[27]						✓	
[5]						✓	
[32]		✓		✓			
[30]							✓

We found that those approaches where numerical quantities are used to specify one value, and compute any decision based on only that representation (*e.g.*, [26]) are inline with current trends of some artificial intelligence-based mechanisms using a data-oriented approach, which makes a strong difference for the treatment of a human value from a software agents with cognitive architectures perspective. In this regard, our results are inline with some reviews in the Machine Learning area where is surveyed how human values are used in those data-oriented approaches, see [7, 18].

3.4 RQ4: What Type of Computational Mechanisms *families* for Decision-Making are Used for Selecting/Deciding a Value-Based *output*?

Key Findings
– Authors propose novel algorithms for decision-making based on BDI-like reasoning mechanisms.
– An abstract decision-making process named Value-based Reasoning in [5] is foundational for some general frameworks.
– *Off-the-shelf* Game Theory and Machine Learning approaches are used for value-based and value-oriented decision-making.

We found that there are different computational mechanisms that are suitable for decision-making based on those values captured or represented using different underlying approaches (RQ3). In Table 5, we summarize the findings of those *families* of computational mechanisms used in the selected articles. Based on these findings, we highlight two main trends:

Table 5. Families of computational mechanisms for value-based decision-making

Computational mechanisms							
Ref	Reinforcement learning (Q-learning)	Recurrent Neural Networks	Linear programming	Tailored reasoning	Value-based Reasoning	Game Theory	Multi-objective optimization
[45]			✓				✓
[52]	✓						
[49]					✓		
[37]				✓			
[4]					✓		
[36]				✓			
[26]						✓	
[23]						✓	
[33]				✓			
[6]				✓			
[12]						✓	
[31]		✓					
[27]				✓	✓		
[5]					✓		
[32]				✓			

- Novel decision-making processes tailored to value-based computations. We found that the majority (6/15) of computational mechanisms are tailored to solve the challenge of selecting an *output* (*e.g.*, an action) based on those captured or represented values, see [6,27,32,33,36,37]. Most of these approaches are related to *reasoning* mechanisms where *BDI-like* control loops are tailored to include values in the decision-making process.
- Abstract computational mechanisms for value-oriented reasoning. We found that the work of Value-based Reasoning in [5] has been foundational for other approaches. In [5], Bench-Capon introduces a *formal argumentation theory* mechanism for reasoning about arguments that capture abstract representations of human values. We found that this value-oriented reasoning process is further extended by other approaches mechanisms such as [4,27] and [49].
- Game Theory and Machine Learning (ML) mechanisms for value-based decision-making. In our survey, we found that value-oriented and value-based decision-making is performed using some well-established ML mechanisms such as *reinforcement learning* [52] and *neural networks* [31], as well as for some approaches of Game Theory such as the work presented in [23,26].

4   Discussion

In general, our findings reflect a trend for embedding human mental states in software agents extending the well-established theories covering *beliefs*, *desires*, and *intentions* (BDI) (*e.g.*, [11,13,20]). In summary, when RQ1 was addressed we found that the notion of *values* has two major directions, authors use the established theory of values by Schwartz in [42], or an abstract interpretation of them without considering any specification or restriction that particular theories from psychology or philosophy establish. Then, when we addressed RQ3, we found that authors *simplify* the concept of a value to *match* that representation with a definite feature in the underlying specification for capturing that information, for example, considering a value as an additional quantity in propositional or rule-based language, or as a specific value in a range that. Such a simplification is not surprising given that most of the cognitive architectures for software agents require a complexity reduction to be a tractable computational problem. In this context, we found that there is not a unique tendency in the selected articles when families of decision-making algorithms were considered (RQ4); in the following sections, we will discuss this particular finding in detail. Finally, we found that authors tend to use well-established and mature software tools, and platforms to build those value-oriented or value-based decision-making algorithms (RQ2).

In the following, we address RQ1-4 in detail.

4.1 Human Values Theories Used in Decision-Making Algorithms of Software Agents

In our review, we found two specific trends: 1) most of the computational mechanisms for decision-making in value-oriented software agents use or acknowledge Schwartz's theory of basic human values, and 2) Authors of some selected articles use an abstract notion of what values are when no cognitive architectures of software agents are used. The **impact** of these findings is relevant to the software community in at least two directions:

- **Decision-making algorithms integrating human values considering Schwartz's theory in** [42] *favored* specific features in the Schwartz theory, at the same time that ignore others. In most of the selected articles [30–32, 45, 49], authors do not consider the proposed main features of the value conception in Schwartz's theory as a joint set (values are beliefs, values refer to desirable goals, values transcend specific actions and situations, etc. in [44]). Instead, authors tend to use those characteristics that *fit* in their computational specification disregarding the others, for example, in [49], it is argued that the best way to incorporate values into a cognitive agent architecture is to make values *basic* mental attitude along with beliefs, desires and intentions, which is reduced to a *same-level* representation of different mental states. We found this interpretation in other works considering values as attitudes, beliefs, traits, or even norms (see *e.g.*, [36,52]). In this respect, the Schwartz theory establishes that a crucial way in which attitudes, beliefs, traits, or norms differ from values is that they vary on another scale, so it is measured differently [44]. Moreover, for those authors considering BDI-related models [36,37,52], Schwartz notices that beliefs are ideas about how true it is that things are related in particular ways (*e.g.*, "war never solves problems" or "Africa is larger than Europe"). Beliefs vary in how certain we are that they are true, and unlike values, beliefs refer to the subjective probability that a relationship is true, not to the importance of goals as guiding principles in life [44].
- **Lack of computational formalisms for assessing rational decisions when BDI is extended with values**. In the software agents literature using the BDI framework, it is well-established some formal principles (mathematical requirements) that were highlighted from the philosophy field (*e.g.*, the *asymmetry thesis* in [11]) ensure that an agent will select the "best" action

based on their actual mental states. For example, Bratman in [11] argues that it is *irrational* for an agent to intend to do an action and also believe that it *will not* do it. Bratman states also an agent should not have *intention-belief inconsistency*. For example, if *Robbie the Robot* intends to serve beer and also believes that it will not serve beer, it would be considered as an irrational behavior [40]. In this context, computational principles have been proposed for the BDI model ensuring an acceptable behavior of those BDI agents (see formalisms in [10,24,40]). In our review, we found that when BDI extensions are proposed with human values, no author paid attention to how such representation of values integrated into other mental states will fulfill already established principles or additional that could emerge when these mental states are integrated in a decision-making process.

4.2   Software Tools and Platforms Used in Decision-Making Algorithms

The *maturity* of the tools and platforms for implementing decision-making algorithms was one of the interesting findings in our review. In Table 2 we showed that most of these established platforms have been continuously updated over the years, with additional extensions of the reasoning mechanisms, as well as adapting the software development practices. We can mention at the moment of writing this article, Jadex [35] and JaCaMo [8] were recently updated, integrating more complexity and features into those platforms. We acknowledge that NetLogo [51] is an important, and long-standing platform used not only for implementing decision-making algorithms but also as a tool for *social agent-based modeling* (ABM), which can be considered as a sub-field of the software agents research area. In the ABM context, we acknowledge that such simulations deal with large amounts of agents (possibly in millions) that cannot be modeled within some of the previous aforementioned platforms. An ABM review in [1] highlights the variety of tools used for simulations, which mentioned a BDI-ABM integration in [46], where simulation agents are integrated into BDI control loops. These types of BDI-ABM alternatives were explored in a survey by Adam et al. in [2] from a methodological perspective.

4.3   Representing and Capturing Human Values

The findings of our review show that specification languages such as *propositional logic* or *logic programming* extensions such as AgentSpeak [39] are the most preferred approaches to represent and capture values. We acknowledge that more *atomic* representations such as those using numerical measures, in line with some current trends in the Machine Learning field, are also used in value-oriented decision-making approaches. We highlight here some of these works. In [49], it is argued that the best way to incorporate values into a cognitive agent architecture is to make values a *basic* mental attitude, considering the belief-desire-intention

(BDI) model [11]. The authors in [49] use classical propositional logic as a language ($\mathcal{L}$) to describe and capture the notion of a human value, with a syntax as the three *predicates* $promote(v, \rho, \phi)$, $demote(v, \rho, \phi)$ and $weight(v, \phi)$, where $v \in V_C$ is a value from a set of the ten Schwartz values, ρ is a propositional variable in the language $\mathcal{L}$, and $\phi \in [0, 1]$ represents to what degree a state of the world promotes or demotes a value [49], and $weight()$ represents the extent the agent holds a value important. In the same line, the work of Rahimi et al. in [37] presents a value-driven agent architecture called SMASH is proposed where the loop for action decision-making (the selection of the best action) is made in four steps (layers), through value-reasoning, then, goal-reasoning, planning, and acting. In this setting, the value-reasoning layer in [37] considers a set of ordered values, which order varies considering the *user's context* and *preferences*. *Value-ordering rules* (VO) in [37] have a syntax *condition* → *body* where a *condition* is a *first-order logical formula* stating if the rule is active in the current context. The value-based reasoning system presented in [4] has as a foundation for the value-orientation the work of Bench-Capon in [5] from the *argumentation theory* context, where an action can be analyzed in terms of its relevant values, and classical logic is used to represent abstract values.

Different from previous rule-based systems to capture values, in [26] the authors extended an Agent-based Modeling framework (ABM) considering utility functions from *Game Theory* where *fairness*, *conformity*, and *altruism* as values were used to compute a *universal* utility function including different value-oriented *payoffs* to calculate a reward for the agent. Similarly, in [23], the authors tested the hypothesis that agents have *fairness* as a *moral value* and that the transgression of this triggers *guilt* feelings in them. The *game-theoretic* model in [23] assumes that a *player* has two different *motivational systems*: an *endogenous* motivational system determined by the player's *desires*, and an *exogenous* motivational system determined by the player's *moral values*.

In summary, our findings show that several mechanisms for capturing and representing human values are used for value-oriented decision-making in software agents, but in general, the addition of values for the decision-making process does not imply new underlying specifications, rather authors use *off-the-shelf* languages and models to capture values.

4.4 Types of Algorithms for Value-Based or Value-Oriented Decision-Making

When we considered RQ4, looking for the specific computational mechanisms for decision-making used to select the "best" action, or in general any *outcome* from a given framework, we found unsurprisingly that most of the authors propose extensions of well-established theories or frameworks, with special focus on BDI-like reasoning mechanisms. This finding is expected given that BDI has been an established framework in computer science since the 1990s. We found that other abstract approaches for reasoning, such as the work of Bench-Capon in [5] named Value-based Reasoning, have been influential and are not directly connected to the formal argumentation field. Following the line of that AI field, we found that in [27], a formal argumentation framework for *practical reasoning* is presented, where a *Pareto optimality* relationship is considered, hypothesizing that decisions by practical argumentation must satisfy Pareto optimality. More specifically, consequences of practical argumentation are decisions of a *course of action* that an agent or a group of agents takes. Those decisions strongly depend on desires, aims, or values that the agent has. In such a setting, agents are certain to avoid Pareto improvable decisions because if it is not Pareto optimal, there exists another decision that makes some agents better off and no one worse off [27]. This Pareto optimization framework coincides with the Value-based Argumentation in the sense that these approaches try to create computational mechanisms where human values are generalized (no details of what value is or preferences among them).

Following another *family* of knowledge representation and reasoning (KRR), we found a *graph theory* approach that was introduced in [32], where the authors suggested a graph framework where human values (specifically from the taxonomy in Schwartz [43]) are represented in a graph model containing *value nodes* representing the Schwartz values, with an associated *importance* weight; *property values* whose satisfaction (or degree of satisfaction) can be automatically verified in a given system [32]. In this research, Osman et al. suggest a *light* version of an ontology for capturing values in the sense of Schwartz, but no semantics are proposed to make an automated inference on that graph.

In our review, we found that several decision-making approaches are tailored to adapt the specific notion of value in their specifications, such as the work in [6,33,52]. More specifically, in [33], agents have *internal states* from which "negative", "neutral" and "positive" results (actions) are computed considering a Partial Observable Markov Process (POMDP), which is useful for agents that have to choose optimal actions in partially observable stochastic domains. Pereira et al., designed agents with different *personality traits*, such as *egoism, altruism, equilibrium fanaticism*, and *tolerance*. The authors in [33], proposed an algorithm to map a POMDP *policy graph* to BDI plans for the agent, using AgentSpeak with Jason to make a prototype of their approach. In [52], the concept of *social values* was defined as standards that individuals and groups employ to shape the form of social order, *e.g.*, *fairness* and *justice*. Then, the authors used a BDI control loop mechanism for their implementation, which is a similar strategy found in [6], where a BDI architecture of an agent was extended with values (named V-BDI), considering that values represent abstract and permanent needs of the user that the agent should satisfy [6]. Moreover, Benzi et al. stated that the role of those values is to modulate the behavior of the other three mental attitudes (*w.r.t.*beliefs, desires, and intentions), according to the specific hierarchy of values. Different than other BDI models using values, the work in [6] uses values to choose the most appropriate intentions to achieve a given desire, meaning that it is used to "filter" those intentions aligned with the given values. The authors in [6] used Jadex to implement their framework.

5   Conclusion

In this review, we revise trends of computational mechanisms for decision-making in value-oriented or value-aligned software agents. We highlight the trends, but also we point out specific gaps in how values are represented, selected, evaluated, and implemented.

Key major findings were that most of the authors either adopt or acknowledge Schwartz's theory of basic human values [42,43], or use an *abstract* notion of human values without referencing specific theories from psychology or philosophy. The implications of our findings suggest that most of the computational mechanisms simplify the complexity of mental states described in Schwartz's theory, often disregarding key features that Schwartz suggests as key as a collective (see [44]). We found also authors oversimplify the notion of values without specifying or restricting them according to established theories. The review also found that established software tools and platforms are commonly used to build value-oriented or value-based decision-making algorithms. Our review found that most authors propose extensions of well-established theories or frameworks, particularly the Belief-Desire-Intention model, however, our analysis suggests that most of these mechanisms disregard key features of the underlying BDI framework proposed by Bratman in [11], where agents should follow some rationality principles such as the *asymmetry thesis* to create sound plans. As future work, we want to expand this review with additional sources that were not obtained from the selected databases, acknowledging the work of related fields such as ABM for simulations.

Acknowledgments. Guerrero's and Dignum's work was supported by the WASP (Wallenberg AI, Autonomous Systems and Software Program) and WASP-HS (WASP-Humanities and Society) programs with the project numbers: 570011330 and 570011505 respectively. Tzeng's and Pastrav's work was supported by WASP with the project numbers: 570011331 and 570011332, respectively.

Disclosure of Interests. The authors have no competing interests to declare that are relevant to the content of this article.

References

1. Abar, S., Theodoropoulos, G.K., Lemarinier, P., O'Hare, G.M.P.: Agent based modelling and simulation tools: a review of the state-of-art software. Comput. Sci. Rev. **24**, 13–33 (2017). https://doi.org/10.1016/j.cosrev.2017.03.001
2. Adam, C., Gaudou, B.: BDI agents in social simulations: a survey. Knowl. Eng. Rev. **31**(3), 207–238 (2016). https://doi.org/10.1017/S0269888916000096
3. Amouroux, E., Chu, T.-Q., Boucher, A., Drogoul, A.: GAMA: an environment for implementing and running spatially explicit multi-agent simulations. In: Ghose, A., Governatori, G., Sadananda, R. (eds.) PRIMA 2007. LNCS (LNAI), vol. 5044, pp. 359–371. Springer, Heidelberg (2009). https://doi.org/10.1007/978-3-642-01639-4_32

4. Badea, C.: Have a break from making decisions, have a mars: the multi-valued action reasoning system. In: International Conference on Innovative Techniques and Applications of Artificial Intelligence, pp. 359–366. Springer, Cham (2022)

5. Bench-Capon, T.J.M.: Value-based argumentation frameworks. In: Benferhat, S., Giunchiglia, E. (eds.) 9th International Workshop on Non-Monotonic Reasoning (NMR 2002), 19–21 April, Toulouse, France, Proceedings, pp. 443–454 (2002)

6. Benzi, F., Fogli, D., Guida, G.: Towards natural interaction with smart homes. In: CHItaly 2017: Proceedings of the 12th Biannual Conference on Italian SIGCHI Chapter, pp. 1–6. Association for Computing Machinery, New York (2017). https://doi.org/10.1145/3125571.3125581

7. Birhane, A., Kalluri, P., Card, D., Agnew, W., Dotan, R., Bao, M.: The values encoded in machine learning research. In: Proceedings of the 2022 ACM Conference on Fairness, Accountability, and Transparency, pp. 173–184 (2022)

8. Boissier, O., Hübner, J.F., Ricci, A.: The jacamo framework. In: Social Coordination Frameworks for Social Technical Systems, pp. 125–151 (2016)

9. Bordini, R.H., Hübner, J.F.: A java-based interpreter for an extended version of agentspeak. University of Durham, Universidade Regional de Blumenau, vol. 256 (2007)

10. Bordini, R.H., Moreira, Á.F.: Proving BDI properties of agent-oriented programming languages: the asymmetry thesis principles in AgentSpeak(L). Ann. Math. Artif. Intell. **42**(1), 197–226 (2004). https://doi.org/10.1023/B:AMAI.0000034527.45635.e5

11. Bratman, M.: Intention, Plans, and Practical Reason. Harvard University Press, Cambridge (1987)

12. Davis, N., Dermody, B., Koetse, M., van Voorn, G.: Identifying personal and social drivers of dietary patterns: an agent-based model of dutch consumer behavior. J. Artif. Soc. Soc. Simul. **27**(1) (2024). https://doi.org/10.18564/jasss.5020

13. Davis, W.A.: A causal theory of intending. Am. Philos. Q. **21**(1), 43–54 (1984)

14. Debreu, G.: Theory of value: an axiomatic analysis of economic equilibrium, vol. 17. Yale University Press (1959)

15. Dignum, V.: Responsible autonomy. In: Sierra, C. (ed.) Proceedings of the Twenty-Sixth International Joint Conference on Artificial Intelligence, IJCAI 2017, Melbourne, Australia, 19–25 August 2017, pp. 4698–4704. ijcai.org (2017). https://doi.org/10.24963/ijcai.2017/655

16. Dignum, V.: Responsible artificial intelligence: how to develop and use AI in a responsible way, vol. 1. Springer (2019)

17. Dixon, M.L., Christoff, K.: The lateral prefrontal cortex and complex value-based learning and decision making. Neurosci. Biobehav. Rev. **45**, 9–18 (2014)

18. Dotan, R., Milli, S.: Value-laden disciplinary shifts in machine learning. In: FAT* 2020: Proceedings of the 2020 Conference on Fairness, Accountability, and Transparency, p. 294. Association for Computing Machinery, New York (2020). https://doi.org/10.1145/3351095.3373157

19. Epstein, J.M., Axtell, R.: Growing artificial societies: social science from the bottom up. Brookings Institution Press (1996)

20. Ferrero, L.: Can i only intend my own actions? Oxford Studies in Agency and Responsibility, vol. 1, pp. 70–94 (2013)

21. Friedman, B., Kahn, P.H., Borning, A., Huldtgren, A.: Value sensitive design and information systems. In: Doorn, N., Schuurbiers, D., van de Poel, I., Gorman, M.E. (eds.) Early engagement and new technologies: Opening up the laboratory. PET, vol. 16, pp. 55–95. Springer, Dordrecht (2013). https://doi.org/10.1007/978-94-007-7844-3_4

22. Fritzsche, D.J.: A model of decision-making incorporating ethical values. J. Bus. Ethics **10**, 841–852 (1991)

23. Gaudou, B., Lorini, E., Mayor, E.: Moral guilt: an agent-based model analysis. In: Advances in Social Simulation, pp. 95–106. Springer, Berlin (2014). https://doi.org/10.1007/978-3-642-39829-2_9

24. Guerrero, E., Lindgren, H.: Practical reasoning about complex activities. In: Demazeau, Y., Davidsson, P., Bajo, J., Vale, Z. (eds.) PAAMS 2017. LNCS (LNAI), vol. 10349, pp. 82–94. Springer, Cham (2017). https://doi.org/10.1007/978-3-319-59930-4_7

25. Haidt, J., Graham, J., Joseph, C.: Above and below left-right: ideological narratives and moral foundations. Psychol. Inq. **20**(2–3), 110–119 (2009)

26. Jäger, G., Reisinger, D.: Can we replicate real human behaviour using artificial neural networks? Math. Comput. Model. Dyn. Syst. (2022). https://doi.org/10.1080/13873954.2022.2039717

27. Kido, H.: Practical argumentation semantics for pareto optimality and its relationships with values. In: McBurney, P., Parsons, S., Rahwan, I. (eds.) ArgMAS 2011. LNCS (LNAI), vol. 7543, pp. 28–45. Springer, Heidelberg (2012). https://doi.org/10.1007/978-3-642-33152-7_3

28. Kitchenham, B.: Procedures for performing systematic reviews. Keele University, Keele, UK, vol. 33, pp. 1–26 (2004)

29. Meglino, B.M., Ravlin, E.C.: Individual values in organizations: concepts, controversies, and research. J. Manag. **24**(3), 351–389 (1998)

30. Mercuur, R., Dignum, F., Kashima, Y.: Changing habits using contextualized decision making. In: Jager, W., Verbrugge, R., Flache, A., de Roo, G., Hoogduin, L., Hemelrijk, C. (eds.) Advances in Social Simulation 2015. AISC, vol. 528, pp. 267–272. Springer, Cham (2017). https://doi.org/10.1007/978-3-319-47253-9_23

31. Mogles, N., Padget, J., Gabe-Thomas, E., Walker, I., Lee, J.H.: A computational model for designing energy behaviour change interventions. User Model. User-Adap. Inter. **28**(1), 1–34 (2017). https://doi.org/10.1007/s11257-017-9199-9

32. Osman, N., D'Inverno, M.: A computational framework of human values. In: AAMAS 2024: Proceedings of the 23rd International Conference on Autonomous Agents and Multiagent Systems, pp. 1531–1539. International Foundation for Autonomous Agents and Multiagent Systems (2024). https://doi.org/10.5555/3635637.3663013

33. Pereira, D.R., Gonçalves, L.V., Dimuro, G.P., Costa, A.C.R.: Towards the self-regulation of personality-based social exchange processes in multiagent systems. In: Zaverucha, G., da Costa, A.L. (eds.) SBIA 2008. LNCS (LNAI), vol. 5249, pp. 113–123. Springer, Heidelberg (2008). https://doi.org/10.1007/978-3-540-88190-2_17

34. Poel, I.: Design for value change. Ethics Inf. Technol. **23**(1), 27–31 (2018). https://doi.org/10.1007/s10676-018-9461-9

35. Pokahr, A., Braubach, L., Lamersdorf, W.: Jadex: a BDI reasoning engine. Multi-agent programming: languages, platforms and applications, pp. 149–174 (2005)

36. Rahimi, H., Trentin, I.F., Ramparany, F., Boissier, O.: Q-smash: Q-learning-based self-adaptation of human-centered internet of things. In: IEEE/WIC/ACM International Conference on Web Intelligence and Intelligent Agent Technology, pp. 694–698 (2021)

37. Rahimi, H., Trentin, I.F., Ramparany, F., Boissier, O.: SMASH: a semantic-enabled multi-agent approach for self-adaptation of human-centered IoT. In: Dignum, F., Corchado, J.M., De La Prieta, F. (eds.) PAAMS 2021. LNCS (LNAI), vol. 12946,

pp. 201–213. Springer, Cham (2021). https://doi.org/10.1007/978-3-030-85739-4_17

38. Rangel, A., Camerer, C., Montague, P.R.: A framework for studying the neurobiology of value-based decision making. Nat. Rev. Neurosci. **9**(7), 545–556 (2008)

39. Rao, A.S.: Agentspeak (l): BDI agents speak out in a logical computable language. In: European Workshop on Modelling Autonomous Agents in a Multi-Agent World, pp. 42–55. Springer (1996)

40. Rao, A.S., Georgeff, M.P.: Decision procedures for BDI logics (1998)

41. Rokeach, M.: The nature of human values. Free press (1973)

42. Schwartz, S.H.: Universals in the content and structure of values: theoretical advances and empirical tests in 20 countries. In: Advances in Experimental Social Psychology, vol. 25, pp. 1–65. Elsevier (1992)

43. Schwartz, S.H.: Basic human values: theory, methods, and application. Basic Human Values, pp. 1000–1023 (2007)

44. Schwartz, S.H.: An overview of the schwartz theory of basic values. Online Read. Psychol. Cult. **2**(1), 11 (2012)

45. Serramia, M., et al.: Moral values in norm decision making. In: Autonomous Agents and Multi-Agent Systems (AAMAS 2018) (2018)

46. Singh, D., Padgham, L., Logan, B.: Integrating BDI agents with agent-based simulation platforms. Auton. Agent. Multi-Agent Syst. **30**(6), 1050–1071 (2016). https://doi.org/10.1007/s10458-016-9332-x

47. Steg, L., De Groot, J.I., Dreijerink, L., Abrahamse, W., Siero, F.: General antecedents of personal norms, policy acceptability, and intentions: the role of values, worldviews, and environmental concern. Soc. Nat. Resour. **24**(4), 349–367 (2011)

48. Steg, L., Perlaviciute, G., van der Werff, E., Lurvink, J.: The significance of hedonic values for environmentally relevant attitudes, preferences, and actions. Environ. Behav. **46**(2), 163–192 (2012). https://doi.org/10.1177/0013916512454730

49. Szabo, J., Such, J.M., Criado, N.: Understanding the role of values and norms in practical reasoning. In: European Conference on Multi-Agent Systems, pp. 431–439. Springer (2020)

50. The MathWorks Inc.: Matlab version: 9.13.0 (r2022b) (2022). https://www.mathworks.com

51. Tisue, S., Wilensky, U.: Netlogo: a simple environment for modeling complexity. In: International Conference on Complex Systems, vol. 21, pp. 16–21. Citeseer (2004)

52. Tzeng, S.T.: Engineering normative and cognitive agents with emotions and values. In: Proceedings of the 21st International Conference on Autonomous Agents and Multiagent Systems, pp. 1878–1880 (2022)

53. Van De Schoot, R., et al.: An open source machine learning framework for efficient and transparent systematic reviews. Nat. Mach. Intell. **3**(2), 125–133 (2021)

54. Wohlin, C.: Guidelines for snowballing in systematic literature studies and a replication in software engineering. In: Proceedings of the 18th International Conference on Evaluation and Assessment in Software Engineering, pp. 1–10 (2014)

Modelling Moral Decision-Making in a Contractualist Artificial Agent

Giovanni Dalmasso[1], Luis Marcos-Vidal[1], and Clara Pretus[1,2(✉)]

[1] Hospital del Mar Research Institute, Barcelona, Spain
clara.pretus@uab.cat
[2] Department of Psychobiology and Methodology of Health Sciences, Universitat Autònoma de Barcelona, Barcelona, Spain

Abstract. As artificial intelligence (AI) systems become increasingly integrated into our daily lives, ensuring their ethical behavior is paramount. This paper introduces a novel approach to embedding moral cognition in AI based on contractualism, an ethical theory that deems actions appropriate if they can be justified based on the set of norms that govern interactions between pairs of agents. Our model, embodied in a robotic cleaning agent named Sweepy, makes decisions based on a combination of predefined norms and dynamic user feedback. This hybrid decision-making process allows Sweepy to align its behavior with individual user preferences, thus enhancing user satisfaction. Through extensive simulations, we demonstrate Sweepy's ability to learn and adapt its actions across different scenarios, illustrating the model's robustness and flexibility. This study highlights the advantages of the contractualist approach over utilitarian and deontological models, particularly in their support of user autonomy and fairness. Our findings underscore the need to develop AI systems capable of making ethically sound decisions in complex, real-world environments, paving the way for more trustworthy and user-centric AI applications.

Keywords: Moral Artificial Agent · Contractualism · Moral AI · Ethical Decision-Making

1 Introduction

1.1 Artificial Moral Systems

In recent years, artificial intelligence (AI) has made significant strides in integrating into various aspects of society, particularly through the use of generative AI. This technological revolution is impacting multiple sectors, including education [23], healthcare [2], and science [22]. The importance of these advances is highlighted by recent initiatives by international organizations that aim to establish guidelines for trustworthy AI [8,20]. These guidelines outline the essential

---

G. Dalmasso and L. Marcos-Vidal—Equal Contribution.

N. Osman and L. Steels (Eds.): VALE 2024, LNAI 15356, pp. 155–175, 2025.
https://doi.org/10.1007/978-3-031-85463-7_10

features that AI systems must have to be considered trustworthy. Trustworthy AI is fundamentally based on reliability, that is, it should perform the tasks it is designed for efficiently and reliably [24]. In some applications, such as face-detection machine learning algorithms, accurate performance alone may be sufficient to establish trustworthiness. Although ethical considerations like the diversity of training data are important, they are typically separate from the decision-making process of the AI system once it is deployed. However, in scenarios where AI actions directly impact humans, it is crucial that the AI model determines the rightness or wrongness of its actions. Therefore, for AI to be truly trustworthy, it must possess moral cognition capabilities that adhere to fundamental ethical principles.

Two common approaches to implementing morality in AI are utilitarianism and deontology [4]. Utilitarianism suggests that the best action is the one that generates the greatest overall good, focusing on the consequences of actions [18]. In contrast, deontology assesses actions based on their adherence to a set of rules or norms rather than their outcomes [1]. These ethical theories are readily applicable to AI: utilitarianism leverages AI's computational abilities to maximize positive outcomes, while deontology specifies which actions are prohibited or required.

Utilitarianism and deontology have significant limitations when applied to AI systems, especially when it comes to guaranteeing human autonomy and fairness, two crucial applied ethics principles. On one hand, utilitarianism focuses on aggregated benefits across individuals thus overlooking individual preferences. It also neglects the principle of fairness, which concerns the distribution of burdens and benefits, as long as the majority benefits (but see also [7]). Additionally, utilitarianism does not account for intentions or accountability. Since these concepts are central to human morality, AI systems based solely on consequentialism can feel dehumanizing [10]. As a result, people may perceive AI as having reduced moral agency and exhibit less trust in these systems. On the other hand, deontology's focus on adherence to moral rules can be rigid and lack context sensitivity. Although this approach ensures that certain actions are inherently prohibited or required, it may fail to accommodate the nuances of specific situations and individual relationships. Thus, AI systems based solely on deontological principles might struggle to adapt their actions to diverse and dynamic environments.

How can we create systems that prioritize human autonomy and fairness while reducing dehumanization? While the use of contractualist theory in AI ethics is largely unexplored, related concepts have been touched upon in multi-agent systems research. For example, a framework for the negotiation of norms between agents was proposed in [17], and the balance between the adherence to rules and the explanations in robotics was explored in [3] both of which echo ideas aligned with contractualism. Similarly, a framework for ethical decision-making in autonomous systems, focusing on dynamic behavioral adaptation to ethical norms was proposed in [9]. However, these works do not explicitly employ contractualism and are primarily theoretical, lacking practical application in embodied agents such as robots. Our work advances this research by directly integrating contractualist reasoning into a physical robot, thereby illustrating both the potential and challenges of applying this approach in real-world scenarios.

In this paper, we present a model of moral cognition for AI based on contractualism. Contractualism in the broad sense is a set of ethical theories that define morality in terms of agreements between free and equal individuals. However, in this article, we refer to contractualism in the narrow sense, namely, the normative ethical theory described by T.M. Scanlon in 1998 [15]. One of the desirable properties of this contractualist theory for AI applications is that it is not a political theory about what every agent in a system agrees upon (such as Rawls'), but it can be conceptualized as an epistemic theory about how an individual must behave based on principles others could not reasonably reject [15, 16]. For now on, when we mention contractualism, we will refer to this specific theory.

Contractualists consider an action appropriate if it can be justified to its recipient based on the terms of the specific relationship the agent has with the recipient [15]. Justification can be based on self-centered and other-centered reasons. For instance, someone may have a given preference not because it benefits them but because it benefits others. This attribute allegedly makes aggregation redundant. However, in the case where the moral agent is an artificial system, self-centered reasons lose importance because the human always has priority over the AI system. Thus, the justification of an action must be based on the preferences of AI users. These properties make contractualism especially suitable for supporting autonomy and fairness in human-AI interactions.

Contractualism, in this context, is grounded in the assumption that moral actions are justified by the agreements between agents, typically in a dyadic relationship. However, this theory can be extended to multiagent systems, where norms are negotiated and enforced within a broader social context. The current implementation focuses on dyadic interactions, where the AI model aligns its actions with the preferences of a single user. Nevertheless, contractualist principles could be generalized to scenarios involving multiple agents, where the appropriateness of actions is evaluated not just in terms of individual preferences, but also in relation to a collective agreement or societal norms. This expansion could involve modeling more complex social contracts, where multiple norms interact and are enforced within a community of agents, whether human or artificial.

Contractualism can be differentiated from other contract-based theories in that it emphasizes the rights and obligations of individuals negotiated within specific social relationships ("What we owe each other"). It is also different than utilitarianism because it evaluates actions within their specific context instead of focusing on their outcomes (consequences). For instance, a contractualist agent recognizes that it is wrong for someone to punch someone else even if they miss. In this sense, it is similar to deontology, as it assesses an action against a set of norms. However, unlike deontology, these norms are dynamic and context-sensitive. An example of this dynamic nature is evident that multiple agents have different preferences, leading to diverse norms governing their interactions.

We propose an implementation of a moral artificial system based on contractualism. To achieve this, we first outline the criteria a moral agent must meet to be considered "contractualist". To our knowledge, there are no previous implementations of contractualism in artificial agents. We then introduce an artificial system designed to fulfill these criteria, describing it both theoretically and mathematically. Finally, we test the system using simulated data to demonstrate its behavior in various situations.

2   A Contractualist Model of Moral Cognition for AI

2.1   Conceptual Model

In this section we will describe a moral system that is based on contractualism. As mentioned above, contractualism is based on three main characteristics: (1) evaluation of actions *per se* and not their consequences, (2) adaptive computation of the suitability of actions depending on who the moral patient is and (3) justification of its decision based on other-centered reasons. We believe that a deontological-like system addresses (1), since it uses norms to evaluate the appropriateness of actions *a priori*. However, contractualism diverges from traditional deontological AI by requiring norms to prohibit an action for some recipients while allowing it for others (to comply with (2)). Therefore, we use norms that can be adapted to different individuals for the decision-making process of our artificial system. Finally, justification (3) arises naturally from the decision-making process in the sense that an action is justified based on the "believed" relevance of the norms it is related to. That is, an action is performed if it does not violate any norm or if the norms it violates are not relevant to the recipient of the action. Thus, the function of the moral model of this system is to inhibit "immoral" or inappropriate behaviors.

This inhibitory approach to morality allows for the flexible deployment of other components of the system, which may be responsible for proposing the evaluated actions (e.g., sweeping someone's room in case of a cleaning AI system), as well as detecting contextual information about the action. If the action affects a human, the morality module is "activated" and the moral evaluation process begins. The purpose of this process is to assess whether the action is appropriate or not in a given context based on an appropriateness score. We define this appropriateness score as a combination of norms related to the action weighted by their relevance for the action patient. For example, if the cleaning AI needs to sweep someone's room, one norm can be cleaning on weekend, and another norm to clean when there is a visitor in the room. The appropriateness of the action will depend on how relevant these two norms are for the room's owner (the moral patient).

In our proposed system norms are predefined, which may change in future versions of the system. Additionally, we also assume that contextual information is available, including the relation between the norms and the evaluated action, as well as the identification of the moral patient from a stack of individuals. Thus, the elements that the model needs to estimate are how relevant these norms are for the moral patient (the room's owner) and how they are combined (the relative weight of each norm). To preserve the human-centric nature of contractualism, these parameters are learned directly from human feedback [6]. In case of negative feedback, the action can be justified in terms of the relevance of the assumed norms that were violated for the patient. This justification depends on the parameters of the model, which are communicated to users in natural language [21]. A schematic representation of this model is shown in Fig. 1. In the rest of this section, we present an example of how to implement this contractualist moral agent.

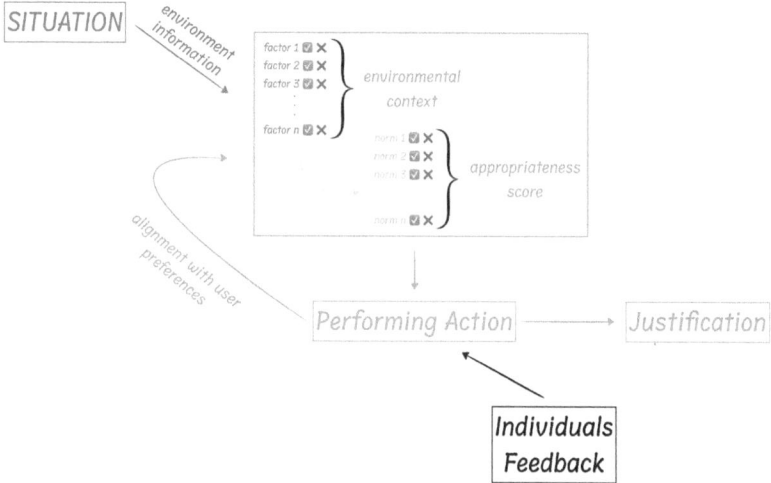

Fig. 1. Schematic representation of the contractualist moral cognition model for AI.

The methodology integrates autonomous decision-making, user interaction, and feedback-based learning. In this section we will describe how to optimize the cleaning schedule of an autonomous contractualist robot. Using feedback and continuously updating its parameters, the system aims to align its actions with user preferences, improving the overall user experience. This approach demonstrates the potential of adaptive learning algorithms in practical applications involving human-robot interactions.

2.2   Mathematical Model

This section elaborates on the mathematical framework employed to simulate and scrutinize the decision-making mechanism of a contractualist cleaning robot (*Sweepy*), which interacts with individual users. The cardinal aim is to enhance Sweepy's cleaning choices based on user feedback, thereby maximizing user satisfaction over time as measured by the alignment of Sweepy's parameters with the user's preferences.

Cleaning Robot. Sweepy is designed to autonomously determine which are the acceptable times to clean a room, considering both the current situation and (past) individual user feedback. The robot comprises two modules: the situation evaluator and the appropriateness calculator.

1. *Appropriateness*: The appropriateness module serves as an internal moral evaluation system, represented by the function $A_R^i(t, v, w)$. This function evaluates the appropriateness of cleaning at a given time t, considering specific conditions. The equation is as follows:

$$A_R^i(t, v, w) = \left(1 + vC^i + wK^i\right) f^i(t) \tag{1}$$

where the parameters are defined as follows:
   - $f^i(t)$: denotes the cleaning preference of user i over the course of the hours of the day t. This time norm, modeled as a continuous function over a 24-hour cycle, is predefined based on hypothetical scenarios but could be adapted using real-world user data by evaluating satisfaction scores at different times.
   - C^i: a norm adjustment scalar that represents the relevance of the "visitor" norm for user i.
   - K^i: a norm adjustment scalar that represents the relevance of the "weekend" norm for user i.
   - v: a binary indicator denoting whether the user has a visit (1 if visit, 0 if alone).
   - w: a binary indicator for the type of day (1 if weekend, 0 if weekday).

   The parameters $f^i(t)$, C^i, and K^i are initialized with baseline values and dynamically adjusted by the robot to align with the preferences of the user (i) currently considered.

   The choice of this specific functional form to represent norms is motivated by its flexibility in capturing the varying importance of norms across different contexts and users. The scalar norm adjustments in the function allow for dynamic tuning, reflecting how the significance of each norm can change based on user feedback. This approach, while formal, provides a systematic method for generalizing the representation of norms, ensuring that the model can adapt to a wide range of user preferences and scenarios. Future work could explore alternative functional forms or incorporate machine learning techniques to further enhance this adaptability.

2. *Situation* (Room): This module is responsible for monitoring the environmental context, providing Sweepy with essential information regarding the time of day, whether the user considered (i) has a visit, and whether it is the weekend. This situational awareness allows Sweepy to make informed decisions about when to perform cleaning tasks. In our example, this module provides i, t, v, and w to the appropriateness calculator.

Sweepy's operation is guided by its moral appropriateness and situational context. User feedback on the appropriateness of Sweepy's actions enables the robot to continually refine its decision-making process [5].

Through the integration of its internal modules and the incorporation of user feedback, Sweepy ensures that its cleaning schedule is both contextually appropriate and tailored to the user's specific preferences. This approach improves overall user satisfaction and improves efficiency in maintaining a clean environment.

Decision-Making Process. Sweepy's decision-making algorithm synthesizes real-time feedback and situational variables to dynamically adjust its $A_R^i(t, v, w)$. This ensures that cleaning operations are optimized to improve user satisfaction, aligning Sweepy's cleaning schedule with user preferences and situational demands.

Epsilon-Greedy Strategy: Sweepy employs an epsilon-greedy strategy to decide whether to clean the room [19]:

$$\begin{cases} \text{random choice} & \text{if } \varepsilon > \text{ random(0,1)} \\ \text{exploit } (A_{\text{clean}}^i > A_{\text{not clean}}^i) & \text{otherwise} \end{cases}$$

where A_{clean}^i and $A_{\text{not clean}}^i$ are the expected feedback values of the individual (i) for cleaning and not cleaning, respectively. The exploration parameter ε decays over time as $\varepsilon \leftarrow \lambda\varepsilon$, allowing Sweepy to gradually shift from exploration to exploitation, thereby refining its decision-making process to consistently enhance user satisfaction.

Expected Feedback: The expected feedback for cleaning and not cleaning is estimated as:

$$\begin{cases} \text{expected clean} & = A_R^i(t, v, w) \\ \text{expected not clean} & = 0 \end{cases}$$

The expression "expected not clean $= 0$" implies that if the robot decides not to clean, there is no positive or negative feedback expected from the user. This baseline assumption simplifies the decision-making process, although future versions of the model could incorporate more nuanced outcomes for inaction.

Sweepy uses this information to balance exploration (trying new actions) and exploitation (choosing the best-known action).

2.3   Feedback and Parameter Update

The robot's parameters are iteratively updated based on the feedback received by the individual from its actions [13]. Specifically, feedback is modeled as a function of the user's observed satisfaction with robot actions, which is inferred from predefined preference functions. This feedback loop allows the robot to adjust its cleaning schedule in subsequent iterations with the goal of maximizing user satisfaction over time. Although the feedback mechanism is inspired by previous work on reinforcement learning [13], this implementation specifically tailors it to ethical decision making in a contractualist framework.

For each individual (i), the robot computes its appropriateness value $A_R^i(t, v, w)$ at time t, given the indicators v (whether the individual has a visit), w (whether it is a weekend) and the individual's feedback F. Based on these, it can compute the error (δ) as the difference between the feedback (F) received and the robot's computed appropriateness value ($A_R(t, v, w)$):

$$\delta = F - A_R^i(t, v, w)$$

The error is then normalized to ensure stable updates:

$$\hat{\delta} = \frac{\delta}{\max(1, |\delta|)}$$

Parameter Update: Sweepy updates its function $f^i(t)$, the constant C^i, and the constant K^i based on the normalized error and the partial derivatives of the appropriateness function with respect to each parameter using gradient descent [11]. The updates for each parameter are as follows.

$$f^i(t) \leftarrow f^i(t) + \eta_f \hat{\delta}$$
$$C^i \leftarrow C^i + \eta_C \hat{\delta} \qquad \text{if } v = 1$$
$$K^i \leftarrow K^i + \eta_K \hat{\delta} \qquad \text{if } w = 1$$

where η_f, η_C, η_K are the learning rates.

2.4   Justification

Together with every decision, Sweepy sends a friendly message that explains in plain language what led to the decision to clean or not clean the room. Since Sweepy employs an epsilon-greedy strategy, as explained earlier, the decision-making process can fall into two main categories: a random decision (exploratory strategy) or a decision based on exploiting acquired knowledge (exploitative strategy).

In the case of a random decision, where Sweepy is exploring different actions to gather more information, the messages are straightforward. One of them might look like the following:

```
message: Hi there! I'm Sweepy, your friendly cleaning
    robot. Today, I'm in an adventurous mood, so I
    decided to clean up. Exploring different options
    helps me learn what makes you happy.
```

If Sweepy uses its accumulated knowledge to make a decision, the message is more informative and tailored to reflect the reasoning behind the action. These messages might provide insight into why the particular time was chosen based on past feedback and learned preferences. An example of these messages might be:

```
message: Hello! It's Sweepy here.
It's 7:00, and I've decided it's the perfect moment to
    tidy up! My experience tell me that cleaning when:
- it's 7:00
- you have a visit
- it's a weekday
usually brings a smile to your face.
According to my records, the benefit of cleaning now is
    quite high with an expected appropriateness score
    of 99.14%.
I'm confident that a cleaner space will make your day
    brighter!

message: Hi! Sweepy here.
It's 23:00, and after thinking it over, I decided not
    to clean right now.
Given that:
- it's 23:00
- you are alone
- it is a weekday
cleaning doesn't seem to have significant benefits
    based on my past records. The expected
    appropriateness score is indeed only 17.33%.
So, I'll take a break and be ready for the next best
    opportunity to clean!
```

These messages are generated from predefined templates that are populated with context-specific information, such as the time of day, presence of visitors, and day of the week. These templates are designed to communicate the robot's decision process clearly and transparently to the user. These friendly and informative messages not only help users understand the robot's actions but also foster a sense of engagement and transparency in the robot's operations. By communicating the rationale behind its decisions, Sweepy ensures that users are kept informed and involved in the optimization process, thereby enhancing user satisfaction and trust in the system. Future work could involve the development of more sophisticated natural language generation systems to create fully dynamic messages based on real-time data.

2.5   Iterative Simulation Process

The iterative simulation process is designed to emulate the decision-making and learning behavior of a robotic cleaning agent (Sweepy) in a dynamic environment. We detail the three main steps of the iterative process, explaining the rationale and methodology behind the robot's decisions and parameter updates.

1. *Random Selection of Hour, Visitor Indicator, Weekend Indicator:*

At the beginning of each iteration, three key variables (hour of the day, visit, weekend) are randomly selected to simulate varying conditions throughout the day for every individual:

- Hour of the Day t: an integer t is randomly selected from the range 0 to 23, representing each hour of a 24-hour day. This selection ensures that the robot encounters different times of day across iterations, capturing diurnal variations in cleaning preferences.
- Visitor Indicator v: a binary variable v is randomly chosen, where $v = 1$ indicates that the user has a visit, and $v = 0$ indicates that the student is alone. This binary choice models the varying social contexts in which the robot might operate.
- Weekend Indicator w: a binary variable w is randomly selected, where $w = 1$ signifies a weekend, and $w = 0$ signifies a weekday. This variable introduces variability in the robot's operational environment, accounting for different behaviors and routines on weekends versus weekdays.

2. *Decision-Making Process:*
   Sweepy uses these variables to decide whether to clean the room. The decision-making process is governed by an epsilon-greedy strategy, which balances exploration (random choices) and exploitation (optimal choices based on current knowledge).
   Cleaning Decision: Sweepy determines whether to clean the room of the individual (i) based on the values of t, v and w. In addition, a justification message is generated. Sweepy's learning policy evolves as it assimilates feedback from the environment.

3. *Feedback and Parameter Update:*
   Depending on the cleaning decision, the robot either receives feedback and updates its parameters or records a lack of action. In the current theoretical model, Sweepy's feedback mechanism is simulated by predefined user preference functions, which allow the robot to adjust its cleaning behavior in a controlled environment. In a real-world application, this feedback could be generated through direct user interaction, such as pressing a button to indicate "start cleaning" or "stop cleaning". This would provide dynamic feedback data, enabling the system to better adapt to actual user preferences. Future developments of this model could involve collecting real-time feedback, ensuring a closer alignment with real user behavior and preferences.
   - If Sweepy Decides to Clean:
     - Feedback: Sweepy receives feedback from the individual (i), which is a function of t, v, and w. This feedback reflects the appropriateness of the cleaning action, given the individual's preferences and the contextual factors.
     - Parameter Update: Sweepy updates its internal parameters $f^i(t)$, C^i, and K^i based on the received feedback adjusting them to minimize the error between the expected and received feedback.
   - If Sweepy Decides Not to Clean:
     - Feedback: a *None* value is recorded indicating that no feedback was received because no action was taken.

This iterative simulation process continues for a predetermined number of iterations, allowing Sweepy to adapt its cleaning strategy over time.

3   Use of the Model

To evaluate the model's performance, we investigated two distinct scenarios, *Case 1* and *Case 2*, each involving an individual with different cleaning preferences across the 24-hour daily cycle, $f_1(t)$ and $f_2(t)$.

The individual's *appropriateness*, $A_I(t, v, w)$, is defined similarly to the robot's appropriateness of Sect. 2.2:

$$A_I(t, v, w) = (1 + vC + wK)\, f(t) \tag{2}$$

where the parameters retain the same definitions as the one of the robot.

In this formulation, the basic user's cleaning time preference $f(t)$ is adjusted by whether the user has any visits (C) and whether the cleaning day is a weekend (K). Furthermore, the influence of these components on the appropriateness can be deduced from (2) as follows:

$$\alpha_f = \frac{f(t)}{A_I(t, v, w)}, \qquad \alpha_C = \frac{C}{A_I(t, v, w)}, \qquad \alpha_K = \frac{K}{A_I(t, v, w)}.$$

Case 1: the individual's cleaning preference function, $f_1(t)$, exhibits an undulated form with a peak preference hour at $T_p = 7$. This function is mathematically defined as follows:

$$f_1(t) = \cos^2\left[\pi\left(\frac{t}{24} - \frac{T_n}{2\pi}\right)\right] \tag{3}$$

where

$$T_n = 2\pi\left(\frac{T_p}{24}\right)$$

represents the normalized peak time for a 24-hour cycle, expressed in radians (Fig. 2).

Case 2: the cleaning preference function, $f_2(t)$, is characterized by a repeating squared pattern, defined as a piece-wise function that repeats every 6 h:

$$f_2(t) = \begin{cases} 1.0 & \text{if } t\%6 < 2 \\ 0.0 & \text{if } t\%6 \geq 2 \end{cases} \tag{4}$$

where

$$t\%6 = t - 6\left\lfloor \frac{t}{6} \right\rfloor$$

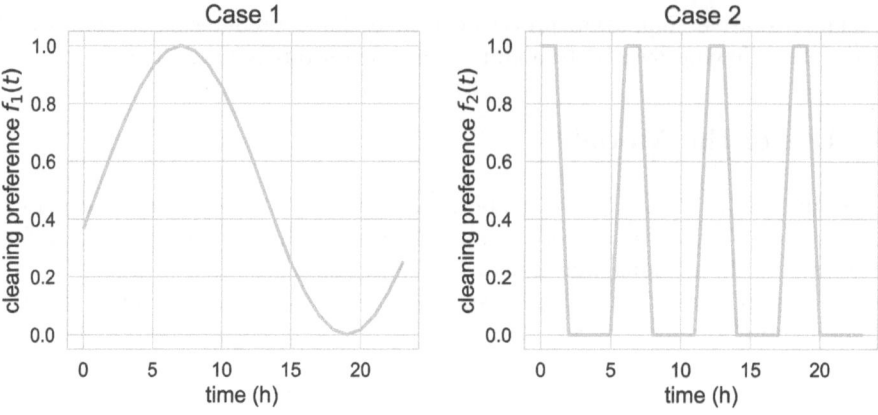

Fig. 2. Cleaning preference functions for the two scenarios. Left: undulating pattern (*Case 1*) and right: repeating squared pattern (*Case 2*).

and $\lfloor \frac{t}{6} \rfloor$ denotes the floor function, which provides the largest integer less than or equal to $\frac{t}{6}$ (Fig. 2).

In both cases, the values of the norm adjustment scalars are set as $C = -0.3$ and $K = 0.08$. These coefficients are based on preliminary simulations that aimed to balance the influence of social context (visitor presence) and temporal context (weekend / weekday) on the suitability of cleaning actions. These parameters were chosen to reflect the general expectation that cleaning is less appropriate when visitors are present (hence a negative C value) and slightly more appropriate on weekends (hence a positive K value). These values can be adjusted on the basis of specific user preferences or empirical data in real-world implementations. However, it is important to note that these values represent the user real preferences, not Sweepy's knowledge about them. Sweepy will estimate their values from the feedback after each interaction.

Thus, as illustrated in Fig. 3 and Fig. 4, combining the indicators av (whether the individual has a visit) and w (whether it is a weekend) results in four different modulations of the student appropriateness $A_I(t)$:

– alone, not weekend
– alone, weekend
– visit, not weekend
– visit, weekend

To evaluate the adaptive learning capabilities of the robotic cleaning agent, Sweepy, we initialized the robot's parameters with constant values: $f^i(t) = C^i = K^i = 0.5$. This baseline allows the robot to begin learning and adapting its behavior from a neutral starting point. The learning rates are set to $\eta_f = \eta_C = \eta_K = 0.5$ to allow significant adjustments in response to feedback during the early stages of learning. The performance of Sweepy's learning algorithm was evaluated over 500 iterations, during which the robot continually updated its parameters $f^i(t)$, C^i, and K^i based on the feedback received from the individual.

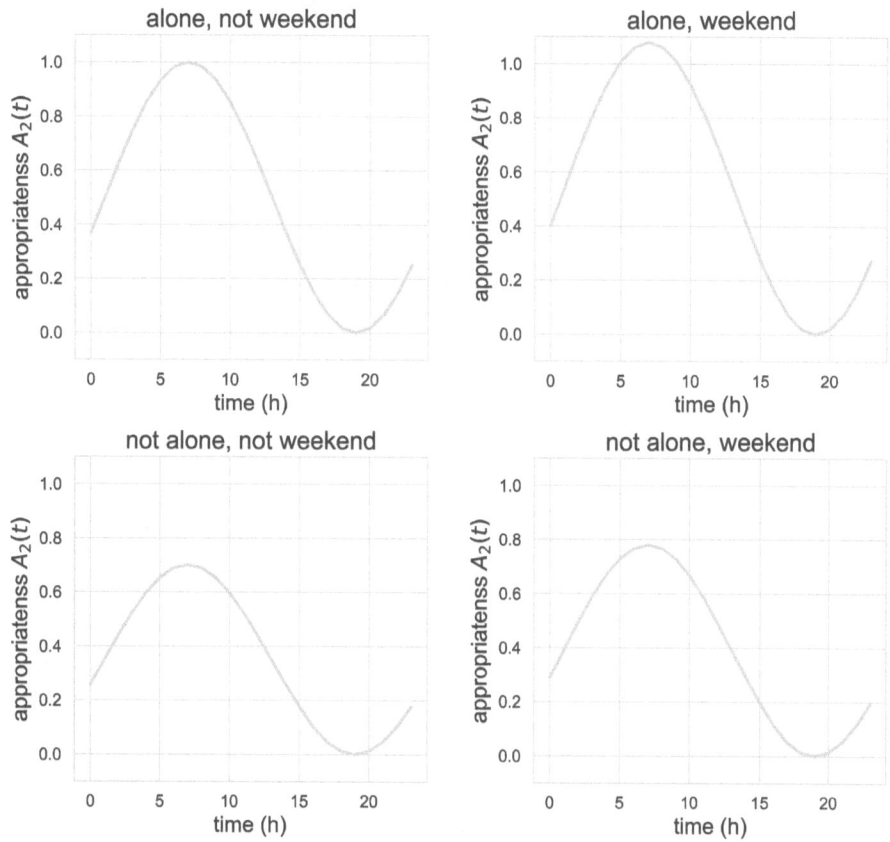

Fig. 3. Modulations of appropriateness in *Case 1*, showing variations based on social and temporal contexts.

Figure 5 and Fig. 6 illustrate the evolution of the parameters $f^i(t)$, C^i, and K^i over time and across iterations in the two cases.

Examining the evolution of the parameters, it can be seen that $f^i(t)$, initially set at 0.5, evolves significantly as Sweepy learns the cleaning preferences of the user throughout the day (Fig. 5 and Fig. 6 top left). These plots show the hourly changes within a 24-hour cycle and the adjustments made over 500 iterations. The undulating and piecewise characteristics of $f(t)$ indicate that Sweepy is becoming increasingly adept at learning optimal cleaning times based on user preferences.

The initial modulator C^i starts at 0.5 and undergoes substantial adjustments throughout the iterations. The left plots of Fig. 5 and Fig. 6 illustrate the progression of C^i, reflecting Sweepy's learning about the appropriateness of cleaning actions when the user is has visit. As shown, C^i fluctuates and gradually stabilizes, suggesting that the robot effectively learns to modulate its cleaning behavior based on the presence of others.

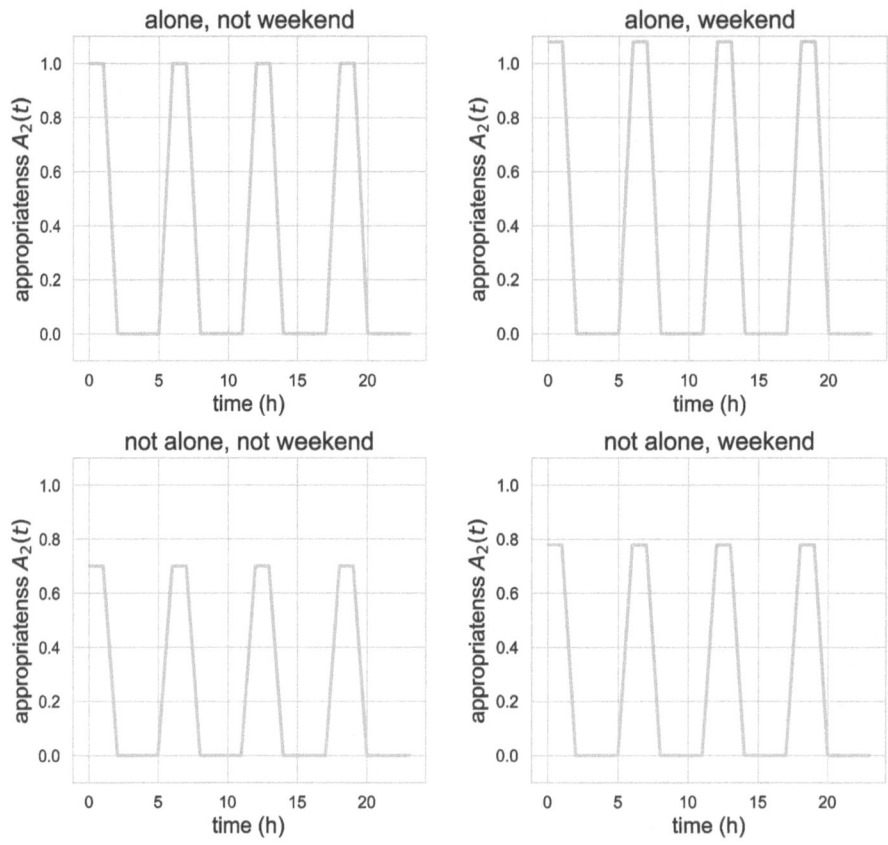

Fig. 4. Modulations of appropriateness in *Case 2*, showing variations based on social and temporal contexts.

Similarly, the initial value of K^i is 0.5, and its evolution is depicted in the right plots of Fig. 5 and Fig. 6. K adjusts over iterations, capturing Sweepy's learning about the appropriateness of cleaning actions during weekends. The adjustments in K^i demonstrate how the robot refines its understanding of different temporal contexts and adapts its behavior accordingly.

During the 500 iterations, the parameters $f^i(t)$, C^i, and K^i exhibit significant changes, showcasing the robot's ability to adapt its decision-making process to maintain acceptable cleaning operations. The gradual stabilization of these parameters indicates that Sweepy effectively learns from feedback and fine-tunes its actions to enhance user satisfaction.

In general, the iterative learning process and the corresponding evolution of the parameters demonstrate the robustness of the Sweepy learning algorithm. Adaptive adjustments highlight the robot's ability to personalize its cleaning schedule based on user preferences and situational variables, thus maintaining its performance in a dynamic environment.

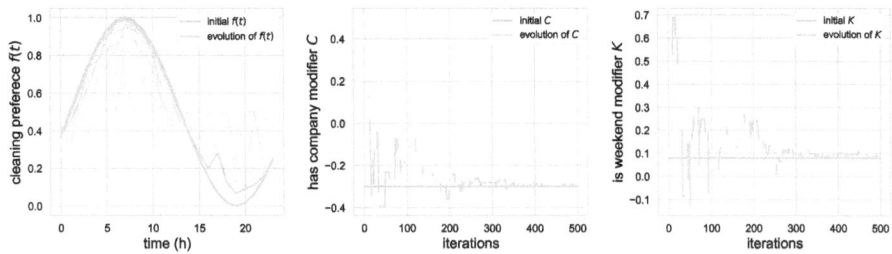

Fig. 5. Evolution of parameters $f^i(t)$, C^i, and K^i over 500 iterations in *Case 1*.

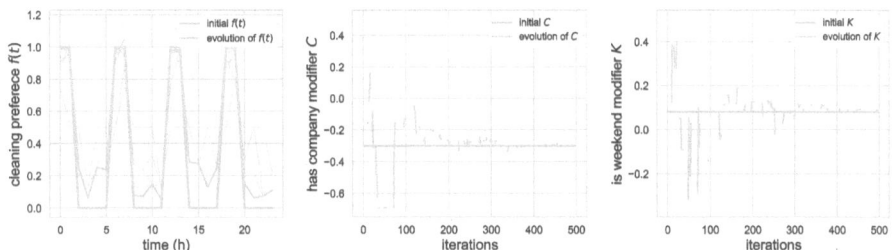

Fig. 6. Evolution of parameters $f^i(t)$, C^i, and K^i over 500 iterations in *Case 2*.

A detailed view of Sweepy's iterative received feedback and the decision pattern are shown in Fig. 7 and Fig. 8. The evolution of feedback and decision-making behavior over the iterations is pivotal in understanding how the robot adapts its decision-making over time based on feedback and changing situational variables providing significant insights into Sweepy's learning dynamics.

The single feedback instances and cumulative feedback are tracked across 500 iterations (left plots Fig. 7 and Fig. 8). Initially, the feedback values exhibit considerable variability, reflecting the robot's exploratory actions. Sweepy begins by testing a wide range of cleaning actions, leading to scattered feedback results. However, as the iterations progress, the feedback values start to converge. This convergence signifies an improvement in user satisfaction as the robot refines its actions to better align with user preferences. The cumulative feedback plot demonstrates a steady increase over time, underscoring the overall improvement in Sweepy performance. This upward trend indicates that the robot's learning algorithm effectively integrates user feedback to maintain its cleaning strategy within an acceptable range.

In addition to feedback, the hourly distribution of cleaning decisions made by Sweepy throughout the iterations is shown (right plots Fig. 7 and Fig. 8). Initially, Sweepy's cleaning decisions are dispersed over various hours, indicating its exploratory phase. This broad distribution is necessary for the robot to gather sufficient data on user preferences at different times of the day. As iterations advance, a more distinct pattern emerges with cleaning decisions becoming concentrated around specific hours. This concentration reflects the robot's learned preferences, aligning more closely with the peak cleaning times favored by the user. Sweepy's ability to identify and adapt to these optimal cleaning windows demonstrates its evolving proficiency in decision-making.

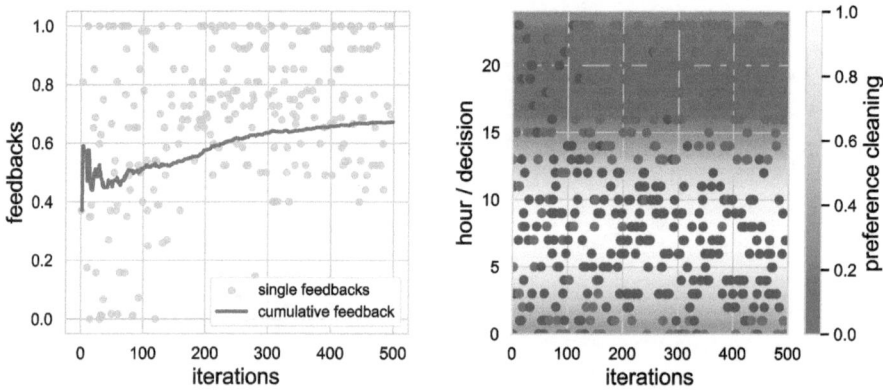

Fig. 7. *Case 1*: Evolution of feedback and cleaning decisions.

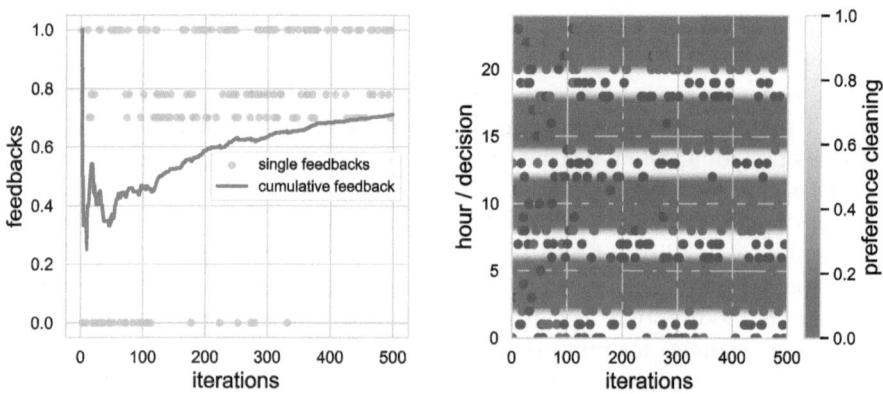

Fig. 8. *Case 2*: Evolution of feedback and cleaning decisions.

The general patterns observed in the parameter evolution, feedback and decision plots highlight the iterative and adaptive nature of Sweepy's learning algorithm. Dynamic adjustments in parameters such as $f^i(t)$, C^i, and K^i showcase Sweepy's ability to respond to varying user feedback and situational contexts. These adjustments are essential to fine-tune the robot decision-making process, ensuring that it remains effective and user-centered.

During the 500 iterations, the gradual stabilization of the parameters and the convergence of feedback values demonstrate the robustness of Sweepy's learning mechanism. Initially, Sweepy operates in an exploratory phase, testing different actions to gather feedback. As it accumulates data, the robot transitions to an exploitative phase, performing actions that align with the user preferences learned. This transition is reflected in the convergence of cumulative feedback and the stabilization of parameter values, indicating that Sweepy has effectively learned to maintain its cleaning strategy within an acceptable range based on user feedback.

4 Discussion

We present an AI agent that can discern appropriate actions based on a con-tractualist framework. This artificial moral system fulfills the three conditions we that propose make a system contractualist: (1) evaluation of the actions *per se* and not their consequences, (2) adaptive computation of the appropriateness of actions depending on who the moral patient is, and (3) transparent justification of its decision based on other-centered reasons. Our implementation of this type of system exhibited morally acceptable behavior, as evidenced by a reduction in negative feedback from users during the learning process.

The simulations demonstrated that using a contractualist approach enabled the robotic cleaning agent, Sweepy, to effectively learn and adapt to different user preferences in two distinct scenarios. In both cases, Sweepy showed a significant improvement in aligning its cleaning actions with user preferences, as evidenced by the evolution and stabilization of the parameters $f^i(t)$, C^i, and K^i over 500 iterations. The undulating and piecewise characteristics of $f(t)$ highlighted Sweepy's capability to identify and adhere to appropriate cleaning times based on user feedback. Additionally, the adjustments in C^i and K^i illustrated the robot's learning regarding the appropriateness of cleaning actions in different social and temporal contexts. It is important to note that while in the example of this study the norms are the hour of the day, if the agent is alone or if it is weekend day, the model can be generalize to other norms for different applications, since it only learns the weight of each norm and how to combine them.

The contractualist approach offers a unique contribution to the moral decision-making framework by simulating a social contract between the AI sys-tem and the user, in which the AI model respects user autonomy and fairness by aligning its actions with context-specific norms and individual preferences. While Sweepy does not engage in a literal social contract, the contractualist framework guides its decision-making process to ensure that its actions are jus-tified and ethically sound. This contrasts with utilitarian models that prioritize aggregate benefits and deontological models that apply fixed rules irrespective of the moral patient's preferences. As a disadvantage, the complexity of the contractualist model significantly surpasses that of traditional deontological and utilitarian frameworks due to the increased number of parameters and their dynamic adjustments. Deontological and utilitarian models are computationally less intensive. Deontological models rely on fixed norms equally applied to all situations, while utilitarian models focus on maximizing overall good with fewer variables. In contrast, the Sweepy model must continually update and refine its parameters based on individual user feedback and contextual factors, leading to a higher computational load. This requires a robust computational infrastructure capable of handling real-time data processing and adaptation. Thus, computational cost remains a significant consideration, especially when scaling the system to multiple users or more complex environments.

Although the paper contrasts contractualism with utilitarianism, a broader discussion of consequentialism is necessary to fully understand the implications of these ethical frameworks. Consequentialism, in its various forms, prioritizes outcomes and often involves the aggregation of individual utilities to maximize overall welfare. This approach, however, raises questions about value commensurability—how different values or preferences can be compared and aggregated. Contractualism, in contrast, avoids these issues by focusing on the justification of actions within specific relationships, rather than attempting to aggregate values across a population. This distinction is crucial, as it highlights how contractualism can respect individual autonomy and fairness without reducing ethical decisions to a mere calculation of aggregated benefits.

While the current implementation does not fully realize the dynamic and context-sensitive norms that differentiate contractualism from deontological approaches, it lays the groundwork for future developments. The key contribution here is the introduction of a framework where norms can, in principle, be adjusted based on user feedback, paving the way for a more personalized and context-aware ethical decision-making process. Unlike deontological models that apply rules uniformly, our approach is designed to learn the norms from the feedback, thereby gradually aligning with each user's specific preferences. From a different perspective, we can see deontology as an ontology of norms that are applied to the whole system, while contractualism (at least the version that we have implemented) is an epistemology in which the agent learns the appropriateness of each norm from and for each other agent. Thus, the current implementation allows for regulating dyadic interactions, even though contractualism can also be applied to determine norms in the ontological sense.

Future work should include comparative simulations to quantitatively assess the computational demands and ethical performance of contractualist models against deontological and utilitarian models, providing insights into the trade-offs between computational cost and the ethical robustness of AI systems. One way to reduce the computational cost of our system is to include initial templates of norm preferences to be used with unknown individuals. This strategy is grounded in the fact that when we (as moral agents) know a new person we are not blindfolded to the actions this person could accept. There are common preferences among humans, and they can be used for quicker parameter optimization as well as to reduce negative feedback in the first interactions. However, this approach has to be used only under uncertainty conditions, since the goal of our system is to adapt to individual preferences and not universal ones. For more accurate initialization templates, social categories can also be used, since preferences across norms tend to correlate within the same social group. That is, some norms are culturally dependent and thus will be related to social group categorizations.

The use of social templates takes advantage of common underlying features between norms, which can be related to values. Value is defined here as something that helps choose one thing over another [14]. As an example, imagine a situation where someone gives negative feedback to any action affecting their physical integrity. In that situation, that person *values* has physical integrity. So, a model can exploit these commonalities between norms to create accurate initial templates and reduce its estimation time. Previous norm-value alignment models [12, 17] could link values with norms in our system.

In this initial implementation of Sweepy, we did not take into account the type of relationship between the agent and the moral patient, which is central to contractualism [15]. We wanted to test the model in a simple situation with only two individuals who hold the same type of relationship with Sweepy. Future versions of Sweepy should implement the type of relationship it holds with each moral patient as a modulator of each norm relevance. Identifying the type of relationship between the agent and the patient could also provide initial templates of norms preferences, which could later be individualized to given moral patients. For instance, in our simulation scenario we could add workers of the building to whom Sweepy may have different obligations than the hosts.

Despite promising results, there are several limitations to the current model and simulation. One primary concern is the potential bias in user feedback, such as confirmation bias, recency bias, social desirability bias, sampling bias, and feedback fatigue, which could skew the learning process. Mitigating these biases involves strategies like ensuring diverse user participation, anonymizing feedback, and using algorithms to detect and adjust for biases. Additionally, the simulation's simplicity may not fully capture the complexity of real-world scenarios, where user preferences can be more nuanced and variable.

One of the key aspects of implementing contractualist theory in AI systems is managing the life-cycle of norms, which includes their design, promulgation, activation, and derogation. In our model, the norms are initially predefined, but can evolve based on user feedback, which serves as a mechanism for "promulgation" and "activation". Compliance is monitored through the continuous feedback loop, where the AI model adjusts its behavior to align with the user's expectations, effectively "enforcing" the norms. However, the model currently does not explicitly address the derogation of norms and when and how a norm should be overridden or discarded. This could be an area for future research, where norms are treated as more dynamic entities, closely tied to evolving user values and preferences. Furthermore, the relationship between norms and values in this model is crucial, as values guide the prioritization and adjustment of norms. Future iterations of the model could further explore how values influence the life-cycle of norms, especially in complex, multi-agent environments.

Future research should focus on addressing these limitations and expanding the model's applicability. Enhancing the robustness of the feedback mechanism to account for potential biases is crucial. In addition, extending the model to include more complex and varied scenarios will provide a better understanding of its applicability in the real world. Real-world testing in different environments, such as healthcare and customer service, will also be essential to validate the model's effectiveness. Further exploration of hybrid ethical frameworks that combine the strengths of contractualism with other ethical theories could also offer new insights and improvements.

Integrating moral cognition into AI systems is imperative as these systems become more embedded in our daily lives. The contractualist approach, as demonstrated by Sweepy, offers a promising pathway to developing AI that respects user autonomy and fairness. By learning from user feedback and providing transparent justifications for its actions, Sweepy exemplifies how AI can achieve trustworthy and ethical decision-making. The continued refinement and testing of such models will be vital in ensuring that AI systems contribute positively to society.

Acknowledgments. Funded by the European Innovation Council (EIC) under the Horizon Europe research and innovation programme (Grant agreement No. 101070930). Views and opinions expressed are, however, those of the authors only and do not reflect those of the European Union or the European Innovation Council. Neither the European Union nor the granting authority can be held responsible for them.

References

1. Alexander, L., Moore, M.: Deontological ethics. In: The Stanford Encyclopedia of Philosophy (Winter 2021 Edition), Edward N. Zalta (ed.) (2023)
2. Ali, O., et al.: A systematic literature review of artificial intelligence in the healthcare sector: benefits, challenges, methodologies, and functionalities. J. Innov. Knowl. **8**, 100333 (2023)
3. Arnold, T., Kasenberg, D., Scheutz, M.: Explaining in time: meeting interactive standards of explanation for robotic systems. ACM Trans. Hum. Robot Interact. **10**(3), 1–23 (2021)
4. Bakiner, O.: What do academics say about artificial intelligence ethics? An overview of the scholarship. AI Ethics **3**, 513–525 (2023). https://doi.org/10.1007/s43681-022-00182-4
5. Pattern Recognition and Machine Learning. ISS, Springer, New York (2006). https://doi.org/10.1007/978-0-387-45528-0_9
6. Breazeal, C.: Toward sociable robots. Robot. Auton. Syst. **42**(3–4), 167–175 (2003)
7. Card, D., Smith, N.A.: On consequentialism and fairness. Front. Artif. Intell. **3** (2020). https://doi.org/10.3389/frai.2020.00034
8. European Commission: Coordinated plan on artificial intelligence 2021 review (2021)
9. Dennis, L., Fisher, M., Slavkovik, M., Webster, M.: Formal verification of ethical choices in autonomous systems. Robot. Auton. Syst. **77**, 1–14 (2016)
10. Dietvorst, B.J., Bartels, D.M.: Consumers object to algorithms making morally relevant tradeoffs because of algorithms' consequentialist decision strategies. J. Consum. Psychol. **32**, 406–424 (2022). https://doi.org/10.1002/jcpy.1266
11. Goodfellow, I., Bengio, Y., Courville, A.: Deep Learning. MIT Press (2016)

12. Montes, N., Sierra, C.: Value-Guided Synthesis of Parametric Normative Systems, pp. 907–915 (2021)
13. Murphy, K.P.: Machine Learning: A Probabilistic Perspective. MIT Press (2012)
14. Parks, L., Guay, R.P.: Personality, values, and motivation. Pers. Individ. Differ. **47**, 675–684 (2009). https://doi.org/10.1016/j.paid.2009.06.002
15. Scanlon, T.: What We Owe to Each Other. Belknap Press of Harvard University Press (1998)
16. Scanlon, T.: Moral Dimensions: Permissibility, Meaning. Belknap Press of Harvard University Press, Blame (2008)
17. Sierra, C., Osman, N., Noriega, P., Sabater-Mir, J., Perelló, A.: Value alignment: a formal approach. arXiv preprint arXiv:2110.09240 (2021)
18. Sinnott-Armstrong, W.: Consequentialism. In: The Stanford Encyclopedia of Philosophy (Winter 2023 Edition), Edward N. Zalta & Uri Nodelman (eds.) (2023)
19. Sutton, R.S., Barto, A.G.: Reinforcement Learning: An Introduction. MIT Press (2018)
20. UNESCO: Recommendation on the ethics of artificial intelligence (2021)
21. Wallach, W., Allen, C.: Moral Machines: Teaching Robots Right from Wrong. Oxford University Press (2008)
22. Wang, H., et al.: Scientific discovery in the age of artificial intelligence. Nature **620**(7972), 47–60 (2023). https://doi.org/10.1038/s41586-023-06221-2
23. Wang, T., et al.: Exploring the potential impact of artificial intelligence (AI) on international students in higher education: generative AI, chatbots, analytics, and international student success. Appl. Sci. **13**, 6716 (2023). https://doi.org/10.3390/app13116716
24. Zanotti, G., Petrolo, M., Chiffi, D., Schiaffonati, V.: Keep trusting! A plea for the notion of trustworthy AI. AI Soc. (2023). https://doi.org/10.1007/s00146-023-01789-9

Satisfaction in Negotiation by Structured Values and Propositions

Adam Wyner[1]([envelope])[iD] and Tomasz Zurek[2][iD]

[1] Department of Computer Science, Swansea University, Swansea, UK
a.z.wyner@swansea.ac.uk
[2] Complex Cyber Infrastructure, Informatics Institute, Faculty of Science, University of Amsterdam, Amsterdam, Netherlands
t.a.zurek@uva.nl

Abstract. In the course of dialogues such as negotiations about what to do, agents take turns to exchange propositions, starting from some initial disagreement and aiming at agreement. It is claimed that propositions are often associated with personal values. An agent's *underlying* purpose in the dialogue is to see to it that the agreement best satisfies their values, leading to a course of action that is in some sense consistent with them. However, in the literature, the relationships between propositions and values is often not transparent. In the Value-based Formal Reasoning model, these relationships are formalised. However, as an abstract model, it rather strict. It would seem that a more lenient and flexible model is called for, particularly with the aim of attaining agreement amongst agents. This flexible model enables agents to, in effect, "trade off" propositions that are associated with less important values for those that are more important. This paper contributes a formal representation of values in a set-theoretic lattice and associates sets of values with sets of propositions. It provides a formal mechanism to represent negotiation, wherein agents can achieve a maximally satisfying result relative to their particular sets of values. The proposal allows agents to agree on propositions, yet disagree on values.

Keywords: reasoning with values · negotiations · formal model

1 Introduction

Agents carry on dialogues of a variety of types, among which we can find negotiations (cf. Section 2). Initially, the parties start out with some difference of opinion, expressed in terms of propositions. We can assume that the aim of the negotiation is to arrive at some joint agreement, that is, some propositions that they both sufficiently accept. The role of values in dialogues has been pointed out in Perelman [11]:

If men (*sic*) oppose each other concerning a decision to be taken, it is not because they commit some error of logic or calculation. They discuss

N. Osman and L. Steels (Eds.): VALE 2024, LNAI 15356, pp. 176–192, 2025.
https://doi.org/10.1007/978-3-031-85463-7_11

apropos the applicable rule, the ends to be considered, the meaning to be given to values, the interpretation and characterisation of facts.

For the purposes of this paper, we consider personal values such as presented in Schwartz's value theory [12]. The context of this research is computational argumentation, particularly as it relates to values, e.g., [4]. The central question which is addressed in this paper is: *given that the agents share propositions which could be discussed, what underlies the choice of propositions that are discussed by each and which guides the agents to a negotiated agreement?*

Agents may negotiate over what to do, i.e., as in practical reasoning. For instance, agents might wish to make a plan to go together to a restaurant. Consider a dialogue between two agents, where they initially do not agree about which restaurant to go to. Alternative propositions are proposed and counter-proposed until, at some point, they agree on some restaurant to go to. More specifically: $agent_i$ says *I've already been to Joe's restaurant, let's go to Jill's restaurant instead.*, $agent_j$ suggests *Jill's restaurant is too expensive, I'd prefer Bob's restaurant.* $Agent_i$ counters *Bob's has a poor hygiene rating, let's go to Mary's,* to which $agent_j$ retorts *Who cares if it has poor hygiene, the food tastes great! But, OK, let's go to Mary's.* And perhaps finally, they agree to go to Mary's restaurant. Some of the values associated with their statements are explicit, reflecting such matters as *novelty, cost, health,* while others are implicit, e.g., what is it about Mary's restaurant that justifies the final agreement. One has the sense that the agents weigh these values differently, e.g., one agent cares more about the hygiene rating than another, and they both seem to care highly about going together. Intuitively, values are used, explicitly or implicitly, to select amongst the propositions put forth in the negotiation. Moreover, there appears to be some trade off amongst the values in order to arrive at agreement. The framework proposed below formalises these intuitions.

In our framework, we formalise a notion of *satisficing agreement.* In order for an $agent_i$ to attain agreement with another $agent_j$, $agent_i$ may have to neglect some of their values; that is, in reaching agreement $agent_i$ cannot insist on upholding all their values, but may sacrifice less important values in order to focus on more important values. From $agent_i$'s point of view, it is a satisfactory rather than ideal result. In our approach, an agent reaches a *satisficing agreement* where $agent_i$ agrees with $agent_j$ on that set of propositions which maximise the number of values of most importance to each agent. There are other notions possible for satisficing, e.g., being personally happy, serving a social group, or others. These are not under consideration here.

Values may relate to other topics in ethics, e.g., *deontology* (what is obligatory, prohibited, or permissable), *virtue* ethics (the personal traits of a person), and *consequentialism* (the consequences of some action). We do not here consider these topics. Relatedly, there are ethical paradoxes, such as the so-called *trolley problems,* which we do not treat. Our proposal aims to describe and model the application of values in negotiations.

In this paper, we propose a novel, formal framework for associating propositions with values in the context of negotiation. The proposal builds on prior work [16, 17, 21]. This paper does not present a dialogue protocol that mimics the incremental exchange of propositions as in the simple, informal example previously. Rather, it presents a novel approach to formally explain how: agents may start with disagreement and then agree, where one agent comes to agree with another agent by a process of selecting from amongst a set of values. We call this negotiation, as it correlates with the initial state and goals of negotiation. Importantly, while agents may not satisfy all of their values, they can reach an agreement that represents their most highly held values.

The paper is an advance over [16, 17, 21], which presented a *maximalist* position in terms of one set of values and all propositions that meet the values. The proposal here introduces *intermediate* positions, which allows much greater flexibility and supports basic aspects of negotiation. The framework contributes a formal representation of values in a lattice, an association of sets of values with sets of propositions, and a formal mechanism to represent negotiation between agents as *satisficing* with regards to values.

In Sect. 2, we contextualise negotiation with respect to other dialogue types and protocols. In Sect. 3, we outline the technical details of the Value-based Formal Reasoning (VFR) from [16, 21], which provides basic types and functions that are the basis for the advance in this paper. There is insufficient space in this paper to motivate and exemplify VFR, which can be found in the cited works. The main body of the paper starts in Sect. 4, wherein we provide the framework of values in a lattice and propositions relative to the subsets of values. Against this framework, we outline negotiation and agreement in Sect. 5. Related work is discussed in Sect. 6 and compared to our framework. The paper summarises and outlines future work in Sect. 7.

2   Dialogue Types and Dialogue Protocols

While the longer outlook of this work is to integrate value-based reasoning with dialogue types and protocols, the aim in this paper is to provide the formal, conceptual foundation for negotation dialogues. Nonetheless, some remarks about dialogue types and dialogue protocols are relevant to set context.

The well-known Walton-Krabbe typology of dialogue types [13] are differentiated in terms of an *initial* situation and a *goal*:

- Persuasion: *initial* conflict of opinion; *goal* resolve the conflict.
- Negotiation: *initial* conflict of interest; *goal* make a beneficial agreement.
- Inquiry: *initial* lack of knowledge; *goal* growth of knowledge.
- Deliberation: *initial* need for action; *goal* to decide on the action.
- Information-seeking: *initial* ignorance about information; *goal* understanding about information.
- Eristic: *initial* antagonism between parties; *goal* to accommodate parties.

The dialogue types are high level, only describing the initial and goal states. Dialogue protocols aim to provide the formal means to move incrementally from the initial state to the goal by using the resources to hand and along with some strategy [5,10]. Dialogue types and protocols are highly relevant to argument.

As discussed further in Sect. 3 and 6, approaches to computational argumentation do not take into consideration the role of values in the *construction* of arguments, but only in their evaluation, e.g., [2]. In [16], values are used to construct arguments from propositions which are relative to values. However, as noted in Sect. 3 and 6, this is inflexible, maximalist, and unrepresentative of aspects of argumentation. To make a more flexible and less maximalist approach, we structure values and propositions as in Sect. 4.

Returning to dialogue types and protocols, the aim of the current work is to provide agents with the means to find a common ground, understood as a set of propositions both agents hold, such as might be accomplished in a negotiation or persuasion dialogue. Crucially, the means to achieve agreement is relative to values. An agent's maximalist position on values would only block such common ground, given the differences between agents. While this is the aim, the current work only addresses the initial and goal states of a negotiation dialogue rather than the incremental turn-taking steps as found in some dialogue protocols, though see Algorithm 1 in Sect. 5.

3   Background on Value-Based Formal Reasoning

In this section, we provide the formal background on the relationship between an agent's values and the propositions compatible with the agent's values as found in [16,17,21], which we refer to as the Value-based Formal Reasoning model (VFR). There is insufficient space in this paper to motivate and exemplify VFR. The main novel contribution of the paper starts in Sect. 4, which is then used in the context of negotiation and agreement in Sect. 5.

3.1   Agents, Propositions, Values, and Weights

Below we develop a value-based language for knowledge bases and reasoning. We assume:

- `Agent`, where each element is an agent.
- `Prop`, where each element is a proposition.[1]
- `Value`, where each element of `Value` is an abstract object that expresses a value concept such as *freedom*, *security*, etc.
- `Scale`, which is a totally ordered, finite set of scalar elements. For the sake of this model, we understand Scale to be a set of integers.
- `Weight` is of type `Scale | ?`. The question mark "?" indicates that a weight is indeterminate (not relevant).[2] While there may be alternative interpretations of 'weights', here they reflect the relative 'importance' to an agent, e.g., *family*

---

[1] We simplify using "proposition", which could Prolog atoms. Truth-conditions are not germane here.

[2] Due to this, many propositions might be neutral with respect to values.

might be a very important value and *personal status* very unimportant.[3] As ? is unordered with respect to other elements of `Scale`, any expression comparing ? to the other entity is false.

With the following definitions, we construct $\mathtt{PropBaseTaint}_{agent_h}$, which represents a set of type `Prop` that is *sufficiently* compatible with the values of $agent_h$. This is less restrictive approach than `PropBaseClean` introduced in [21].

An agent's *value profile*, `AgentValueToWeight`, indicates the degree of importance that the agent ascribes to a value, where the higher the weight, the more important and the lower the weight the less important. Given an agent and value, the value can only have one weight, which avoids conflicts; `AgentValueToWeight` is a total function.

$$\mathtt{AgentValueToWeight} = (\mathtt{Agent} \times \mathtt{Value}) \to \mathtt{Weight}$$

An agent's value profile bears a subscript, e.g., $\mathtt{AgentValueToWeight}_{agent_k}$ for agent $agent_k$. Given the ? weight, the importance an agent associates with a value can be indeterminate, that is, the agent has no specific association with respect to the value. Any two agents may ascribe different weights to the same value.

Since differences in `AgentValueToWeight` of particular agents represent differences in the levels of importance the agents associate with the values, they can be seen as subjective or personal value profiles of those agents. An agent assesses an element of type `Prop` with respect to an element of type `Value` and an element of type `Weight` with a total function:

$$\mathtt{AgentValuePropWeight}: (\mathtt{Agent} \times \mathtt{Value} \times \mathtt{Prop}) \to \mathtt{Weight}$$

This expresses an agent's disposition towards a proposition with respect to values and weights. While `AgentValuePropWeight` is a total function, the use of ? signals that there may be propositions which are not meaningfully assessed.

The association of a proposition with a particular value and weight appears in [20] and in work on case-based reasoning with factors and values [3][4].

The functions `AgentValueToWeight` and `AgentValuePropWeight` are taken to be conceptually distinct. In particular, we interpret `AgentValueToWeight` to indicate the importance that the agent ascribes to the value, where the higher the weight, the more important, and the lower the weight, the less important, relevant, or disposed. It is a predicate that expresses a disposition of the agent in general about a value. In contrast, we interpret `AgentValuePropWeight` to indicate an agent's assessment of the `value` and `weight` ascribed to a particular proposition from `Prop`.

`AgentValueToWeight` expresses an agent's "ideal" and "global" view on values, while `AgentValuePropWeight` expresses an agent's assessment of particular propositions in terms of their association with a value.

---

[3] Just what alternatives one considers might depend on the aims of analysis.

[4] Here, weight represents the level of satisfaction of value with respect to a given proposition, in contrast to [6].

To reflect an agent's value-based *world view*, we gather all the propositions that are "compatible" with an agent's values. There could be a number of ways to model what it means to be compatible. In VFR [16], this means that the weight an agent assigns to a proposition relative to a value must not be less than the weight that agent assigns to that value in general. The proposition must "pass" the filter of acceptability relative to the agent's value profile.

However, propositions can be indeterminate with respect to the weight on values; that is, not every proposition needs be value-weighted. Given ? is unordered with respect to weights, such a proposition always passes an agent's filter.

A set $\texttt{PropBaseClean}_{agent_h}$ contains all and only those propositions which pass the value-weight in the value profile for $agent_h$ for all values.

$\texttt{PropBaseClean}$ is of type $\texttt{Prop}$.[5]
Where $agent_\alpha$ is a variable for elements of type $\texttt{Agent}$, p_β is a variable for elements of type $\texttt{Prop}$, and v_γ is a variable for elements of type $\texttt{Value}$, the definition relative to an $agent_\alpha$ is:
$\texttt{PropBaseClean}_{agent_\alpha} =$
$\{p_\beta | \neg(\texttt{AgentValuePropWeight}(agent_\alpha, v_\gamma, p_\beta) <$
$\texttt{AgentValueToWeight}(agent_\alpha, v_\gamma))\}$

This is a strict, formally convenient definition, which assesses all propositions and creates a set of only those propositions that pass the agent's value filter. Such an approach is, however, too strict and *maximalist*. In "real life", reasoning is usually more lenient and flexible allowing for the demotion of some values in order to promote some other ones. Demotion of a value means to considering the value to be of lesser relevance or importance and consequently the related propositions to be of lesser relevance or importance; promotion of a value means the converse. The proposal in Sect. 4 gives this a formal meaning and provides a more flexible approach appropriate for dialogue.

Values and weights discriminate amongst propositions. For a particular agent, a lower weight on a particular value implies that there is a lower discriminatory threshold on the acceptability of propositions, which themselves are associated with that value and the weight. Simply put, if an agent has a lower weight on a particular value, then more propositions may pass the filter, as they have higher weights on the same value. The higher the weight means that an agent has higher standards with respect to the value; there is greater discrimination such that fewer propositions pass the filter.

We assume $\texttt{PropBaseClean}$ represents *static* (all at once) and *private* (inaccessible to others) associations of value-weights to expressions by an agent, which contrasts to the publicly reported (i.e., accessible to others) reasoning chains (see [16,21]). Note that we do not analyse whether the propositions in $\texttt{PropBaseClean}$ are true or believed to be true, the set presents propositions which the agent can accept in the light of his/her value profile. In this approach, $\texttt{PropBaseClean}$ only represents propositions which the agent accepts in relation to their value profile, not concepts related to truth or belief.

---

[5] We indicate variables with Greek subscripts and constants with Latin subscripts.

4   Structuring Sets of Values and Propositions

In this section, we provide definitions for structuring sets of values and propositions, then an example.

4.1   Definitions of Structure

Values in a Lattice From the set of values $\texttt{Value}$, $\{v_i \ldots v_j\}$, we form the powerset, $\wp(\text{Values})$, $\mathcal{V}$, which is the set of all subsets of values. This gives us a *lattice* as in Fig. 1. A lattice is a set partially ordered by inclusion, e.g., $(\mathcal{V}, \leq)$, where for each two-element subset of $\mathcal{V}$, $\{a,b\} \subseteq \mathcal{V}$ for a, b $\in \mathcal{V}$, the set has a unique *supremum* (the join or least upper bound; denoted by a $\vee$ b; the union) and a unique infimum (the meet or greatest lower bound; denoted by a $\wedge$ b; the intersection).

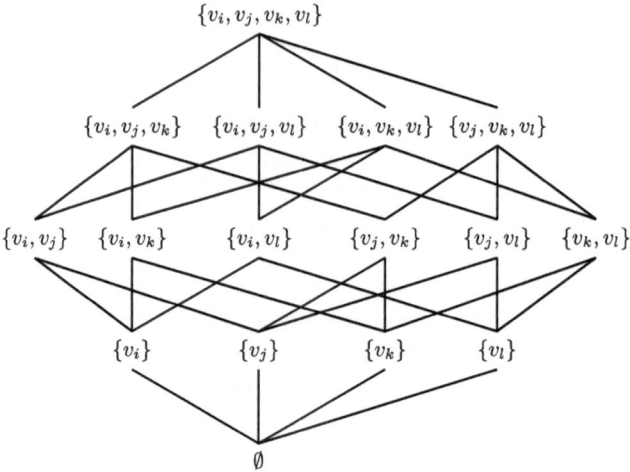

Fig. 1. Lattice of Values

Note that we are analysing a set $2^{|\texttt{Value}|}$ of values, which could be problematic in the light of computational complexity. It is worth noticing, however, that in real life, the number of values taken into consideration is not very high, therefore the number of subsets of all values should not be critically problematic.

Values and Propositions Much like $\texttt{PropBaseClean}$, we can filter propositions relative to sets of values, here elements of $\mathcal{V}$.

The VFR model allows for treating some values as not relevant for a given agent. Moreover, it also allows one to evaluate that an agent treats a proposition as not relevant with respect to a particular value. For the sake of simplicity and without losing meaning, if for an agent and value, the output is

? (i.e., `AgentValueToWeight`(agent,value)=?), then propositions pass the filter with respect to that value. Similarly, if for an agent, value, and proposition, the output is ? (i.e., `AgentValuePropWeight`(agent,value,prop)=?), then this proposition passes the filter.

Sets of Propositions Relative to Sets of Values. By $PropBase_{agent_\alpha}^\eta$, where $\eta \in \mathcal{V}$, we denote a set of propositions selected on the basis of value set η of $agent_\alpha$.

Definition 1. *For every* $\eta_i \in \mathcal{V}$,
$PropBase_{agent_\alpha}^{\eta_i} =$
$\{p_\beta | \forall_{v_\gamma \in \eta_i}, \neg(\textbf{\textit{AgentValuePropWeight}}(agent_\alpha, v_\gamma, p_\beta) <$
$\textbf{\textit{AgentValueToWeight}}(agent_\alpha, v_\gamma))\}$

$PropBase_{agent_\alpha}^{\eta_i}$ contains all propositions which pass the filter with respect to every value from set eta_i for $agent_\alpha$. In this sense, we provide an agent's *intermediate positions* in that propositions are assessed with respect to some subset of Value. This contrasts with the *maximalist position* of Sect. 3.

In the lattice, we have sets of values from singletons to the set of all values. The correlated sets of propositions are all of the same type Prop, but associated with and filtered by different sets of values. The sets incrementally become more *stringently* filtered with respect to the agent's values, from least stringent to most stringent, where the latter is just PropBaseClean. In other words, the set of propositions must pass more stringent value filters the more values are considered.

If PropBaseClean is the most stringently filtered set of propositions, we can define a relation of a less stringently filtered PropBase, which is relative to the sets of values under consideration:

Definition 2. *For all* $PropBase_{agent_\alpha}^{\eta_i}, PropBase_{agent_\alpha}^{\eta_j}$:
$PropBase_{agent_\alpha}^{\eta_i}$ *lessStringent* $PropBase_{agent_\alpha}^{\eta_j}$ *iff* $\eta_i \subset \eta_j$.

We also have the inverse *moreStringent*. An example appears in Subsect. 4.2.

Ordering Sets of Values. At this point, we have sets of props filtered with respect to different sets of values. However, we know that some values are more *important* (have a greater weight) to an agent than other values, which is given by `AgentValueToWeight`. Relatedly, a prop which *passes* on a more important value we take to be more important to the agent; in effect, the proposition *inherits* its importance from the related importance of the value.

There seem to be two ways to indicate this. Either we could specifically pass the weight of value to the proposition or we could order the sets of propositions according to the value weights. The former might be useful and make information transparent, but it violates a design principle (cf. [16,17,21]) that values (and by extension the weights associated to them) are private to an agent in the course of reasoning, action, and dialogue. That is, we take it that agents do not overtly say *P is important to me to extent i on value j*; though granted, there are sometimes expressions of ranking about statements, e.g., *importantly* or *it is key that* and similar. Nonetheless, given this (design principle), we will follow through on the second approach.

To compare the sets with respect to the weights, we find the sum of the weights of all values in the set and relative to an agent:

Definition 3. *Suppose an agent* $a \in Agent$, $\forall v_\gamma \in \eta_i$, *and weight* $w \in Weight$, *and* $\Sigma_{v_\gamma \in \eta_i} (AgentValueToWeight(a,v_\gamma))$ *represents sum of the weights of all values in* η_i.

Definition 4. *For* $\eta_i, \eta_j \in \mathcal{V}$:

- $\eta_i \succeq_a \eta_j$ *iff* $\Sigma_{v_\gamma \in \eta_i} (AgentValueToWeight(a,v_\gamma)) \geq$
  $\Sigma_{v_\delta \in \eta_j} (AgentValueToWeight(a,v_\delta))$
- $\eta_i \succ_a \eta_j$ *iff* $\Sigma_{v_\gamma \in \eta_i} (AgentValueToWeight(a,v_\gamma)) >$
  $\Sigma_{v_\delta \in \eta_j} (AgentValueToWeight(a,v_\delta))$
- $\eta_i \equiv_a \eta_j$ *iff* $\Sigma_{v_\gamma \in \eta_i} (AgentValueToWeight(a,v_\gamma)) \equiv$
  $\Sigma_{v_\delta \in \eta_j} (AgentValueToWeight(a,v_\delta))$;

This is a partial order of sets of values given the weights on the values. It would seem that ordering the sets relative to sums of weights indicates a preference of one set over another. As shown below, this establishes an ordering amongst sets of values that might not match the lattice ordering in Fig. 1.

4.2 Example of an Agent's Values, Weights, Sets of Values, and Sets of Propositions

For each set of values, we can provide the weight of the set and the set of propositions which pass the filters on each value in the set. The set of propositions can be also represented as a lattice. Here, we simply provide outcomes rather than the computational mechanisms behind calculating such sets.

Example 1. We assume:

- η represents set of values.
- Σ_η yields the sum of the value-weights of the values in η. For the example, we assume the `AgentValueToWeight` for v_i, v_j, v_j, and v_k are, respectively, 0, 1, 2, 1.
- PropBase$^\eta_{agent_i}$ represents the set of props that pass the agent's filter relative to the values in η, which is calculated per set of values as in Defnition 1.

Proposition 1 (Monotonicity of PropBase$^\eta_{agent_\alpha}$ relative to η).
For $\eta \subset$ *Value*, $\delta \subset$ *Value*, $\delta \subseteq \eta$, *and* $\forall_{p_\phi} \in$ *Prop*,
if $p_\phi \in$ *PropBase*$^\eta_{agent_\alpha}$, *then* $p_\phi \in$ *PropBase*$^\delta_{agent_\alpha}$.
This follows straightforwardly from Definition 1.

Table 1. Agent$_i$ Values η, Sum of Value Weights Σ_η, and Propositions Relative to Values from set η

Label	η	Σ_η	PropBase$^\eta_{agent_i}$
A	$\emptyset$	0	$\{p_1, p_2, p_3, p_4, p_5\}$
B	$\{v_i\}$	0	$\{p_2, p_3, p_4, p_5\}$
C	$\{v_j\}$	1	$\{p_1, p_3, p_4, p_5\}$
D	$\{v_k\}$	2	$\{p_1, p_2, p_4, p_5\}$
E	$\{v_l\}$	1	$\{p_1, p_2, p_3, p_5\}$
F	$\{v_i, v_j\}$	1	$\{p_3, p_4, p_5\}$
G	$\{v_i, v_k\}$	2	$\{p_2, p_4, p_5\}$
H	$\{v_i, v_l\}$	1	$\{p_2, p_3, p_5\}$
I	$\{v_j, v_k\}$	3	$\{p_1, p_4, p_5\}$
J	$\{v_j, v_l\}$	2	$\{p_1, p_3, p_5\}$
L	$\{v_k, v_l\}$	3	$\{p_1, p_2, p_5\}$
M	$\{v_i, v_j, v_k\}$	3	$\{p_4, p_5\}$
N	$\{v_i, v_j, v_l\}$	2	$\{p_3, p_5\}$
O	$\{v_i, v_k, v_l\}$	3	$\{p_2, p_5\}$
P	$\{v_j, v_k, v_l\}$	4	$\{p_1, p_5\}$
Q	$\{v_i, v_j, v_k, v_l\}$	4	$\{p_5\}$

In Table 1, the sets PropBase$^\eta_{agent_i}$ represent the *clean* sets relative to each η; that is, the propositions in PropBase$^\eta_{agent_i}$ pass the value filter of every value relative to the η as per Definition 1. We see that values play a role of constraining sets of propositions: the more values an agent applies in filtering propositions, the more constrained (i.e., as a subset) the set of propositions (i.e., *moreStringent*). As can be seen, a lattice is induced by Definition 1, though in a sense inverse to the values lattice; that is, from the empty set of values, we have a set of all propositions (least stringent); and from the set of values, we have the (singleton) set of propositions which pass all values, the infimum of the lattice of propositions (most stringent).

5   Negotiation and Agreement

Extent of (Dis)Agreement There are various generic ways to understand (dis)-agreement amongst agents. We outline some of these, then turn to a specific way to find agreement using Algorithm 1.

In the simplest version, two agents agent$_\alpha$ with η_i and agent$_\beta$ with η_j, agree on propositions where:

$$\text{PropBase}^{\eta_i}_{agent_\alpha} = \text{PropBase}^{\eta_j}_{agent_\beta}$$

In such a case, they symmetrically agree on everything. Note, however, that agreement is about the propositions, not the values. We have assumed that an agent's values are *opaque* to other agents; that is, `AgentValueToWeight` and `AgentValuePropWeight`, which are used to calculate the PropBases, are *only* available to the agent and not to other agents. What agents negotiate and agree on is only the set of propositions.

Alternatively, they could agree on some propositions or none. These are ordered by extent of agreement from less to more:

- Agree on some but not all props (non-empty intersection):
  $(\text{PropBase}_{agent_\alpha}^{\eta i} \cap \text{PropBase}_{agent_\beta}^{\eta j} \neq \emptyset)$ &
  $(\text{PropBase}_{agent_\alpha}^{\eta i} \neq \text{PropBase}_{agent_\beta}^{\eta j})$
- One set includes the other (subset):
  $(\text{PropBase}_{agent_\alpha}^{\eta i} \subset \text{PropBase}_{agent_\beta}^{\eta j})$
- Disagree on all (empty intersection):
  $(\text{PropBase}_{agent_\alpha}^{\eta i} \cap \text{PropBase}_{agent_\beta}^{\eta j}) = \emptyset$
- Disagree on some (non-empty intersection):
  $\neg[(\text{PropBase}_{agent_\alpha}^{\eta i} \cap \text{PropBase}_{agent_\beta}^{\eta j}) = \emptyset]$

For the sake of this work, the aim is that one agent ($agent_\alpha$) agrees with respect to another agent ($agent_\beta$); that is, $agent_\alpha$ agrees with all propositions introduced by $agent_\beta$. This is a kind of asymmetrical agreement (accommodationist) in which only one agent steps back from his values in order to find agreement. We assume that:

Definition 5 *$Agent_\alpha$ agrees with $Agent_\beta$ if:*
$$PropBase_{agent_\beta}^{\eta j} \subseteq PropBase_{agent_\alpha}^{\eta i}$$

Note that the agreement explicitly relates to propositions and only implicitly to values or value-weights.

Following the above:

Definition 6 *$Agent_\alpha$ disagrees with $Agent_\beta$ if:*
$$\exists_{p_\phi \in PropBase_{agent_\beta}^{\eta j}} \; s.t. \; p_\phi \notin PropBase_{agent_\alpha}^{\eta i}$$

A more sophisticated analysis, including symmetrical agreement and negotiations, will be discussed in a future work.

Finding Agreement. The agents try to find sets of propositions with increasing agreement from least to more, and perhaps to all. The agents would use the lattice structure of propositions. As noted above and to reduce complexity in the presentation, we assume that one agent's position is fixed and another varies. While there are a variety of strategies possible, we give one: the agent seeks a position which not only maximises the set of propositions in agreement, but also maximises with respect to their most highly weighted (in sum) set of values.

On the basis of the above we assume that one agent ($agent_\beta$) has a fixed $\text{PropBase}_{agent_\beta}^{\eta j}$. The other agent ($agent_\alpha$) finds all sets of their PropBases which include $\text{PropBase}_{agent_\beta}^{\eta j}$. Then the agent finds those PropBases where the sum on the value weight is maximal (max) amongst the available sets. Note that this is not a negotiation, because it is one-sided (only one agent is looking for agreement) and it is not built incrementally (step-by-step) as in normal dialogues. Yet, it relates to the basic attribute of negotiation in terms of the initial situation (difference) and goal (agreement).

Below we present a simple algorithm which returns the `PropBaseTaint-Success`. It finds a set of propositions of agent$_\alpha$ which agrees with agent$_\beta$ and which is the *best* in terms of agent$_\alpha$'s values.

Basic assumptions:

– We have two agents, agent$_\alpha$ and agent$_\beta$, where agent$_\alpha$ aims to accommodate to the propositions of agent$_\beta$.
– The agents start with disagreement (see Definition 6); that is, agents disagree with their PropBaseCleans.
– The algorithm terminates with agreement on propositions, where one agent agrees with another, i.e., ($\texttt{PropBase}^{\eta_i}_{agent_\alpha} \subseteq \texttt{PropBase}^{\eta_j}_{agent_\beta}$) and the value weights associated with $\texttt{PropBase}^{\eta_i}_{agent_\alpha}$ is highest in the designated set.
– Selections are based on sets of propositions.
– CANDIDATE is initially $\emptyset$
– $\textbf{add}(\texttt{PropBase}^{\eta}_{agent_\alpha}, \text{CANDIDATE})$ is a function that adds set $\texttt{PropBase}^{\eta}_{agent_\alpha}$ to the set CANDIDATE. In other words, CANDIDATE is a (possibly empty) set of `PropBases`.
– $\textbf{max}_{Agent_\alpha}(\text{CANDIDATE})$ is a function returning the most preferred PropBase for a given agent, i.e. a PropBase which has a highest sum of value weights of relative to set of values η:
$$\textbf{max}_{agent_\alpha}(\text{CANDIDATE}) =$$
$$\{\texttt{PropBase}^{\eta}_{agent_\alpha} | \neg \exists_{\texttt{PropBase}^{\phi}_{agent_\alpha} \in CANDIDATE}($$
$$\texttt{PropBase}^{\phi}_{agent_\alpha} \succ_{agent_\alpha} \texttt{PropBase}^{\eta}_{agent_\alpha}) \}$$

Algorithm 1. Finding Agreement Algorithm

Require: $\exists_{p_\phi \in \texttt{PropBase}^{\eta_j}_{agent_\beta}}$ s.t. $p_\phi \notin \texttt{PropBase}^{\eta_i}_{agent_\alpha}$

  CANDIDATE = {}
  for all $\eta \in 2^{VALUE}$ **do**
  if $\texttt{PropBase}^{\eta_j}_{agent_\beta} \subseteq \texttt{PropBase}^{\eta}_{agent_\alpha}$ **then**
      $\textbf{add}(\texttt{PropBase}^{\eta}_{agent_\alpha}, \text{CANDIDATE})$
  end if
  for all $\texttt{PropBase}^{\eta}_{agent_\alpha} \in \textbf{max}_{agent_\alpha}(\text{CANDIDATE})$ **do**
      $\texttt{PropBaseTaintSuccess}_{agent_\alpha} \leftarrow \texttt{PropBase}^{\eta}_{agent_\alpha}$
      Return($\texttt{PropBaseTaintSuccess}_{agent_\alpha}$)

Note that function **max** may return different sets of propositions which have equal sums of value weights. The preference of a given agent may depend on different criteria (for example the number of values taken into consideration). We explore this in future work.

The analysis gives us a precise, formal notion of *satisficing agreement*; namely, `PropBaseTaintSuccess` is that set of propositions which maximise the values that the agent holds most important, even if some other values might need to be sacrificed to do so and all values are not considered. It is good enough to reach agreement, but not ideal from the point of view of that agent, which is represented by *PropBaseClean*.

6   Related Work

As noted previously, this paper builds on [16,17,21], which share the background outlined in Sect. 3; in those works, the set of propositions is used to construct knowledge bases, then on top of them arguments [16,21] and actions [17]. The main aim of this paper is to further articulate the relation of sets of values and sets of propositions themselves, which we can use to express a notion of *satisficing agreement*. In future work, we would look to extend the framework discussed here to other topics. We are not aware of other works which similarly construct sets of propositions related to an agent's values.

Nonetheless, a number of models of reasoning with values have been introduced in recent years. Some of them are related to value-based argumentation and practical reasoning. Although they discuss various aspects of value-based reasoning, most (if not all) of them do not relate to the situation in which an agent, in order to find agreement with other agents, has to sacrifice one or more of his values (one can call it a *dirty compromise*). To situate this work, we briefly discuss several approaches to values in reasoning.

The role of values in argumentation has been discussed in many papers. One of the most influential approaches are Value-based Argumentation Frameworks (VAFs) [4], where the author extended Dung's abstract argumentation frameworks [8]. Values, in this work, are used to establish preferences between arguments. Moreover, [4] also introduces the concept of audience which is an ordering between values. This concept represents disagreement about preferences amongst values, which impact on argument attacks; this is similar, to some extent, to the concept of individual PropBases in VRF.

The differences are, however, significant. Firstly, in VRF, values are used in structured, not abstract, models. Moreover, instead of preferences between values used to define audiences in [4], values in VRF are used as filters which remove propositions which do not fit to the agent's value profile. In VRF, values are private and inaccessible for others, while in [4] they are used explicitly to justify preferences. Approaches similar to VAF appear in argumentation schemes and papers devoted to practical reasoning (e.g. [1,14]). None of these approaches allow for the sacrificing some values to achieve a goal.

An approach to model value based argumentation in ASPIC+ has been presented in [18]. This model has some points which are worth discussing. Firstly, the authors distinguish the concept of context, which is used to represent different parties in a discourse. The context contains value-based orderings between norms. These orderings allow for differentiating parties (agents). [18] introduces also the concept of consensus which is similar to our concept of satisficing agreement, but without the possibility of sacrificing some values to find an agreement. Apart from general similarities, there are significant differences between VRF and [18]. The most important is that our model separates values from the construction of arguments (see [16]). Although values may influence the construction of arguments, we cannot infer the values from the propositions without knowing the `AgentValueToWeight` and `AgentValuePropWeight` functions; this would appear to correspond to human argumentation, where we do not necessarily know which values influenced an agent's arguments. In [18] values are explicitly involved in the argumentation mechanism, which is not clearly consistently accessible in everyday discourse. .

Most existing approaches to value-based reasoning use an ordering between values. For example, [15] augment a Belief-Desire-Intention framework with values, where valuings indicate preferences amongst outcomes. The treatment of values is somewhat similar to our approach in that they are abstract properties associated with propositions, but they introduce conditional orderings over effects on values caused by decision options; these are not necessary in our model and would seem to introduce a high degree of complexity. Technically, in our model, we also construct an ordering, but this is an ordering between sets of values on the basis of their relative importance, thanks to which we can easily compare every possible set of values. Moreover, [15] does not give any tool allowing for sacrificing values to achieve a certain goal.

Values appear in discussions about actions in multi-agent systems with Action-based Alternating Transition Systems with values (AATS+V) [2]. Essentially, an AATS+V expresses actions as transition functions from state to state, where states are sets of propositions. Values are a set of abstract objects. A valuation function describes whether a state transition promotes or demotes the value; in a sense, it is a preference over actions. However, the values relate to states as wholes, i.e., a set of propositions. Thus, it is unclear just what it is about the states, i.e., particular propositions, such that the transition promotes or demotes the value. In AATS+V actions promote, i.e. increase the levels of satisfaction with respect to values, without considering that a given value can be already promoted to the satisfactory level (drinking one beer can promote happiness, but drinking 8 beers not, as it will result in hangover). In other words, AATS+V does not allow for expressing whether a given value reaches a necessary level of satisfaction. An extended version of AATS+V [2] introduces the mechanisms called 'maximisers' and 'satisficers', which are similar to concepts in this paper. However, these mechanisms are very complex, and it seems problematic to represent relations between a given value, value promotion, and levels.

Preferences are considered in AI across topics, where choices made between objects and preference is a comparative ordering of the objects [7]. In our proposal, there is no direct comparison between objects (propositions) and an ordering over them. Rather, values filter propositions according to the value profile of the agent; this identifies the belief set that the agent uses for reasoning. Ordering, created on the basis of relative value importance, is used to choose the most satisficing set of propositions which allows for agreement.

Our model shares some similarities with two value-based decision making models: [20] and later [9], which were constructed on the basis of similar assumptions. Firstly, both models are rooted in Schwartz value theory [12] ([9] focuses strictly on the list of values introduced in Schwartz, et al., while [20] has more abstract character without specifying concrete values). Secondly, both models assume that the thresholds on the levels of the satisfaction of values can function as a motivation of the decisions made by an agent. The differences between these models are in the details of formal machinery used to model the analysed phenomena and in the burden of analysis: [20] focuses on the decision making process, while [9] on the relations between values. The most similar to our approach is [19], which is based on a formal model from [20], where [20] is discussed from the point of view of various ethical theories. The relation of ethical theories and computational theories with values is elaborated in [17], which addresses so-called *consequentialist ethics*. None of the above models allows for what we call *dirty compromise*, i.e. the possibility of dropping some values in order to find a agreement.

7   Conclusions

The paper presents a framework which provides for sets of values that generate alternative sets of propositions. The sets of values represent different commitments to the values and give rise to different sets of associated propositions. This then allows a systematic way of expressing the idea that agents negotiate towards agreement explicitly using propositions yet implicitly based on their values. Agreement of one agent with another may require some sacrifice of values, but in such ways as to maximise significant values.

We aim to use this basis to further explore the role of values in dialogue and action. Real negotiations deploy turn taking and variation, which require heuristics, strategies, search, and optimisation, which may be found amongst game-theoretic approaches. Notions of balancing may play an important role, that is, where agents make choices about what propositions to maintain or sacrifice relative to what is available and the other agent's choices. Other dialogues type could be explored.

More speculatively, there is an intuition that the conceptual framework could be used to express the relationship between ideologies in terms of values and the expressions tied to those ideologies; it would appear that the more rigorous the ideology (more highly weighted values maintained) the more succinct and limited are its expressions.

References

1. Atkinson, K., Bench-Capon, T.: States, goals and values: revisiting practical reasoning. In: Proceedings of 11th International Workshop on Argumentation in Multi-Agent Systems (2014)
2. Atkinson, K., Bench-Capon, T.J.M.: Value-based argumentation. FLAP **8**(6), 1543–1588 (2021)
3. Bench-Capon, T., Prakken, H., Wyner, A., Atkinson, K.: Argument schemes for reasoning with legal cases using values. In: Proceedings of the 14th Conference on Artificial Intelligence and Law, pp. 13–22. ACM, New York, NY, USA (2013)
4. Bench-Capon, T.J.M.: Persuasion in practical argument using value-based argumentation frameworks. J. Log. Comput. **13**(3), 429–448 (2003)
5. Bentahar, J., Moulin, B., Belanger, M.: A taxonomy of argumentation models used for knowledge representation. Artif. Intell. Rev. **33**, 211–259 (03 2010)
6. Chorley, A., Bench-Capon, T.J.M.: An empirical investigation of reasoning with legal cases through theory construction and application. Artif. Intell. Law **13**(3–4), 323–371 (2005)
7. Domshlak, C., Hüllermeier, E., Kaci, S., Prade, H.: Preferences in AI: an overview. Artif. Intell. **175**(7–8), 1037–1052 (2011)
8. Dung, P.M.: On the acceptability of arguments and its fundamental role in non-monotonic reasoning, logic programming and n-person games. Artif. Intell. **77**(2), 321–358 (1995)
9. Heidari, S., Jensen, M., Dignum, F.: Simulations with values. In: Verhagen, H., Borit, M., Bravo, G., Wijermans, N. (eds.) Advances in Social Simulation, pp. 201–215. Springer International Publishing, Cham (2020)
10. McBurney, P., Parsons, S.: Dialogue Game Protocols. In: Huget, M.-P. (ed.) Communication in Multiagent Systems. LNCS (LNAI), vol. 2650, pp. 269–283. Springer, Heidelberg (2003). https://doi.org/10.1007/978-3-540-44972-0_15
11. Perelman, C.: Justice, law, and argument: Essays on moral and legal reasoning, vol. 142. Springer Science & Business Media (2012)
12. Schwartz, S.: An overview of the Schwartz theory of basic values. Online Readings in Psychology and Culture **2**(1) (2012)
13. Walton, D., Krabbe, E.: Commitment in dialogue: basic concepts of interpersonal reasoning. University of New York Press (1995)
14. van der Weide, T.L., Dignum, F., Meyer, J.-J.C., Prakken, H., Vreeswijk, G.A.W.: Practical reasoning using values. In: McBurney, P., Rahwan, I., Parsons, S., Maudet, N. (eds.) ArgMAS 2009. LNCS (LNAI), vol. 6057, pp. 79–93. Springer, Heidelberg (2010). https://doi.org/10.1007/978-3-642-12805-9_5
15. Winikoff, M., Sidorenko, G., Dignum, V., Dignum, F.: Why bad coffee? explaining BDI agent behaviour with valuings. Artif. Intell. **300**, 103554 (2021)
16. Wyner, A., Zurek, T.: On legal teleological reasoning. In: Sileno, G., Spanakis, J., van Dijck, G. (eds.) Legal Knowledge and Information Systems - JURIX 2023. Frontiers in Artificial Intelligence and Applications, vol. 379, pp. 83–88. IOS Press (2023)
17. Wyner, A.Z., Zurek, T., Stachura-Zurek, D.: Towards a formalisation of value-based actions and consequentialist ethics. CoRR **abs/2403.16719** (2024)
18. Yu, Z., Ju, S., Chen, W.: Context-based argumentation frameworks and multi-agent consensus building. J. Logic Comput. **34**(2), 199–228 (10 2023)
19. Zurek, T., Stachura-Zurek, D.: Applying ethics to autonomous agents. In: Bylina, J. (ed.) Selected Topics in Applied Computer Science, pp. 199–222. Wydawnictwo UMCS, Lublin, Poland (2021)

20. Zurek, T.: Goals, values, and reasoning. Expert Syst. Appl. **71**, 442–456 (2017)
21. Zurek, T., Wyner, A.: Towards a formal framework for motivated argumentation and the roots of conflict. In: Grasso, F., Green, N.L., Schneider, J., Wells, S. (eds.) Proceedings of the 22nd Workshop on Computational Models of Natural Argument, CMNA@COMMA 2022, Cardiff, Wales, September 12, 2022. CEUR Workshop Proceedings, vol. 3205, pp. 39–50. CEUR-WS.org (2022)

Towards the Incorporation of Social Values in Automated Negotiation Strategies

Laura Rodriguez Cima$^{(\boxtimes)}$, Dave De Jonge, and Nardine Osman

IIIA-CSIC, Barcelona, Spain
laura.rodriguez@iiia.csic.es

Abstract. In today's society, aligning AI with social values is a major concern. Researchers are exploring various approaches to ensure AI systems adhere to human values, developing technologies that not only optimise performance but also promote social well-being. Traditional automated negotiation primarily focuses on agents optimising their individual outcomes. However, introducing social values, such as fairness, complicates the negotiation process as agents must balance personal gains with collective well-being and equitable outcomes. This paper presents initial research on developing negotiation strategies that prioritise both individual payoffs and social values. We explore the theory behind these strategies, propose initial models incorporating social values into utility functions, and present preliminary experimental results using simple use cases. Our experiments demonstrate that agents operating in social mode exhibit fairer behaviours, emphasising equitable outcomes over individual gain. Furthermore, our findings suggest several requirements for implementing our value-aware negotiation models, including the necessity for agents to have some information about others' preferences, and a general commitment to social considerations. This paper represents our first steps towards more comprehensive solutions, with future work aimed at extending our investigations to more complex scenarios.

Keywords: Automated Negotiation · Value-driven AI

1 Introduction

Traditional automated negotiation focuses primarily on agents aiming to optimise their own outcomes [2,14]. However, when social values are introduced, the negotiation process becomes more complex as agents must consider changes in the social context and the fairness of offers. Social values influence how outcomes are perceived, requiring agents to balance their personal gains with the collective well-being and equitable distribution of resources. This added layer of consideration increases the complexity of negotiations.

Our objective is to develop negotiation strategies for agents that prioritise not only the maximisation of their individual payoffs but also social values such as fairness.

© The Author(s), under exclusive license to Springer Nature Switzerland AG 2025
N. Osman and L. Steels (Eds.): VALE 2024, LNAI 15356, pp. 193–207, 2025.
https://doi.org/10.1007/978-3-031-85463-7_12

Fairness is a subjective value that varies from one individual to another, thus there are different ways to express it in computational terms. Some of the most commonly assumed definitions in automated negotiations consider the Nash bargaining Solution [15] or the Kalai point [16] as fair outcomes. Therefore, the level of fairness is computed by the distance to these points, and the closer the agreements are to these points, the fairer the outcome. However, we consider that, as fairness may be perceived differently by different individuals, different agents should be allowed to have different concepts of fairness, which may even change over time, similar to real life. This approach also allows us to investigate models that incorporate other values, apart from fairness.

While this problem can be approached by modelling the agents' preferences through utility functions that incorporate all relevant values, and subsequently applying standard utility-based negotiation techniques, we argue that such an approach requires agents to adjust their utility functions during the negotiation process. This adjustment implies that this kind of negotiation is truly different from traditional negotiation scenarios.

In this paper, we will explore the theory behind such negotiation strategies, propose initial models for incorporating social values into utility functions, and present preliminary experimental results using simple use cases to demonstrate the practical implications. Our aim is to contribute to the field of automated negotiation by providing strategies for developing agents that consider both individual and social factors, recognising that this work represents only the first steps towards more comprehensive solutions.

2   Conceptual Analysis

2.1   Social Negotiation Use Case

To illustrate the concept of social negotiations, we consider an agricultural cooperative formed by a group of farmers that collectively work together and pool their resources for mutual benefit. Farmers join forces in a cooperative to achieve common goals and share resources with the aim of enhancing their overall economic well-being. In an agricultural cooperative, individual farmers are members that participate actively in the cooperative's activities. They contribute resources and they have a say in the decision-making process. By collaborating, farmers can achieve economies of scale, reduce costs, and gain access to services and opportunities that may not be available to them individually.

This use case provides a *task assignment problem* that includes a set of *agents* or *farmers*, where each farmer owns: a finite set of *resources* (implements) such as plows, harrows or planters, and a set of *tasks* to be completed, such as irrigation, harvesting or planting. The goal of such a problem is to re-assign each task and each resource to a new farmer.

In order to work together in cooperation, farmers negotiate over how they will divide their tasks and equipment among themselves. Since this is a highly complex scenario with an astronomically large number of possible agreements, the farmers will be aided by an electronic *mediator* that will propose potential deals to the farmers. In order to achieve successful outcomes, the mediator has to make proposals that take into account the values of the farmers. Specifically, the values considered in this context, expressed as desirable properties, are:

- **Equality**: The outcome should ensure that each farmer benefits similarly.
- **Global welfare**: The outcome should maximize the total financial benefit for all farmers combined.
- **Sustainability**: The outcome should minimize pollution, even if it results in slightly lower financial gains.
- **Trust**: The outcome should foster resource-sharing based on the trustworthiness of others.

In this paper, we show that in such a negotiation scenario the agents will need to readjust their utility functions during the negotiation process to consider social context and fairness in the offers, ultimately aiming for agreements that **benefit all parties involved while aligning with intended values**.

2.2 Payoff Vs. Utility

In our research we differentiate between two important concepts: *payoff* and *utility*. When talking about payoff, we refer to a tangible commodity, such as money. According to our definition of payoff, it is always a quantity that can be objectively measured. In principle, high payoff is considered a good thing, so in general agents prefer outcomes that yield higher payoffs. However, this may not be the agents' *only* motivation. That is, when agents make their decisions, they may also care about other values such as fairness and sustainability, which means that they may prefer a solution that is more fair or sustainable over another solution that yields higher payoff.

Utility, on the other hand, is a more abstract concept. Utility is, *by definition*, the quantity that an agent aims to maximise. That is, an agent will *by definition* always prefer a solution that maximises her utility, no matter what. It should therefore reflect all the decision making of the agent. If an agent cares about many different aspects, such as payoff, fairness and sustainability, then each of these aspects should be included in the definition of her utility function. Furthermore, utility is in general not something that can be directly measured. It can only be *calculated*, from other, more concrete concepts that can be measured.

In other words, if *payoff* can be compared to *money*, then *utility* can be compared to *happiness* or *satisfaction*.

Our goal is to model interactions between agents that do not only care about their payoffs, but also about social values, such as fairness.

For example, suppose that Alice and Bob just finished their dinner at a restaurant and they negotiate about who pays the bill. The negotiations could proceed as follows:

- **Alice**: Let me pay the bill.
- **Bob**: No, I invited you for this dinner, so I will pay.

- **Alice**: But you already paid for our dinner last week, so really I should pay the bill.
- **Bob**: Well, okay, but last week's dinner was much cheaper, so let me at least pay for the drinks today.
- **Alice**: Okay, that seems fair :)

Notice that in this negotiation each of the agents aims to maximise its own costs, and therefore *minimise* its own payoff. This is not contradictory to utilitarian negotiations, as long as we model each agent's utility function as being proportional to the payoff of the *other* agent.

Just like in traditional automated negotiations, we will assume that agents do not have full knowledge of each others' utility functions. This is because agents may not be entirely social, so they still partially aim to maximise their individual payoff, and therefore are not willing to share their utility functions. Moreover, utility functions may be too complex for humans to specify as an exact formula, as in the agricultural use case, which makes it hard for them to communicate their preferences in a precise manner.

It is important to recognise that this dynamic, where agents may prioritise fairness but lack insight into each other's utility functions, can lead to **paradoxical situations**. For example, consider a scenario where a third party proposes to distribute $1000 between Alice and Bob, offering $900 to Alice and $100 to Bob. From a purely financial point of view, Alice should be happy with the deal. However, in a social setting, Alice might reject the offer because she believes it to be unfair to Bob. On the other hand, Bob might actually accept it, believing that Alice needs the money more than him. This illustrates how one agent may reject a deal because she thinks it is unfair to the other agent, while the other agent actually does not perceive it as unfair. Initially, the agent may see this as a form of courtesy, but if the opponent finds the proposal genuinely acceptable, then the agent has no more reason to reject the deal. **We argue that this problem is inherent to all negotiations where agents care about fairness.**

3   Related Work

Automated negotiation has been widely studied and applied across various domains, including e-commerce [9], computer networks [10], supply chain management [11], or resource/task allocation [12,13]. In these contexts, agents act on behalf of individuals or organisations, leveraging algorithms to make decisions, propose offers, and accept or reject agreements.

Although agents primarily aim to maximise their own benefits, they must also consider the benefits of their opponents to identify mutually beneficial proposals, necessitating cooperation to achieve mutually advantageous outcomes. We can find different proposals where social agents assume a cooperative behaviour [17, 18], in which it is typically assumed by the authors that both parties employ the same cooperative strategy.

Sanchez-Anguix *et al.* introduce a social agent to be used within realistic agent societies where cooperative behaviour is not assumed by all parties [19]. Their agent is supported by a portfolio of strategies, a novel tit-for-tat concession mechanism, and a frequency-based opponent modelling mechanism capable of adapting its behaviour based on the opponent's actions and negotiation state. However, their approach still relies on the existence of a pre-defined notion of fairness (distance to the Nash- or Kalai-point) that is imposed onto the agents 'from above'.

A key aspect of our research is the relationship between payoff and utility, fundamental concepts in automated negotiation, game theory, and multi-objective decision making. This relation has been widely examined in literature. For instance, in adaptive learning models, where players adjust their strategies based on past experiences, Xie challenges the common assumption that monetary payoff directly corresponds to utility [20]. Xie's work demonstrates that imposing this assumption can lead to significant biases in both in-sample estimations and out-of-sample predictions. Our research follows the same approach where payoff refers to a tangible benefit, such as money, while utility is a more abstract concept that reflects an overall satisfaction, considering both material gains and others.

Thus, while there has been significant research on social agents and cooperative negotiation, existing approaches often impose a fixed concept of fairness, limiting the agents' ability to reflect diverse individual values in negotiation processes. This limitation presents a critical gap, as it restricts the adaptability of agents to the personalized notions of fairness or other values. Addressing this gap is crucial for developing trustworthy and reliable AI systems that not only fulfill human needs but also respect and align with human values.

Our research is motivated by the need to create value-aware systems that allow each agent to define its own individual concept of fairness, rather than conforming to a predefined standard. By enabling agents to incorporate and reason about diverse values, our approach enhances the adaptability and realism of automated negotiation systems. This aligns with the broader goal of ensuring that AI systems take value-aligned decisions, interpret human behavior in terms of values, and enrich human reasoning by enhancing value-awareness.

4   Formal Preliminaries

The research area of automated negotiation traditionally involves multi-agent systems in which each agent is driven by self-interest. Despite having conflicting objectives, these agents must collaborate to reach outcomes that are mutually advantageous. An illustrative example is the negotiation between a car buyer and a seller over the vehicle's price, though the scenarios studied are often far more intricate.

Typically, automated negotiation assumes the presence of a finite set of **agents** $\{a_1, a_2, \ldots, a_n\}$, and a set of potential **offers** Ω that the agents can present to one another. An offer ω can be represented as a tuple $\omega =$

$(x_1, x_2, \ldots, x_m)$, where each x_j corresponds to a value assigned to the j-th attribute of the negotiation. The set of all possible offers, Ω, is the space of all such tuples that agents can propose.

Each agent a_i has a distinct **utility function** u_i that assigns a utility value to each offer $\omega \in \Omega$: $u_i : \Omega \to \mathbb{R}$; it's typically assumed that agents lack knowledge of each other's utility functions and reservation values. During negotiations, agents adhere to a specified protocol [1], which dictates the timing and conditions under which offers can be proposed or accepted, and when an agreement becomes binding. Additionally, there is generally a pre-defined deadline T. If an agreement is not reached by this deadline, the negotiation is considered unsuccessful, and each agent a_i receives a utility value rv_i, known as the **reservation value**. Consequently, a rational agent will reject any offer yielding less utility than its reservation value.

Therefore, an offer ω is deemed **rational** for agent a_i if $u_i(\omega) \geq rv_i$, and it is **individually rational** if it is rational for every agent involved in that offer and for at least one of those agents a_i, we have $u_i(\omega) > rv_i$.

Definition 1. A *negotiation scenario* N comprises:

- A finite set of agents $\{a_1, a_2, \ldots, a_n\}$.
- A set of offers Ω.
- For each agent a_i, a utility function $u_i : \Omega \to \mathbb{R}$.
- For each agent a_i, a reservation value $rv_i \in \mathbb{R}$.
- A negotiation protocol.
- A deadline T.

5 The Social Approach

5.1 A Model of Social Negotiations

To design agents that prioritise fairness and address the paradoxical situations described in Sect. 2.2-where an agent might reject an offer because it seems unfair to other agent, even if the other agent does not perceive it as unfair-we adopt an approach in which each agent uses a single utility function that incorporates both a payoff component and considerations of fairness.

Let x denote an offer, and let $p_j(x)$ represent the payoff that agent a_j receives from that offer.

We assume that the utility function u_j of each agent a_j is given by a weighted sum of two components: an *individual utility*, u_j^i, and a *social utility*, u_j^s:

$$u_j(x) = w_j^i \cdot u_j^i(x) + w_j^s \cdot u_j^s(x) \tag{1}$$

Although the expressions of these components may vary, for simplicity, let's consider that the individual utility is just the agent's own payoff, and that the social utility is given by the minimum of the individual utilities of all agents (i.e. the agents prefer fair solutions in which no agent receives significantly less than others):

$$u_j^i(x) = p_j(x) \tag{2}$$

$$u_j^s(x) = \min_{a_k \in A} u_k^i(x) \tag{3}$$

In traditional negotiations, each agent knows its own utility function u_j, and initially knows nothing about the utility function of its opponent. The agent then tries to learn the opponent's utility function based on the proposals received from the opponent. The key distinction in our approach lies in the interdependence of utility functions. As Alice learns about Bob's individual utility u_B^i, her own utility function u_A is affected, since her social utility u_A^s depends on Bob's individual utility u_B^i through Eq. (3).

5.2   Example: Split-The-Pie

Let's consider a scenario where Alice and Bob are dividing a pie, and each offer x represents the fraction of the pie assigned to Alice, ranging from 0 to 1. For instance, $x = 0.4$ implies Alice receives 40% of the pie, leaving the other 60% for Bob.

For each agent, the payoff is simply the part of the pie they get assigned:

$$p_A(x) = x$$

$$p_B(x) = 1 - x$$

Alice's individual, social and total utility, are given by (1), (2) and (3), and she assumes that the same holds for Bob's utilities.

Now, suppose that Bob proposes $x = 0.9$, i.e. that Alice gets 90% of the cake. Alice rejects this proposal because she thinks that this is unfair (it yields low social utility and therefore low utility to her overall). However, Bob explains that he is not very hungry after a recent lunch, and therefore he cannot eat more than 10% of the cake (assuming the cake cannot be stored so any any uneaten portion must be discarded). This means that Bob's individual utility is constrained by his appetite and actually given by:

$$u_B^i(x) = 10 \cdot \min\{\ 0.1\ ,\ p_B(x)\ \}$$

That is, Bob achieves maximum individual utility when he gets 10% of the pie, and any larger portion will not increase his individual utility any further.

When Alice learns that Bob cannot eat more than 10% of the pie, she updates her expression of Bob's individual utility. Since Alice's social utility depends on Bob's individual utility, this also affects Alice's own utility. She therefore recalculates her own utility for this offer and now realises that it actually yields the highest possible utility, so she accepts the offer.

6   Split-The-Pie Case Simulation

In this section, we present a simulation conducted to experiment with our theoretical framework and explore the practical implications of social negotiation strategies, focusing on the Split-The-Pie scenario. The simulation aimed to observe how agents, equipped with initial beliefs about each other's preferences and a commitment to social considerations, would reach agreements. By varying parameters such as the weights assigned to individual and social utilities, we gained insights into the effectiveness of the proposed social negotiation model.

In order to develop our agents and build the simulated negotiation scenario we used Genius (General Environment for Negotiation with Intelligent multipurpose Usage Simulation) [5], a Java-based negotiation platform to develop general negotiating agents and create negotiation scenarios.

6.1   Negotiation Scenario

The simulated negotiation scenario is as follows:

- **Agents**: $\{Alice, Bob\}$.
- **Issue**: the portion of the pie assigned to Alice, x.
- A set of **offers** Ω.
- A **utility function for Alice**:

$$u_A(x) = w_A^i \cdot u_A^i(x) + w_A^s \cdot u_A^s(x)$$

where:

$$u_A^i(x) = x \tag{4}$$
$$u_A^s(x) = \min\{u_A^i(x), u_B^i(x)\} \tag{5}$$

- A **utility function for Bob**:

$$u_B(x) = w_B^i \cdot u_B^i(x) + w_B^s \cdot u_B^s(x)$$

where:

$$u_B^i(x) = 10 \cdot \min\{1 - x, 0.1\} \tag{6}$$
$$u_B^s(x) = \min\{u_A^i(x), u_B^i(x)\} \tag{7}$$

- For each agent α_i, a **reservation value** equal to 0.
- **Negotiation protocol**: Alternating Offers Protocol (AOP) [1], in which agents can make a bid, accept the most recent bid or walk way (i.e., end the negotiation without an agreement) when it is their turn.
- A **deadline** T.

Both agents operate in a 'social mode,' incorporating a social utility factor into their utility calculations, as outlined by equations (1), (2) and (3).

6.2   Negotiation Algorithm

In order to let the agents negotiate we implemented a new variant of the MiCRO strategy [7], that takes into account that the agent's own utility function may change during the negotiations. Each agent runs an instance of this algorithm.

Bidding Strategy. The original MiCRO Bidding strategy operates as follows: whenever the opponent proposes a new offer, MiCRO replies with a new offer from the list of possible bids, selecting the one with the highest utility not yet proposed. When the opponent repeats an earlier offer, MiCRO responds with an offer randomly chosen from those it has already proposed previously.

Our agents, however, use a small variation of the MiCRO Bidding strategy, with the difference that each time the opponent model is updated, it recomputes the total utility for all offers and resorts the list of possible bids. This is necessary because a change in the model of the opponent's individual utility function also causes a change in the agent's own utility function, as discussed above.

Acceptance Strategy. Our algorithm applies the standard acceptance strategy that accepts any received offer if and only if it is better than or equal to the lowest offer it is, at that time, willing to propose.

Opponent Model. We developed personalised Opponent Models for our agents that adapt to the current scenario. Although these algorithms are simple and cannot be generalised to other agents or scenarios, this approach enables us to simulate the current use case and provide an initial assessment of our proposed model's performance. We leave the development of a proper domain-independent opponent-modelling algorithm for social negotiations as future work.

In Bob's opponent model, Alice's individual utility u_A^i is represented by the portion of the pie assigned to her. Conversely, in Alice's opponent model, Bob's individual utility u_B^i is calculated as the complement of her own individual utility (i.e. the portion of the pie assigned to him). Alice updates her opponent model upon receiving an offer from Bob, learning that Bob's individual utility for the received offer is the maximum he can obtain.

7   Experiments

To gain initial insights into the performance of our social negotiations model, we conducted several experiments. These experiments simulated a scenario where a pie needs to be divided between Alice and Bob, considering the following conditions:

- Both agents operate within a 'social environment,' prioritizing fairness along-side individual benefit.
- Bob has recently eaten lunch and is unable to eat more than 10% of the pie.

– The pie cannot be stored, so any uneaten portion must be discarded.

The scenarios were simulated as described in the previous section, with variations in the weights assigned to individual and social utilities of the agents across different experiments.

We experimented with different weights to analyse the negotiation process under various conditions: when both agents are acting socially, when neither is acting socially, and when only one agent is acting socially. Table 1 summarises the analysed scenarios.

Table 1. Weights of Individual and Social Utilities for Different Experiments

Experiment	Scenario	Alice weights	Bob weights
1	Non-social Alice	$w_A^i = 0.8$	$w_B^i = 0.8$
	Non-social Bob	$w_A^s = 0.2$	$w_B^s = 0.2$
2	Social Alice	$w_A^i = 0.2$	$w_B^i = 0.8$
	Non-social Bob	$w_A^s = 0.8$	$w_B^s = 0.2$
3	Non-social Alice	$w_A^i = 0.8$	$w_B^i = 0.2$
	Social Bob	$w_A^s = 0.2$	$w_B^s = 0.8$
4	Social Alice	$w_A^i = 0.2$	$w_B^i = 0.2$
	Social Bob	$w_A^s = 0.8$	$w_B^s = 0.8$

8   Results

Figure 1 shows the final agreement reached in each scenario, in terms of portion of pie assigned to Alice and Bob.

Although the final result is the same in three out of four scenarios, it is crucial to understand the differences between the negotiation processes that leads to these outcomes.

– **Scenario 1 (Traditional Negotiations)**: As neither agent is operating in social mode, the negotiation proceeds traditionally. Alice starts by proposing bids that are most beneficial to her. Since Bob is content with 10% of the pie, he accepts the first offer that meets or exceeds this amount. Consequently, Alice receives 90% of the pie, and Bob receives 10%.
– **Scenario 2**: In this scenario, Alice operates in social mode and initially proposes what she perceives as the fairest distribution, 50% for each. However, Bob, not operating in social mode, behaves as he would in traditional negotiations and accepts this first offer because it is equal or greater than his minimum expectation of 10%. Despite being unable to consume 50% of the pie, Bob accepts the offer, resulting in 40% of the pie being discarded.

Fig. 1. Final Agreement in each Scenario

- **Scenario 3**: In this scenario, Alice, not in social mode, starts by proposing bids most advantageous to her. Bob accepts the first offer that meets or exceeds his expectation of 10%. Thus, Alice receives 90% of the pie, and Bob receives 10%.
- **Scenario 4 (Social Negotiations)**: In this case, both agents operate in social mode. Alice begins by proposing what she considers the fairest distribution, 50% each. However, Bob, unable to consume more than 10% of the pie, does not accept any offer exceeding this amount.

As illustrated, although the outcomes may appear similar, each scenario reflects the expected behaviours, demonstrating how agents prioritise fairness over individual benefits when acting in social mode.

It is important to recognize that this preliminary exploration is limited to fairness, treating it as a standalone desirable property. Future work will expand on this by incorporating a multi-value utility function in which agents can look into a mix of values, similar to the more complex social negotiation scenario discussed in Sect. 2.1. In that broader context, agents will consider a range of values, including equality, global welfare, sustainability and trust.

9   Discussion

The primary insights extracted from these results, highlighting the differences in behaviour between traditional and social negotiations, are summarised in Fig. 2:

1. **Proposal Side**: In traditional negotiations, agents begin with proposals that are most beneficial to themselves (e.g., Alice proposes a large portion for herself) and gradually make concessions until an agreement is reached. In contrast, in social negotiations, agents may start with proposals they believe to be fair based on the information available (e.g., Alice proposes a 50/50 split).
2. **Acceptance Side**: In traditional negotiations, agents accept offers that meet or exceed their minimum expectations (e.g., Bob accepts 50% because it is more than the 10% he wants). Conversely, in social negotiations, agents may not accept offers that exceed their requirements (e.g., Bob refuses any offer giving him more than 10% of the pie).

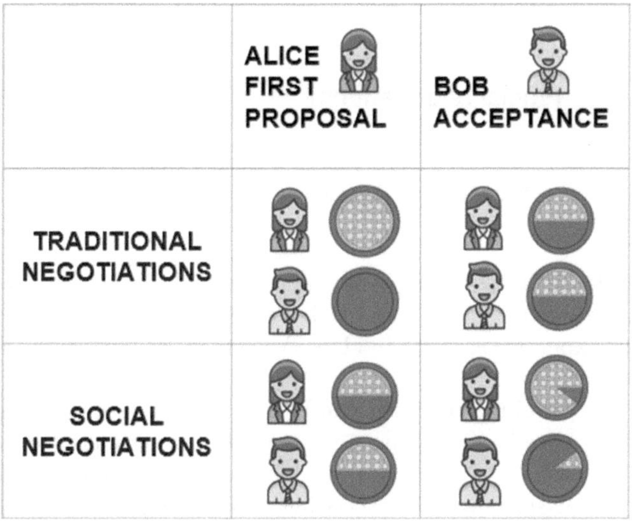

Fig. 2. Key Differences Between Traditional and Social Negotiations.

Although the outcomes in this simple example often resemble those of traditional negotiations, this should not diminish the potential importance of social negotiation in more complex situations. The similarity in results here is due to the straightforward nature of the example, where the agents' preferences and utility functions are relatively basic. In more complex scenarios, involving a broader range of values, the outcomes are likely to differ more significantly from those in traditional negotiations.

In addition, insights from our simulation suggest several requirements for incorporating fairness into negotiations:

1. **Initial Belief of Opponent's Preferences**: To start negotiations with the most socially optimal proposals, agents need to have some initial belief about their opponent's preferences and, therefore, the opponent's individual utility. This contrasts with traditional negotiations, where typically agents initially know nothing about the opponent's utility function and build an opponent model based on the received proposals.
2. **Knowledge Acquisition of Specific Opponent Preferences**: In addition to having an initial belief of opponents' preferences, agents need to acquire knowledge about specific preferences of the opponent in order to adjust their utilities accordingly. For example, in the previous scenario, Alice needs to learn that Bob's maximum utility is reached when he gets 10% of the pie.
3. **Commitment to Social Considerations**: To reach the best agreement in social terms, all agents need to operate in a 'social mode' and incorporate a social factor into their utility computation. If any agent does not consider fairness, it can exploit the willingness of others to concede, leading to unfair agreements.

We argue that this lack of knowledge about others' preferences can be addressed by incorporating a communication mechanism. Such a mechanism would enable agents to exchange preference information and build effective opponent models, facilitating the negotiation of socially optimal proposals. This mirrors real-life negotiations, where agents are interested in fairness and likely to share their needs to reach a fair agreement.

10 Conclusions

This paper presents initial research on developing negotiation strategies for agents that prioritise not only maximising individual payoffs but also considering social values such as fairness.

Our experiments highlighted the main differences on behaviour between traditional and social negotiations: agents operating in social mode exhibited fairer behaviours, beginning with proposals aligned with perceived fairness and prioritising equitable outcomes over individual gain.

Additionally, insights from our simulations revealed several requirements for successfully implementing our model. In contrast to what is typically assumed to happen in traditional negotiations, in social negotiations we need agents to have some information about others' preferences, to be able to identify fair agreements. Furthermore, to achieve the best agreement in social terms, all agents need to commit to social considerations and operate fairly.

While this paper represents preliminary work on value-aware negotiation, further research is needed to refine and expand these models. We aim to extend our investigations to more complex scenarios, such as the agricultural cooperative use case discussed in Sect. 2.1, by incorporating multi-value utility functions that address a broader range of values.

Acknowledgments. This work was supported by a Ramón y Cajal research grant from the Spanish Ministry of Science and Innovation (RYC2022-035229-I) and by Grant no. TED2021-131295B-C31 funded by MCIN/AEI /10.13039/501100011033 and by the European Union NextGenerationEU/PRTR.

Disclosure of Interests. The authors have no competing interests to declare that are relevant to the content of this article.

References

1. Rosenschein, J.S., Zlotkin, G.: Rules of Encounter. The MIT Press, Cambridge, USA (1994)
2. Fatima, S., Kraus, S., Wooldridge, M.: Principles of Automated Negotiation. Cambridge University Press, Cambridge (2014)
3. Jennings, N.R., Faratin, P., Lomuscio, A.R., Parsons, S., Wooldridge, M., Sierra, C.: Automated negotiation: prospects, methods and challenges. Group Decis. Negot. **10**, 199–215 (2001). https://doi.org/10.1023/A:1008746126376
4. Baarslag, T., Hindriks, K., Hendrikx, M., Dirkzwager, A., Jonker, C.: Decoupling negotiating agents to explore the space of negotiation strategies. In: Studies in Computational Intelligence, vol. 535, pp. 61–83. Springer, Heidelberg (2014). https://doi.org/10.1007/978-4-431-54758-7_4
5. Lin, R., Kraus, S., Baarslag, T., Tykhonov, D., Hindriks, K., Jonker, C.M.: Genius: an integrated environment for supporting the design of generic automated negotiators. Comput. Intell. **30**(1), 48–70 (2014). https://doi.org/10.1111/j.1467-8640.2012.00463.x
6. Aydogan, R., Festen, D., Hindriks, K., Jonker, C.: Alternating offers protocols for multilateral negotiation. In: Studies in Computational Intelligence, vol. 674, pp. 153–167. Springer, Heidelberg (2017). https://doi.org/10.1007/978-3-319-51563-2_10
7. De Jonge, D.: An analysis of the linear bilateral anac domains using the MiCRO benchmark strategy. In: Proceedings of the Thirty-First International Joint Conference on Artificial Intelligence, IJCAI-22, pp. 223–229. International Joint Conferences on Artificial Intelligence Organization, Vienna (2022). https://doi.org/10.24963/ijcai.2022/32
8. De Jonge, D.: Theoretical Properties of the MiCRO Negotiation Strategy. Preprint (2024)
9. Cao, M., Luo, X., Luo, X.R., Dai, X.: Automated negotiation for e-commerce decision making: a goal deliberated agent architecture for multi-strategy selection. Decis. Support Syst. **73**, 1–14 (2015). https://doi.org/10.1016/j.dss.2015.02.012
10. De la Hoz, E., Gimenez-Guzman, J.M., Marsa-Maestre, I., Orden, D.: Automated negotiation for resource assignment in wireless surveillance sensor networks. Sensors **15**(11), 29547–29568 (2015). https://doi.org/10.3390/s151129547

11. Fiedler, A., Sackmann, D.: Automated negotiation for supply chain finance. In: Mes, M., Lalla-Ruiz, E., Voß, S. (eds.) Computational Logistics. Springer, Cham (2021). https://doi.org/10.1007/978-3-030-87672-2_9

12. Krainin, M., An, B., Lesser, V.: An application of automated negotiation to distributed task allocation. In: 2007 IEEE/WIC/ACM International Conference on Intelligent Agent Technology (IAT'07), pp. 138–145 (2007). https://doi.org/10.1109/IAT.2007.28

13. Eshragh, F., Pooyandeh, M., Marceau, D.J.: Automated negotiation in environmental resource management: review and assessment. J. Environ. Manage. **162**, 148–157 (2015). https://doi.org/10.1016/j.jenvman.2015.07.051

14. Vente, S., Kimmig, A., Preece, A., Cerutti, F.: The current state of automated negotiation theory: a literature review. arXiv preprint arXiv:2004.02614 (2020)

15. Nash, J.: The bargaining problem. Econometrica **18**, 155–162 (1950). In: Kuhn, H.W. (ed.) Classics in Game Theory, pp. 5–13. Princeton University Press, Princeton (1997). https://doi.org/10.1515/9781400829156_007

16. Kalai, E., Smorodinsky, M.: Other solutions to Nash's bargaining problem. Econometrica **43**(3), 513–518 (1975). https://doi.org/10.2307/1914280

17. Chen, J.-H., Chao, K.-M., Godwin, N., Soo, V.-W.: A multiple-stage cooperative negotiation. In: Proceedings of the IEEE International Conference on e-Technology, e-Commerce and e-Service (EEE '04), pp. 131–138 (2004). https://doi.org/10.1109/EEE.2004.1287299

18. Zheng, S., Xiang, Y., Shi, L., Liao, K., Yang, J., He, Z.: A cooperative game-based negotiation strategy of electric vehicle discharging price. In: 2019 IEEE Sustainable Power and Energy Conference (iSPEC), pp. 2437–2442 (2019)

19. Sanchez-Anguix, V., Tunali, O., Aydoğan, R., Julian, V.: Can social agents efficiently perform in automated negotiation? Appl. Sci. **11**(13), 6022 (2021). https://doi.org/10.3390/app11136022

20. Xie, E.: Monetary payoff and utility function in adaptive learning models. Bank of Canada Staff Working Paper, no. 2019-50. Bank of Canada, Ottawa (2019). https://doi.org/10.34989/swp-2019-50

Context Matters: Contextual Value-Based Deliberation in Water Consumption Scenarios

Luis Oliva-Felipe[1,2]([✉]) [ID], Inês Lobo[3] [ID], Jack McKinlay[4] [ID], Frank Dignum[5] [ID], Marina De Vos[4] [ID], Ulises Cortés[1,2] [ID], and Atia Cortés[2] [ID]

[1] Knowledge Engineering and Machine Learning Group (KEMLG), Department of Computer Science (CS), Universitat Politècnica de Catalunya—BarcelonaTECH (UPC), Barcelona, Spain
luis.javier.oliva@upc.edu
[2] Barcelona Supercomputing Center (BSC), Barcelona, Spain
[3] INESC-ID and Instituto Superior Técnico, University of Lisbon, Lisbon, Portugal
[4] University of Bath, Bath, UK
[5] Umeå University, Faculty of Science and Technology, Department of Computing Science, Umeå, Sweden

Abstract. Values and context are important in an agent's decision-making process. Individuals may prioritise values differently, and changing context can also necessitate different considerations. In this paper, we use Schwartz's theory of basic human values to define ethical values and introduce a preorder to model an agent's relative preference among those values. We characterise context using this preorder, which can then be used in socio-technical systems as part of the autonomous agents' deliberation process. We also define the transition between contexts as shifts in value order. To illustrate our approach, we implement this preorder in a domestic water-consumption scenario featuring two towns whose citizens make daily decisions regarding showering, considering visitors, drought rules, and sports activities. Our results demonstrate how our model can effectively represent value orders and integrate them into agents' decision-making processes. This approach also allows us to characterise contexts, understand how these contexts affect agents' behaviour, and assess the impact of shifting contexts. We observe that the value order influences the dynamics of context transitions, making some value orders more prone to shift than others.

Keywords: value-awareness · agent decision-making · value-based context

1 Introduction

There has been a growing interest in modelling behaviour based on values emerging in recent research. Values can be seen as stable drivers that determine at a high level a person's preferred actions. However, these values, such as *universalism*, are very abstract, and their translation into preferences between actions is not always clear. For example, universalism would imply a concern for the wider society, but this could have different interpretations for different situations and people.

To illustrate how values can be translated and cause decision-making conflicts, consider a case where universalism, benevolence and hedonism are important for a person.

N. Osman and L. Steels (Eds.): VALE 2024, LNAI 15356, pp. 208–222, 2025.
https://doi.org/10.1007/978-3-031-85463-7_13

Should they be supportive of their community (*i.e.*, be benevolent) and fill their swimming pool to allow neighbourhood children to cool off during a heatwave, or should they be more concerned about the universalism-based impacts of water conservation, adhere strictly to water restrictions, and leave the pool covered to conserve water for the greater good? Additionally, they might face the dilemma of watering their garden, which provides personal pleasure by keeping it as a small haven, versus adhering to water restrictions to conserve water for the community or, if these measures allow a certain flexibility, choosing between the garden or the swimming pool.

However, this also depends on the context. Maybe the person relies on the swimming pool for physical therapy, which is crucial for their health, or perhaps their vegetable garden is a significant source of their family's nutrition. These personal needs make it harder to follow water restrictions strictly. Alternatively, in a scenario where there is an ongoing severe drought, the urgency of conserving water might be more pronounced, making universalism values more salient.

The particular context makes some values more salient than others. Therefore, one can say that value prioritisation in making choices changes between different contexts.

To maintain the focus on values, in this paper we assume that it is clear when the context changes, either because the environment changes (*e.g.*, a drought starts) or a new regulation comes into play (*e.g.*, a prohibition to refill swimming pools or water gardens in a drought situation). In these cases, a person goes from one context to another rather than participating in several contexts simultaneously. The latter happens, for example, when one talks with one's boss at a Christmas party. This is both a party context and a work context. We assume that the person can determine the most salient context.

The goal of this paper is to present our framework for modelling values and value orders as part of the agents' deliberation. We also use value orders to characterise contexts and a mechanism to represent changes in context when an agent's decision requires choosing one. We demonstrate its applicability using a water-consumption scenario based on comparing two towns with different contexts. Our empirical results show that our model can reflect the impact of value orders and the relative difficulties in moving between different types of value orders with equal ease. Since values are not all independent, some orderings facilitate a change of value priorities better than others.

2 Background

The two main elements our agents use in the simulation are values and contexts. In this section, we give a very brief introduction to both. Contexts have been defined by [16] and are used to provide the deliberation with tangible elements that are distinct in different situations. They are things like time, location, and so on. In [3], some issues are identified about how to recognise a context and know when it changes. In [7], it is shown how contexts can be used in agent-based simulation deliberations. For simplicity, in the current paper, we only use the different value priorities to distinguish contexts. For other types of agent-based approaches in the water domain, see [4], which focuses on norm-aware simulation. Although norms may promote values, these are not explicitly represented in the deliberation. In a similar fashion but agnostic to the domain, [8] proposes using explicit value-awareness to assess which norms are being promoted/demoted.

These approaches focus on the normative aspect. Our proposal focuses on values only and the effects on agents' decisions on themselves, also exploring the different value dispositions (*i.e.*, value orders) and assessing their differences. Which introduces the second element of our framework, the use of values in the agent's deliberation. Values are abstract concepts that represent the assessment or evaluation of a state of the world on various criteria associated with those values.

The need to use ethical decision-making in agents has been highlighted in [1] where it is discussed the use of explicit ethical values in the agent's deliberation process (or explicit ethical machines). What is interesting about using values, at least according to Schwartz [11, 12], is that there is a universal set of abstract values that can be attributed to people. Cervantes [2] also differentiate the use of ethical values in artificial agents, distinguishing those that possess implicit values given by the programmer, agents that have explicit values as part of the deliberation but not implicitly hard-coded in the actions but as first-order elements. They also define the concept of full ethical agents, which only applies to humans. In other words, explicit ethical agents use the concepts as part of their logic, implementing an ethical approach. Differences between people stem not from having different values but from giving different priorities to these values. This makes it possible to use values as a starting point to compare behaviours. The downside of Schwartz's value theory is that the defined values are very abstract and thus not directly related to behaviour. Several steps are needed to translate abstract values into more concrete values and ultimately into behavioural choices. How people ground abstract values into concrete choices for action can also differ. Therefore, there is a need to describe this whole system precisely and unambiguously before it can be used for practical purposes. Some work formally describing the relation between abstract values and actions has been developed using value trees in Weide [14]. We use the work of Heidari [5] that shows how values can be incorporated in the agent deliberation.

Fig. 1. Schwartz's circumplex model of basic values.

There, a function τ is defined to relate the set of values in Schwartz's model (see Fig. 1) ($Values = V_1, V_2, \ldots, V_{10}$) to an importance value (*i.e.*, salience) for each $V_i \in Values$:

$$\tau : Value \rightarrow Importance, \text{ where}$$

$$\begin{cases} Value \in [V_1, V_2, \ldots, V_{10}] \\ Importance \in [0, 100] \end{cases} \tag{1}$$

This importance function is a numerical assessment, ranging from 0 to 100, that quantifies the significance of a value for a given agent (*i.e.*, how often a given value has to be satisfied or how salient it is), such that a higher numerical value indicates greater importance.

Besides this function, [5] defines two more conditions to represent how values are related to each other according to the circumplex defined in Schwartz's theory. For these conditions, they assume "...*each value has the same distance with its neighbours*", representing this by the constant c:

Condition 1: $\forall i, j \in [1, 10] : 0 \leq |\tau(V_i) - \tau(V_j)| \leq m_{i,j}$

$$\text{where } m_{i,j} = \begin{cases} (|i - j| * c) \text{ if } |i - j| \leq 5 \\ (10 - |i - j| * c) \text{ if } |i - j| > 5 \end{cases} \tag{2}$$

Condition 1 shows that the range of differences in value importances is narrower the closer the values are to each other on the circumplex model.

Condition 2: $$\begin{cases} \tau(V_i) > 50 \text{ if } \tau(V_j) = 0 \\ 100 - \frac{c}{2} \leq \tau(V_i) + \tau(V_j) \leq 100 + \frac{c}{2} \text{ if } \tau(V_j) \neq 0 \\ \qquad \qquad \qquad \text{ and } \tau(V_i) \neq 0 \\ \text{where } j = (5 + i)\%10 \end{cases} \tag{3}$$

Condition 2 should be understood as follows: if a given value V_i is not present in the model, then $\tau(V_i) = 0$ and its complement is required to have a high importance value (if it is in the model) so that it can have effects on the behaviour of the system [6]. If both values are in the model, their summed importance is bounded above and below. This indicates that the importance of values should be complementary to each other to represent conflicting relations between them. Taken together, these conditions constrain the range these value importances can take.

3   Theoretical Model

The model presented in this paper contains two main elements: values and context. The values used in our model are based on Schwartz's theory of basic values [12], which is a well-established and accepted theory in the community. Three of these basic values were selected, and for each of these, a more specific value was proposed to align with our scenario (see 4):

- **Universalism**: This value is represented as Environmentalism (E), promoting the reduction of resource consumption (*e.g.*, water).
- **Hedonism**: This value is denoted as Comfort (C), driving agents to have more enjoying experiences (*e.g.*, having long showers).

– **Benevolence**: Represented as Relatedness (R), this value signifies agents' social relations (*e.g.*, potentially more visitors staying at agents' homes).

Our model defines a context as a specific preorder function that establishes a value ordering within the model, accounting for a preference within these values. This preorder, therefore, represents the hierarchy among values, where some are considered more relevant than others in the given context.

Each agent is characterised by the above three values, represented as V_1, V_4, and V_{10}[1], and a context of their own (referred to as original context) representing the preorder of these three values that is generated when the agent is initialised. For instance,

$$V_i \gtrsim V_j \gtrsim V_k, \text{ for pairwise distinct } i, j, k \in [1, 10] \subseteq \mathbb{N} \tag{4}$$

defines a context in our model, which says that V_i is more relevant than V_j, and V_j is more relevant than V_k.

Assuming the concepts described by [5]: value importances as defined by the τ function (Eq. 1) and the conditions to constrain those value importances - **compatibility relation** and **conflicting relation** (Eqs. 2 and 3), we relate the **value order** with the τ function,

$$V_i \gtrsim V_j \gtrsim V_k \equiv \tau(V_i) \geq \tau(V_j) \geq \tau(V_k),$$
$$\text{for pairwise distinct } i, j, k \in [1, 10] \subseteq \mathbb{N} \tag{5}$$

effectively moving from a preorder to a partial order and adding an additional condition that constrains value importances ranges. Different contexts (*i.e.*, different value orders) would imply different τ functions, that is, an agent may have to re-map value importances if a different value order is affecting that agent.

For simplicity, we will use the letters E, R, and C to represent the importance given to the values Environmentalism, Relatedness, and Comfort, respectively, instead of $\tau(V_1)$, $\tau(V_4)$, $\tau(V_{10})$. A string containing these letters will be used in the same order as the value order to simplify this representation further. For instance, $\tau(V_1) \geq \tau(V_{10}) \geq \tau(V_4)$ can be represented as $E \geq R \geq C$ or simply as ERC. The permutation of these three value representations in different positions yields six value orderings: ERC, ECR, REC, RCE, CER, and CRE. The previous conditions (Eq. 2-5) impose constraints on the importance ranges that each value can assume within the model for each possible combination.

Consequently, we can refine the characterisation of an agent and define it by its original value order and the importance assigned to each value that ensures consistency with the prior conditions.

An agent may encounter multiple contexts in parallel, having to determine which one among these to prioritise and employ. Once the conflict is solved and a context is chosen, the agent will shift from its own context to that one. We define the set of possible contexts as $\mathcal{C}$.

We use function σ to represent the process of shifting from one context to another:

---

[1] Indexes are significant since they are used later to order values according to Schwartz's circumplex representation. We denote Universalism as V_1, Hedonism as V_4 and Benevolence as V_{10}.

$$\sigma : \mathcal{C} \to \mathcal{C}$$
$$V_i \succsim V_j \succsim V_k \to V_a \succsim V_b \succsim V_c,$$
for pairwise distinct $i, j, k \in [1, 10] \subseteq \mathbb{N}$
and $\{a, b, c\}$ a permutation of $\{i, j, k\}$.
$$\tag{6}$$

Shifting to another context implies rearranging the agent values (*i.e.*, moving its values into a different order), where any V_x could occupy any possible position (*e.g.*, ERC transitioning to CRE). Applying the τ function (Eq. 5) with function σ, we can state that such transition would be

$$\tau(V_i) \geq \tau(V_j) \geq \tau(V_k) \to \tau'(V_a) \geq \tau'(V_b) \geq \tau'(V_c),$$
for pairwise distinct $i, j, k \in [1, 10] \subseteq \mathbb{N}$ and $\{a, b, c\}$
a permutation of $\{i, j, k\}$.

where τ' is the importance of the values in the new context reflecting the different order of the values; that is, shifting to a new context implies the agent will use a new τ function to remap value importances in such a way that it complies with the new value order. It is sensible to assume that modifying a value importance may imply some effort (*e.g.*, changing a habit, increasing awareness towards your own actions), that is:

Effort: $\mathcal{C} \times Importances \times \mathcal{C} \to \mathbb{N}$
$$< V_i \succsim V_j \succsim V_k > \times (\tau(V_i), \tau(V_j), \tau(V_k)) \tag{7}$$
$$\times < V_a \succsim V_b \succsim V_c > \to \mathbb{N}$$

This function uses the agent's importance values, its original context, and the value order of a target context to calculate the effort required to temporarily change value importances to comply with that target context. Once the context is no longer applicable, the agent's value order defaults to its original context and original importances. To quantify this effort, we assume it is linearly proportional to the change in importance. That is, modifying value importance by ten units requires more effort than just doing it by one unit. We represent this with the following equation:

$$E_i * w_1 + E_j * w_2 + E_k * w_3 \tag{8}$$

In this equation, E_x represents the amount of importance increased or decreased for each V_x to make the new importances consistent with Eq. 4. Such an amount depends on the new positions that each value has adopted in the new context. We assume that the effort of changing a value is proportional to the position the value occupies in the original value order. The variables w_n represent weights that embody this assumption - moving a value from a higher position in the original value order (*e.g.*, V_i) requires more effort than doing so for a value in a lower position (*e.g.*, V_k). That is, modifying the importance of a value that occupies a high position in the value order implies it is a core value compared to the values that come after and, therefore, modifying it is more difficult than doing so for a value that is in a lower position in the value order. Therefore, $w_1 > w_2 > w_3$.

To provide actual values for these weights in our experiments, we opted to use a golden ratio proportion since it is a common ratio in nature. It is possible to use other proportions as long as they comply with the previous equation. Therefore:

$$w_x = \phi^{N-x}, \text{ where N is the amount of}$$
$$\text{values being considered and } x \in [1, N] \subseteq \mathbb{N} \tag{9}$$
$$\text{In our case, } w_1 = 2.671, w_2 = 1.618, w_3 = 1$$

This effort function helps gauge how much effort an agent must invest in changing its context, allowing for a simple way to manage the conflict of selecting a context. As a target context, six possible value orders may occur, determining which values should be modified. Table 1 summarises these different situations. The first column contains the value orders in terms of the agent's values (*i.e.*, V_i, V_j, V_k) whose original context is $V_i \geq V_j \geq V_k$, to clearly show the reordering that implies shifting to a different context. In all cases, we assume there are different options for modifying value importances to shift from one value order to another. The second column presents the description of the best option that optimises the effort and the effects on the value importances, given the new value order that rearranged them as such. The last column gives the equation that measures the effort of that best option. Once the agent has changed context, its importances are temporarily modified accordingly (we refer to them as the actual context/value order the context that the agent shifted to, and the changed importances as actual importances).

Table 1. Considering the original context as $V_i \geq V_j \geq V_k$, the first column shows the effect of applying one of the six possible parallel contexts as the shift destination. The second column describes the changes to make to modify value importances and comply with the new value order (*i.e.*, τ' has to map new value importances to account for these changes). The last column provides the expression that returns the effort required to shift.

Destination context	Changes	Effort required
$V_i \geq V_j \geq V_k$	None	0
$V_i \geq V_k \geq V_j$	Raise V_k to V_j	$\lvert\tau(V_k) - \tau(V_j)\rvert * w_3$
$V_j \geq V_i \geq V_k$	Raise V_j to V_i	$\lvert\tau(V_j) - \tau(V_i)\rvert * w_2$
$V_k \geq V_i \geq V_j$	Raise V_k to V_i	$\lvert\tau(V_k) - \tau(V_i)\rvert * w_3$
$V_j \geq V_k \geq V_i$	Raise V_j, V_k to V_i	$\lvert\tau(V_j) - \tau(V_i)\rvert * w_2+$ $\lvert\tau(V_k) - \tau(V_i)\rvert * w_3$
$V_k \geq V_j \geq V_i$	Raise V_k, V_j to V_i	$\lvert\tau(V_k) - \tau(V_i)\rvert * w_3+$ $\lvert\tau(V_j) - \tau(V_i)\rvert * w_2$

4 Scenario

The scenario is set at a time when there is a change from a situation of scarce rain to a drought that affects a territory in a non-uniform way. It consists of an agent-based model of domestic water management with multiple households. Households are evenly distributed between two towns (Town$_1$ and Town$_2$). Water consumption is measured in terms of showers taken by household members, with shower units serving as the standard measurement for such consumption. We distinguish between three types of showers (no shower, short shower, and long shower) with associated shower units (0, 1, and 3 units, respectively). Agents decide their daily shower type, consuming more or less water depending on their values and the current context (*i.e.*, value order). During the simulation, Town$_1$ enacts policies to promote water-saving awareness because of drought during summer. Households may receive visitors that the hosts will try to accommodate. Also, agents may practice sports, which affects the type of shower they will take. The primary objective of this scenario is to illustrate how variations in the context can result in different water consumption patterns. Specifically, it aims to show *how* changes in context can effectively reduce water consumption.

The process starts by determining if there is any parallel context: Firstly, the appearance of visitors in the household and the hosts wanting to accommodate them, introduces a randomly generated context for a whole week, thus making agents in that household deal with a parallel context in their decisions. This context is randomly generated using a discrete uniform distribution across all six possible value orders. The probability of having visitors depends on the household's agents' importances for Relatedness (R) and Comfort (C). Since this affects the household collectively, we assume the importance values for R and C used when determining the arrival of visitors, are the highest ones amongst the agents living in that household, considering each value individually. Using a sigmoid function (see Eq. 10), we model how households with higher Comfort (relative to Relatedness) prefer having fewer visitors, and higher Relatedness would result in a higher probability of having visitors. The 0.05 factor in the exponential was determined empirically to achieve an appropriate smoothness in the curve.

$$p = 1/1 + e^{-0.05(R-C)} \qquad (10)$$

Town$_1$ enacts drought measures in summer that are represented as a parallel context for all agents in that town (*i.e.*, Town$_1$ enables the value order ERC, to promote water saving measures, hence the Environmentalism value placed in first place and Comfort in last place).

Each individual will compute the effort of moving from its original context to each possible parallel context, if any. The parallel context needing the least effort to shift to is the one selected. We assume an agent tries to move to any available parallel context and not remain in its original context as long as the effort is below a certain effort threshold. This threshold is represented as a parameter of our model. Lower values of this threshold imply the agent will shift only to contexts that require less effort. This parameter allows us to fine-tune experiments where the effort to shift contexts can be low, thus representing cases where the agents may find shifting to contexts is not that cumbersome or the other way around, where the effort to shift is so high that they shift fewer times.

Once the shift to the selected (actual) context is done and value importances are changed, the agent uses these new (actual) importances to select the kind of shower; the agent may decide not to change from its original context since the effort is higher

---

Algorithm 1. shouldIShower(E, C)

Input: $E : \tau(Environmentalism), C : \tau(Comfort)$
Output: Shower decision

```
 1: if E > C then
 2:    if Bernoulli((100 − E)/100) = 1 then
 3:       if Bernoulli((E − C)/100 + 0.5) = 1 then
 4:          long_shower
 5:       else
 6:          normal_shower
 7:       end if
 8:    else
 9:       no_shower
10:    end if
11: else if C > E then
12:    if Bernoulli(C/100) = 1 then
13:       long_shower
14:    else
15:       if Bernoulli((C − E)/100 + 0.5) = 1 then
16:          no_shower
17:       else
18:          normal_shower
19:       end if
20:    end if
21: else
22:    normal_shower
23: end if
```

---

than the mentioned threshold. This selection is performed according to Algorithm 1, treating the choice as a decision tree. The first branch focuses on a water-saving attitude $(\tau'(E) > \tau'(C)$, thus generating more normal or no-shower decisions. The second branch, $(\tau'(C) > \tau'(E))$, on the contrary, generates longer showers. In every case, we use a Bernoulli function based on the relative difference in the value importances of Environmentalism and Comfort to randomly choose whether to shower more or less.

Lastly, an individual may do sports, thus requiring increasing the length of the shower (from No shower to Short shower, and from Short shower to Long shower; if s/he was already taking a long shower, it is not further increased), we represent this with a sports probability equal for all agents.

The arrival of visitors and this sport probability factor add stochastic elements to the scenario. The visitors randomly add a context that agents may shift to, and the sports factor adds stochasticity to the length of showers they take. Both account for factors that the scenario may not have explicitly considered and which may have a similar effect.

4.1   Experiment Results

The model and scenario presented have been implemented in NetLogo [15] and executed with 240, 960 and 2600 households, containing an average of 2.3 individuals (*i.e.,* around 550, 2200 and 6000 agents). The representation for each value order is evenly distributed among individuals for the whole system. An execution run represents a year in which agents make decisions on a weekly basis. The experiment sweeps through the sports factor, from 0.0 to 0.3, with 0.05 steps. It also sweeps the effort threshold to shift contexts from 0 to 130, with steps of five. We selected this range for the effort threshold so it starts at zero, where almost no shifts are performed, to 130, which allows any shift (*i.e.*, according to the maximum value importance differences using our proposed effort function. It is possible, at zero when all importances are equal, that shifts occur. Each configuration is executed ten times with different random seeds. All these parameters make for 5670 experiment executions. In these experiments, we aim to show that contexts, defined as value orders, have an impact on water consumption and how context shifts produce significant changes in that consumption. Moreover, we also aim to show how certain contexts are capable of making more shifts because of the value order itself, resulting in a structural characteristic coming from the representation of Schwartz's circumplex model and the value order.

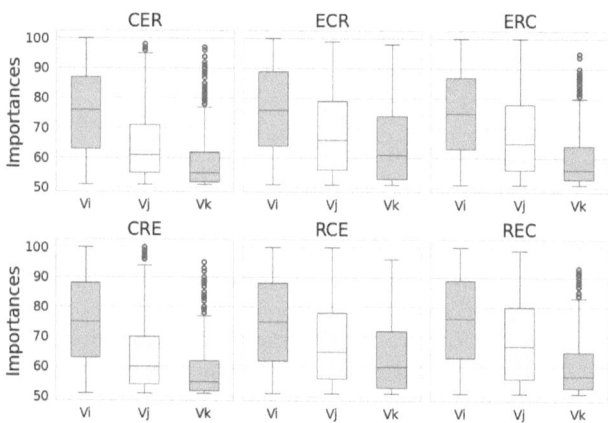

Fig. 2. Boxplots for baseline value importances, by value order. Observe how the distribution of importances depends on the value order. Boxes have been arranged in terms of the relative position of C in contexts. Having C in the middle produces fewer outliers; also, the boxes overlap more. Depending on the value order, the importance ranges are significantly different. This directly affects the effort to shift context, according to our definition of σ.

Observing Fig. 2, we can see how value importances are distributed along the range [51, 100]. V_i is not restricted and ranges uniformly. However, for V_j and V_k their range depends on which value they represent. In general, depending on the relative position of where C is located in the value order, we can notice how R and E will see their ranges modified. For CER and CRE, C restricts their ranges on the lower part. The value represented by V_k has a small box since, according to Eq. 2, it cannot be more than twenty units further. Something similar happens with ERC and REC, but in this case, since C is at the end, E and R have a wider range. Lastly, when C is in the middle, we find that its range is restricted to the small range defined by V_i and V_k. This will have a significant impact since it implies that value importance differences are smaller and, therefore, the effort to shift will be small as well thus making these contexts to be more prone to change.

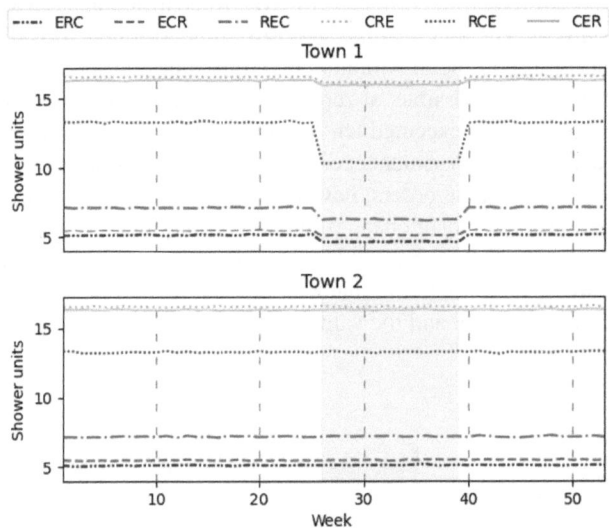

Fig. 3. Data belongs to experiments with effort threshold between 5 and 30, and sport factor between 0.1 and 0.3. Summer season has been highlighted (weeks 26–39) when Town$_1$ enacts drought measures (ERC context). Notice how all contexts exhibit a reduction in shower units in that period. Also, notice the differences between the two groups of value orders: ERC/ECR/REC and CRE/CER/RCE. The former are water savers, and the latter are water spenders. The differences between those two groups respond to the relative positions of C and E. Town$_2$ also exhibits a difference in water consumption due to value order. The difference between RCE and CRE/CER is relevant. Even though in those cases, C is higher than E, being C in the middle produces shorter showers.

For instance, compare CER and RCE in Fig. 3 for Town$_2$. Although the relative positions of E and C remain the same, the position of R determines the value importances of these values. Specifically, if R is in the first or last position, it creates a wider or narrower range for the value importances of C and E. This directly affects the difference between τC and τE and, consequently, the length of the shower. Also in Fig. 3, we can observe how agents adapt their water consumption habits in Town$_1$, which is affected by water restrictions during summer. Not only are agents with a value ordering starting with C the ones consuming more shower units, but they also show a less consequential reaction to the limitation policies encoded as a context with a specific value order (*i.e.*, ERC). A similar low descent in water consumption is observed in ERC and ECR because these two contexts already consume a low amount of shower units. One would argue why ERC exhibits a decrease; this is because, before summer, visitors may induce a change of context for those agents that have similar value importances for the three values. In that case, the agent will shift to the visitor's context. In summer, since Town$_1$ context is added, those agents will have always a parallel context at effort zero. It is significant the reduction in consumption for RCE. Examining Fig. 4 we can see the reason. This figure shows for each week, and for each original value context, the percentage of shifts to contexts that tend to save or spend water (shorter versus longer showers), and shifts to Town$_1$ context; it also shows the mean shower units. There, ERC (as well as RCE) exhibits a higher amount of shifts compared to the other value orders. That is due to the relative position of C, whose value importance range is enclosed by E and R. This makes the value importance differences used to compute the effort to shift, to be smaller than other contexts (see Table 1). This is more evident during the summer season, where context ERC is always parallel and is massively chosen. On the contrary, for CER and CRE, Town$_1$ context is not that popular to shift to since it still requires a significant effort higher than the threshold, explaining the small decrease in shower units.

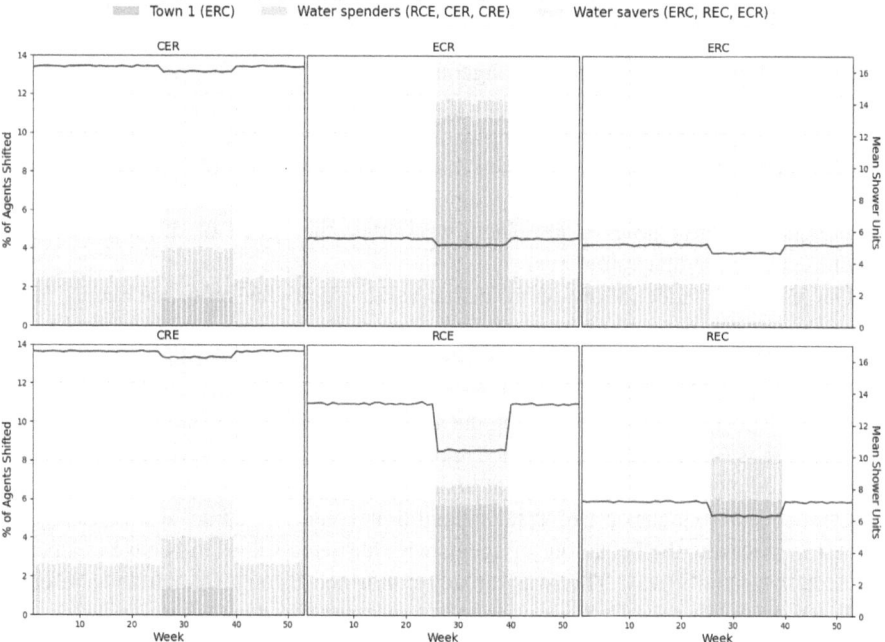

Fig. 4. On the left y-axis, the percentage of shifts towards other contexts; we grouped contexts into water savers ($ERC/REC/ECR$) and water spenders $RCE/CER/CRE$. In darker green, shifts to Town$_1$ context (ERC). On the right y-axis, mean shower units. Data is displayed for all weeks in the simulation. Summer season has been highlighted in yellow (weeks 26-39). Data belongs to experiments with an effort threshold between 5 and 30 and a sports factor between 0.1 and 0.3. Each subplot focuses on Town$_1$ agents with a specific original context (in the title). Notice the shower unit reduction that takes place in summer. For the ERC subplot, the Town$_1$ context is not reflected since it is always chosen and is not considered a shift. In all cases, the changing context has produced a clear effect; observe how the context with C in the mid position of the value order have a higher amount of shifts, indicating that these value orders need less effort to shift. (Color figure online)

Results show that context directly impacts agent behaviour towards water consumption (*i.e.*, having shorter or longer showers, if any). Figure 3 shows how agents with a value order that prioritises Environmentalism (E) over Comfort (C) spend significantly fewer shower units across all weeks of the year. Moreover, value importances ranges are constrained by the conditions that represent the circumplex model of values and the value order. These constraints limit the range of value importances so that the relative position of those two values, in the value order, significantly affects the number of shower units. More importantly, our findings suggest that value ordering also affects the capacity to shift from one context to another, which produces changes in that consumption. Given that the effort of shifting depends on the value importance differences, the narrower the value importances ranges are, the easier to shift. Therefore, the effects of Eqs. 2 and 3 along the value order impact water consumption and the capacity to shift whenever a parallel context occurs.

5   Conclusions and Future Work

This paper shows how we can model agents behaving under different contexts. These contexts modify agents' behaviour when deciding what action to perform (*e.g.*, length of shower). Using Schwartz's circumplex model along with Heidari's equations and τ importance function, we have defined these contexts in terms of preorder of ethical values (namely Universalism (E), Hedonism (C) and Benevolence (R)) thus adding a preference towards those values. Then, we studied the effects of shifting them and, therefore, changing that value order.

Our proposed model allows us to define value orders that influence agents' decisions. Decoupling the actions from the value order distinguishes values and value priorities from the agent's disposition towards the actions it may take in an explicit way. That is, we can define the agent's value order and, independently, using value importance, the disposition when performing the action (*e.g.*, deciding which kind of shower, which depends on the value importance and not the value relative position). This may be considered close to the concept of attitude defined by Schwartz [12, p.16].

Our decision to focus on Universalism and Benevolence as values was driven by the interest in assessing the behaviour of agents with altruistic values to behave in an environmentally friendly way. This was already confirmed through quantitative research by [9, 10]. By adding the Hedonism value, we introduced a dimension of egoistic goal (*i.e.*, prioritising pleasure or self-gratification) that, despite not being opposite to Universalism or Benevolence, offered room for flexibility as the element leveraging them in our model. However, it would be interesting to study how value orderings would be affected by the addition of new values, in particular those that clearly confront E and C in Schwartz's circumplex model, such as Power or Self-direction. Such addition would significantly constrain value importances and, therefore, agents' behaviour (*i.e.*, opposed values according to Eq. 3 have to balance their importances between them). In our case, context shifts were limited to the conditions of 2 that defined that E's and R's importances should be close. Adding new values would open the window to higher variability in value ordering and presumably more complexity in predicting agents' behaviour, increasing, for instance, the complexity of computing the effort to shift contexts.

Limitations of the Model. Our value model assumes homogeneous values since the effort of modifying a value's importance is the same, independent of the value itself. Value importances are constrained by the c factor described in [6]; such a factor assumes the value importances relations between values are also constant and uniform. It is possible that in certain situations the effort to change is negligible (*e.g.*, short periods with a value order changed or non-significant situations). Those cases are accounted for by a high effort threshold. However, we have not explored how representative those situations are. We have assumed all effort threshold levels uniformly when designing the experiments. Finally, we assumed the agents would always try to shift context whenever there were parallel contexts, and the effort to shift was below the effort threshold. We acknowledge a more realistic process for selecting which context the agent should choose is possible. However, adopting this assumption allowed us to focus on the impact of shifting context and value orders.

This work has served as a first approach to observe how a small group of values have a clear impact on agent's behaviour in a given context. When modelling, there is always the compromise between complexity, realism, and what elements do we want to capture to achieve the model's goals. Adding more values would clearly add much more complexity for computing the effort to shift contexts. In our example, we have used three values, two being close and a third one being not strictly opposed to the other two. One question arises as what if the model have used two confronted values, that is, if value importances ranges have been affected by the second part of Eq. 3. Applying that, it is possible to see that either value importance ranges would have been affected to be either very close or very far away of each other, thus promoting extreme behaviours.

Finally, it is worth mentioning that certain value orders may appear more frequently in societies [13], which is something to consider when using this model regarding the distribution of different value orders.

Acknowledgments. The authors would like to thank the **HumanE-AI-Net** project, which received funding from the European Union's Horizon 2020 research and innovation programme under grant agreement **952026**, for supporting the efforts made on this paper. This work has been partially supported by the **AI4CCAM** (Grant agreement ID: **101076911**), which funded Luis Oliva's efforts. National funds supported it through Fundação para a Ciência e a Tecnologia (FCT) with reference **UIDB/50021/2020**, which funded Inês Lobo's efforts, thus acknowledging her FCT grant (**2021.04796.BD**). This research is supported by UK Research and Innovation grant number **EP/S023437/1**, which funded Jack McKinlay's efforts.

References

1. Anderson, M., Anderson, S.L.: Machine ethics: creating an ethical intelligent agent. AI Mag. **28**(4), 15–15 (2007)
2. Cervantes, J.A., López, S., Rodríguez, L.F., Cervantes, S., Cervantes, F., Ramos, F.: Artificial moral agents: a survey of the current status. Sci. Eng. Ethics **26**(2), 501–532 (2020)
3. Edmonds, B.: Complexity and context-dependency. Found. Sci. **18**, 745–755 (2013)
4. Gómez-Sebastià, I., Oliva-Felipe, L., Cortés, U., Verdaguer, M., Poch, M., Rodríguez-Roda, I., Vázquez-Salceda, J.: A Norm-Aware Multi-agent System for Social Simulations in a River

Basin, pp. 67–90. Springer International Publishing, Cham (2017). https://doi.org/10.1007/978-3-319-42993-9_4, https://doi.org/10.1007/978-3-319-42993-9_4

5. Heidari, S.: Agents with Social Norms and Values: A framework for agent based social simulations with social norms and personal values. Ph.D. thesis, Utrecht University (2022)
6. Heidari, S., Jensen, M., Dignum, F.: Simulations with values. In: Verhagen, H., Borit, M., Bravo, G., Wijermans, N. (eds.) Advances in Social Simulation: Looking in the Mirror, pp. 201–215. Springer International Publishing, Cham (2020). https://doi.org/10.1007/978-3-030-34127-5_19
7. Jensen, M., Vanhée, L., Dignum, F.: Dynamic context-sensitive deliberation. In: Multi-Agent-Based Simulation, MABS 2023 (2023)
8. Montes, N., Osman, N., Sierra, C., Slavkovik, M.: Value engineering for autonomous agents. arXiv preprint arXiv:2302.08759 (2023)
9. Oreg, S., Katz-Gerro, T.: Predicting proenvironmental behavior cross-nationally: Values, the theory of planned behavior, and value-belief-norm theory. Environ. Behav. 38(4), 462–483 (2006)
10. Primc, K., Ogorevc, M., Slabe-Erker, R., Bartolj, T., Murovec, N.: How does Schwartz's theory of human values affect the proenvironmental behavior model? Baltic J. Manage. 16, 276–297 (2021). https://api.semanticscholar.org/CorpusID:234256765
11. Schwartz, S.H.: Universals in the content and structure of values: Theoretical advances and empirical tests in 20 countries. In: Zanna, M.P. (ed.) Advances in experimental social psychology, Advances in Experimental Social Psychology, vol. 25, pp. 1 – 65. Academic Press (1992)
12. Schwartz, S.H.: An overview of the Schwartz theory of basic values. Online Read. Psychol. Cult. 2(1), 0919–2307 (2012)
13. Schwartz, S.H., Bardi, A.: Value hierarchies across cultures: Taking a similarities perspective. J. Cross Cult. Psychol. 32(3), 268–290 (2001)
14. Weide, T.V.D.: Arguing to motivate decisions. Ph.D. thesis, Utrecht University (2011)
15. Wilensky, U.: Netlogo. Center for Connected Learning and Computer-Based Modeling, Northwestern University, Evanston, IL (1999). http://ccl.northwestern.edu/netlogo/
16. Zimmermann, A., Lorenz, A., Oppermann, R.: An operational definition of context. In: International and Interdisciplinary Conference on Modeling and Using Context, pp. 558–571 (2007)

Ethical Issues, Including Explainability

Opportunities and Challenges of the Use of Forgetting in Symbolic XAI

Joaquín Arias[1]([⊠]) [ID], Sara Degli-Esposti[2] [ID], Jose Walter Hernández-Pérez[1] [ID], Luciana Fidilio-Allende[1] [ID], and Sascha Ossowski[1] [ID]

[1] CETINIA, Universidad Rey Juan Caros, Madrid, Spain
joaquin.arias@urjc.es
[2] Institute of Philosophy, Spanish National Research Council (CSIC), Madrid, Spain

Abstract. The increasing use of artificial intelligence systems (especially those based on black-box algorithms) in decision models that affect humans is leading to an increase in demand for explainable AI (XAI) and models aligned with human values and norms. Recently, symbolic reasoning approaches, such as Answer Set Programming (ASP), have re-emerged as an alternative solution to create transparent and interpretable models more easily auditable. However, this explainability may expose private information (with ethical and legal implications). Although it is possible to manipulate the justifications (to hide sensitive information), ASP forgetting techniques are gaining relevance because they allow to remove such information from the models as well, thus allowing to audit them without compromising the users' privacy and comply with GDPR data minimization principle. On the other hand, black box models cannot provide such explanations, so to ensure privacy preservation a naive approach is to learn Machine Learning (ML) models using a dataset from which sensitive attributes are removed, but this solution may affect accuracy. In this paper we present Privacy-ML, a complex scheme that is trained with sensitive information but then does not require such information when performing classification (improving the accuracy of naive approaches). Additionally, we have identified that a Privacy-ML based on Inductive Logic Programming can also be used by a malicious agent in combination with forgetting to obfuscate their deceptive profiling practices in such a way that it cannot be directly detected by someone reading the explanations it produces or by auditing the model.

1 Introduction

The automation of decision-making through AI can be dangerous when the system is opaque, used at scale and its decisions can violate people's rights or liberties [14]. Research unveiling algorithmic biases in ML, human-computer interaction, recommender systems, and information retrieval focuses on bias detection, fairness management, and model or outcome explainability [13]. The advantage of symbolic AI approaches resides into the possibility of designing

N. Osman and L. Steels (Eds.): VALE 2024, LNAI 15356, pp. 225–239, 2025.
https://doi.org/10.1007/978-3-031-85463-7_14

simple, transparent systems that can be audited and interpreted by end-users. Promoting a reliable AI, focused on humans, is of foremost importance because autonomous AI systems may cause significant harm.

Value-awareness engineering [12] is an approach that claims that it is possible to formally represent values and factor them in the decision-making process of machines, paving the way to some sort of *machine morality*. AI systems, even if they are value-aware, can only be perceived as trustworthy by users if they can be auditable and explainable. The DARPA Explainable Artificial Intelligence (XAI) challenge [9], for instance, aims to create AI systems whose learned models and decisions can be understood by end users. This includes seeking methods to increase the interpretability of models, designing effective explanation interfaces, and understanding the psychological requirements of effective explanations. Value-aware systems should be more transparent and interpretable than other systems thanks to the use of logical reasoning during the creation of the algorithms. By interpretability, we mean 'the ability to explain or to present in understandable terms to a human' [6]. In the case of recommendation systems, it is especially important that the system is capable of explaining itself and justifying –in a human-understandable manner– why it makes specific recommendations; these explanations should include the values and norms that influenced the reasoning process, among other considerations.

Many studies demonstrate that wide reliance on observational user behavior data in recommender systems can be a major source of bias that creates distortions and negative effects on individuals [5]. Consequently, there is an increased interest in the topic of how to avoid bias and build recommender systems that enact the values of the individuals and societies that they serve [16]. Within this line of studies, it is worth exploring the contribution of logic-based programming to explainable AI. As an example, the notion of *fidelity* has been proposed as a metric for evaluating how close the explanation is to the internal decision-making process of Graph Neural Networks [10].

Here we draw insights from previous work on computational legal reasoning with s(LAW) [3] to focus specifically on the protection of special categories of data – as defined in Art. 9 of the General Data Protection Regulation (GDPR) – by using *forgetting* [19]. ASP forgetting techniques have already been proposed to preserve the privacy of victims of gender violence in the automated allocation of school places [7]. Besides being used as a privacy-preserving tool, here we argue that forgetting can also be used to hide deceptive profiling practices, where profiling refers to any form of automated processing of personal data to evaluate certain personal aspects relating to a natural person.

Table 1. High-risk AI systems referred to in Article 6(2) of the AI Act

	Areas	Example of AI Systems used
1	Biometrics	Remote biometric identification systems; biometric categorization; emotion recognition
2	Critical infrastructure	AI used as safety components in the management and operation of critical digital infrastructure, road traffic, or in the supply of water, gas, heating or electricity
3	Education and vocational training	AI used to determine access or admission, evaluate learning outcomes, assess the appropriate level of education that an individual will receive, monitor and detect prohibited behaviour of students during tests
4	Employment, workers management and access to self-employment	AI used to analyse and filter job applications, to promote or terminate work-related contractual relationships, to allocate tasks based on individual behaviour or personal characteristics, to monitor and evaluate staff performance
5	Access to and enjoyment of essential private services and essential public services and benefits	AI used to evaluate the eligibility of natural persons for essential public assistance benefits and services; the creditworthiness of natural persons or to establish their credit score; and IA to be used for risk assessment and pricing and to evaluate and classify emergency calls
6	Law enforcement	Polygraphs or similar tools and AI used to assess a person's risk of becoming the victim of criminal offences; to evaluate the reliability of evidence in the course of the investigation of criminal offences; to assess the likelihood of a natural person of offending or reoffending; to profile natural persons
7	Migration, asylum and border control management	AI system to assess security risk, a risk of irregular migration, or a health risk; to detect, recognise or identify natural persons

2   Background: (Symbolic) ML + Forgetting

In this paper, we initially focus on machine learning algorithms, such as linear regression, that can learn from and make predictions about data. Linear regression is a supervised machine learning algorithm that learns from labeled data sets.

Additionally, we explore Symbolic Machine Learning Algorithms, such as the family of FOLD-R algorithms [17], that focus on representing human-readable concepts, such as the logic behind the interactions between the objects in a problem. These algorithms can extract from a given dataset the relationship between the different attributes of its instances. These relationships are modeled as rules in a logic-based model, which then can be executed as Answer Set Programs.

Answer Set Programming (ASP) is a logic programming approach based on the stable model semantics [8] which supports non-stratified negations. One notable reasoner of ASP is s(CASP) [2], a goal-directed interpreter that supports ASP programs with constraints and is capable of generating (human-understandable) explanations for its answers [1]. This ability allows us to generate value-aligned decisions in a transparent manner [4].

As we mentioned before, these justifications can potentially expose sensitive data, violating the current legislation or/and violating the privacy of the owners of the information. A straightforward way to avoid this is to exploit the s(CASP) directive `#show` and the flag `--short`, and thus directly manipulate the resulting justifications. However, the sensitive data can still be exposed when inspecting the underlying program.

To preserve privacy in the models in a more robust manner, s(CASP) has been extended with f_{CASP} [7], a forgetting operator that performs syntactic transformation to remove information from a given ASP program, without altering the answers it provides. In particular, s(CASP) can invoke the forgetting operator using the flag `forget`, as the operator has been implemented as part of the s(CASP) ciao compiler, available at https://pages.software.imdea.org/ciao-lang/sCASP.

3   AI Legal Requirements wrt Privacy

Art. 22 of GDPR already demands to implement transparency procedures for decisions based solely on automated processing, including profiling. The EU Artificial Intelligence Act, which was approved by the Council of the EU on May 21, 2024, in recital 42 explicitly says that "Natural persons should never be judged on AI predicted behavior based solely on their profiling, personality traits or characteristics, such as nationality, place of birth, place of residence, number of children, level of debt or type of car, without a reasonable suspicion of that person being involved in a criminal activity based on objectively verifiable facts and without human assessment thereof". The regulation considers high-risk AI systems intended to be used for the profiling of criminal suspects and potential victims, monitoring students' behavior, filtering job applications, evaluating or terminating job candidates, and so on. In all these examples, the use of sensitive data to classify people or make decisions that affect them requires the development of transparent, interpretable, and auditable AI systems.

Table 1 provides an overview of high-risk AI systems that require cautionary measures following the EU AI Act in Annex III. In general, any AI systems that pose a risk of harm to health and safety or an adverse impact on fundamental rights can be considered high risk. It also forbids AI systems that infer the emotions of a natural person in the areas of workplace and education institutions. It is also important to remember that Art. 9 of the GDPR imposes additional precautionary measures on the processing of personal data revealing racial or ethnic origin, political opinions, religious or philosophical beliefs, or trade union membership, as well as on the processing of genetic data, biometric data for the purpose of uniquely identifying a natural person, data concerning health or data concerning a natural person's sex life or sexual orientation.

4   Privacy-ML: Scheme Design

In this section, we will describe the architecture of different Machine Learning (ML) models where we focus on two different goals: (i) preserve user's sensitive information (to avoid biased classification and/or discrimination), and (ii) improve accuracy wrt. classification labels introduced considering this sensitive information (even if it is biased):

- First, we describe $\mathrm{ML}_0^{\mathcal{X}}$, a (biased) model trained with a dataset containing a sensitive characteristic whose usage could pose a legal problem, or generate a biased response. In what follows we will refer to this sensitive characteristic as a_k.
- Second, we describe a naive approach, $\mathrm{ML}_{\bar{k}}^{\mathcal{X}}$, that avoids the usage of the sensitive characteristic a_k by directly removing it from the training dataset. As a result, obviously, for the classification of new instances with $\mathrm{ML}_{\bar{k}}^{\mathcal{X}}$, a_k is not required.

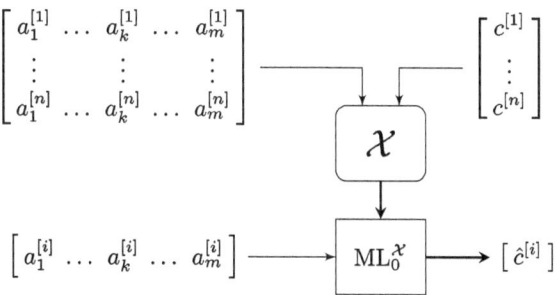

Fig. 1. Design of the (biased) model $\mathrm{ML}^{\mathcal{X}_0}$.

- Then, we describe an auxiliary model, $\mathrm{ML}_k^{\mathcal{X}}$, that is trained to infer the sensitive characteristic a_k from the training dataset without this characteristic.
- Finally, we construct the Privacy-ML scheme combining the auxiliary model $\mathrm{ML}_k^{\mathcal{X}}$, and the (biased) model $\mathrm{ML}_0^{\mathcal{X}}$.

4.1 $\mathrm{ML}_0^{\mathcal{X}}$: The (Biased) Model

First, we assume an AI classification model that has been trained using a (biased) dataset.

The upper part of Fig. 1 shows: (i) the classifier represented as $\mathcal{X}$, (ii) the dataset represented as a matrix of m attributes with n instances $(a_{[1-m]}^{[1-n]})$, and (iii) the classes used as targets represented as a vector of n instances of classes $c^{[1-n]}$. The lower part of Fig. 1 shows the resulting model $\mathrm{ML}^{\mathcal{X}_0}$, which, given a vector of attributes can output the potential class that corresponds to these attributes.

Note that within the training dataset, there exists the attribute a_k that should not be used. As we mentioned before, this is either because it is a sensitive predicate that does not comply with the necessary requisites for its use, or because it is being employed to make biased/discriminative decisions.

4.2 $\mathrm{ML}_k^{\mathcal{X}}$: Naive Approach to Preserve Privacy

To comply with the current regulations on AI systems and data protection in cases where a dataset contains a sensitive attribute, a naive approach consists of simply not using this attribute to avoid discrimination or privacy violations of the users or other third-party agents.

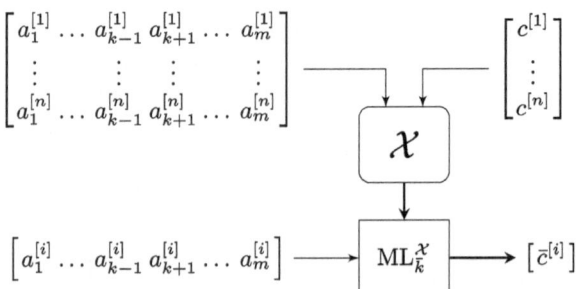

Fig. 2. Design of the naive approach $\mathrm{ML}_k^{\mathcal{X}}$.

The upper part of Fig. 2 shows, as before: (i) the classifier represented as $\mathcal{X}$, (ii) the dataset represented as a matrix of $m - 1$ attributes with n instances $(a_{[1-(k-1),(k+1)-m]}^{[1-n]})$ –note that the sensitive characteristic a_k is not included–, and (iii) the classes used as targets represented as a vector of n instances of classes $c^{[1-n]}$. The lower part of Fig. 2 shows the resulting model $\mathrm{ML}_{\bar{k}}^{\mathcal{X}}$, which, given an instance represented as a vector of attributes (without a_k) can output the potential class that corresponds to this instance.

4.3 $\mathrm{ML}_k^{\mathcal{X}}$: Auxiliary Model to Learn a_k

In this subsection we are concerned with a model that, instead of determining the classes used as targets, is used to infer one of the attributes contained in the dataset. In particular, $\mathrm{ML}_k^{\mathcal{X}}$ will be trained to infer the sensitive information from the data that can be used without ethical and/or legal concern.

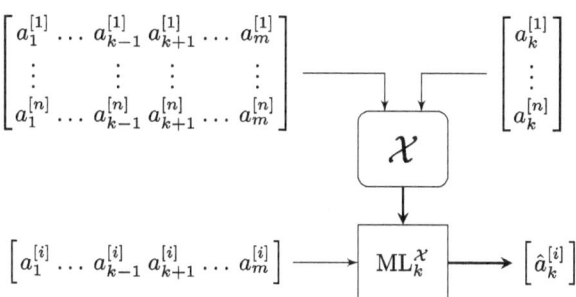

Fig. 3. Design of the auxiliary model $\mathrm{ML}_k^{\mathcal{X}}$.

The upper part of Fig. 3 shows, as before: (i) the classifier represented as $\mathcal{X}$, (ii) the dataset represented as a matrix of $m - 1$ attributes with n instances $(a_{[1-(k-1),(k_1)-m]}^{[1-n]})$ –note that the sensitive characteristic a_k is not included–, and (iii) the attribute a_k used as targets represented as a vector of n instances of classes $a_k^{[1-n]}$. The lower part of Fig. 3 shows the resulting model $\mathrm{ML}_k^{\mathcal{X}}$ which, given an instance represented as a vector of attributes (without a_k), predicts the potential value of a_k that corresponds to this instance.

4.4 The Privacy-$\mathrm{ML}^{\mathcal{X}}$ Scheme

We can now define the architecture of a Machine Learning model that simulates a non-biased model but internally guesses the sensitive attribute and feeds a pre-trained biased model to improve the classification accuracy (considering that the potential bias is desirable).

Note that potential applications of this model include: adjusting customer experience by "guessing" their biased preferences, and protecting discriminated persons (from minorities) without stigmatizing them. I.e., improve clustering without asking for sensitive information (preserving the privacy of the users). As before, Private-$\mathrm{ML}^{\mathcal{X}}$ is a parameterizable scheme, where $\mathcal{X}$ represents the machine learning classifier used to learn the models used in the scheme.

Figure 4 shows that the scheme simulates a single classifier, but internally it contains two models:

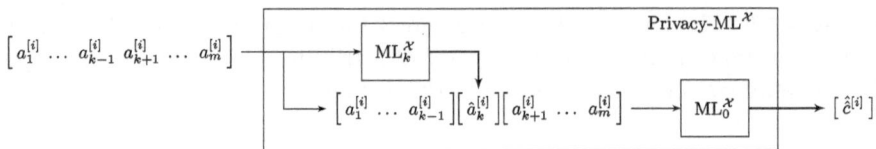

Fig. 4. Privacy-ML$^{\mathcal{X}}$ scheme, an ML model that preserves privacy (and accuracy).

- **ML$_0^{\mathcal{X}}$**, this model has been trained taking into account all attributes available in the data set. Since we assume that the dataset is biased, i.e., it discriminates depending on the attributes a_k.
- **ML$_k^{\mathcal{X}}$**: This model is trained to learn the attribute we want to hide during the inference phase because it is known to be a discriminative attribute, i.e., it learns a_k:

To validate that the ability to hide discriminative attributes is not only real but also worthy, we plan to compare **Privacy-ML$^{\mathcal{X}}$** against **ML$_{\bar{k}}^{\mathcal{X}}$**, the classifier that is trained without considering the discriminative attribute a_k from the data set. We claim that the resulting comparison (on biased datasets) would have the following properties (considering also the accuracy of the original biased ML model, **ML$_0^{\mathcal{X}}$**:

$$\text{Acc}(\text{ML}_0^{\mathcal{X}}, \hat{c}^{[i]}) > \text{Acc}(\text{Privacy-ML}^{\mathcal{X}}, \hat{c}^{[i]}) >> \text{Acc}(\text{ML}_{\bar{k}}^{\mathcal{X}}, \bar{c}^{[i]})$$

5   Vulnerability of XAI to Deceptive Practices

We have claimed in the introduction that forgetting can be used as a deceptive practice. We make this argument based on Crandall's complaint, which asks"Why would you build and operate an expensive algorithm if you can't bias it in your favor?" [15]. The argument explicitly introduces the bad intentions of a legitimate actor developing an AI system for a economic gain and without abiding to social norms or legal rules. This type of actor can use a legitimate tool such as forgetting to deceive other users or external auditors. In this article, we focus on this specific scenario.

First, in Sect. 4.1, we described ML$_0^{\mathcal{X}}$, a system in which an actor has developed an AI system using a dataset that contains a sensitive characteristic whose utilization could lead to legal issues or biased outcomes. The sensitive characteristic will be represented as a_k.

Next, in Sect. 4.2, we have described ML$_{\bar{k}}^{\mathcal{X}}$, a naive AI system that does not employ the discriminating or sensitive attribute a_k. This approach would be the acceptable solution to comply with the regulations on AI and data privacy.

But, even if using the second one would be more ethical, a malicious actor could still violate the law or/and discriminate without such actions being discovered, and while ostensibly complying with the European AI Act. I.e., in Sect. 5.1, we describe a scheme based on Inductive Logic Programming (ILP) that could potentially facilitate this action, let's denote this scheme as Hack-ML^{ILP}, which is composed by the combination of Privacy-ML^{ILP} and the use of the forgetting operator f_{CASP}.

5.1 Hack-ML $=$ Privacy-ML $+$ f_{CASP} (A Real Threat)

Privacy-ML^{ILP} is a specific scheme in which we use the symbolic AI algorithms based on Inductive Logic Programming (ILP) which, as classification models, generates logic programs. Recent ILP proposals, including the FOLD family of algorithms [17,18], can run the learned programs under s(CASP) to generate explanations (in natural language) of the inferred classification. In addition, we could provide the learned logic program(s) to be audited –this possibility is one of the main advantages of ILP over black-box-based learning models in building trust in the system. However, while in the black-box algorithm we do not expect a model audit, this is not the case when dealing with ILP models. Consequently, the Privacy-ML^{ILP} scheme architecture would reveal sensitive information, and the scheme owner/auditor could (maliciously) use it to infer sensitive information from vulnerable users.

Note that Privacy-ML^{ILP} is constructed with two ILP models:

- The first model is learned by ML$_0^{ILP}$ and it is a program with rules of the form:

```
1  class(X, c_1) :- a_3(X,a), a_k(X,b), not a_5(X,d).
```

- The second model is learned by ML$_k^{ILP}$ and it is a program with rules of the form:

```
1  a_k(X, b) :- a_1(X,E), E #> 18, not a_7(X,f).
```

  which in this case we consider it has constraints (which in this example is a linear equation, E #> 18), but more importantly it would be able to infer the sensitive information from the other attributes.
- Finally, another advantage of using ILP over a scheme built using black-box ML models is the possibility of applying forgetting to merge the two models by eliminating any presence of a_k and thus making the existence of a_k go unnoticed during an audit. Merging the above rules invoking f_{CASP} to forget a_k results in:

```
1  class(X, c_1) :-
2      a_3(X,a), a_1(X,E), E #> 18, not a_7(X,f), not a_5(X,d).
```

Note that we have used f_{CASP} [7] to obfuscate this scheme and hide the use of discriminatory features from auditors. We denote the resulting scheme as Hack-ML$_k^{ILP}$, and we claim that since forgetting sensitive information can be seen as a way of obfuscating the model (and its justifications), if we use it to hide evidence in deliberately discriminatory decision-making, it can become a real threat.

Additionally, the last advantage of auditing the resulting ASP programs is the possibility of adapting (biased) rules. Considering Hacking, this ability can be used to include discriminatory rules in non-biased learned models in such a way that after applying f_{CASP} these discriminatory rules cannot be detected later on by the auditors.

Note that, Hack-ML$_k^{\text{ILP}}$, could be potentially used with dataset included in application areas 3 and 4 (e.g., the COMPAS Recidivism Racial Bias data set) and its use in automated administrative legal reasoning with discretion to act as in [3] targets applications in area 6 (see Table 1).

6   Evaluation Experiments

This section reports on our efforts to experimentally validate the conjectures made in Sect. 4 regarding the accuracy of our models. We first outline the implementation of the evaluation environment in Python v.3.12 (more details in requirements.txt) which comprises a training and a testing module. In Sect. 6.2 we report on preliminary evaluation results using the German Credit Data [11] dataset.

6.1   Implementation

The training module, train.py,[1] builds the three binary classifiers: (i) $ML_0^{\mathcal{X}}$, (ii) $ML_{\bar{k}}^{\mathcal{X}}$, and (iii) Hack-ML$^{\mathcal{X}}$, using a linear regression model (later on we plan to parameterize this module to allow the use of other algorithms). Each binary classifier is contained in a class called `BinaryClassifier` which provides methods for fitting the model (called `fit`), making predictions (`predict`), and saving and loading the model from a file (`save_model` and `load_model`, respectively). The class `LinearRegressionBinary` inherits from it, overriding the `predict` method to directly transform the results into binary, encapsulating the `sklearn` `linear_model` class.

The training module performs the following steps:

- First, it loads the dataset and splits the data into training and testing sets to separate relevant features and target variables, ensuring that the bias category is handled appropriately.
- Next, it trains the three ML models: (i) $ML_0^{\mathcal{X}}$ (which uses all features), (ii) $ML_{\bar{k}}^{\mathcal{X}}$ (the model that excludes the bias), and (iii) $ML_K^{\mathcal{X}}$ (which predicts the bias); using, as we mentioned before, the `LinearRegressionBinary` class.
- Finally, we create the Hack-ML^{X} thanks to the `BiasedMlx` class, which is shown in Fig. 5.

The `BiasedMlx` class inherits from `LinearRegressionBinary` (line 1). Then, in lines 2 and 3, we observe that it receives the parameters: (i) `bias_category_tag`,

---

[1] For the reader's convenience, the files linked in this paper are available at http://platon.etsii.urjc.es/~jarias/papers/forgetXAI-vae24/.

```
1    class BiasedMlx(LinearRegressionBinary):
2      def __init__(self, bias_category_tag, bias_category_pos,
3                   missing_feature_model, final_prediction_model):
4        self.bias_category_tag = bias_category_tag
5        self.bias_category_pos = bias_category_pos
6        self.missing_feature_model = missing_feature_model
7        super().__init__(final_prediction_model)
8
9      def predict(self, x):
10       # Predict missing feature
11       y_score_ml_kx = self.missing_feature_model.predict(x)
12       y_score_ml_kx = pd.DataFrame(y_score_ml_kx,
13                         columns=[self.bias_category_tag])
14
15       # Reset the indexes of the DataFrames
16       x.reset_index(drop=True, inplace=True)
17       y_score_ml_kx.reset_index(drop=True, inplace=True)
18
19       # Concatenate the prediction with the original DataFrame
20       x_with_bias_category = pd.concat(
21           [x.iloc[:, :self.bias_category_pos],
22            y_score_ml_kx,
23            x.iloc[:, self.bias_category_pos:]], axis=1)
24
25       # Final prediction using the new DataFrame
26       predictions = super().predict(x_with_bias_category)
27       return predictions
```

Fig. 5. Class `BiasedMlx`

with the name of the biased attribute (ii) `bias_category_pos`, with the column index of the biased attribute (iii) `missing_feature_model`, the auxiliary model $ML_k^{\mathcal{X}}$, and (iv) `final_prediction_model`, the (biased) model $ML_0^{\mathcal{X}}$. Then, in line 11, it uses `missing_feature_model`, which corresponds to the $ML_k^{\mathcal{X}}$ model to predict the bias attribute. In line 20, it concatenates a_k with the passed data set to predict in line 26 using `final_prediction_model`, which corresponds to $ML_0^{\mathcal{X}}$. This results in a framework that receives a dataset without the discriminative attribute a_k, but it is inferred and used in the classification of a model that has been trained with real a_k values.

The testing module, test.py, evaluates the trained models with metrics such as accuracy and recall from `sklearn metrics` (`accuracy_score` and `recall_score`) to assess their effectiveness. Key components in this file include the function that calculates the metrics (`calculate_metrics`), loading our test data and the pre-trained models from their respective files, which are then used to make the predictions and calculate the metrics with the aforementioned function. In our case, we made predictions using a linear regression model.

6.2   Evaluation: Preliminary Results

In this section, we apply the above framework to the case of German Credit Data [11], a publicly available dataset in the domain of bank lending (german_data.csv). Recall that so far we have used the aforementioned initial implementation with a linear regression algorithm, not an ILP-based model.

Figure 6 shows the results obtained from our three models in terms of accuracy and recall. We observe that the use of Hack-ML is similar to the trained classifier without the sensitive attribute (both obtain 76% accuracy). Although these results do not allow us to confirm our hypothesis that the use of Hack-ML would improve the accuracy of a model that does not infer the sensitive attribute, they do allow us to observe its performance on data sets whose potentially sensitive attributes are not strongly correlated with others (note that the accuracy with and without the sensitive attributes are practically equal 76.5% vs. 76.0%).

1	Acc. of ML OX: 0.7650	3	Acc. of Hack MLX: 0.7600	5	Acc. of ML NEG KX: 0.7600
2	Recall of ML OX: 0.9073	4	Recall of Hack MLX: 0.9073	6	Recall of ML NEG KX: 0.9073

Fig. 6. Testing output for German Credit dataset

Figure 7 supports the above conclusion. It shows the result of checking the Correlation Matrix with the target attribute (approval) for the German Credit dataset. None of the attributes has a strong correlation with the target, not even those supposed to be sensitive like sex or Age Group. They only have -0.075493 and 0.023094 respectively. Meaning that German Credit Data is a non-biased dataset.

1	duration_month	-0.214927	10	debtors_guarant	0.025137
2	credit_history	0.228785	11	residence_since	-0.002967
3	purpose	-0.017979	12	property	-0.142612
4	credit_amount	-0.154739	13	other_installment_plans	0.109844
5	Age Group	0.023094	14	housing	0.019315
6	savings_bonds	0.178943	15	nr_credits	0.045732
7	employment_since	0.116002	16	job	-0.032735
8	installment_in_percent	-0.072404	17	nr_dependants	0.003015
9	sex	-0.075493	18	phone	0.036466

Fig. 7. Correlation Matrix of approval for the German Credit dataset.

Note that this evaluation needs to be extended using datasets with bias, and comparing the accuracy of the optimal (biased) classifier, $\mathbf{ML}_0^{\mathcal{X}}$, the naive privacy-preserving approach, $\mathbf{ML}_{\bar{k}}^{\mathcal{X}}$, and the more sophisticated **Hack-ML**$^{\mathcal{X}}$, with regards to the accuracy relations conjectured in Sect. 4. Furthermore, to validate the potential damage of Hack-ML$^{\mathcal{X}}$, an ILP-based classifier should be applied to these datasets. We leave this for future work.

7   Conclusions

The automation of all sorts of processes through AI systems demands us to guarantee, as much as possible, the protection of the people who are affected by the decisions generated by such systems. In this paper, we have outlined the attack scheme Hack-ML in which a machine learning framework can learn a discriminative decision-making model such that it does not need to receive the discriminative feature to make the decision. We conjecture that this can increase distrust in automated systems as long as the authorities do not enforce verification methods (beyond requiring traceability and a readable explanation) to demonstrate that a high-risk AI system ensures reliability (robustness, security, and accuracy) and that it does not entail risks or generate discriminatory results.

According to the AI Act, high-risk AI systems are subject to the following strict obligations before they can be placed on the market:

Ob1 Adequate risk assessment and mitigation systems;
Ob2 High quality of the datasets feeding the system to minimize risks and discriminatory outcomes;
Ob3 Activity logging to ensure traceability of results;
Ob4 Detailed documentation providing all information on the system and its purpose for authorities to assess its compliance;
Ob5 Clear and adequate information to users;
Ob6 Appropriate human oversight measures to minimize risk;
Ob7 High level of robustness, security, and accuracy.

However, obligations Ob1 and Ob2 cannot be audited once the model is built, and obligations Ob4 and Ob7 are independent of the system used and any proposal (whether it has good or bad intentions) would want to be able to satisfy them. Therefore, malicious systems would only have to cover obligations Ob3, Ob5, and Ob6.

As we have argued in this paper, the combination of Privacy-ML^{ILP} with forgetting allows (Ob3) tracing the results –the justification is a trace of the inference based on the model, (Ob5) providing the user with clear and adequate information – one can query why a certain classification is not obtained and the corresponding justification is generated, and (Ob6) the justifications can be generated in natural language to facilitate interaction with humans.

In future work, we plan to validate the existence of this vulnerability with several use cases (using different learning algorithms and different datasets). We will also look into potential countermeasures that allow us to mitigate its negative impact.

Acknowledgments. This work has been supported by grant VAE: TED2021-131295B-C33/C31 funded by MCIN/AEI/ 10.13039/501100011033 and by the "European Union NextGenerationEU/PRTR", by grant COSASS: PID2021-123673OB-C32 funded by MCIN/AEI/ 10.13039/501100011033 and by "ERDF A way of making Europe".

Disclosure of Interests. The authors have no competing interests to declare that are relevant to the content of this article.

References

1. Arias, J., Carro, M., Chen, Z., Gupta, G.: Justifications for goal-directed constraint answer set programming. In: Proceedings 36th International Conference on Logic Programming (Technical Communications). EPTCS, vol. 325, pp. 59–72. Open Publishing Association (2020). https://doi.org/10.4204/EPTCS.325.12

2. Arias, J., Carro, M., Salazar, E., Marple, K., Gupta, G.: Constraint answer set programming without grounding. Theory Pract. Logic Program. **18**(3–4), 337–354 (2018). https://doi.org/10.1017/S1471068418000285

3. Arias, J., Moreno-Rebato, M., Rodriguez-García, J.A., Ossowski, S.: Automated legal reasoning with discretion to act using s(LAW). Artif. Intell. Law **23**, 1–24 (2023). https://doi.org/10.1007/s10506-023-09376-5

4. Arias, J., Moreno-Rebato, M., Rodriguez-Garcia, J.A., Ossowski, S.: Towards value-awareness in administrative processes: an approach based on constraint answer set programming. In: Proceedings of the 39th ACM/SIGAPP Symposium on Applied Computing, pp. 770-778. SAC '24, Association for Computing Machinery, New York, NY, USA (2024). https://doi.org/10.1145/3605098.3636022

5. Chen, J., Dong, H., Wang, X., Feng, F., Wang, M., He, X.: Bias and debias in recommender system: a survey and future directions. ACM Trans. Inf. Syst. **41**(3), 1–39 (2023)

6. Doshi-Velez, F., Kim, B.: Towards a rigorous science of interpretable machine learning. arXiv preprint arXiv:1702.08608 (2017)

7. Fidilio-Allende, L., Arias, J.: f_{CASP}: a forgetting technique for XAI based on goal-directed constraint ASP models. In: Proceedings of XXIII Jornadas sobre Programación y Lenguajes (PROLE 2024). EPTCS (2024)

8. Gelfond, M., Lifschitz, V.: The stable model semantics for logic programming. In: 5th International Conference on Logic Programming, pp. 1070–1080 (1988). https://doi.org/10.2307/2275201

9. Gunning, D., Aha, D.: DARPA's explainable artificial intelligence (XAI) program. AI Mag. **40**(2), 44–58 (2019). https://doi.org/10.1609/aimag.v40i2.2850

10. Himmelhuber, A., Grimm, S., Zillner, S., Joblin, M., Ringsquandl, M., Runkler, T.: Combining sub-symbolic and symbolic methods for explainability. In: Rules and Reasoning: 5th International Joint Conference, RuleML+ RR 2021, Leuven, Belgium, September 13–15, 2021, Proceedings 5, pp. 172–187. Springer (2021)

11. Hofmann, H.: Statlog (German Credit Data). UCI Machine Learning Repository (1994). https://doi.org/10.24432/C5NC77

12. Montes, N., Osman, N., Sierra, C., Slavkovik, M.: Value engineering for autonomous agents. arXiv preprint arXiv:2302.08759 (2023)

13. Orphanou, K., et al.: Mitigating bias in algorithmic systems-a fish-eye view. ACM Comput. Surv. **55**(5), 1–37 (2022)

14. O'Neil, C.: Weapons of Math Destruction: How Big Data Increases Inequality and Threatens Democracy (2017)

15. Sandvig, C., Hamilton, K., Karahalios, K., Langbort, C.: Auditing algorithms: research methods for detecting discrimination on internet platforms. Data Discrimination Converting Criti. Concerns Prod. Inquiry **22**(2014), 4349–4357 (2014)

16. Stray, J., et al.: Building human values into recommender systems: an interdisciplinary synthesis. ACM Trans. Recommender Syst. **2**(3), 1–57 (2024)
17. Wang, H., Gupta, G.: FOLD-R++: a scalable toolset for automated inductive learning of default theories from mixed data. In: International Symposium on Functional and Logic Programming, pp. 224–242. Springer (2022). https://doi.org/10.1007/978-3-030-99461-7_13
18. Wang, H., Shakerin, F., Gupta, G.: FOLD-RM: a scalable, efficient, and explainable inductive learning algorithm for multi-category classification of mixed data. Theory Pract. Logic Program. **22**(5), 658–677 (2022). https://doi.org/10.1017/S1471068422000205
19. Wang, Y., Wang, K., Zhang, M.: Forgetting for answer set programs revisited. In: IJCAI, pp. 1162–1168. Citeseer (2013)

Values-Aligned, Responsible Sharing (VaRS): A Methodology and a Blueprint

Alexandros Nousias(✉)📵, Maria Dagioglou📵, and Georgios Petasis📵

Institute of Informatics and Telecommunications, National Center of Scientific Research "Demokritos", Ag. Paraskevi, Attica, Greece
{alexandros.nousias,mdagiogl,petasis}@iit.demokritos.gr

Abstract. Identifying values as the drivers of human behavior consti-tutes the first step towards responsible and trusted sharing. A value-aligned and responsible sharing schema for AI assets aims to gener-ate, over and above hard law, a 'for benefit' culture and can serve as a driver for responsible AI practices. In the present work, we propose a methodology that allows licensors to self-reflect about their values set with respect to the licensed AI asset, based on Schwartz's personal values vocabulary and convey licensors permissions and restrictions accordingly through licensing. The proposed value-aligned responsible sharing license blueprint integrates the licensor's values along with typical open licens-ing elements (BY-SA-NC-ND) that are employed in a dual form, both for copyright and responsibility (r) treats. We demonstrate the applica-tion of VaRS methodology through the datasets of the VAST project, an EU-funded H2020 research and innovation action. The VaRS blueprint integrates the VAST consortium's responsibility treats and demonstrates how licensors' value-alignment can be reflected in the license.

Keywords: Value-alignment · Value-driven responsible sharing · Open Responsible AI licensing · Soft law

1 Introduction

Delivering ethical, responsible, and trustworthy artificial intelligence (AI) solu-tions is not just a desired characteristic of AI systems any longer, but rather a requirement. For these requirements to be fully materialized, relevant asset owners need to unpack, identify and reflect the varying qualitative properties of the different assets of an AI system, namely the data, the algorithms, the models and the governance practices thereof. Such reflections are subject to appropriate ethical, societal, human rights, privacy or environmental assessments as directly or indirectly introduced by the recently adopted Regulation 2024/1689 on AI [1], relevant legal tools like the General Data Protection Regulation (GDPR), or the 2019/790 Copyright Directive, the new liability rules on products and AI to protect consumers and foster innovation. To that end, different conformity or

N. Osman and L. Steels (Eds.): VALE 2024, LNAI 15356, pp. 240–256, 2025.
https://doi.org/10.1007/978-3-031-85463-7_15

ethical frameworks have come to play, assessing the level of risk in given areas of interest.

In this context, open and responsible AI licences (RAILs) [10] can play a crucial role in the adoption of ethical practices, while maintaining access to state-of-the-art algorithmic models and datasets. RAILs enable AI asset holders to incorporate permissive or restrictive terms on how their assets should or should not be re-used and/or re-purposed, based on their understanding of what constitutes a responsible behaviour, hence imposing contextual behavioural use-based restrictions [10]. The existing RAILS [4,9] integrate aspects of responsibility by taking into account ethical principles, such as the Ethical Charter (EC) adopted by the BigScience community [5]. This Ethical Charter includes values such as inclusivity, diversity, responsibility, etc. However, they do not explicitly refer to these values within the actual licenses, nor introduce a values vocabulary that would allow licensors to clearly transmit their morality (through the licenses) for licensees to reflect upon.

The combination of a licensor's underlying value set and the properties of the licensed asset, namely technical features, legal confrontations and ethical repercussions, as well as the overall concept, if assessed as a whole, should formulate the requirements, objectives and clauses of the final license, under which the licensed asset is distributed and shared. This kind of responsible distribution and sharing comes not as a stand-alone outcome. It requires a moral process. Morality here is not only understood as the licensor's value set, as it applies in a given context, but also as the licensor's capability to produce moral behaviour [18]. Hence, in the present work, we go beyond proposing a blue-print of a RAIL that merely refers to specific values coming from a widely accepted values vocabulary [25]. Our focus also lies on the required moral process that leads to a RAIL.

We propose a methodology that allows licensors to self-reflect about their values set, with respect to the licensed AI asset. The methodology adopts a vocabulary of specific values [25] that is used to trigger self-reflection and convey licensor permissions and restrictions. This approach handles miscommunication regarding the concept of values and their meaning, encourages moral behavior, and produces tangible and tailor-made requirements for specific license clauses. Following a similar procedure, downstream users need: a) to assess whether they respect the values of the licensors, b) to assess whether they are capable of satisfying the responsibility criteria set by them, and c) to conduct their own values-alignment analysis, in order to articulate their values and responsibility treats in context for their derivative works.

The structure of this paper is as follows. Section 2 explores the work related to RAILs and value definitions. Section 3 introduces the proposed methodology of producing value-informed and asset/licensor-tailored requirements for RAIL clauses. It also demonstrates it through a concrete paradigm as explored in the VAST project. Section 4 presents the resulting RAIL blue-print. Section 5 concludes the presented work with a follow-up discussion.

2   Background

Legal systems reflect the constitutionally agreed value system of a given society, organized in a state form. Licenses are voluntarily but still binding instruments for transactions among different types of agents. Apart from the licensed material, the rights and the restrictions they impose, licenses convey a social message, based on a set of guiding values and world perceptions of the licensor and to some extent of the licensee. This is mostly the case in the worlds of open source, remixing and the so called 'free culture' [15].

Open source licenses (i.e. open software licenses like GPL, MIT, BSD or Apache) and open content licenses (i.e. Creative Commons or Open Data Commons licenses) are instruments of this kind of ethic, shaped and governed by the foundational freedoms and constraints of copyright law. This licensing structure is both a legal set of constraints that sets out what developers can and cannot do to prevent uses they view as unethical, and a normative one that frames broader cultural values beyond what the license requires [8]. Open software licenses can be conceived as social institutions setting the norms in specific communities and/or markets [26].

Advances in computing have introduced new challenges in maintaining openness, so the computing community has begun to respond to the conflict between powerful new technologies and the value of openness. A new tension between open and responsible use emerges. Licensing is gradually being transformed from an intellectual property rights management tool, to a mechanism for enabling legally enforceable responsible use, subject to given value sets and ethical schema. In practice, licenses in the context of computing and namely AI, enable AI asset holders to incorporate permissive use clauses, based on their view of how their assets should or should not be re-used and/or re-purposed, while imposing contextual behavioural use-based restrictions [10]. Responsible sharing can be carried out via responsible licensing. Due to the voluntarily 'soft law' character of open licensing the volume of the parties that may enter in such agreements is uncertain. Nevertheless, similar to laws, licenses guide behaviour so as to encourage people to act in a particular manner [6].

The behavioural-use restrictions of Responsible AI Licences' (RAILs) are not limited to the licensed artifact, rather they extend to all downstream uses and/or derivative works thereof. In the event that responsible licenses include open access/free-use terms, this means that the license promotes free use and re-distribution of the applicable artifact, albeit subject to use restrictions [26]. Such a development may qualify RAILs as Open RAILs, subject to the universal requirements of the open source definition as provided by the Open Source Initiative.[1] Open licensing schemas define, on a 'one to many' model, the rules of the game, thus are capable of engineering downstream responsible behaviours in given contexts. The 'responsibility' element attempts to limit usage, based on ethical considerations, such as distribution of untrustworthy information or propaganda, imitation of user characteristics causing third party confusion between

---

[1] https://opensource.org/osd.

AI systems and humans, imitating other persons' likeness, voice or other identifiable characteristics in order to damage their reputation [10].

Like open source licenses, the RAILs are styled as copyright licenses. The ability to enforce them rests on the licensor's ability to prove that they have copyright ownership in the licensed material and that a violation of the RAIL is therefore copyright infringement [26]. RAILs however do not simply operate as copyright licenses. RAILs attempt to assert wider behavioural adaptations that transcend the space of intellectual property, subject a) to the values of the licensor and b) to the legal arrangements introduced by the emerging AI regulatory package. In view of the emerging AI regulatory package, to the extent there is a violation of the responsibility part of the license, fault or no fault based liability of the licensee may arise under tort law as depicted in AI Liability Directive and Revised Product Liability Directive, regardless the license, provided there is damage or harm [2]. This means that under the AI Liability Directive, hard responsibility obligations are binding by law, regardless the contractual arrangements (in other words license terms), if any. Add here the specific obligations of an AI system stakeholder, that come according to the level of risk as identified by the AI Act, responsibility rolls out as a complex legal concept based on the level of risk. Note that the risk levels according to AI Act are: unacceptable, high, limited and minimal risk. High-risk systems must undergo a third-party assessment before they can be sold or used [1].

Licensors of an AI asset are free to assume that their licensed asset is susceptible for high risk uses or to claim the mere action of embedding the licensed asset to an AI system that may constrain their values, as an event of high risk. Hence, the responsibility elements of a RAIL go hand in hand with the risk level of an AI system and the underlying hard law obligations and responsibilities. EU AI Act, Annexes XI and XII state for example that the technical documentation necessary for providers of general purpose AI models (GPAI) includes *"...information on the data used for training, testing and validation, where applicable, including the type and provenance of data and curation methodologies (e.g. cleaning, filtering etc.), the number of data points, their scope and main characteristics as well as the license"*. It is evident that all nodes in the AI value chain, including data providers, need to be transparent in regard to the properties of the licensed asset and their wider sociotechnical and moral concerns.

On the other hand, use based restrictions, although lawful in strict legal terms, they may violate the license terms due to the fact that they compromise the licensor's value set. As Stanford computer scientist Stefano Ermon puts it, the issue of value alignment is *"...to define what exactly these values are because people have different values, come from different parts of the world, and have different socioeconomic backgrounds"*.[2] Hence, such downstream behavioral restrictions need to be properly framed (by the licensor) and fully respected (by the licensee).

The existing RAILS do not explicitly introduce a values vocabulary that licensees may reflect upon. The BigCode OpenRAIL-M license agreement [3]

---

[2] https://futureoflife.org/2017/01/26/stefano-ermon-interview/.

"...embeds a specific set of restrictions for the use of the model in identified critical scenarios. Use restrictions are informed by an evidence-based approach to ML development and use limitations which forces to draw a line between promoting wide access and use of ML against potential societal costs stemming from harmful uses of the openly licensed AI artifact".[3] The BigScience BLOOM RAIL 1.0[4] aims at a free worldwide access to its Large Language Models *"...by taking a multicultural and responsible approach to the development and release of these artifacts".* In the BLOOM RAIL case, the license provides a permissive IP grant, whilst restricting the use of the model for a set of use-cases for which the BigScience community was reluctant to enable, either due to its technical limitations or due to ethical and legal concerns, both based on the community Ethical Charter [5] and the EU AI Act. The Ethical Charter of BigScience defines a list of two kinds of values. Intrinsic values refer to *"what is valuable for its own sake, in itself [...], as an end"* and include inclusivity, diversity, reproducibility, openness, responsibility. Extrinsic values are related to *"...what is valuable as a means, or for something else's work"* and comprise accessibility, transparency, interdisciplinarity and multilingualism.

There is no single topic related to ethical and responsible AI that does not involve multiple references to *(moral) values*: from licences and AI ethics assessment procedures [7,22], to values detection [14,19], inference [16] and alignment in AI [13]. Human morality, including the nature of values, has long been a topic of quest in philosophy and psychology [11]. Values are considered as the forces that guide our actions [25] and drive our moral behaviour (perception, judgment, focus, action) [18]. As such, their impact is manifested in all aspects of our lives, from cultural heritage artifacts [21] to citizen's political behaviour [23] and human interaction with AI.

Discussing about values in socio-technical contexts, such as those related to responsible AI's multiple facets, can quickly turn into a babel of personal perceptions and biases. Situations and contexts are perceived through personal lenses and are verbally expressed through different words (vocabularies), the interpretation (and translation) of which is again personal. A standard list of values, as opposed to an open vocabulary, could be a powerful tool to avoid the aforementioned complexities. Schwartz's theory of personal values [25] offers such a vocabulary that comprises 19 values accompanied with definitions. Schwartz's list of personal values is a research-based, widely used and accepted vocabulary [24] that is currently adopted by many initiatives [20]. Moreover, in contrast to other research based vocabularies it offers a required expressivity [12]. Beyond being a common semantic ground, Schwartz's values can systematically walk one through *"the values and perceptions of other people"* and enhance the consolidation of personal biases [23]. The use of such vocabulary is a quick workaround, of what would (and should) otherwise involve a holistic training about morality and values, to responsibly react to the rapidly evolving field of AI.

---

[3] https://oecd.ai/en/catalogue/tools/bigcode-openrail-m-license-agreement.

[4] https://oecd.ai/en/catalogue/tools/bigscience-bloom-responsible-ai-license-rail-1-0.

The morality of the people is not only related to their values but also their skills in producing moral behaviour. According to Rest [18] the production of moral behaviour comprises four ethical processes: *sensitivity, judgment, focus* and *action*. Considering that drafting a license is a demonstration of moral behaviour, one can assume that a licensor needs to demonstrate expertise in most of the sub-skills pertinent to each process [17]. Ethical action, manifested by the license itself, should resolve conflicts and problems and assert respect. It should support the ethical focus to respecting others and their values, cultivate conscience and ethical behaviours, act responsibly, be a community member. To do so, the process of drafting the license must encourage: a) ethical sensitivity, that is to support taking the perspectives of others, responding to diversity, controlling social bias, interpreting situations, communicating well, as well as b) ethical reasoning, so as to reflect on the processes and the outcomes, and understand ethical problems and consequences.

3   VaRS Methodology

3.1   Values-Alignment Analysis for AI Assets

To capture the values of licensors in a systematic way, there is a need for a methodology that guides licensors (and licensees) through a structured self-reflection about values that encourages moral behaviour [17] as described above. Such methodology should alleviate the complexities of talking about values in terms of used vocabularies or lack thereof, terminology, perception, semantic interpretation and contextual application.

Our proposed methodology aims to support licensors to run a *values-alignment analysis* that captures their values, and as a result the values conveyed (promoted or constrained) through their AI assets. In this way, the final license clauses do not simply provide straight legal terms for the licensed use, rather reflect a deeper linking between the licensed asset, the context, the legal and commercial objectives and the underlying morality. This allows licensors to assert maximum flexibility in drafting (or selecting) licenses while introducing specific use-behaviour, values-aligned restrictions, permissions and endorsements, explicit or implicit. The methodology for analysing the values-alignment for a given AI asset comprises two major dimensions:

1. The use of Schwartz's [25] 19 personal values as a predefined vocabulary that drives the self-reflection process (see Table 1).
2. A structured group discussion during which, involved parties self-reflect and analyse the impact of AI assets by taking the perspectives of people who align or not with each Schwartz's value. For each value, the stakeholders need: a) to reflect on *value-alignment* scenarios; a value is *promoted* or *constrained*, and b) to decide about their related positioning.

To successfully conduct the process, the involved parties need to be familiar with the definitions of Schwartz's values, as introduced in the literature [25], and with practical examples of existing values-alignment analysis. During the first step of the methodology, the group of licensors need to reflect upon the following questions, for each value in the Schwartz's list:

> *In the event that your asset (dataset/code) was used for the development of an AI application/method/system, how would you position yourself in the following two scenarios*:
> – A specific value is promoted. Do you support this or not?
> – A specific value is constrained. Do you accept this or not?

These questions are the product of pilot testing (unpublished data) and reflect the fact that the impact on a value can be either positive or negative depending on the perspective viewed. This procedure, as shown in Fig. 1, guides licensors through different paths of *value alignment* (a value is promoted or not) and *stakeholders' positioning*, leading to three possible outcomes regarding a given AI system (or method, application, etc.) that uses a licensors' asset: a) a system is endorsed if it promotes a value that the licensor also promotes, b) a system needs to be treated as high-risk if it promotes a value that the licensor does not support its promotion, or if it constrains a value, but this is acceptable by the licensor and c) a system can only use the licensed asset in a restricted way if it constrains values that the licensors do not accept to be constrained. The aforementioned outcomes provide a 'soft law' adoption of the 'hard law' AI Act's risk classification as they allow licensors to set the scope of the behavioural restrictions they impose on their AI assets, based on their identified value system and in synch with the AI Act's risk centric logic, in a more personalised way without violating the law. For example, the licensor either adopts the AI Act's risk classification as is, in the case that the values alignment and positioning lead to 'endorsement', or it imposes a stricter treat otherwise. Indicatively, if values alignment and positioning leads to 'treat as high-risk' then even applications that in AI act are considered of no or minimum risk are treated as high-risk. Finally, any application, whatever its risk classification according to the AI act is, can be rendered of 'restricted' use based on the licensor.

Overall, reflection across the paths over values and positioning can lead to clear-cut decisions, if there is (almost) a consensus about a value's positioning. In this case, one of the outcomes in Fig. 1 is opted. Paths over values and positioning that seem to be more susceptible to individual perceptions lead to treat assets that promote or constrain a given value as high-risk.

Note that based on the VaRS blue-print as introduced in the following section, the *licensees* need to analyse the values-alignment of their assets to inform their choices of the use of VaRS licensed asset. In this case for each value in the Schwartz list, the licensees need to reflect upon the following:

> *Does your asset (AI application/method/system): a) Promotes this value? or b) Constrains this value?*

Note that in the case of licensees, given that the object of assessment is a specific application, method or system, all potential types of end-users (primary,

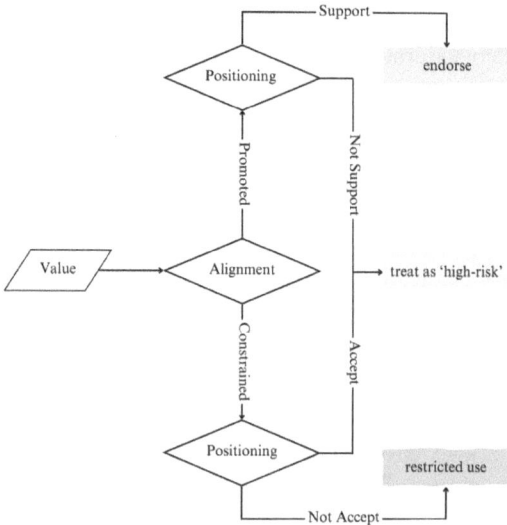

Fig. 1. VaRS methodology. A combination of values-alignment scenarios (promoted or constrained) and the related positioning choices leads to three possible operational outcomes: *endorse, treat as high risk and restricted use.*

secondary, etc.) need to be considered. Following, we present an example of the results of using VaRS method, among VAST consortium as potential licensors of the VAST datasets.

3.2 Use Case: VAST Datasets

About VAST. The present work has been driven by the need to license the datasets produced in the context of the VAST project (Values Across Space and Time), an EU-funded H2020 research and innovation action.[5] VAST has developed methodologies, tools and data infrastructure to capture and digitise the (moral) values of cultural heritage (CH) artifacts, focusing on narratives. Besides annotating artifacts with values, VAST has developed a methodology to capture and digitise the values of citizen's during experiences, such as theatre performances and educational activities. Given the complexity of the task and subjectivity of people's perceptions, VAST methodology, instilled in the ontological specifications [21], deals with three major aspects of a person's interaction with an artifact or experience: a) the participants themselves by considering demographic characteristics, personal values, beliefs, etc., b) the description of the artifact or the experience, and c) the collection of the perceived values.

In general, Digital CH (DCH) data can be quite diverse by nature and biased by definition, often created or collected without computation in mind. VAST offers an extra metadata description by labelling DCH artefacts according to

---

[5] https://www.vast-project.eu/.

the values these data are associated with. As such, the use of VAST DCH data requires additional consideration and responsibility, especially in relation to their use in ML/AI applications, as it may lead to unwanted bias, unfair outcomes, or transformative effects that pose ethical challenges and concerns.

VAST has identified its role in the AI ecosystem and the emerging AI value chains as a responsible provider of potentially sensitive, or high impact, or of significant importance and character datasets. No doubt, this is a challenging positioning that operated as a driver for VAST to work on an informed and responsible data governance basis by a) legally obtaining DCH data, b) generating datasets fit for responsible AI purposes, and c) introducing a values-aligned Open RAILs schema (present work).

Drafting VAST VaRS. Seven consortium partners participated in the procedure introduced above. Most of them had a background in computer science, while one was a law expert. Table 1 shows the results of applying the procedure described above for the case of VAST data sets.

Briefly, VAST datasets include the association of values as perceived by modern audiences to CH artifacts. The numbers in the cells of the table indicate the number of participants that chose a certain path of value alignment and positioning. In our case, we reached a 'clear-cut' decision over a path provided that at least 5 participants agreed to it. Based on this, each cell is colour coded following the categories introduced in Fig. 1, i.e. green for 'endorsement', yellow for 'treat as high-risk' and red for 'restricted use'. Moreover, a few value cases were inconclusive (gray highlighted boxes), and the final related positioning was to include related values-alignment as leading to 'treating as high-risk' permissions. These cases included: Conformity interpersonal constrained and Security personal, Face and Hedonism promoted.

4   The VaRS Blueprint

4.1   General Remarks

The starting point of the VaRS licenses are the very elements and structure of a license in general [10]. The basic structure of a license requires, at minimum, the following:

- Licensor: A person, business or organization with exclusive legal rights over the assets;
- Licensee: A person, business or organization that has been granted legal permission by the licensor;
- Intellectual Property Rights (IPR): Identification of the licensed material and the IPRs thereof;
- Restrictions: geographic, temporal, behavioural, ability to sublicense, royalty terms, etc.

Table 1. VAST consortium's positioning (CP) for the two different values-alignment (VA) scenarios (for each Schwartz value) regarding the VAST datasets, following VaRS methodology. The colours represent the three operational outcomes as per Fig. 1.

Schwartz values	Promoted Support?		Constrained Accept?	
	Y	N	Y	N
Benevolence - Dependability	1	5	5	2
Benevolence - Caring	2	5	5	2
Universalism - Tolerance	7			7
Universalism - Concern	7		1	6
Universalism - Nature	5	2	1	6
Humility	2	5	1	6
Conformity - Interpersonal	1	6	6	1
Conformity - Rules	2	5	3	4
Tradition		7	2	5
Security- Societal		7	5	2
Security - Personal	3	4		7
Face	4	3		7
Power - Resources		7	4	3
Power - Dominance		7	7	
Achievement		7	7	
Hedonism	4	3	6	1
Stimulation	7			7
Self-direction - action	2	5		7
Self-direction - thought	6	1		7

The restrictions delineating how licensed material can be used or repurposed, incorporate a specific set of values and norms that licensor expects the public to respect and follow when using the licensed material. For data and their use in the context of ML/AI, additional licensing options or restrictions regarding the actual uses that are susceptible to licensing could be provided for clarity purposes. Such permissions may refer to usages regarding the licensed data per se, like access, labelling, distribution, and representation. The licensor, however, needs to delineate and grant licenses thereof, for usages of data in conjunction with the ML/AI models. The right to measure the performance of a trained model, the right to enter in model research, to embody the model in a product or a service, or to commercialize the ML/AI output, constitute relevant usage scenarios of this sort. Instead of focusing on usage scenarios, licensors can use their value system as a baseline.

For the rest of this section, the VAST project datasets are used as the use case to present the VaRS blueprint. Nevertheless, the blueprint (next subsection) can be tailored to any asset. The VAST consortium has aimed to maintain an open and permissive character for its licensing schema, while ensuring responsible use of the VAST datasets, either 'as is' or in conjunction with ML/AI models. Via navigating in the Schwartz value framework, the VAST consortium attempted to identify the values that supports to promote or accepts to have them constrained. Subject to this values filter, it was agreed to introduce appropriate requirements, permissions, or restrictions for the following data journeys:

1. Up-streaming data on the VAST platform (a dedicated space developed for the project) from third parties;
2. Responsible downstream sharing formalisations of VAST datasets (i.e. (r)BY, (r)SA, (r)NC, (r)ND - see bellow) connected to the ML/AI lifecycle horizontally (i.e., train, validation, AI model or AI output commercialization) regardless the underlying context of such ML/AI developments;
3. Responsible downstream clauses and/or behavioural use restrictions in random ML/AI contexts.

The objective here is to let the licenses act as informed value carriers and employ tailored restrictions so as to ensure responsible downstream uses in the context of each one of the three points listed above. Point 1 is clear in the sense that for up-streaming data on the VAST platform, specific organizational requirements need to be satisfied (i.e., being a registered user or follow a set metadata or licensing schema). Point 2 provides permissions or restrictions, subject to given values filters with the focus on the phases of the AI system lifecycle, while point 3 focuses on the context.

At the high level, the VAST consortium follows a two fold approach in its licensing scheme as it: a) retains copyright for its generated datasets, which are shared under open licenses, while operating as an open access repository for third party copyrighted material and b) provides a responsibility aspect, subject to its VaRS methodology, as described in Sect. 3. This explicit responsibility aspect for the downstream uses of the licensed material is offered under the typical open licensing options, namely attribution (BY), Non Commercial (NC), Non Derivatives (ND), Share Alike (SA), adjusted accordingly. Following the VaRS methodology, we conclude in the Open Responsibility (r) formalisations below. Off note, (r) here stands for 'Responsible' and operates as an indicator in relation to the typical copyright restrictions of the licenses which are labelled with the typical license elements (BY-SA-NC-ND):

(a) For VAST datasets where the consortium's positioning is 'Endorse' a permissive Responsible Attribution **(r)BY** restriction covers both the IP and the responsibility aspects.
(b) For VAST datasets where the consortium's positioning is 'Treat as High Risk' the licensed material is shared under a **(r)BY-SA**, meaning that the derivative work needs to be treated as High Risk as per the EU AI Act, at all times.

(c) For VAST datasets where the consortium's positioning is 'Restricted Use' the licence restrictions at play would be **(r)BY-NC-ND**, meaning that the licensed material can be used solely for non commercial purposes, namely for scientific and research purposes, while derivatives or further adaptations are explicitly prohibited.

As a background note VAST acknowledges that such a responsible licensing approach can be neither monitored nor enforced in its entirety, i.e. to licensees that operate in different jurisdictions or under a controversial value system or simply aim for 'evil'. However, a scheme like VaRS in a given network with shared values or motives, may arise and generate a 'for benefit' culture that can be a driver for responsible AI practices. The open source software community leads the way in such soft law tactics. Alternatively, identifying generically how VAST datasets can be used in the context of ML/AI may raise awareness and generate trust in networks of shared artifacts, objectives, concerns and values.

4.2   VaRS Blueprint Elements

The VaRS blueprint comprises the following three elements: 'Open', 'Use' and 'Responsible'.

Open.

- Given the licensed material that is data, the license's general approach regarding the copyright aspects will be open and permissive, following the Creative Commons Attribution 4.0 (CC-BY) and Open Data Commons Attribution License, meaning no copyleft elements will be attached, rather solely the attribution of the source (this is the VAST platform) requirement.
- A perpetual, worldwide, non-exclusive, royalty-free, irrevocable copyright license to extract and re-utilize whole or part of the VAST database.
- No sublicense rights are at play. By excluding sub-licensing, the license ensures a direct contractual relationship between the VAST consortium and each registered VAST dataset users, hence optimal enforcement capabilities, since all data users remain in reach of VAST and the license.
- The question remains in the event the licensee wishes to (sub)license the AI model, output or system, which incorporates the VAST dataset.
- Commercial purposes are allowed, solely subject to the Responsible element. Sub-licensing of the commercialized artifact needs to follow the same responsibility element under a Share Alike (SA), licensing restriction. Further scrutiny is required on that ground.

Use.

- Use for the data itself may include: a) access, view, download, b) tag, label or add other metadata, c) make available to third parties, d) otherwise process the data.

- Use for the data in conjunction with ML/AI models may include: a) to train or evaluate a model, b) to enter in model research c) to make the model available to third parties for further research, d) to commercialize either the model or the output thereof.
- Commercialization is subject to scrutiny and the responsibility requirements. On that note further scrutiny on what usage qualifies as commercial is required (i.e., to what extent can a model be embedded in a commercial AI system).

Responsible. Prior to any processing and use of the licensed VAST datasets, licensee needs to apply the VaRS methodology as described in Sect. 3.1, in the context of the secondary uses in place. Subject to the VaRS methodology, VAST data-sets can be used under the following responsibility terms:

1. In the event that the downstream usage promotes a value and the VAST consortium supports this promotion, VAST data sets can be used under **(r)BY**.
2. In the event that the downstream usage constrains a value and the VAST consortium accepts this constrain, or the downstream usage promotes a values and the VAST consortium does not support this, VAST data sets can be used under **(r)BY-SA**. In operational terms this refers to upgrading all downstream AI uses to high risk according to the EU AI Act and address them as such.
3. In the event that the downstream usage constrains a value and the VAST consortium does not accept this, VAST data sets are shared under a **(r)BY-NC-ND** license.

Table 2 provides the licensing scheme that applies for each value of the Schwartz values framework for both the 'promoted' and the 'constrained' scenarios, following VAST Consortium's positioning as per Table 1.

4.3   Further Considerations

Further remarks related to data sharing are listed for data providers/licensors to consider:

- Access to the data can be provided solely to registered users.
- Data that formulate the datasets need to be legally obtained, generated and shared, hence comply with copyrights, privacy rights, personality rights.
- Datasets need to be shared under responsibility and certainty.
- Downstream AI/ML driven permitted uses cannot be contextually agnostic.
- Training GenAI applications needs further examination on the basis of the value-alignment analysis.
- As the case may be appointing internal oversight bodies for assessing the type of candidate downstream uses, the context and the commercial or research character on a case-by-case basis could be an option.
- Dual licensing models, with case specific thresholds of use shall come at play in due course.

Table 2. VaRS Responsible use of VAST datasets

	Value Promoted	Value Constrained
Benevolence - Dependability	(r)BY-SA	(r)BY-SA
Benevolence - Caring	(r)BY-SA	(r)BY-SA
Universalism -Tolerance	(r)BY	(r)BY-NC-ND
Universalism - Concern	(r)BY	(r)BY-NC-ND
Universalism - Nature	(r)BY	(r)BY-NC-ND
Humility	(r)BY-SA	(r)BY-NC-ND
Conformity - Interpersonal	(r)BY-SA	(r)BY-SA
Conformity - Rules	(r)BY-SA	(r)BY-SA
Tradition	(r)BY-SA	(r)BY-NC-ND
Security - Societal	(r)BY-SA	(r)BY-SA
Security - Personal	(r)BY-SA	(r)BY-NC-ND
Face	(r)BY-SA	r)BY-NC-ND
Power - Resources	(r)BY-SA	(r)BY-SA
Power - Dominance	(r)BY-SA	(r)BY-SA
Achievement	(r)BY-SA	(r)BY-SA
Hedonism	(r)BY-SA	(r)BY-SA
Stimulation	(r)BY	(r)BY-SA
Self-direction action	(r)BY-SA	(r)BY-NC-ND
Self-direction thought	(r)BY	(r)BY-NC-ND

- VaRS licensing requires high level metadata schema for optimal labelling and tagging.
- The VAST datasets can be distributed with specific explanations regarding their properties and recommendations in a 'how to sheets' formats (i.e. what means treating a derivative as high risk).
- Enforcement seems not an easy task whatsoever. Data-as-a-Service in an API-based approach could allow for optimal monitoring of downstream uses with the ability to terminate the service in the event of a violation.

5 Conclusions

In the present paper we have proposed a methodology and a license blue-print for value-aligned and responsible sharing (VaRS) over and above the emerging AI regulatory framework, reproducing the legacy and record of the open (source, data, content) licenses under the lenses or responsibility. Our methodology allows licensors, to self-reflect on their values set, with respect to the licensed AI asset, by adopting Schwartz's vocabulary of personal values. This is used to: a) trigger self-reflections and b) convey licensors permissions and restrictions, thus introducing a self-value-driven element in future uses. Following a similar procedure, downstream users need to: a) assess whether they respect the values of the licensors and whether they are capable of satisfying the responsibility criteria set by them, and b) to conduct their own values-alignment analysis in order to identify their own values and responsibility treats for their derivative works.

The present work has been driven by the need to license the datasets produced in the context of the VAST project, an EU-funded H2020 research and innovation action in a responsible, accountable transparent and traceable fashion, so as to allow retrospective AI value chains. VAST datasets include the association of values as perceived by modern audiences to CH artifacts, as well as descriptions (demographics, values, etc.) of involved citizens and the CH artifacts. VaRS licenses provide an Open and Responsible data sharing framework. The typical open licensing elements (BY-SA-NC-ND) are employed in a dual form, both for copyright and responsibility (r) treats. Here, (r)-treats are anchored to the AI Act; a licensed AI asset (e.g. data) may define, shape or influence the AI system's level of risk. VaRS has the potential to extend the AI Act's risk classification mechanism as it may classify a usage as high risk, solely and exclusively under the licensor's values' set. In this way, a licensed AI asset, if not classified objectively (under the AI Act) as high risk, it may be classified as such subjectively (under the VaRS license). A misuse of the license of that sort however, apart from constituting a license breach (under the license use-based restrictions) it may stand as an act of tort (under tort law).

As we enter the AI era, all stakeholders that contribute assets throughout the AI lifecycle have a share and a saying in the AI alignment challenge. VaRS alike methodologies provide the means to accountable, transparent and traceable AI value chains. Future steps of our work include the validation of the VaRS methodology for other AI assets, including other datasets and AI models, as well as the drafting of a full VaRS license (including an easy to read deed, a machine readable deed and a full legal code).

Acknowledgments. This research was co-funded by the European Union in the context of the projects: VAST (grant agreement No. 101004949), TITAN (grant agreement No. 101070658), AI4TRUST (grant agreement No. 101070190) and MANOLO (grant agreement No. 101135782). Views and opinions expressed are, however, those of the authors only and do not necessarily reflect those of the European Union or CNECT. Neither the European Union nor CNECT can be held responsible for them.

Disclosure of Interests. The authors have no competing interests to declare that are relevant to the content of this article.

References

1. Artificial intelligence act, corrigendum, 19 april 2024. interinstitutional file: 2021/0106(cod). https://www.europarl.europa.eu/doceo/document/TA-9-2024-0138-FNL-COR01_EN.pdf. Accessed 14 June 2024

2. Artificial intelligence liability directive. https://www.europarl.europa.eu/RegData/etudes/BRIE/2023/739342/EPRS_BRI(2023)739342_EN.pdf. Accessed 14 June 2024

3. BigCode Model License Agreement - a Hugging Face Space by bigcode — huggingface.co. https://huggingface.co/spaces/bigcode/bigcode-model-license-agreement. Accessed 14 June 2024

4. BigCode OpenRAIL-M — bigcode-project.org. https://www.bigcode-project.org/docs/pages/bigcode-openrail/. Accessed 14 June 2024

5. BigScience Ethical Charter — bigscience.huggingface.co. https://bigscience.huggingface.co/blog/bigscience-ethical-charter. Accessed 14 June 2024

6. Black, J.: Decentring regulation: understanding the role of regulation and self-regulation in a 'post-regulatory' world. Curr. Leg. Probl. **54**(1), 103–146 (2001)

7. Boonstra, M., et al.: Lessons learned in performing a trustworthy AI and fundamental rights assessment. arXiv preprint arXiv:2404.14366 (2024)

8. Coleman, E.G.: Coding Freedom: The Ethics and Aesthetics of Hacking. Princeton University Press (2013)

9. Contractor, D., Ferrandis, C.M., Lee, J., McDuff, D.: From RAIL to Open RAIL: topologies of RAIL licenses - Responsible AI licenses (RAIL) — licenses.ai. https://www.licenses.ai/blog/2022/8/18/naming-convention-of-responsible-ai-licenses. Accessed 12 June 2024

10. Contractor, D., et al.: Behavioral use licensing for responsible AI. In: Proceedings of the 2022 ACM Conference on Fairness, Accountability, and Transparency, pp. 778–788 (2022)

11. Ellemers, N., Van Der Toorn, J., Paunov, Y., Van Leeuwen, T.: The psychology of morality: a review and analysis of empirical studies published from 1940 through 2017. Pers. Soc. Psychol. Rev. **23**(4), 332–366 (2019)

12. Graham, J., et al.: Moral foundations theory: The pragmatic validity of moral pluralism. In: Advances in Experimental Social Psychology, vol. 47, pp. 55–130. Elsevier (2013)

13. Klingefjord, O., Lowe, R., Edelman, J.: What are human values, and how do we align AI to them? arXiv preprint arXiv:2404.10636 (2024)

14. Legkas, S., Christodoulou, C., Zidianakis, M., Koutrintzes, D., Petasis, G., Dagioglou, M.: Hierocles of alexandria at touché: multi-task & multi-head custom architecture with transformer-based models for human value detection. In: Working Notes of the Conference and Labs of the Evaluation Forum CLEF (2024). CEUR Workshop Proceedings, CEUR-WS. org (2024)

15. Lessig, L.: Free Culture: The Nature and Future of Creativity (reprint edition) (2005)

16. Liscio, E., et al.: Value inference in sociotechnical systems. In: Proceedings of the 2023 International Conference on Autonomous Agents and Multiagent Systems, pp. 1774–1780 (2023)

17. Narvaez, D., Bock, T.: Developing ethical expertise and moral personalities. Handbook Moral Char. Educ. **2**, 140–158 (2014)

18. Narvaez, D., Rest, J.: The four components of acting morally. Moral Behav. Moral Dev. Introd. **1**(1), 385–400 (1995)

19. Papadopoulos, G., Kokol, M., Dagioglou, M., Petasis, G.: Andronicus of rhodes at semeval-2023 task 4: transformer-based human value detection using four different neural network architectures. In: Proceedings of the 17th International Workshop on Semantic Evaluation (SemEval-2023), pp. 542–548 (2023)

20. Reitis-Mustenrmann, T., Schulze, B.P., Scharfbillig, M., Stefanovich, N., de, L.B., et al.: Values in news and political manifestos: annotation guidelines (2024). https://doi.org/10.2760/7398
21. Ruskov, M., Dagioglou, M., Kokol, M., Montanelli, S., Petasis, G., et al.: A knowledge graph of values across space and time. In: CEUR Workshop Proceeding, vol. 3536, pp. 8–20. CEUR-WS (2023)
22. Schabus, D.: The IEEE CertifAIEd framework applied to the city of vienna, IEEE SA. https://standards.ieee.org/beyond-standards/the-ieee-certifaied-framework-for-ai-ethics-applied-to-the-city-of-vienna/. Accessed 11 June 2024
23. Scharfbillig, M., et al.: Values and Identities - A Policymaker's Guide. Tech. Rep. KJ-NA-30800-EN-N, European Commission's Joint Research Centre, Luxembourg (2021). https://doi.org/10.2760/349527
24. Schwartz, S.H.: A repository of schwartz value scales with instructions and an introduction. Online Readings Psychol. Cult. **2**(2), 9 (2021)
25. Schwartz, S.H., et al.: Refining the theory of basic individual values. J. Pers. Soc. Psychol. **103**(4) (2012).https://doi.org/10.1037/a0029393
26. Widder, D.G., Nafus, D., Dabbish, L., Herbsleb, J.: Limits and possibilities for "ethical AI" in open source: a study of deepfakes. In: Proceedings of the 2022 ACM Conference on Fairness, Accountability, and Transparency, pp. 2035–2046 (2022)

From the Pascal Wager to Value Engineering: A Glance at AI Risks and How to Address Them

Pablo Noriega[1(✉)] and Pompeu Casanovas[1,2,3]

[1] Artificial IIIA-CSIC, Campus UAB, 08193 Barcelona, Spain
{pablo,pompeu.casanovas}@iiia.csic.es
[2] UAB Institute of Law and Technology, (IIIA-CSIC Associated Unit), Campus UAB, 08193 Barcelona, Spain
[3] La Trobe Law School, Melbourne 610101, Australia

Abstract. There is widespread awareness of the potential undesirable consequences of AI. In this paper we explore the grounds of such concerns from the perspective of risk management. We propose a decomposition of AI risk into three sorts of risk (inertial, disruptive, fundamental) that can be approached in different but complementary ways. From this differentiation we advocate for Value Engineering as a pertinent approach to address fundamental AI risk.

Keywords: AI risk · engineering values in AI artefacts · autonomy · governance · risk-management

1 Motivation

This paper is an invitation to equanimity. We look into the risks associated to AI, delineate a general strategy for dealing with them and focus on the role that value alignment can play in taking care of some of those risks.

There are three main biases in our discussion: First, that the assessment of risk is based on exposure, impact and likelihood. Second, that conventional risk-management approaches and simple common sense are quite useful in the assessment of AI risks and devising adequate strategies to address them. And third, that we focus our attention on *AI artefacts*—for the specific type of risks they pose—, and not on all potential risks associated with AI as a scientific discipline, nor those associated with the social phenomena emerging from human interaction with AI systems.[1]

The argument is structured around four claims: (i) The existential threat of AI is a latent risk that underlies more imminent AI risks, which can be approached through conventional risk management strategies. (ii) By looking

---

[1] We use the expression "AI artefact" to stand for "artificial intelligent system"; that is, a machine based system that exhibits some sort of autonomy, in the sense defined in [39] and discussed below in Sect. 7.

N. Osman and L. Steels (Eds.): VALE 2024, LNAI 15356, pp. 257–275, 2025.
https://doi.org/10.1007/978-3-031-85463-7_16

at the historical adoption of AI as a proxy for AI risk, one can decompose AI risk in three distinct categories: *inertial, disruptive* and *fundamental*. These types correspond to the way that, for forecasting purposes, time series are typically decomposed (trend, intervention and residual). (iii) Each of these three types of AI risk can be addressed with a judicious adaptation of conventional risk management practices. However (iv), fundamental AI risk, which emerges from the inherent autonomy and adaptability of AI artefacts, requires a more circumspect approach. And finally, (v) a prudent strategy to contend with fundamental AI risk is to use ethics and value engineering in particular as means to tame autonomy.[2]

2   From Extinction Threat to Catastrophic Risk

According to Stephen Hawking:
"Success in creating AI would be the biggest event in human history. Unfortunately, it might also be the last ..."[3] [23]

Stuart Russell is more precise:
"Given our current lack of understanding of how to control AGI systems and to ensure with absolute certainty that they remain safe and beneficial to humans, achieving AGI would present potential catastrophic risks to humanity, up to and including human extinction."[4]

Figure 1 describes Russell's view of AI risk. It postulates that: (i) Harm caused by AI may be huge, but it is very unlikely although not impossible; hence (ii) today (t_0) risk is small $(0 < \epsilon)$, and (iii) this situation remains rather stable until a future time, (t_σ), when a *singularity* takes place, namely Artificial General Intelligence (AGI) is achieved and takes control over human affairs.[5]

---

[2] There is a lively ongoing discussion about the interplay between risks, autonomy, values and AI that this paper addresses; for example, [4,22,32,40]. Such interplay is also addressed explicitly in some salient official documents, like [28,38,49] and is at the core of the EU AI Act [15].

[3] The Independent, May 4, 2014. https://www.independent.co.uk/news/science/stephen-hawking-transcendence-looks-at-the-implications-of-artificial-intelligence-but-are-we-taking-ai-seriously-enough-9313474.html (Retrieved Oct 2024).

[4] Stuart Russell. Testimony to the Subcommittee on Privacy, Technology and Law of the US Senate Committee on the Judiciary. Accessible in the web-page of the 25.07.2023 hearing: https://www.judiciary.senate.gov/committee-activity/hearings/oversight-of-ai-principles-for-regulation).

[5] According to S. Ulam, the notion of a technological singularity—the moment (in a distant future) when the evolution of technology surpasses human capabilities—was probably first articulated by J. von Neumann [52]. Shortly after, Turing phrased it in AI terms: *"It seems probable that once the machine thinking method had started, it would not take long to outstrip our feeble powers... At some stage therefore we should have to expect the machines to take control"* [51]. More recently, Vinge, Kurtzweil, Bostrom and others popularised it in connection to chiliastic views like "transhumanism" and "longterminism" [3,11].

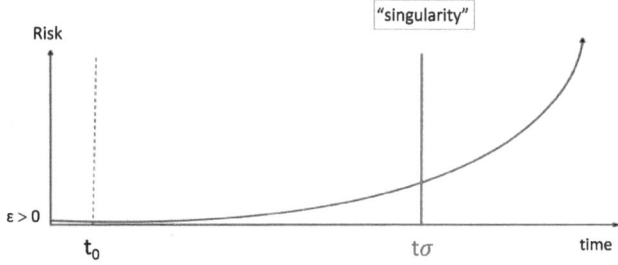

Fig. 1. The AI Singularity according to S. Russell: Currently (t_0), the risk of human extinction due to AI is negligible and will remain so until a future time (t_σ) when AGI is achieved and risk becomes catastrophic.

While Hawkins' assertion articulates a threat, Russell's qualifies it as a latent risk. The advantage of phrasing Hawking's dictum in Russell's terms is that it makes the threat concrete: the extinction of humanity, because of AI, is a future event with an extremely large cost but a very small likelihood.

In spite of the fundamental differences. Russell's phrasing echoes Pascal's Wager as a risk-mitigation approach: "Since we cannot have proof of the existence of God, the rational choice is to live a virtuous life" (Pascal, Blaise, "Infinite-Nothing", §233, in Pascal's Pensées [43]).[6]

Russell's claim provides little guidance to elucidate the likelihood of reaching the singularity but, as Pascal puts it, one can bet on identifying other not latent AI risks and devise ways to manage them. To elucidate what those risks are we can rely on previous experience. Rather than merely contemplating extinction, one can look at how the adoption of AI has evolved over the years and try to identify features that suggest what impact AI has had, what types of hazard AI rises, and identify strategies to anticipate and contend with AI risk. In order to guide that exploration towards an understanding of AI risks and how one can deal with them, we propose to rely on conventional risk-management heuristics. We will actually identify three different classes of AI risk which can be approached through different risk management strategies.

---

[6] The key paragraph reads: "'God is, or He is not.' But to which side shall we incline? Reason can decide nothing here. There is an infinite chaos which separated us. A game is being played at the extremity of this infinite distance where heads or tails will turn up... Which will you choose then? Let us see. Since you must choose, let us see which interests you least. You have two things to lose, the true and the good; and two things to stake, your reason and your will, your knowledge and your happiness; and your nature has two things to shun, error and misery. Your reason is no more shocked in choosing one rather than the other, since you must of necessity choose... But your happiness? Let us weigh the gain and the loss in wagering that God is... If you gain, you gain all; if you lose, you lose nothing. Wager, then, without hesitation that He is.".

3   Addressing AI Risk with a Standard Risk-Management Approach

We understand risk as the expected cost of an adverse but uncertain event. The purpose of risk-management is to reduce those expected costs. This reduction can be achieved with a combination of actions—the *risk-management process*—summarised in Fig. 2.

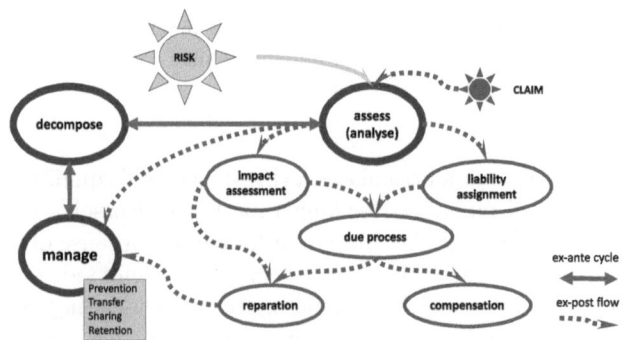

Fig. 2. The risk-management process. It includes an ex-ante cycle where specific risks are identified and analysed in order to define those actions triggered by an actual occurrence of that risk (a "claim").

The process involves the identification and analysis of relevant risks and the specification of those actions that should take place if and when the risk materialises.

A risk is usually analysed through the assessment of five elements: (i) a *haz-ard*—the achievement of AGI; a wrong AI-based diagnosis—; (ii) *exposure* where and how and whom would be affected if the hazard actually takes place—human race; a patient, a pathologist and a hospital—(iii) *impact* the unwanted conse-quences of the materialisation of the risk—AI takes over human affairs; mistreat-ment of the patient—(iv) *likelihood* of the materialisation of the risk—unlikely but not impossible; some measurement of the effectiveness of post-diagnosis treatment—and (v) *liability* a measure of the adverse consequences if and when the hazard materialises—extinction of civilisation; economic and moral damage compensation of malpractice claims.

Since the purpose of risk management is to reduce impact, one would try to distinguish what elements are involved in a *claim* (a presumable materialisation of the hazard, by analogy of insurance terminology) and deal with each separately in order to reduce the overall impact (AGI landmarks; wrong decision model, bad data, equipment malfunction, inadequate medical protocol, and so on).

Each of those fragmented risks should be managed on its own and ultimately put in place the mechanisms to mitigate the actual impacts of its occurrence (as suggested f.i. by Bengio et.al [4]). In the malpractice example the mitigation mechanism might be (i) revise current practice (main steps of the relevant protocol including the AI diagnosis decision-making), (ii) improve oversight, (iii) establish a procedure to deal with malpractice claims, and (iv) buy insurance to cover legitimate malpractice claims.

Once this ex-ante analysis-decomposing-management cycle is ready, the materialisation of a risk (a "claim") triggers a flow of actions that determine its impact, attributes blame, takes measures to compensate the adverse impact of the claim and using this experience improves the overall risk management process.

As we shall see below, a circumspect adaptation of this conventional risk management process can be applied to AI related risks.

4   A 3-Fold Decomposition of AI Risk

Acknowledging that AI risk is correlated with the use of AI, we propose to estimate AI impact (and harm) from historical market information. That is, we can use the time series of the AI market value to identify different sorts of risk that are associated with AI, their sources and impact; and find ways to manage each of them.

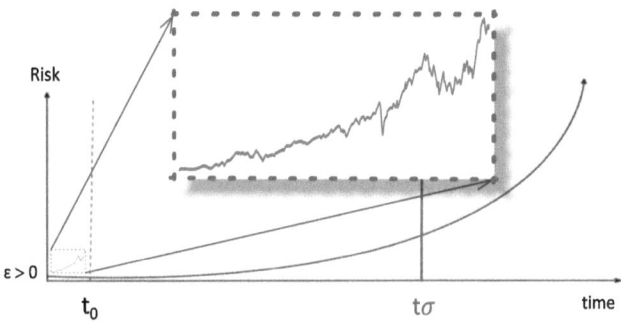

Fig. 3. Future risk can be estimated from historical data.

Customarily, time series (like the one in Fig. 3) can be analysed, for the purpose of forecasting, as a combination of four components: (i) a cyclic component that describes periodic and seasonal influences, (ii) a trend component that describes the long-term orientation of the series, (iii) "interventions", that alter the profile of the series with respect to other components and (iv) the core stochastic (residual) process. Forecast is based on the evolution of each of these components.

Based on the two time series in Fig. 4, we propose to project AI risks onto those time-series components in order to elucidate different sources or types of risk and devise differentiated management strategies.

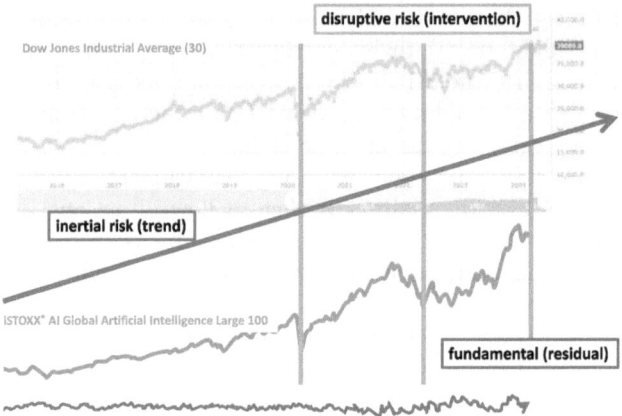

Fig. 4. A decomposition of stock-market prices into three components (trend, interventions and residual) and, by analogy, a decomposition of AI risk as *inertial, disruptive* and *fundamental*). The top graph shows the evolution of the Dow Jones index; the bottom one, the evolution for the same period of an index of one hundred large investors in AI (from: iSTOXX AI Global AI Large 100).

Figure 4 plots two stock-market time series from June 2014 to June 2024: the Dow Jones Industrial Average (30), on top, and the iSTOXX® AI Global Artificial Intelligence Large 100 index (https://stoxx.com/index/ixagal1p/). The top series shows rather clearly the three components we mentioned: an overall ascending *trend* (that absorbs a cyclic time-series component, which is irrelevant for our purposes), two prominent *interventions* (COVID and Fed intervention on interest rates linked with the Ukrainian war), and the underlying *residual* (stochastic) component. The bottom series shows that the segment of the stock market that is most influenced by AI has a patently similar profile. Thus, in the segment of AI companies one can also identify three components: the core stochastic component of the time-series would correspond to the risk that is directly linked with AI: the *fundamental* AI risk. The trend component corresponds to an *inertial* AI risk, which "pushes" the fundamental risk over time. And, finally there is a *disruptive* AI risk that originates from external, unanticipated events (the interventions) that resonate with the fundamental risk and produce significant changes in both fundamental and inertial risks.[7]

Although all AI risks share some common features and basic risk management heuristics apply to all, each of these three types of AI risk has distinguishing

---

[7] Note, that for the two interventions the AI index has a steeper slope and wider variation. Although this difference can be explained in part because of the smaller number of firms in the iSTOXX index, another explanation is the fact that large companies that invest in the development and use of AI—like ALPHABET; AMD; META, NVIDIA and Siemens—have attracted significantly more capital in this later period (see Fig. 5).

features that are amenable not only to further risk differentiation but to a specific risk-management approach.

5   Addressing Inertial AI Risk (tendency)

From the above, we use the label *Inertial AI risk* to capture the underlying trend of the time series and its cyclic (periodic and seasonal) components. Intuitively, inertial risk reflects the historical evolution of risk, independent of the constantly evolving *fundamental risk* and independent of disruptive, unanticipated events coming from exogenous forces or radical AI innovations.

One can identify four main sources of inertial AI risk:

1. *Increase of IT power and online activity*, as enablers of AI innovation, demand and productivity.
2. *Underlying market inertia.* AI investment, development and use are affected by the overall business activity. Hence, to capture the influence of that general activity—that is largely independent of AI proper—one can use market indicators (market trend, cyclic components and interventions), that are extrinsic to AI but may still reflect forces that impinge on AI.
3. *Short term provisos* that influence amount, concentration and sources of investment in AI R+D+T—like regional, national and industry-specific policies, programs, incentives and regulations. Although, in the short term they are disruptive for AI to some extent, they are also an inertial component by affecting direction, development and adoption of AI. Consequently, they are especially significant for the design of medium and long-term AI risk management.
4. *Maturity of AI.* Not only as a scientific discipline but also in terms of ready-use technologies, professional expertise and market development.

The combination of the previous elements determines long term evolution in the adoption of AI, and therefore in its positive and negative impacts.

These elements suggest a cautious, *vigilant* risk-management approach. In practice this amounts to decomposing inertial risk and build on proven risk-management practices to design *ad-hoc* mitigation devices for each of those risk decompositions. For instance, (i) monitor evolution of AI impact through AI observatories, (ii) identify disruptive features in the demand and capitalisation of enabler technologies (e.g., emergence of social networks), (iii) include AI-specific considerations in policies that involve provisos on education and R&D, oversight organisms, and international agreements on these aspects (e.g., NSF and EU projects); and (iv) design AI-specific provisos to articulate some type of long-term responsible AI policy.

6   Addressing Disruptive AI Risk (Interventions)

As suggested by the analogy with time series interventions, disruptive AI risks come from unanticipated innovations, events or circumstances that have a profound effect on the types of AI artefacts that become available, the expectations and the actual use and adoption of AI. Hence affecting the preexisting risk profile.

Interventions can be seen as a sort of crisis. They produce a Thom-like singularity [50] that alters the magnitude and volatility of the AI market and all its subsidiary indicators; hence its *liability*. But they also trigger strong adaptive reactions in demand, supply, policy and social perception.

There are two illustrative historical examples of disruptive AI interventions. The first one is the so-called "AI winter" in the sixties: a substantial decrease in AI investment and development spawned by unfulfilled expectations of the field and a suspension of soft R&D funds. The second is the so-called "Fifth Generation Computer Revolution", in the early seventies, when the convergence of new computer architectures, the consolidation of knowledge-based systems and the expected adoption of AI in manufacturing and strategic decision-making brought in a "spring" of resources, motivation and expectations [17,24,31]. We are arguably in the midst of one. In addition to diffused reactions to Hawking-like concerns, two ostensible arguments back this claim: the distinct alteration of stock prices of three large AI players (Apple, Microsoft and Nvidia) in recent years (Fig. 5), and the dramatic increase in public interest sparked by ChatGPT captured in the OECD's observatory of AI-related news (Fig. 6).[8]

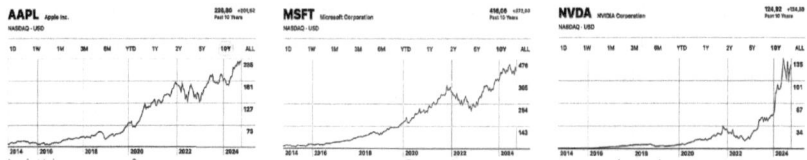

Fig. 5. Evolution of stock prices over the last ten years of Apple, Microsoft and Nvidia. From Apple's *stocks app* (retrieved 14.10.24).

Even a crude description of the current crisis helps illustrate the key dynamics of disruptive AI risk one should address:

1. The convergence of fundamental and inertial risk components
   (a) A fundamental risk component from AI innovations that had been evolving over several years (essentially ML, NLP and MAS), and
   (b) An accelerated inertial risk from:
       i. the sophistication of AI enablers (GPU, "AI chips", cloud computing) that is being driven by the colossal requirements of AI processing.
       ii. The availability of massive digital content (text, images and knowledge);
       iii. Added thrust from the adoption of AI enabled applications.

---

[8] Some voices claim that the current AI disruption is bringing the singularity closer. As close as the next decade [4]. We claim that such urgency needs to be reined in with equanimity.

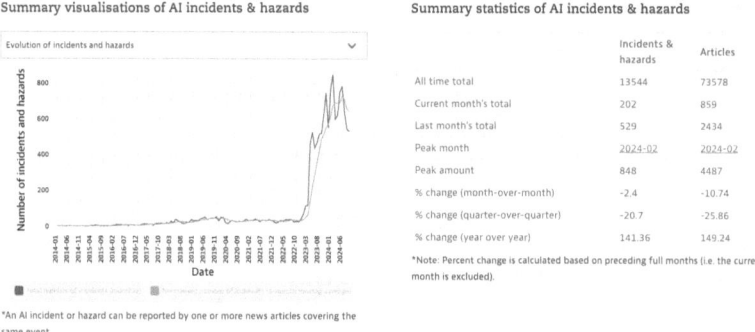

Summary visualisations of AI incidents & hazards

Summary statistics of AI incidents & hazards

	Incidents & hazards	Articles
All time total	13544	73578
Current month's total	202	859
Last month's total	529	2434
Peak month	2024-02	2024-02
Peak amount	848	4487
% change (month-over-month)	-2.4	-10.74
% change (quarter-over-quarter)	-20.7	-25.86
% change (year over year)	141.36	149.24

*Note: Percent change is calculated based on preceding full months (i.e. the current month is excluded).

*An AI incident or hazard can be reported by one or more news articles covering the same event.

Fig. 6. OECD's automated monitor of AI news and hazards from public sources. From https://oecd.ai/en/incidents (retrieved 14.10.24).

2. Landmark success cases (from *Jeopardy and Alpha-Go* to *ChatGPT*) that stimulated important advances in different AI technologies and gave public visibility to AI.
3. An unprecedented market impact and speed of adoption.
4. Inordinate concentration of knowledge, capital and capital investment in very few dominant AI firms.
5. A swift reaction of stakeholders (academia, industry, authorities, press and public) stimulated by risk aversion, ambition and lack of information.

In light of the speed and force of the current disruption, it seems advisable to embark in a *reactive* risk-management strategy with two aims in sight: on one hand, to identify specific potential harms and elucidate what are the main factors that are playing out risk in the current disruption; and, on the other hand, identify stakeholders and their interests, in order to articulate adequate institutional mechanisms to manage the associated risks, and to address liability and accountability in particular.

Hence, a prudent risk-management strategy would suggest the following reactive actions:

- Identify potential impacts, triggering events and conditions.
- Adapt successful risk-management strategies and mechanisms from other risk-prone technologies and professional practices (health, energy, finance, genetics).
- Dilute risk concentration through incentives for start-ups and commit public investment in research and innovation on the disruptive topics.[9]

---

[9] This device reduces AI's negative impact and amplifies potential benefits by enlarging the set of stakeholders (those who possess knowledge, resources and competence to identify and contend with emerging risks and opportunities) and fostering a social appropriation of value form these innovations. As a side effect it discourages premature release of technology.

- Adequate legal procedures to support impact assessment and attribution of liability on AI-based claims, in order to guarantee accountability and foster risk mitigation.
- Analyse the role of AI in systemic risks (finance, health, energy, environment, defence, security) and take relevant protective measures.
- Develop new institutional frameworks to design and implement risk control policies.

7   Addressing Fundamental AI Risk

Fundamental AI risk is the one that derives directly from the deployment of AI systems and is not included in the previous two sorts. This is the risk that is intrinsic to AI and therefore difficult to characterise *a priori*. Nevertheless, one can still advance a preventive risk-management approach by trying to elucidate where the risk originates and analyse the forces at play. A sensible heuristic to find that source is to identify what makes AI different from other disciplines, or better yet, what are the most salient features that distinguish AI systems from other. We find that the following characterisation [39] is a good starting point:

"An AI system (AIS) is a machine-based system that, for explicit or implicit objectives infers, from the input it receives, how to generate outputs such as predictions, content, recommendations, or decisions that can influence physical or virtual environments. Different AI systems vary in their levels of autonomy and adaptiveness after deployment".

This OECD definition carries three important implications. The first one is that from an AI risk-management perspective, the key aspect to address is *autonomy*. That is, the capability—engineered into AI systems—of making decisions that affect the world without direct intervention of humans [10]. The second one is that fundamental AI risk resides in AI artefacts. It resides not in the potential impact of *AI as a scientific discipline* concerned with understanding intelligence in the wide sense, nor is it about the *social phenomena* that result from the interaction between humans and artificial autonomous artefacts. The third one leads to preventive outlook: in the context of risk-management, one can understand autonomy along two well-established notions of autonomy and deal with each separately. Namely, (i) Autonomy as a relationship of delegation between a *principal and an agent*, in the traditional legal and economics sense; and (ii) autonomy of a individual in the form of *moral agency*, in the philosophical and cognitive sense.

Autonomy as Delegation. This notion of autonomy presumes two parties: a *principal* and an *agent*. The principal holds some capabilities, entitlements or authority that enables it to perform certain actions whose consequences the principal is liable for. Delegation, in this case, is a procedure through which some of those capabilities, entitlements or authority are passed onto an agent who will now be enabled to execute some actions on behalf of the principal.[10]

The key issue to keep in mind in delegated autonomy is that delegation of autonomy concerns not only the capability of "acting in representation of", but it also involves an actual allocation of *liability*.[11]

This type of delegation of autonomy between principal and agent has a long tradition and has been the source of several devices to support risk management tasks. Three examples serve to illustrate this form of delegation: (i) A car manufacturer delegates onto a car dealer the capability of selling cars, provide maintenance and acknowledge when a certain failure is covered by the manufacturer's guarantee. (ii) Highway police has the authority, empowered by administrative public laws, to assess traffic violations and to enforce norms to prevent life-threatening situations. (iii) A pathologist may delegate the task of screening tissue samples to an AI-based diagnostics system to simplify triage (identify positive cases and discard the rest).

In rough terms, the car dealer will be liable for the costs of poor repairs, not the manufacturer; and a policeman will be liable for any harm that is the consequence of a misinterpretation of its entitlement to use force, i.e. its abuse of power. Example (iii), illustrates how, in medical practice and other similar domains, risk-management is used to decompose risk in order to put appropriate risk mitigation devices in place and attribute different liabilities to the different stakeholders involved in the harm resulting behaviour. Namely, the pathologist is entitled to delegate the decision to label a sample "positive" because such delegation is part of the approved medical protocol and because the hospital has allowed the use of the specific AI system in this protocol. The hospital, in turn allows the use of the particular AI system because, in addition to the endorsement of the use of an automated diagnostics in the medical protocol, the supplier of the specific AIS provides some guarantees that the systems works properly. Similarly, the supplier signs a contract with the hospital that reflects its own confidence on the proficiency of the AI system, which is eventually based on proper testing and sound science and engineering. The point is that, in spite of this chain of entitlements, the pathologist is that the pathologist would never relinquish its moral and professional responsibilities for a botched diagnosis, nor the hospital its clinical and reputational ones. Nevertheless, the patient,

---

[10] From a legal perspective, delegation must be differentiated from *legal empowerment*. "Delegation" presupposes an already established power, which is delegated to another physical (individual) or moral person (an institution or organisation). "Empowerment" refers to the constitutive act of attributing to a person or an organization certain normative capacities, i.e. "powers", without the need for prior delegation.

[11] In our context, "liability" refers to the legal responsibility, to the economic cost attached to a harmful behaviour, and also to the associated social and moral damages. The issue of liability and rendering liable parties accountable has received attention not only in law but also in economics, see for instance [13,14,26]. It is worth noting too that, from a legal point of view, there is a well-known tradition linking accountability and autonomy with causation and liability.

the pathologist and the hospital can avoid financial stress with a malpractice insurance policy, whose cost reflects the guarantees and liability clauses the supplier is contractually bound to assume, the quality of the clinical practices in the hospital and the professional standing of the pathologist.

Autonomy as Moral Agency. Moral agency is understood as the capability of an individual to choose behaviour—make "moral choices" based on some notion of right and wrong—and being accountable for the harmful consequences of those choices. Depending on the requirements one imposes on the decision-making process one can debate whether or not, or in what sense animals, children, disabled persons and autonomous artificial systems have moral agency.

The attribution of moral agency to artefacts has been discussed at large. Some opinions are negative: only humans can hold moral agency, not computers, qualified as 'entities', not as 'agents' [7,8,25,29,42]. Others are more favourable [44,48]. For instance, Floridi and Saunders [18] contend that moral agency is a matter of "level of abstraction". They claim that the concept of moral agent does not require the preconditions of exhibiting free will, mental states or responsibility. Their guidelines for "agenthood" are: *interactivity* (response to stimulus by change of state), *autonomy* (ability to change state without stimulus) and *adaptability* (ability to change the transition rules by which state is changed) at a given level of abstraction. Thus, under these assumptions, moral agency may hold for AI systems as well.

From a classical Multi-Agent Systems perspective, Falcone and Castelfranchi [16] contend that it is possible to analyse the adjustable autonomy of an agent both by considering the level of delegation allowed to the contractor (agent) by the principal, and the possibility for the contractor itself to adjust its own autonomy by restricting or by expanding the received delegation. Falcone and Castelfranchi claim that "in studying how to adjust the level of autonomy and how to arrive to a dynamic level of control, it could be useful an explicit theory of delegation able to specify different kinds and levels of autonomy".

Essentially, what matters in this form of delegation of autonomy is not only the debatable possibility of the "personhood" or even "legal personhood" [1,27]. The issue that truly matters is to determine whether an artificial system would have, *de facto*, the responsibility for any harm its actions may produce. In other words, in order to mange risk, the fundamental problem in artificial moral agency is the proper assessment and allocation of liability in order to render such agent accountable.

Dealing with Harm: Liability and Reparation. We claimed that autonomy is the source of fundamental AI risk and we mentioned two forms of autonomy in AIS: delegation and moral agency. In both cases there are essentially two risks: misuse and malfunction of the artefact.

On the surface, both forms of autonomy can be addressed in a similar way because the ex-post risk-management process starts in both cases by identifying *liability*. That is, assessing the level of harm and attributing responsibility (recall Fig. 2). Once liability (harm and responsibility) is established, a process of reparation can be activated, which is essentially two-fold: compensation of damage and mitigation.

While this ex-post claim management process applies in most situations, its actual execution needs to take into account three salient considerations. The first one is that the impact of the misuse or the malfunction—that is, the severity of each casualty (or claim), the number of casualties and the expected reparation costs—needs to be articulated in the materialisation of each hazard (a given "claim") both to assess actual and potential liabilities, and to devise commensurable reparation processes. The second one is that the conventions and principles to assess liability and address reparation may differ substantially depending on the domain of use of the AIS (health, transportation, civil rights, defence). Finally, in order to implement the claim settlement process (assessment, attribution and reparation), one needs to account for the socio-legal environment where harm is taking place.

Fortunately, it is often the case that in order to establish liability (harm and responsibility) and render guilty parties accountable (blame assignment, reparation measures and enforcement), one can rely on conventional means like contracts, regulations, oversight and insurance, following a conventional due process. However, for some special cases of AI misuse or malfunction, new *ad-hoc* due processes might be needed. Such new due processes ought to be responsive to the impact and domain considerations mentioned above. Moreover, some new non-standard cases will need a more sophisticated analysis of the "value chain" of stakeholders involved in order to properly establish collective and individual liability, as well as the respective reparation processes.[12]

8   Risk Control and Value Engineering

Although in this paper we circumvent further elaboration of the risk management process for autonomous AIS, we turn our attention, however briefly, to a time-honoured tool to address autonomy, which is *governance*. Instead of reacting to claims, governance assumes a proactive role. Governance prevents harm by imposing restrictions or dissuading undesirable behaviour, while also creating incentives and facilitating courses of action to foster desirable behaviour. This proactive role can be explicitly linked with ethical considerations (as we will argue below).

Conventional governance principles and practices are relevant, once again, to the management of fundamental AI risk. Either by adapting conventional governance means—like standards, best practices, rules and regulations as well as enforcement and oversight frameworks—or, by developing analogous new ones [9]. Nevertheless, one can also look into the unconventional idea of making use of AI to govern artificial autonomous systems. One particular approach to

---

[12] See *Recital 20* of the Artificial Intelligence Act [15]) that acknowledges the need of refining such notions and links the overall process to compliance and a better understanding of the "AI value chain".

the governance of AI autonomy is to rely on ethics as a form of control. The gist of this approach is sketched in Fig. 7.

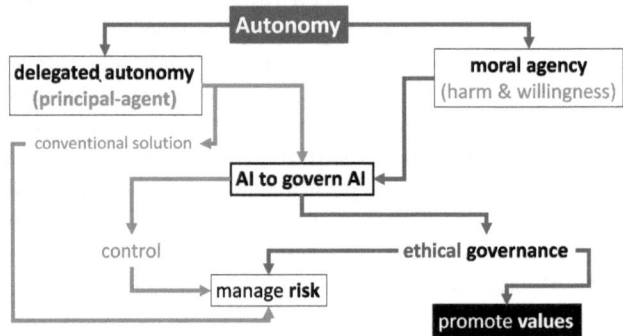

Fig. 7. While conventional practices and means can be adapted judiciously to the governance of artificial delegated autonomy, the deployment of AI means to govern moral autonomy in AIS is a distinct possibility. One venue in this approach is to design AIS that are aligned with human values.

Although AI based AIS governance in general, and ethics-based AI governance in particular, can be approached from several fronts, there are two distinct but complementary salient subproblems: (i) imbuing ethical notions into the self-governance of autonomous agents and (ii) imbuing ethical notions into the governance of the collective interactions in online hybrid human AI social systems [30, 36, 37].

The general problem of ethics-based AI governance can be framed as a *value alignment problem*: to find ways of guiding behaviour (individual or collective) towards outcomes that are consistent with some values. Value alignment, in the context of AI, can be made explicit as the problem of "designing autonomous artificial systems whose behaviour is objectively aligned with explicit human values" [19, 45–47, 53]; VAP, for brevity.

VAP can be approached as an engineering problem: how to implement the means to govern the behaviour of an AIS so that the satisfaction of an explicit set of values can be objectively assessed [41]. By acknowledging the correspondence of harm and value, VAP translates, for the purpose of risk-management, into the challenge of designing and implementing governance devices into AIS so that explicit risks are objectively avoided.[13]

What we are in fact claiming is that if one can align an AIS to avoid an explicit risk, it is because the degree to which that risk is avoided in that AIS

---

[13] In not all that dissimilar spirit, there have been three other proposals to govern autonomy in which values play some role: superalignment, constitutional AI and risk-level safeguards for "agentic AI" [2, 5, 6, 12, 20, 21, 33].

can be objectively assessed; hence the actual harm can be objectively assessed. That is, risk-bound AIS can be designed if value-aligned AIS can.[14]

This interpretation of VAP from a risk-management perspective does not solve the general problem of fundamental AI risk but it is a promising incursion in that direction: It provides the basis for the design of risk-bound AIS those for which liability can be objectively assessed, accountability can be objectively attributed and the corresponding reparation procedures can be put in place.

This last observation leads to another argument in favour of addressing risk-management as values-based governance: the possibility not only of addressing liability, by avoiding objective harm, but actually achieving benefits by objectively accruing value [34].

9   Closing Remarks

We understand that the commitment of the AI community should be to responsible AI development. We propose to instrument this responsibility through a discerning attention to the management of AI risks.

1. We have approached AI risks from a risk-management perspective and identified three main types of risk that are associated with AI (*inertial, disruptive* and *fundamental*). We sketched a tentative strategy to address each of them (vigilant, reactive and preventive).
2. In particular, we are convinced that the AI community has the salient responsibility of addressing the fundamental risks associated with autonomy in AI artefacts. We argue that the challenge of developing *risk-bound AIS* (as a value engineering problem) is a sensible step in that direction.
3. We advocate for a long-term perspective: The judicious strategy to deal with AI risk—including latent risk however large it may be—is to develop institutional frameworks to design and implement AI risk control policies. Risk control policies that should look into ways of (i) developing risk-commensurable governance that is responsive to differentiated risks, and (ii) enabling reliable national and international due processes to deal with AI induced harm, including means to render risk-enhancing stakeholders accountable.
4. The fact that conventional risk-management practices may apply to AI risks provides grounds for cautious confidence, suggests guides for their prudent adaptation to AI, and motivates a road-map for the type of research, institutional and market developments needed to avert extreme risks.
5. AI development and use comes with unavoidable risks, but also with benefits. Whatever strategy to contend with AI risk we choose, it should encompass a sound strategy to offset any potential harm with actual benefits.
   In this respect, we urge our colleagues to invest a systematic effort in the development of AI artefacts that align with human values. We argue that value aligned AIS, in addition to their risk-taming role, can be designed to achieve objective social benefits.

---

[14] Of course this claim can only be validated up to the properties of the engineering process or the methodology that is used to engineer that particular risk [34,35,37].

In sum, the design of value-aligned artificial intelligence systems is at the foundation for the development of beneficial AI.

Acknowledgments. We wish to thank Jean-Gabriel Ganascia, Ramon López de Mántaras, Mustafa Hashmi, Ho-Pun Lam, and Louis de Koker for their helpful comments. Research for this paper is supported by EU (Horizon-EIC-2021-Pathfinder challenges-01) Project VALAWAI 101070930; the EU Next Generation EU/PRTR program; the Spanish (MCIN/AEI) project VAE TED2021-131295B-C31, CSIC's (Bilateral Collaboration Initiative i-LINK-TEC) project DESAFIA2030 BILTC22005 and the IDT Research Group of Excellence UAB-CSIC (SGR 00532 2022-24).

References

1. Anderson, M., Anderson, S.L.: Machine ethics: creating an ethical intelligent agent. AI Mag. **28**(4), 15 (2007)
2. Bai, Y., et al.: Constitutional AI: harmlessness from AI feedback (2022). https://doi.org/10.48550/arXiv.2211.2212.08073
3. Bales, A., D'Alessandro, W., Kirk-Giannini, C.D.: Artificial intelligence: arguments for catastrophic risk. Philos. Compass **19**(2), e12964 (2024)
4. Bengio, Y., et al.: Managing extreme AI risks amid rapid progress. Science **384**(6698), 842–845 (2024)
5. Bowman, S.R., et al.: Measuring progress on scalable oversight for large language models (2022). https://doi.org/10.48550/arXiv.2211.03540
6. Brenneis, A.: Assessing dual use risks in AI research: necessity, challenges and mitigation strategies. Res. Ethics (2024). https://doi.org/10.1177/17470161241267782
7. Brożek, B., Janik, B.: Can artificial intelligences be moral agents? New Ideas Psychol. **54**, 101–106 (2019)
8. Bryson, J.J., Diamantis, M.E., Grant, T.D.: Of, for, and by the people: the legal lacuna of synthetic persons. Artif. Intell. Law **25**(3), 273–291 (2017). https://doi.org/10.1007/s10506-017-9214-9
9. Casanovas, P., Hashmi, M., de Koker, L., Lam, H.P.: A three steps methodological approach to legal governance validation (2024). https://doi.org/10.48550/arXiv.2407.20691
10. Castelfranchi, C., Falcone, R.: From automaticity to autonomy: the frontier of artificial agents. Agent Autonomy 103–136 (2003)
11. Chalmers, D.J.: The singularity: a philosophical analysis. In: Science Fiction and Philosophy: From Time Travel to Superintelligence, pp. 171–224 (2016)
12. Christian, B.: Alignemt problem: machine learning and human values. W W Norton, S.l. (2021). oCLC: 1233266753
13. Daughety, A., Reinganum, J.: Economic analysis of products liability: theory, pp. 69–96. Edward Elgar Publishing (2013). https://doi.org/10.4337/9781781006177.00011
14. Daughety, A.F., Reinganum, J.F.: Markets, torts, and social inefficiency. Rand J. Econ. **37**(2), 300–323 (2006). https://doi.org/10.1111/j.1756-2171.2006.tb00017.x

15. European Commission: Regulation (EU) 2024/1689 of the European parliament and of the council of 13 June 2024 laying down harmonised rules on artificial intelligence (artificial intelligence act) (text with EEA relevance) pe/24/2024/rev/1. https://eur-lex.europa.eu/eli/reg/2024/1689/oj

16. Falcone, R., Castelfranchi, C.: Levels of delegation and levels of adoption as the basis for adjustable autonomy. In: Congress of the Italian Association for Artificial Intelligence, pp. 273–284. Springer (1999)

17. Feigenbaum, E.A.: Stories of AAAI-before the beginning and after: a love letter. AI Mag. **26**(4), 30 (2005)

18. Floridi, L., Sanders, J.W.: On the morality of artificial agents. Mind. Mach. **14**(3), 349–379 (2004)

19. Gabriel, I.: Artificial intelligence, values, and alignment. Minds Mach. **30**(3), 411–437 (2020). https://doi.org/10.1007/s11023-020-09539-2

20. Ganguli, D., et al.: The capacity for moral self-correction in large language models (2023). https://doi.org/10.48550/arXiv.2302.07459

21. Ganguli, D., et al.: Red teaming language models to reduce harms: methods, scaling behaviors, and lessons learned (2022). https://doi.org/10.48550/arXiv.2209.07858

22. Giudici, P., Centurelli, M., Turchetta, S.: Artificial intelligence risk measurement. Expert Syst. Appl. **235**, 121220 (2024). https://doi.org/10.1016/j.eswa.2023.121220. https://www.sciencedirect.com/science/article/pii/S0957417423017220

23. Hawking, S., Russell, S., Tegmark, M., Wilczek, F.: Stephen hawking: 'transcendence looks at the implications of artificial intelligence - but are we taking AI seriously enough?'. The Independent (2014). (Retr. Oct 2024)

24. Hendler, J.: Avoiding another AI winter. IEEE Intell. Syst. **23**, 2–4 (2008). https://doi.org/10.1109/MIS.2008.20

25. Himma, K.E.: Artificial agency, consciousness, and the criteria for moral agency: what properties must an artificial agent have to be a moral agent? Ethics Inf. Technol. **11**(1), 19–29 (2009). https://doi.org/10.1007/s10676-008-9167-5

26. Hua, X., Spier, K.E.: Holding platforms liable. HKUST Business School Research Paper No. 2021-048, (2022). https://doi.org/10.2139/ssrn.3985066

27. IEEE: Ethically aligned design, version 2 (2017). https://ethicsinaction.ieee.org/. Accessed 13 June 2019

28. International Standards Office (ISO) and International Electrotechnical Commission (IEC): International standard ISO/IEC 23894: Information technology - artificial intelligence - guidance on risk management (first edition) (2023). https://cdn.standards.iteh.ai/samples/77304/cb803ee4e9624430a5db177459158b24/ISO-IEC-23894-2023.pdf

29. Johnson, D.G.: Computer systems: moral entities but not moral agents. Ethics Inf. Technol. **8**, 195–204 (2006)

30. King, T.C., et al.: Automated multi-level governance compliance checking. Auton. Agents Multi-Agent Syst. 1–61 (2017)

31. Lenat, D.B., Feigenbaum, E.A.: On the thresholds of knowledge. In: IJCAI, vol. 87, pp. 1172–1176 (1987)

32. Lockey, S., Gillespie, N.M., Holm, D., Someh, I.A.: A review of trust in artificial intelligence: challenges, vulnerabilities and future directions. In: 54th Hawaii International Conference on System Sciences, HICSS 2021, Kauai, Hawaii, USA, 5 January 2021, pp. 1–10. ScholarSpace, (Retr. Oct 2024) (2021). https://hdl.handle.net/10125/71284

33. METR (Model Evaluation and Threat Research): Responsible scaling policies (RSPS). https://metr.org/blog/2023-09-26-rsp/. Accessed 18 Oct 2024

34. Noriega, P., Plaza, E.: The use of agent-based simulation of public policy design to study the value alignment problem. In: Casanovas, P., de Koker, L., et al. (eds.) Proceedings of Selected Papers of the Workshop on Artificial Intelligence Governance Ethics and Law (AIGEL 2022). CEUR Workshop Proceedings, vol. 3531, pp. 130–139. CEUR-WS.org, (Ret. Oct 2024) (2022). https://ceur-ws.org/Vol-3531/SPaper_10.pdf

35. Noriega, P., Plaza, E.: On autonomy, governance, and values: an AGV approach to value engineering. In: Osman, N., Steels, L. (eds.) Value Engineering in Artificial Intelligence, pp. 165–179. Springer, Cham (2024). https://doi.org/10.1007/978-3-031-58202-8_10

36. Noriega, P., Verhagen, H., Padget, J., d'Inverno, M.: Design heuristics for ethical online institutions. In: Ajmeri, N., Morris Martin, A., Savarimuthu, B.T.R. (eds.) Coordination, Organizations, Institutions, Norms, and Ethics for Governance of Multi-Agent Systems XV, pp. 213–230. Springer, Cham (2022)

37. Noriega, P., Verhagen, H., Padget, J., d'Inverno, M.: Addressing the value alignment problem through online institutions. In: Fornara, N., Cheriyan, J., Mertzani, A. (eds.) Coordination, Organizations, Institutions, Norms, and Ethics for Governance of Multi-Agent Systems XVI, pp. 77–94. Springer, Cham (2023)

38. OECD: OECD Framework for the Classification of AI systems. OECD Digital Economy Papers (323) (2022). https://doi.org/10.1787/cb6d9eca-en. https://www.oecd-ilibrary.org/content/paper/cb6d9eca-en

39. OECD: Explanatory memorandum on the updated OECD definition of an AI system (2024). https://doi.org/10.1787/623da898-en. https://www.oecd-ilibrary.org/content/paper/623da898-en. Accessed September 2024

40. Orwat, C., Bareis, J., Folberth, A., Jahnel, J., Wadephul, C.: Normative challenges of risk regulation of artificial intelligence and automated decision-making. CoRR abs/2211.06203 (2022). https://doi.org/10.48550/arxiv.2211.06203

41. Osman, N., Steels, L. (eds.): Value Engineering in Artificial Intelligence - First International Workshop, VALE 2023, Krakow, Poland, 30 September 2023, Proceedings, Lecture Notes in Computer Science, vol. 14520. Springer, Cham (2024). https://doi.org/10.1007/978-3-031-58202-8

42. Parthemore, J., Whitby, B.: What makes an agent a moral agent? Reflections in machine consciousness and moral agency. Int. J. Mach. Conscious. 05(02), 105–129 (2013). https://doi.org/10.1142/S1793843013500017

43. Pascal, B.: Pascal's pensées; introduction by T.S. Eliot, translated by W.F. Trotter in 1910 (1958)

44. Powers, T.M.: On the moral agency of computers. Topoi 32(2), 227–236 (2013). https://doi.org/10.1007/s11245-012-9149-4

45. Russell, S.: Of Myths and Moonshine. A conversation with Jaron Lanier, 14-11-14. The Edge (2014). https://www.edge.org/conversation/the-myth-of-ai#26015. Accessed Oct 2024

46. Russell, S.: Provably beneficial artificial intelligence. The Next Step: Exponential Life, BBVA-Open Mind (2017)

47. Russell, S.: Human compatible: AI and the problem of control. Penguin, UK (2019)

48. Sullins, J.P.: When is a robot a moral agent. Int. Rev. Inf. Ethics 6(12), 23–30 (2006)

49. Tabassi, E.: Artificial intelligence risk management framework (AI RMF 1.0) (2023-01-26 05:01:00 2023). https://doi.org/10.6028/NIST.AI.100-1

50. Thom, R.: Les singularités des applications différentiables. In: Annales de l'institut Fourier, vol. 6, pp. 43–87 (1956)

51. Turing, A.M.: Intelligent machinery, a heretical theory. Philos. Math. **4**(3), 256–260 (1996)
52. Ulam, S.: Tribute to john von neumann. Bull. Am. Math. Soc. **64**(3), 1–49 (1958)
53. Vamplew, P., Dazeley, R., Foale, C., Firmin, S., Mummery, J.: Human-aligned artificial intelligence is a multiobjective problem. Ethics Inf. Technol. **20**(1), 27–40 (2018). https://doi.org/10.1007/s10676-017-9440-6

Author Index

N. Osman and L. Steels (Eds.): VALE 2024, LNAI 15356, pp. 277–278, 2025.
https://doi.org/10.1007/978-3-031-85463-7